ts ∎

EIGHTH EDITION

CONTEMPORARY AMERICAN SPEECHES

A Sourcebook of
Speech Forms and Principles

RICHARD L. JOHANNESEN

Northern Illinois University

R. R. ALLEN

University of Wisconsin

WIL A. LINKUGEL

University of Kansas

FERALD J. BRYAN

Northern Illinois University

KENDALL/HUNT PUBLISHING COMPANY
4050 Westmark Drive   Dubuque, Iowa 52004-1840

CHAPTER SEVEN   SPEECHES THAT AFFIRM PROPOSITIONS OF POLICY _____ 249

CHAPTER EIGHT   SPEECHES THAT INTENSIFY SOCIAL COHESION _____ 353

Alternate Topical Contents

Note: Asterisked speeches are "paired" speeches that present differing views on essentially the same general topic.

Technology and the Environment

Contemporary Morals and Values

Preface ■

This edition, like the first seven editions of *Contemporary American Speeches*, is dedicated to the belief that acquisition of speaking skills is best achieved through three complementary lines of study: *theory*, from which the student may gain a basic understanding of the speech act; *example*, through which the student may evaluate precept in the light of real and varied instances of public discourse; and *practice*, in which the student may apply rhetorical principles to the creation of speeches. This book is primarily designed to contribute to the second of these lines of study, *example*.

Teaching by example is an ancient practice. Isocrates used the study of speeches as one of his principal teaching devices. Cicero, himself an assiduous student of speeches, advocated the study of Greek and Roman speech models to all aspiring orators. Quintilian said, "It is from . . . authors worthy of our study that we must draw our stock of words, the variety of our figures and our methods of composition." Chauncey Goodrich noted that "He who would teach eloquence must do it chiefly by examples." Edmund Burke studied Demosthenes; Daniel Webster studied Burke; and Woodrow Wilson studied Webster.

In producing an eighth edition of *Contemporary American Speeches*, we again faced the critical question of which speeches to retain and which ones to replace. As we have done with earlier editions, we approached this problem by surveying as many users of the previous editions as we could, asking them to tell us which speeches they found especially useful and which ones they felt could be discarded. We have also been guided by our own teaching experience, noting those addresses that generated much student discussion and comprehension of speech principles.

For our purpose, *contemporary* includes the sixties, seventies, and eighties with primary emphasis on the nineties. Five of the speeches in this edition are from the sixties and seventies, five are from the eighties, and 29 are from the nineties. Forty-one percent of the speeches are new to this edition. Three speeches have continued through all eight editions: Martin Luther King's "I have a Dream," Douglas MacArthur's "Farewell to the Cadets," and John F. Kennedy's "Inaugural Address." In an effort to keep this edition at a reasonable length, and thus at at reasonable price, we have added fewer speeches than we eliminated.

We have continued the diversity of "voices" represented in the seventh edition. Certainly the political spectra of Democrat-Republican and liberal-conservative are represented. Thiry-six percent of the speakers are women. Twenty-six percent of the speakers are African American, Hispanic/Latino(a) American, and Native American.

Again we have "paired" speeches that present differing viewpoints on essentially the same general topic: Mario Cuomo and Phyllis Schlafly on what values should be taught in the public schools; Russell Train and Virginia Postrel on values central to the environmental movement; Diane Ravitch and Molefi Asante on multiculturalism in education; Faye Wattleton and Jerry Falwell on legalized abortion; Kathleen Brown and Pete Wilson on illegal immigration; and Robert Dole and Nadine Strossen (in separate chapters) on sex and violence in the entertainment media.

Each chapter essay develops criteria that the student may use in exploring and evaluating the speeches. The suggestions "For Further Reading" at the end of each chapter have been updated. The introductory headnotes that precede each speech provide background information and pose thought provoking suggestions and questions to stimulate student analysis of each address. Some headnotes have been updated. In some headnotes we undertake at length our own analysis of a speech to illustrate a few of the ways in which a rhetorical critic might describe, interpret, and evaluate important elements of the speech.

Whether the teacher chooses to emphasize speech forms or speech principles, this book should prove useful. As in previous editions, we have included an Index of Rhetorical Principles which notes the passages in each speech that best illustrate the major speech principles discussed in modern speech textbooks.

This book also can serve as the core textbook in a course in Contemporary Public Address. While we have continued to emphasize speech forms and principles, in this edition more than in previous editions we have included speeches by well-known speakers. And always we have sought speeches that typify current public scrutiny of some of society's most pressing questions. The speech forms themselves assure coverage of the spectrum of contemporary public address. Knowledge, facts, values, problems, and policies have always been rhetoric's essence. At the same time, ceremonial address continues to be a vital form for social cohesion.

We again wish to acknowledge our indebtedness to the many people and sources who have given us permission to reprint speeches in this book. *Vital Speeches of the Day* continues to be an important source for representative speeches on current issues. We are also grateful for the recommendations that have been so thoughtfully provided by colleagues.

R. L. J.
R. R. A.
W. A. L.
F. J. B.

Chapter One

Why Study Speeches?

> *Only as the constant companions of Demosthenes,*
> *Cicero, Burke, Fox, Channing, and Webster can we*
> *hope to become orators.*
>
> *Woodrow Wilson*

The primary purpose of *Contemporary American Speeches* is to present a collection of speeches for student analysis and evaluation. Just as Woodrow Wilson considered the study of speeches essential to his personal development as a speaker, we hope that this chapter will stimulate your thinking about the importance of such study in your own intellectual life.

We Study Speeches to Increase Our Knowledge of Humanity

One of the purposes of a college education is to encourage students to ponder the nature of their own humanity. In most degree programs, students are encouraged to engage in liberal studies as a complement to the sequence of professional courses that leads to specialized careers. A professional person is, after all, a person: a lawyer is a person who practices law, a teacher is a person who teaches, a doctor is a person who practices medicine, a scientist is a person who studies the physical world in which we live. Through liberal studies, students are encouraged to develop insights regarding the potentialities and limitations of the human condition. Through such knowledge, a system of values should emerge that provides the basis for future decisions, both professional and personal.

Students may take varied paths in their efforts to understand what it means to be human. Each liberal study holds such promise—and rightfully so. Nothing thought or made or done by people is alien to the student in search of human understanding. Emerson said: "Raphael paints wisdom; Handel sings it; Phidias carves it; Shakespeare writes it; Wren builds it; Columbus sails it; Luther preaches it; Washington arms it; Watt mechanizes it." In each of these studies, students may find evidence of the creative struggle of human beings with their environment. And from each of these studies, students may gain insights into their own lives.

In the liberal arts tradition, speeches deserve to be studied because they are a unique form of human expression. No other artifact of social life reflects the same exact process. A painting encompasses the elements of thought and form; yet a speech is composed of language. A poem embraces thought, language, and form; yet a speech is conveyed by sound. Theatre makes use of thought, language, form, and sound; yet a speech is at once more urgent and real, more literal and spontaneous. A speech is a unique product of human creativity; it calls for special understanding as does a painting or a poem, a statue or a scroll.

Speeches have a quality that makes them especially deserving of study by students in search of human understanding; speeches are highly transparent. They are the product of human beings in dynamic confrontation with ideas and audiences. In speeches, students will find men and women articulating the noble ideals of our civilization and making enlightened judgments on the great social, moral, and political issues of our own and other times. In speeches, students will also find men and women degrading our common humanity and concocting themes of hatred and bigotry. In speeches, the potentialities and limitations of the human condition are clearly reflected.

We Study Speeches to Derive Standards for the Critical Appraisal of Public Discourse

Few will question the claim that the quality of our public dialogue is not what it might be. In lecture halls, we have grown accustomed to speakers who are dull, disorganized, and unclear. In chambers of social decisionmaking, we have come to accept as the norm underdeveloped ideas expressed in careless language and sloppy speech. And even at moments of public ceremony, we expect speeches that are trite and mundane when what is called for is an inspiring rearticulation of our social purpose and identity.

As members of audiences, we have come to demand too little of those who address us. Through the study of speeches, we may develop higher standards for the public dialogue. We may come to demand more of those who address us, both in terms of the merit of their ideas and their means of public expression.

The study of speeches offers a broad familiarity with the crucial issues of humanity. Our communion with the past, the freedom of our citizens, the quality of our private and public life, our hopes for the future—all of these are evident in the public dialogue. Through an awareness of the significant issues of our own and other times, students may come to reject trivial issues and petty thoughts as unworthy of public attention.

Through the study of speeches, students may also acquire insights regarding the habits of intellect through which responsible speakers examine, test, and temper ideas. Through such knowledge, they may appraise the worth of a speaker's critical processes. They may test the sufficiency of the speaker's proof. They may deny the specious inference and the faulty deduction. They may reject simplistic answers to complex social questions.

But the enlightened critic must not stop here. Public discourse does not exist in a social vacuum. It is not soliloquy, but purposive address seeking to impart to its hearers some knowledge or interpretation, some value or course of action. Public discourse always seeks to influence the hearer and to change his or her behavior— whether cognitive or overt. If ideas are to have social utility, they must be transformed from private conceptions into meaningful public statements. Speakers must so develop and project their thoughts that direction is given to those who listen. They must choose from a complex of elements those most likely to give energy and vitality to their ideas in a particular public context.

Through the study of speeches, students will come to realize that speakers can adapt ideas to audiences in meaningful and socially productive ways. While recognizing the shortcomings of the public intellect, they will know that speakers have made complex ideas clear. While recognizing that speakers have exploited public avarice and ignorance in achieving personal power, they will know that other speakers have fostered social excellence. While recognizing that speeches have embodied appeals to low motives and base instincts, they will know that oratory has sometimes inspired audiences to act in accord with the noble ideas of humanity.

The dimensions of rhetorical choice are numerous. In Chapter 2, you will be introduced to thirteen questions which will guide your study of the means speakers employ in rendering their ideas clear, persuasive, and memorable. As you apply these questions to speeches, you will develop an increased appreciation for the artistry which undergirds effective public communication. As you witness speakers conveying the essence of significant thoughts with skill and integrity, you will have cause to reject other speakers whose expressions are feeble, whose appeals are base, whose strategies are unethical, and whose purposes are suspect.

We Study Speeches to Enlarge and Deepen Our Understanding of Rhetorical Theory

The student of speech, faced with a body of precepts set forth in a contemporary basic public speaking textbook, will often fail to assign importance to the ideas expressed. The text, it may seem, is too firm in its adherence to inviolate rules, too committed to the perpetuation of useless names and distinctions, and too verbose in the expression of common sense. Any body of principles divorced from the context that gave it being may seem drab and useless. But if these principles are viewed in their proper context, they tend to become meaningful and even intellectually stimulating.

Rhetorical theory was born of the attempt of people to systematize their observations of the purposive and dynamic public interactions of other people. In the fifth century B.C. the first body of rhetorical precepts emerged from Corax's observations of the attempts of his fellow citizens of Syracuse to give social order to a society newly emerged from tyranny. In the centuries that followed, countless other people recorded their observations of identifiable speech principles. While those who followed owed a great debt to those who preceded them, each generation of theorists sought to redefine and reconceptualize the art of speaking in a manner consistent with their own perceptions of public address as it occurred in their own cultures and in their own times.

Authors of modern public speaking textbooks must also acknowledge their debt to the great rhetorical tradition. Their task, however, is not the perpetuation of "the intellectual faults of eminent men." Rather, they seek to test and temper the principles of the art of public communication. They must blend with the old the particular insights of the new—insights gleaned from the scholarship of their own and related disciplines, insights gathered from their own judicious observation of public discourse. Building on the rhetorical philosophies of the past with a knowledge of the present, modern theorists seek to create not a memorial to the past but a structure consistent with the needs and realities of the present. Such work is vital and meaningful, not drab or devoid of intellectual stimulation.

Is it strange that what is bright with intellectual challenge in process often seems boring in product? Not really. The excitement of the intellectual search for precepts by one person is easily lost when relegated to a body of generalizations for the consumption of another. It is not that the theory is bad; it is just that theory alone, divorced from the world from which it was abstracted, is inadequate.

Would it not be best, then, for the student of speech to seek out his or her own precepts? Not really. The perceptive student, skilled in listening to popular instances of communication and afforded such great examples as Burke, Churchill, and Roosevelt, could derive his or her own theory of speech. But at what expense of time? At what expense to progress? Each student would have to begin anew the quest for order and meaning, as helplessly alone as if no one else had ever walked the same path.

While the problem is not fully solved by presenting the student with the generalizations of another's mind, concisely arranged, neither is it fully solved by presenting the student with a body of speech masterpieces, past and present, with the caution to keep "an open mind and vigilant eye." The study of a public speaking textbook is, like the study of examples of public discourse, one important element in the training of the student of public speaking. Preference for one should not lead to a discarding of the other. A public speaking textbook is a body of generalizations drawn from the author's contemplation of the long tradition of rhetorical theory, the scholarship of the day, and his or her own perceptions of human communication. It exists not to inhibit but to stimulate. Intelligent students will put the precepts of a textbook to the pragmatic test of actual public life. They will realize, as did Quintilian, that "rhetoric would be a very easy and small matter, if it could be included in one short body of rules, but rules must generally be altered to suit the nature of each individual case, the time, the occasion, and the necessity itself. . . ." By testing the generalizations of a textbook in the light of real and varied instances of public discourse, students will learn to challenge, question, and compare and, ultimately, develop for themselves a theory of speech that is both comprehensive and personal.

We Study Speeches to Develop an Appreciation for Eminence in Public Address

In 1852, Chauncey Goodrich, Professor of Rhetoric at Yale College, reviewed his teaching philosophy in the preface to his work *Select British Eloquence*. He wrote:

> My object was not only to awaken in the minds of the class that love of genuine eloquence which is the surest pledge of success, but to aid them in catching the spirit of the authors read, and, by analyzing passages selected for the purpose, to initiate the pupil in those higher principles which (whether they were conscious of it or not) have always guided the great masters of the art, till he should learn the *unwritten* rules of oratory, which operate by a kind of instinct upon the mind, and are far more important than any that are found in the books.

This passage has merit today for students who would be more than followers of blueprints. It recommends that students develop an appreciation for eminence in public address, a love of eloquence, by looking beyond textbook principles to the unwritten rules of the art. It suggests the importance of developing a sense of the rightness, or the strength, or the felicity of a thought or an expression through exposure to speeches. Such an appreciation of eminence serves to inspire students to seek in their own works only the highest level of excellence.

Students who have come to acquire this appreciation for eminence will reject trivial subjects. They will understand that a concern for significant ideas has been at the heart of great oratory since ancient times. Demosthenes spoke for the freedom of a city. Churchill spoke for the survival of a nation. Roosevelt spoke for human freedom. Kennedy spoke for peace in a divided world. Rhetorical eminence presupposes worthy ideas to express, ideas that merit the attention and efforts of the speaker and the concern of the audience.

But rhetorical excellence also requires eloquence in expression. Given significant ideas, great public address demands an expression that renders the idea in a striking and compelling way, giving it life and vitality. Stephen Spender once wrote a poem called *I Think Continuously of Those Who Were Truly Great*. As public speakers, students may find great inspiration from the speeches of people who surpassed the ordinary and achieved new heights in skillful and effective communication.

The dimensions of rhetorical excellence are diverse. Some speakers are models of eminence in delivery. Billy Graham, to whom charisma is often attributed, is a model of both vocal and physical involvement and intensity. Barbara Jordan, who captured the spirit of the 1976 Democratic Convention, is known for her vocal precision and overall dynamism. Paul Harvey, with his distinctive oral style, has captivated generations of Americans via radio. Student speakers, finding inspiration in the delivery of able speakers, may seek in their own delivery the same sense of dynamism and involvement.

Students may also gain inspiration from those who use language in lively and memorable ways. The history of public discourse is rich with examples of language which illuminated thoughts in compelling ways: Roosevelt dispelled panic with the expression, "The only thing we have to fear is fear itself"; Churchill imparted strength with the expression, "This was their finest hour"; Kennedy inspired dedication with the expression, "Ask not what your country can do for you—ask what you can do for your country"; Martin Luther King generated hope with the expression, "I have a dream." Students who are exposed to eminence in language usage may acquire an intimate sense of the rightness, appropriateness, and artistry of language that will help them to give greater force to their own ideas.

In the study of speeches, students may also find eminence in ordering ideas, marshalling supporting materials, and enlisting the emotions of audiences. Having acquired an appreciation for eloquence, students may demand more of themselves at those moments when they give public expression to their ideas.

Conclusion

The study of speeches can play an important role in the intellectual development of contemporary college students. Through such study we may expect to *increase our knowledge of humanity, to derive standards for the critical appraisal of public discourse, to enlarge and deepen our understanding of rhetorical theory,* and *to develop an appreciation for eminence in public address.*

For Further Reading

ON SPEECH AS A HUMANE STUDY

Linkugel, Wilmer A., and Johannesen, Richard L. "The Study of Masterpieces of Public Address." *Southern Speech Journal,* Summer 1960, pp. 289–97. Presents the rationale for the scrutiny of noted speeches in the classroom.

Nichols, Marie Hochmuth. *Rhetoric and Criticism.* Louisiana State University Press, 1963. Chapter 1 analyzes rhetoric and public address as a humane study—as a study of people making enlightened choices in a rhetorical context.

Walter, Otis. *Speaking Intelligently.* Macmillan, 1976. Chapter 1 examines the role of rhetoric as a force in the growth of civilization.

Wilson, John F., Arnold, Carroll C., and Wertheimer, Molly. *Public Speaking as a Liberal Art.* 6th ed. Allyn and Bacon, 1990. Chapter 1 examines speech as a liberal study showing people apprehending truths about themselves and their environment and communicating them to others.

ON THE CRITICAL ANALYSIS OF SPEECHES

Cathcart, Robert. *Post Communication: Rhetorical Analysis and Evaluation.* 2nd ed. Bobbs-Merrill, 1981. A brief but very useful treatment of speech criticism.

Walter, Otis M., and Scott, Robert L. *Thinking and Speaking.* 5th ed. Macmillan, 1984. Chapters 11 and 12 present advice on analysis of speeches and arguments.

Wilson, John F., Arnold, Carroll C., and Wertheimer, Molly. *Public Speaking as a Liberal Art.* 6th ed. Allyn and Bacon, 1990. Chapter 11 presents a methodology for the critical appraisal of speeches.

ON RHETORICAL THEORY

Aristotle. *Rhetoric.* The definitive ancient treatise on the art of rhetoric.

Clark, Donald Lemen. *Rhetoric in Greco-Roman Education.* Columbia University Press, 1957. Chapter 2 explains what the ancients meant by rhetoric. Chapter 4 presents the five ancient rhetorical canons of invention, organization, style, delivery, and memory. Chapter 5 discusses how the ancients used speech models for study and emulation.

Golden, James et al., eds. *The Rhetoric of Western Thought.* 6th ed. Kendall/Hunt Publishing Company, 1997. A collection of original and reprinted essays that trace the development of theories of rhetoric from Greco-Roman times to the present.

Wilson, John F., Arnold, Carroll C., and Wertheimer, Molly. *Public Speaking as a Liberal Art.* 6th ed. Allyn and Bacon, 1990. Appendix A presents an overview of the historical development of rhetorical theory.

ON EMINENCE IN PUBLIC ADDRESS

Bryant, Donald C. *Rhetorical Dimensions in Criticism.* Louisiana State University Press, 1973. Chapter 6 explores the concept of "eloquence" in discourse.

Osborn, Michael. *Orientations to Rhetorical Style.* Science Research Associates, Modcom Modules in Speech Communication, 1976. A 35 page booklet that discusses the significance, techniques, and abuses of language choices in discourse.

Jamieson, Kathleen Hall. *Eloquence in an Electronic Age.* Oxford University Press, 1988. Assesses the functions, forms, and quality of contemporary American public address.

Wilson, John F., Arnold, Carroll C., and Wertheimer, Molly. *Public Speaking as a Liberal Art.* 6th ed. Allyn and Bacon, 1990. Chapter 9 discusses the nature of oral and written style, resources of language, and criteria of effective style.

Chapter Two

The Analysis of Speeches

Because communication is a powerful force, we need profound and searching insight into communications— into their truth or falsity, their wisdom or stupidity, their profundity or emptiness, into their subtle greatness or disguised and hidden meanness. Since we need such insights, we need critics of rhetoric and communications. In a democratic society, rhetorical criticism is especially important, for in a democracy, all individuals must understand and judge what they hear and read. Therefore, we all must be, at times, our own rhetorical critics.

Otis M. Walter and Robert L. Scott

This book is a collection of speeches that exemplify the major forms and principles of public address in contemporary American society. A rationale for the study of speeches has been presented in the preceding chapter; it thus remains for us to place in perspective the underlying philosophy and the procedural patterns for the use of this book.

The Art of Rhetoric

Rhetoric is a term with varied and vague meanings today. Major dictionaries, reflecting the popular confusion, list numerous definitions. Among those commonly cited are the following: the speech of stereotyped politicians—empty, misleading, insincere, and high-flown; an oratorical display or exaggeration; highly figurative language, commonly called "purple patches"; the art of prose writing; and, originally, the art of oratory. *Rhetoric, oratory,* and *eloquence* all come from roots meaning *to speak.* Quintilian, the Roman schoolmaster, placed the art of rhetoric at the center of his educational system. Aristotle thought that rhetoric had the capacity to prevent the triumph of fraud and injustice, to instruct popular audiences, to help persons see both sides of an issue, and to help provide a dignified and distinctive means of self-defense.

As used in this book, *rhetoric* is the art of selecting, adapting, and communicating ideas primarily through verbal means to achieve a desired response from a specific audience. The rhetorical act involves making choices related to both the matter of communication—what subjects may be chosen, what issues they embrace, and what values they embody—and the manner of communicating perceptions in order to produce a desired effect. It is important to the welfare of a democratic society that both of these types of choices be enlightened and ethical. Interest in the effectiveness of rhetorical techniques must not outstrip concern for their ethical use. Ethical judgments about rhetorical means employed to achieve ends or judgments of the ethics of the ends cannot be escaped. Each of us must decide for ourself the ethical balance point between our own idea in its pure form and that idea modified to achieve maximum impact on the specific audience.

In seeking to define the nature of rhetoric, theorists have identified those dimensions common to all instances of public discourse. First, there is a person with an idea and a speech purpose—the *speaker.* Governed by personal physical, intellectual, and experiential characteristics, the speaker seeks to choose, structure, and present the message so as to elicit a desired response. Next, there is the *audience,* whose members see the rhetorical context through individual lenses. They may view the speaker as expert, trustworthy, and of good will, or they may set up emotional blocks to the message because the speaker's image and reputation strike them unfavorably. They may view the speaker's thesis as interesting, wise, accurate, and of unquestionable merit, or they may erect barriers to the message because the speaker's ideas run contrary to the beliefs, attitudes, and values that their personal experiences have dictated to them. Finally, there is the *situation* in which the speech occurs: a place—a college classroom, the United States Senate, an ancient synagogue, or London's Hyde Park; a time—fourth century Athens, twentieth century Washington, before lunch or after, November 22, 1963, December 7, 1941; an occasion—a prep-school commencement, a Rotary Club meeting, a Presidential inaugural, a murder trial, a United Nations Security Council meeting, a business association luncheon, or a scientific conference.

In addition to the dimensions of speaker, audience, and situation, speech theorists have identified four variables common to the speech itself. In attempting to promote a desired response, the speaker makes choices about each of these four variables. Through the process that rhetoricians call *invention*, or the discovery and selection of the central idea and its supports, the speaker utilizes appropriate evidence, reasoning, and appeals to audience motives and values to substantiate the message. The remaining three variables relate to transmission of the idea. The speaker selects relevant patterns of *organization* to provide structure and design. Furthermore, the speaker employs impelling symbolization through *language* best suited to himself or herself, to the subject, to the audience, and to the situation. Finally, the speaker uses *delivery* to get the idea across to the audience. Whether he or she uses the impromptu, extemporaneous, manuscript, or memorized methods of delivery, the speaker employs both voice and body to reinforce the meaning and feeling embodied in the message.

Standard speech textbooks contain general principles on these dimensions and variables as they pertain to all types of speeches. By including these principles, these books seek to provide a foundation for purposive and responsible public address that you may use as a guide for your speaking behavior. We will not discuss all of these principles. Rather, we will present examples of speeches illustrating them. Additionally, the introduction to each chapter will focus on the nature of the constraints that influence the speaker's choices in adapting principles to that speech form.

The Forms of Speeches

Since ancient times, scholars have sought to classify those social contexts that give rise to public discourse. They have done so in order to understand the nature of the rhetorical act and to formulate principles by which it might be taught. In 336 B.C. Aristotle saw men in law courts trying to secure justice concerning past actions. Accordingly, he identified one class of speeches as *forensic*. In a second instance, he witnessed men deliberating about problems and the best courses of action for their solution. He saw statesmen in the political assembly giving counsel and advice about the practicality and desirability of future policies. He saw men in legislative chambers seeking to exhort or dissuade those who could decide future action. These speeches he classified as *deliberative.* Finally, he observed men at ceremonial gatherings praising the virtuous and eulogizing the noble dead. At other times he beheld men launching vitriolic attacks against others at public gatherings. These speeches of praise and blame he labeled *epideictic.*

As Aristotle profited from appraising the speeches of his day, so too may the modern scholar of rhetoric profit from an examination of contemporary speeches. As we survey twentieth century public address, we see people in public gatherings translating technical information into popular terms; we see others describing an experience or event. At other times we see people publicly probing for definitive meanings, searching for the causes of natural and social phenomena, dispelling stereotypes, and seeking out the implications of things and events. We classify such speeches as attempts to increase *understanding.* In other situations, we see lawyers seeking decisions on the guilt or innocence of their clients, politicians asking for acceptance of what they validate as facts, and citizens arguing over the "real" cause of something. These speakers are *affirming propositions of fact.* On some occasions, we witness speakers urging adoption of new standards for human behavior, and we see drama and literary critics applying criteria to art forms to establish a judgment about their quality. When people seek to formulate or change human values or to apply standards as measurements of quality, we label their efforts *affirming propositions of value.* In some instances, we observe speakers seeking to make people vitally aware of problems that hinder personal and social fulfillment. These persons are *creating concern for problems.* In still other situations, we see persons advocating programs for the solution of perplexing problems and for the ultimate betterment of society. This effort we call *affirming propositions of policy.* Finally, we see speakers on ceremonial occasions asking for a unity of spirit or for a reenergizing of effort or commitment. When a person urges increased dedication to the existing values of a group, we label that purpose *intensifying social cohesion.*

Some Guidelines for Analysis of Speeches

As a type of rhetorical criticism, the analysis of speeches is not a fool-proof, mathematically precise act of description and calculation. An act of criticism is, by its very nature, an act of persuasion and argument. As a critic you apply standards, make claims, and offer support for those claims. As a critic you argue for the reasonable probability, not absolute certainty, of your descriptions and judgments. In addition, your own beliefs and predispositions will influence your selection and application of a framework for criticism. Such influential factors would include your assumptions about the nature and sources of reality and truth, the ways in which humans derive reliable knowledge, the basis of ethics, and the capacities that mark the essence of human nature. In turn the critical framework that you employ will focus your analysis *toward* some aspects while at the same time deflecting your attention *away from* other aspects. And another critic employing a different critical perspective might reasonably describe and evaluate a particular speech differently than you.

Each of the remaining chapters in this anthology is introduced by a brief essay setting forth guidelines for analyzing the speeches which illustrate that form. At this point we will limit ourselves to suggesting some potential general dimensions and questions for use in judging speechmaking.[1]

Our suggestions are not intended as a definitive statement on speech criticism. They simply are some starting points for possible use in assessing speeches inside and outside the classroom. We do not view this set of guidelines as the only method or the "best" method of speech analysis. Other useful approaches for the criticism of speeches are described in some of the Sources for Further Reading at the end of this and subsequent chapters.

Obviously, in assessing a specific speech, each dimension or question would not be of equal importance. You might, for instance, consider reasonableness and ethicality more crucial than language and delivery. The criteria you use for evaluation should be those particularly appropriate for both the general speech form and the specific speech. Furthermore, consider how dimensions and questions may point to an interaction of factors. How might a listener's value system influence her or his perception of what is reasonable? Or how might a speaker's attitude toward an audience influence that speaker's credibility or perceived ethicality?

As you analyze a particular speech, you may find that some aspects of it are so prominent and worthy of note that they "invite," indeed they "demand," your critical attention. Aspects of a speech may be noteworthy, for example, because they are so frequent, so obvious, so unique, so subtle, so probably effective, so superbly handled, so poorly done, or so detrimental to effectiveness. Based on the general nature of the speech and the rhetorical aspects that invite your critical attention, you probably will select for use only some of the following dimensions or questions.

In presenting an oral or written analysis of a speech, the quality of your criticism will be improved if you discuss *both* strengths and weaknesses; criticism is not solely the making of negative judgments. In addition, quality is improved by specifying, explaining, and justifying the lines of inquiry, framework for analysis, or standards for evaluation you will utilize.

---

[1] Some of the following material is adapted from the contributions of Richard L. Johannesen for *Principles and Types of Speech Communication,* Seventh Edition, by Alan H. Monroe and Douglas Ehninger, pp. 245–47, 249–57, 453–63. Copyright © 1974, 1967, 1962, 1955, 1949, 1939, 1935 by Scott, Foresman and Company.

1.   **To what factors in the immediate occasion or more general relevant situation does the speaker seem to be responding?**

Speechmaking is situationally motivated and a speaker makes choices of communicative ends and means in response to a set of circumstances and to a specific audience. Hence, it is well to begin an analysis of most speeches by discussing the societal milieu, the nature of the physical and ideological setting, and the probable causes that led up to the speech. How might factors in the occasion or prevailing ideological climate have influenced the speaker's purpose and/or methods? To what in particular does the speaker seem to be responding: To a problem, opportunity, lack of information, duty, challenge, ceremonial obligation, attack, issue, or routine invitation?

What is the nature and significance of the specific audience addressed by the speaker? Consider the relevance of such matters as size, age, sex, occupation, educational background, memberships in organizations, ethnic background, and knowledge of the subject of the speech. Is the primary audience the one physically present, or is it perhaps one to be exposed "second-hand" through the various mass media, or is it one "observing" a confrontation between a speaker and audience? Are there any secondary audiences intended for the message?

Sometimes the impact of a speech is influenced by such factors in the occasion as time of day, room acoustics and seating arrangement, preceding and following speeches, and audience customs and expectations. Clearly the expectations for a presidential inaugural address and for a political rally speech differ. Depending upon the role the audience expects a speaker to fulfill (such as leader, advisor, expert, lecturer, intruder, spokesperson for them or others), they may expect different evidence, appeals, proposals, language, and delivery. How adequately a speaker handles questions and answers in a forum period after the speech may influence audience perceptions of the speech.

The speech may play a role in some larger campaign of communication or in the activities of a particular social movement. Is the speaker a spokesperson in behalf of some group or other person and thus probably less free to voice entirely his or her own viewpoint? Is the speech a major effort to be supplemented by other modes of communication? Is it one in a planned series of addresses on the subject? Is the central communication thrust on this subject being carried out through other modes and channels with this speech as only a minor part of the total program? What influence might presentation via radio and/or television have on the impact of the speech?

2.   **What seem to be the speaker's general and specific purposes?**

Typical general purposes are to entertain, to present information and increase understanding, to reinforce existing beliefs and values, to change values and beliefs, and to secure overt action. Consider whether the speaker's intent seems to be identification and agreement, shock and arousal, or confrontation and alienation. What more concrete outcome does the speaker seem to want from his or her audience? What exactly does the speaker want the audience to believe, feel, or do? Does the specific purpose seem appropriate for the subject, audience, and occasion?

Given the audience and relevant circumstances, probe whether the speaker's purposes appear realistic and achievable. Remember that countermessages from other communicators, or unexpected and uncontrollable events, may work on listener's minds to weaken the impact of the speaker's message. Remember, also, that some situations are not altered very easily through public speech. No matter what is said to some audiences, for instance, they may refuse to modify their strongly held beliefs, values, and actions. And some audiences may believe, accurately or inaccurately, that they do not possess the power, authority, skill, money, or facilities to adopt the speaker's idea.

3.   How does the speaker capture and sustain audience attention and interest?

No matter how sincere the speaker's intent, no matter how sound her or his reasoning, no matter how worthwhile the message, if the audience's attention is not aroused at the outset and maintained throughout, the speaker's efforts are doomed to failure. If no one listens, belief and action cannot be influenced as the speaker hopes. In the content, language, and delivery of the speech, are such interest-factors as conflict, suspense, familiarity, novelty, humor, action, curiosity, and concreteness capitalized on? Is interest heightened through such means as narration of a story, vivid description, analogy, contrast, hypothetical and factual examples, and extended illustrations?

4.   How does the speaker strive to insure that the audience clearly understands the message as intended?

Assess the probability that listeners will know exactly what the speaker is asking of them and concretely how to help implement that idea or proposal. Judge whether ideas are presented accurately and clearly and whether extremes of complexity and simplification are avoided. If ambiguity seems employed intentionally, what factors in the subject or occasion might account for or even justify it? How adequately does the introductory portion of the speech gain attention, challenge the audience, lead smoothly into the topic, or create goodwill for the speaker and topic? How adequately does the conclusion summarize basic ideas, convey a sense of completion, leave the listeners in an appropriate mood, or stimulate acceptance of the central belief or action sought? Consider what patterns of organization the speaker uses to foster unity and clarity: chronological, spatial, problem-solution, general-to-specific or vice versa, cause-effect, examination of alternatives, and so forth. If the speech lacks clear structure, is this apparently due to speaker ineptness or may there be some justification for it?

To promote understanding, how does the speaker utilize such devices as repetition, restatement, transitions, internal summaries, parallel phrasing, numerical "signposts," itemization, association with the familiar, examples and illustrations, questions and answers, statistics, and definitions. Some definitions are "objective" in the sense that they report widely accepted, noncontroversial meanings current with experts or with the public. Other definitions are "persuasive" in the sense that the speaker is asking the audience to accept her or his particular meaning as the correct or appropriate definition for a concept which is subject to challenge or controversy. How does the speaker employ audiovisual aids and vocal-physical delivery to increase understanding? If appropriate, how adequately does the speaker answer such standard questions as who, what, where, when, why, and how?

5.   **To what degree might listeners perceive the speaker's proposal (idea, belief, policy) as sound and reasonable?**

Bear in mind that accepted standards of reason, logic, and soundness may vary from one audience to another, from one culture to another, or between fields of discourse (such as politics, religion, natural science, law, historiography). As a critic you may wish to apply to the message some "universal" or "traditional" tests of soundness for evidence and reasoning. But also consider whether such tests are appropriate for the specific speech situation or subject matter. Furthermore, an audience may not make a sharp distinction between so-called logical and emotional appeals. For instance, a set of statistics showing a high probability of listeners being stricken with some form of cancer during their lifetime may be perceived by them as both logical and emotional; for them it simply is a reasonable item of support.

Assess how adequately the speaker employs evidence and reasoning to demonstrate that his or her proposal actually will work, will solve the problem, will be efficient, and will not be too costly. Is the proposal feasible despite such potential limitations as minimal time, personnel, or finances? Evaluate the soundness of the factual examples, expert testimony, literal analogies, statistics, and cause-effect reasoning the speaker employs. Is the speaker's idea consistent with the relevant beliefs and attitudes of the audience? If not, is such inconsistency seemingly due to speaker ineptitude or planned to serve some persuasive function? Is there a legitimate connection between the speaker's idea or purpose and the audience's relevant needs, motives, goals, and emotions? Are listeners made to "feel" a personal stake in the outcome? Has the speaker exaggerated the connection or appealed to irrelevant needs?

What premises or fundamental beliefs are verbalized by the speaker as underpinnings for further argument? Implicitly undergirding the speaker's ideas, are there any unstated assumptions, any unspoken basic beliefs, values, premises, or stereotypes? Are such unstated assumptions probably omitted to avoid scrutiny by the audience or because the speaker and audience already share the assumption? Consider in what ways the spoken and unspoken assumptions reflect the speaker's conception of reality, truth, dependable knowledge, goodness, religion, or the essence of human nature. What might be the intended function or unintended impact of omission of an expected idea or of silence on a controversial issue?

6.   To what degree do the speaker's ideas harmonize with the audience's relevant values?

A value, for our purposes, is defined as a conception of "The Good" or "The Desirable." Honesty, fairness, honor, efficiency, progress, economy, courage, safety, prudence, and patriotism all are examples of possible values for persons. In numerous speeches throughout his two terms as president, Ronald Reagan stressed a cluster of "traditional" American values: family, neighborhood, work, patriotism, peace, and freedom. A value may function either generally, as a goal motivating our behavior, or specifically, as a standard we use to assess the acceptability of means to accomplish ends. We might, for instance, recognize that a policy or solution is efficient and economical, but reject that program for being dishonest and inhumane. Frequently dominant personal or group values are reflected in slogans or mottos: "Liberty, Equality, Fraternity"; "Duty, Honor, Country"; "Law and Order"; "Law and Order with Justice"; "Freedom Now"; "All Power to the People"; "Peace with Honor."

Values are not proved or disproved in quite the same way as "factual" matters. We measure the length of a table with a ruler to demonstrate that it is indeed one meter long. But it is difficult, if not impossible, to measure precisely degrees of beauty, courage, and honesty. And proposed measures of freedom, progress, or efficiency often themselves are controversial. As a culture or subculture develops, a given value becomes accepted as functional for that group. Naturally, the values which predominate often vary from one culture to another. One culture may hold punctuality as a basic value, for example, while another deems being on time of little importance. We develop our own individual value systems in the context of larger cultural and subcultural value systems.

Usually we *rank* the values we hold into a rough *hierarchy* so that some values to which we are committed take precedence over others. In fact, in *The New Rhetoric*, philosopher Chaim Perelman argues that a "particular audience is characterized less by values it accepts than by the way it grades them." Note also that in a specific situation several audience values may come into conflict, thus forcing a choice of one value over another in making a decision. The audience may continue to believe in both values, but temporarily set one aside in favor of the other. For instance, a speaker may advocate in a given situation adherence to honesty over efficiency, patriotism over self-concern, economy over education, or humaneness over frankness.

A warning is in order. A speaker often overtly appeals to a seemingly potent value to which the audience *says* it is committed. But do not assume that the audience always will *act* in accordance with the declared value. In a particular instance the audience may perceive some other value as more important; they may not *apply* the value appealed to and to which they in general are devoted.

In assessing the various value appeals of a speaker, consider the general approach used. Is the aim to get listeners to adopt a new value to replace an outmoded one, perhaps through a redefinition of the meaning we should have for the original value-word? Is the speaker urging acceptance of her or his value judgment of something as an accurate and appropriate judgment? In what ways does the speech function to reinforce and reenergize values already held by the audience? Is the speaker creating concern for a problem by showing that relevant audience values are being threatened or violated? Is the speaker advocating adoption of a policy or solution in part because it harmonizes with or fosters relevant audience values? By exploring such questions, you can move toward an understanding of specific techniques through which a speaker attempts to link an idea or proposal to potent audience values.

7.   To what degree is the speaker perceived as a credible source on the subject?

The positive or negative perceptions that listeners have of a speaker's personal qualities play a major role in determining whether they will accept his or her information, arguments, or proposal. Ancient Greek and Roman rhetorical theorists called this concept *ethos* and identified its three major elements as good sense, good character, and good will. Contemporary communication scholars use such labels as source credibility, image, and reputation to describe audience attitude toward the speaker; they have identified expertness and trustworthiness as the two most potent dimensions of speaker credibility. Listeners assess a speaker's *expertness* by making judgments about competency, experience, and knowledge of the subject. *Trustworthiness* is a quality audiences attribute to a speaker whom they perceive as honest, dependable, sincere, fair, and similar to them in values, beliefs, and background. Researchers have identified a moderately influential dimension, often called *dynamism*, rooted in how alert, energetic, firm-minded, and interesting an audience considers a speaker. And informed observation would suggest that listeners evaluate a speaker's *good will* toward them by judging her or his friendliness, likability, and concern for them.

Ethos is variable rather than static. A speaker's credibility might vary from one audience to another, from one decade to another, or from one subject to another. Different cultures or subcultures may prize different personal qualities as constituting positive *ethos*, or an audience may perceive different qualities as relevant on different topics. The *ethos* attributed to a speaker by listeners will fluctuate during presentation of the speech as the audience judges use of evidence and reasoning, motivational appeals, language, structure, and vocal-physical delivery. Sometimes speakers directly attempt to foster positive *ethos* with an audience by overtly mentioning experiences or qualifications as marks of their expertise or by quoting or indicating associations with persons whose *ethos* with the audience already is high. A speaker's *ethos* level at the conclusion of the speech is an outcome of interaction of her or his reputation (prior audience knowledge of speaker's views, accomplishments, associations, and personality) with the audience's assessment of how well the speaker performed during the speech itself.

Although high *ethos* will not guarantee speaker success, markedly low source credibility usually thwarts a communicative effort. No matter how *actually* sound and ethical are a speaker's program, information, arguments, and appeals, if the audience *perceives* the speaker as incompetent, unethical, untrustworthy, bored, overly nervous, or aloof, then her or his message probably will have little of the desired impact.

8.   What attitudes toward his or her audience does the speaker seem to reveal?

A speaker's attitude toward an audience reflects his or her view of the listener's personal worth and abilities as well as an indication of the speaker's orientation or stance toward the audience. First, attempt to isolate how the speaker's attitude orientation is revealed in communicative choices, strategies, and techniques. Such reflections may be inferred from verbal and nonverbal elements such as word choice, level of abstraction, types of examples, specificity of analysis, emphasis given to items, vocal pitch and quality, facial expression, and directness of eye contact.

Second, attempt to identify the attitudinal stances characteristic of all or parts of the speech. Is the attitude that you perceive probably the one perceived by the audience, the one intended by the speaker, and a sincere index of his or her "real" view? Are any of the speaker's attitudinal stances especially ethical or unethical? Our discussion later in this chapter of question #13 on ethical standards for assessing public discourse may help you consider this issue. Your efforts may be aided by considering to what degree the speech reveals one or more of the following attitude clusters: (1) respect, equality, understanding, honesty, genuineness, concern for audience welfare and improvement, sincerity, openness to new views, trust, selflessness, empathy, helpfulness, humility; (2) prudence, moderation, indifference, aloofness, unconcern, apathy, disinterest, blandness, coldness; (3) objectivity, neutrality; (4) self-aggrandizement, ego-satisfaction, personal "showing off," pretentiousness; (5) superiority, domination, exploitation for personal gain, deception, insincerity, dogmatism, coercion, facade, judgmentalism, arrogance, contempt, condescension, possessiveness, selfishness; (6) aggressiveness, abrasiveness, hostility, nonconciliation, insult, derogation, curtness; (7) inferiority, supplication, pleading, deference; (8) defensiveness, competitiveness, fear, distrust, suspicion; (9) conciliation, consensus, cooperation, identification.

Third, explore in what ways the speaker's attitude toward the audience seems to reflect personal philosophy; beliefs about human nature, society, reality, values, and ethics are some elements of such a philosophy. Does the attitude reflect optimism or pessimism toward human capabilities and potential? Does the speaker see humans as capable of reflective self-decision or only of being coerced or dominated? An attitude might indicate a belief that reality and knowledge are perceived and attained with certainty or with much relativism and uncertainty. Attitudes of cynicism, duplicity, and domination may stem from a commitment to the end justifying the means.

Fourth, probe how the speaker's attitude toward an audience relates to her or his purposes and motives. Does the attitude revealed appear to reinforce or to thwart achievement of the speaker's intended purpose? Is there any verbal and nonverbal inconsistency between the speaker's attitude and the apparent intended meaning of the speech? Does a perceived attitude of insincerity, unconcern, or superiority contradict words proclaiming sincerity, concern, or equality?

Finally, attempt to assess the influence of the speaker's attitudinal stance on the effects or consequences of the speech. Does the attitude seem appropriate for the speaker, subject, audience, and occasion? What effects might the speaker's attitude have on the audience's beliefs, feelings, and actions? Listeners' perception of a speaker's attitude toward them may influence their estimate of expertness, trustworthiness, goodwill, and similarity to them. Attitudes of dominance, superiority, or aloofness, for example, may contribute to people's doubts about the speaker's sincere concern for their welfare.

9.   **In what ways does the speaker's language usage contribute to clarity, interest, and persuasiveness?**

Consider whether the language is appropriate for the speaker, audience, subject, and occasion. Examine the communicative function served by stylistic resources such as repetition, restatement, rhetorical question, comparison, contrast, parallel structure, antithesis, alliteration, analogy, metaphor, imagery, personification, or narration. Do any stylistic devices seem ornamental or "added on" primarily for "showing off"? What does the speaker's language reveal about him or her personally or about the speaker's view of the audience? How do language choices compare with those the speaker reasonably might have made? What stylistic alternatives seem available to the speaker and why might the speaker have made particular choices? If the speaker's language is militant and abrasive, why might this choice have been made? If obscene words are used, what might be their intended function and actual impact?

Why might the speaker rely heavily on one particular stylistic device? If use of metaphors is a major stylistic characteristic, are they largely trite and overly familiar, or are they fresh and insightful for that particular audience? Might the audience have expected to be addressed in familiar, even stereotyped, metaphorical images? If there is a dominant or thematic metaphor woven throughout the speech, what might be its significance? What functions might be served by a speaker's heavy reliance on "god terms" and "devil terms," on value-laden concepts with intense positive or negative meanings? In what ways are names, labels, and definitions employed to channel perceptions—to direct attention toward or away from both relevant and irrelevant aspects of persons and programs? Remember, also, that public tastes in rhetorical style vary from era to era and even between different audiences in the same era. For the particular speech you are analyzing, consider what might be the most appropriate standards of stylistic judgment.

10. In what noteworthy ways does the speaker's delivery of the speech contribute to clarity, interest, and persuasiveness?

Do nonverbal elements of speech presentation reinforce or conflict with the speaker's verbal meaning? Does the speaker's vocal and physical delivery convey one meaning while his or her words convey another? If so, which would the audience probably believe and why? Does the manner of delivery seem appropriate for the speaker, subject, audience, and occasion? Examine the roles of loudness, vocal pitch, vocal quality, pauses, and rapidity in the presentation. How do the speaker's posture, gestures, facial expression, and eye contact help or hinder effectiveness? Are there any distracting mannerisms of vocal or bodily delivery that hinder audience attentiveness or comprehension? Explore also the communicative functions of various nonverbal cues accompanying the speech. Examine the possible intended and unintended implications of music, flags, banners, salutes, emblems, lapel pins, mode of dress, and pictures of family or revered persons.

11. What rhetorical strategies seem noteworthy because of their frequent use, apparent function in the speech, or probable effectiveness?

This line of inquiry obviously builds upon insights and questions from previously suggested guidelines for analysis. But such a scrutiny of concrete strategies will aid you as practitioner and critic of public discourse to see more clearly how others have approached different audiences and situations. The strategies briefly explained here are not offered as an exhaustive list but only as some possibilities. Strategies typical of discourse about values, problems, and solutions are discussed briefly in later chapters which focus on that type of speechmaking.

In the *this-or-nothing* strategy the speaker evaluates leading alternative solutions to a problem, shows in turn why each is unworkable or inappropriate, and finally presents his or her policy as the only sound remaining choice. *Visualization* involves painting a vivid word picture of the positive consequences of adopting or negative results of rejecting a proposal. Sometimes speakers use the *scapegoat* technique wherein they shift all responsibility or blame for problems or faults afflicting their own group onto the shoulders of some other person or group depicted as the embodiment of evil. As a variation of scapegoating, a *conspiracy* appeal claims that the cause of problems facing the group resides in a powerful, widespread, organized, secret effort of some other person or group.

The strategy of *persuasive definition* finds a speaker offering the audience her or his particular meaning as the correct or appropriate definition for a concept which actually is open to challenge or controversy. A speaker might employ *association* to emphasize values, beliefs, experiences mutually held with the audience and/or with persons and programs esteemed by the audience. *Disassociation* involves the speaker's repudiation of relationships with or favorable views toward undesirable people, ideas, or policies. In a strategy of *differentiation,* the speaker avoids guilt or responsibility by arguing the rationale that the action or belief under attack is different or unique from some other state of affairs which may be open to condemnation. Finally, there is a strategy of *transcendence* in which speaker and audience, or opposing groups, are to submerge, at least temporarily, differences of opinion or policy in the name of some commonly agreed upon higher value or goal: national security, political party unity, victory, humanitarianism, or national honor.

12.   As best you can determine, what are some of the effects or consequences of the speech?

Often it is very difficult to determine exact and certain causal connections between a specific speech and later outcomes. And an effect may be the result of a number of rhetorical and nonrhetorical events. Remember, too, that a speech may have consequences never intended by a speaker; these, also, can be scrutinized. You may attempt to assess the effects of a speech by noting the impact on the immediate audience, the long-term impact on the policies and ideology of society-at-large, the impact on persons in positions of public opinion leadership, the influence on experts, and the reactions of news media reporters. You might also explore whether the speaker's aim has been achieved, whether the speaker's ideas have been verified by later historical events, or whether the audience's expectations have been met. Sometimes virtually nondetectible shifts in audience attitudes and beliefs may occur, such as from a favorable to a strongly favorable position. Finally, you may want to consider the influence of the speech on the *speaker.* Did it enhance or lower the speaker's reputation? How did the speech affect the speaker's subsequent rhetoric and actions?

Did the speaker in any way become trapped by his or her own rhetoric? When speakers publicly become "locked in" to a position, later modification may be difficult.

13.   What ethical judgments seem appropriate regarding the speaker's purposes, arguments, appeals, and strategies?

Ethical judgments focus on degrees of rightness and wrongness in human behavior. A speech is designed by one person (sometimes with the aid of a speechwriter or speechwriting team) to influence the lives of other persons. And a speaker makes conscious choices concerning specific ends and communicative techniques to achieve those ends. Potential ethical issues regarding means and ends seem inherent in any act of speechmaking. But how those issues are to be faced and resolved (by speaker, listener, and critic) is not clear-cut.

Traditional American textbook discussions of the ethics of public speaking, argumentation, and persuasion often include lists of standards to be applied in assessing the ethicality of an instance of discourse. What follows is Johannesen's synthesis and adaptation of a half-dozen or so typical traditional lists of ethical criteria for public discourse.[2] Such ethical criteria usually are rooted in a commitment to values deemed essential to the health and growth of our political-governmental system of representative democracy. Obviously other cultures and other governmental systems may embrace basic values that lead to quite different standards for public discourse.

Even within our own society, the following criteria are not necessarily the only or best ones possible; they are suggested as general guidelines rather than inflexible rules, and they may stimulate discussion on the complexity of judging the ethics of communication. Consider, for example, under what circumstances there may be justifiable exceptions to some of these criteria. Also bear in mind that one difficulty in applying these criteria in concrete situations stems from differing standards and meanings people may have for such key terms as: distort, falsify, rational, reasonable, conceal, misrepresent, irrelevant, and deceive.

1.   **Do not use false, fabricated, misrepresented, distorted, or irrelevant evidence to support arguments or claims.**
2.   **Do not intentionally use specious, unsupported, or illogical reasoning.**

---

[2] For example, see the following sources: E. Christian Buehler and Wil A. Linkugel, *Speech Communication for the Contemporary Student* (Harper and Row, 1975), pp. 30–36; Robert T. Oliver, *The Psychology of Persuasive Speech*, 2nd ed. (Longmans, Green, 1957), pp. 20–34; Wayne Minnick, *The Art of Persuasion*, 2nd ed. (Houghton Mifflin, 1968), pp. 278–287; Henry Ewbank and J. Jeffrey Auer, *Discussion and Debate*, 2nd ed. (Appleton-Century-Crofts, 1951), pp. 255–258; Wayne Thompson, *The Process of Persuasion* (Harper and Row, 1975), Ch. 12; Bert E. Bradley, *Fundamentals of Speech Communication*, 4th ed. (Wm. C. Brown Company Publishers, 1984), pp. 20–29.

3. Do not represent yourself as informed or as an "expert" on a subject when you are not.
4. Do not use irrelevant appeals to divert attention or scrutiny from the issue at hand. Among appeals that commonly serve such a purpose are: "smear" attacks on an opponent's character; appeals to hatred and bigotry; god and devil terms that cause intense but unreflective positive or negative reactions; innuendo.
5. Do not ask your audience to link your idea or proposal to emotion-laden values, motives, or goals to which it actually is not related.
6. Do not deceive your audience by concealing your real purpose, by concealing self-interest, by concealing the group you represent, or by concealing your position as an advocate of a viewpoint.
7. Do not distort, hide, or misrepresent the number, scope, intensity, or undesirable features of consequences or effects.
8. Do not use "emotional appeals" that lack a supporting basis of evidence and reasoning, or that would not be accepted if the audience had time and opportunity to examine the subject themselves.
9. Do not oversimplify complex, gradation-laden situations into simplistic two-valued, either-or, polar choices.
10. Do not pretend certainty where tentativeness and degrees of probability would be more accurate.
11. Do not advocate something in which you do not believe yourself.

To assess the degree of ethicality of specific *appeals to values,* consider the following questions that are rooted in standards central to ethical communication in our representative democracy: honesty, relevance, accuracy, fairness, and reasonableness. To what degree do the value appeals serve as relevant motivational reinforcement for a point or proposal that has an independent basis in reasonable evidence? To what degree do the value appeals serve a legitimate function of promoting social cohesion, of reinforcing audience commitment to ideas they already believe? With what degree of appropriateness are the consequences of commitment to the values clarified? To what degree do the value appeals serve as substitutes, as pseudoproof, for the factuality of an assertion? To what degree do the value appeals divert attention from more fundamental, pressing, or controversial matters? To what degree do the value appeals seem to promote, intentionally or not, unreflective stimulus-response reactions when the occasion demands reflective judgment?

What are the ethical implications of the *power relationships* urged or reinforced? In what ways do the language, structure, evidence, and arguments in the speech attempt to alter or reinforce power relationships? What persons, groups, ideas, or institutions are given legitimacy, approval, rights, superiority, or status either overtly or because their role is unquestioned? Which are directly or indirectly delegitimized, disapproved, trivialized, or denied rights? What relevant ones are ignored or dismissed as insignificant because they are not mentioned or taken into account?

We now turn to a list of some questions that we hope will stimulate your examination of various ethical issues as you assess a particular speech. To what degree should ethical standards for judging speeches be relative, flexible, and situation bound, or universal, inflexible, and absolute? Should there be different ethical standards for speechmaking in different fields such as politics, business, education, and religion? Should ethical standards for communication directed at children be higher than for messages aimed at adults? To what degree should ethical standards for public communication differ from or be similar to those appropriate for interpersonal and small group communication?

To what degree, if any, does the worthiness of the speaker's end justify the employment of communication techniques usually deemed ethically suspect? Does the sincerity of the speaker's intent release him or her from ethical responsibility for means and effects? Under what circumstances might intentional use of ambiguity be considered ethical? Should "tastefulness" and "tactfulness" be included or excluded as *ethical* criteria for assessing speeches? To what degree and for what reasons might we consider the use of "sexist" and "racist" language as unethical?

Conclusion

Sonja K. Foss, a contemporary rhetorical critic, reminds us: "We live our lives enveloped in symbols. How we perceive, what we know, what we experience, and how we act are the results of our symbol use and that of those around us. . . . One of the ways we can use to discover how symbols affect us is rhetorical criticism. We engage in the process of rhetorical criticism constantly and often unconsciously, but with some formal training we can become more adept and discriminating in its practice."

By focusing on contemporary American speeches, this book necessarily focuses on one particular kind of rhetorical practice. Speeches still form a significant portion of our communication environment, an environment constantly bombarding us with data, appeals, reasons, and judgments. Whether a speech seeks to create understanding, to advocate or reinforce values and value judgments, to resolve "factual" disputes, to generate concern for problems, or to secure acceptance of solutions—that speech seeks a specific response from a specific audience. Thus such speeches inherently involve some degree of "persuasive" intent, some degree of conscious concrete influence.

As responsible citizens in a representative democracy, we are expected to develop skills in communicating our ideas and choices on matters of personal and public concern. Also we are expected to become discerning consumers of communication, to become perceptive evaluators of messages we receive. We have a social responsibility to become intelligent and ethical speakers and listeners. Part of this responsibility has been summarized forcefully by a contemporary rhetorical critic, Karlyn Kohrs Campbell: "Never has the need to understand the nature of persuasive discourses and to develop techniques and standards by which to analyze and evaluate them been more crucial. . . . In short, we shall have to become working rhetorical critics."

For Further Reading

ON THE ART OF RHETORIC

Brockriede, Wayne. "Dimensions of the Concept of Rhetoric." *Quarterly Journal of Speech,* February 1968, pp. 1–12.

Foss, Sonja K., Foss, Karen A., and Trapp, Robert. *Contemporary Perspectives on Rhetoric.* 2nd ed. Waveland Press, 1991. A thorough exploration of the implications for rhetorical theory of the works of Kenneth Burke, I. A. Richards, Richard M. Weaver, Stephen Toulmin, Chaim Perelman, Ernesto Grassi, Jurgen Habermas, and Michel Foucault.

Johannesen, Richard L., ed. *Contemporary Theories of Rhetoric: Selected Readings.* Harper and Row, 1971. An anthology including the works of Kenneth Burke, I. A. Richards, Richard M. Weaver, Chaim Perelman, Stephen Toulmin, and Marshall McLuhan.

ON THE ETHICS OF RHETORIC

Jaksa, James A., and Pritchard, Michael S. *Communication Ethics: Methods of Analysis.* 2nd ed. Wadsworth Publishing Co., 1994. Includes chapters on moral reasoning, the principle of veracity, and procedures for justifying ethical judgments.

Johannesen, Richard L. *Ethics in Human Communication.* 4th ed. Waveland Press, 1996. Explores varied perspectives, issues, and examples to foster skill in assessing degrees of ethicality.

Larson, Charles U. *Persuasion: Reception and Responsibility.* 7th ed. Wadsworth, 1995. Includes a chapter by R. L. Johannesen on "Perspectives on Ethics in Persuasion."

ON THE FORMS OF SPEECHES

Allen, R. R., and McKerrow, Ray E. *The Pragmatics of Public Communication.* 3rd ed. Kendall/Hunt Publishing Company, 1985. Chapters 7–9 discuss informative, persuasive, and ceremonial speeches.

Campbell, Karlyn Kohrs, and Jamieson, Kathleen Hall. *Deeds Done In Words: Presidential Rhetoric and the Genres of Governance.* University of Chicago Press, 1990. Examines such forms of presidential discourse as inaugural addresses, state of the union messages, farewell addresses, and war rhetoric.

Walter, Otis M., and Scott, Robert L. *Thinking and Speaking.* 5th ed. Macmillan, 1984. Chapters 6–10 discuss speeches that deal with problems, causes, solutions, values, and definitions.

ON THE INVENTION OF SPEECH IDEAS

LeFevre, Karen Burke. *Invention as a Social Act.* Southern Illinois University Press, 1987. Examines invention as an interactive process involving the individual rhetor, small numbers of collaborators, and society-at-large.

Corbett, Edward P. J. *Classical Rhetoric for the Modern Student.* 3rd ed. Oxford University Press, 1990. Chapter 2 contains intensive discussion of the discovery of arguments.

McCroskey, James C. *An Introduction to Rhetorical Communication.* 6th ed. Prentice-Hall, 1993. Chapter 10 offers suggestions on invention.

Wilson, John F., Arnold, Carroll C., and Wertheimer, Molly. *Public Speaking as a Liberal Art.* 6th ed. Allyn and Bacon, 1990. Chapters 4–6 examine the basic processes of invention, including some general thought lines to aid the speaker in finding appropriate ideas and arguments.

Winterowd, W. Ross. *Contemporary Rhetoric: A Conceptual Background with Readings.* Harcourt, Brace, Jovanovich, 1975, pp. 39–162. Twelve essays focus on invention.

ON THE CRITICAL ANALYSIS OF SPEECHES

Andrews, James R. *The Practice of Rhetorical Criticism.* 2nd ed. Longman, 1990. This textbook presents standards and sample analyses of public addresses.

Campbell, Karlyn Kohrs. *Critiques of Contemporary Rhetoric.* Wadsworth, 1972. Chapters 1–3 consider in some detail the process of rhetorical criticism.

Johannesen, Richard L. "Attitude of Speaker Toward Audience: A Significant Concept for Contemporary Rhetorical Theory and Criticism," *Central States Speech Journal,* Summer 1974, 95–104.

Brock, Bernard L., Scott, Robert L., and Chesebro, James, eds. *Methods of Rhetorical Criticism: A Twentieth Century Perspective.* 3rd ed. Wayne State University Press, 1990. An anthology of essays illustrates varied approaches to the theory and practice of rhetorical criticism.

Cooper, Martha. *Analyzing Public Discourse.* Waveland Press, 1989. Of special interest are Chapters 7–9 on ethics, ideology/propaganda, and freedom of speech.

Foss, Sonja K. *Rhetorical Criticism: Explorations and Practice.* 2nd ed. Waveland Press, 1996. Presents critical methods that focus on context, message, or rhetor. Types of criticism illustrated are: neo-Aristotelian, generic, feminist, metaphoric, narrative, fantasy theme, pentadic, and cluster.

Hart, Roderick P. *Modern Rhetorical Criticism.* Scott, Foresman/Little, Brown, 1990. Describes the rhetorical and critical perspectives; presents forms of criticism that analyze situations, ideas, argument, structure, and style; illustrates specialized forms of criticism (role, cultural, dramatistic, ideological).

Rybacki, Karyn, and Rybacki, Donald. *Communication Criticism: Approaches and Genres.* Wadsworth, 1991. Chapters 3–7 cover various methods and perspectives for criticism and Chapter 8 focuses on the rhetoric of public speaking.

Chapter Three

Speeches That Increase Understanding

> *Because information can change society, and because the amount of information doubles every eight years, our culture, if it is to become enriched and improved by its information, needs speakers and writers to digest and assimilate information and to present it to us with clarity.*
>
> *Otis M. Walter*

The Nature and Importance of Speeches That Increase Understanding

Americans have long valued the broad diffusion of knowledge. This value is founded on the premise that our social and political systems function most effectively when all citizens possess the knowledge that is the basis for intelligent decision making. Without affirming or denying this premise, one can note the diverse institutions that pay tribute to its worth. Our vast system of public education, the media of mass communication, and public and private agencies for information dissemination all justify their existence, at least in part, by the premise.

In contemporary America, the broad diffusion of knowledge is becoming increasingly difficult. Alvin Toffler, in his popular book *Future Shock,* observes:

> Today change is so swift and relentless in the techno-societies that yesterday's truths suddenly become today's fictions, and the most highly skilled and intelligent members of society admit difficulty in keeping up with the deluge of new knowledge—even in extremely narrow fields.[1]

In response to this challenge, Otis Walter, in the quotation that headnotes this chapter, calls for a generation of communicators who can digest and assimilate the explosion of knowledge and render it useful for others who must know. As the rate of new knowledge continues to accelerate, and as local, national, and world problems become increasingly complex, speeches that increase understanding must continue to grow in number and significance.

Speeches that serve this function may be of different kinds. Lectures, intelligence briefings, reports of research findings, treasurers' reports, the happy chef show, and the evening TV weather report are all instances of this genre. Whenever speakers seek to create in the minds of their listeners an understanding of an event, concept, phenomenon, object, process, or relationship, they may be viewed as seeking to increase understanding.

In certain instances, increasing understanding is a speaker's *primary* speech purpose. A professor of history, for example, may be totally content if his students understand the major forces which contributed to the beginning of the Civil War. A computer systems engineer may be fully satisfied if installation procedures are understood by technical personnel. An accountant may be adequately rewarded if a company's executive officers understand the implications of a new federal tax regulation.

In other instances, increasing understanding is a speaker's *ancillary* purpose. For example, a sociologist may describe an event in order that he may urge social reform. A civil rights leader may narrate a story of social injustice in order to elicit a

---

[1] Alvin Toffler, *Future Shock* (New York: Bantam Books, 1971), p. 157.

greater commitment to social tolerance. A senator may explain a piece of legislation as a prelude to urging its adoption.

From the perspective of the audience, it is often difficult to determine the extent to which a speech increases understanding rather than serving some other major purpose. Audience members listening to the same speech may come away feeling informed, persuaded to a new point of view, or even inspired to recommit their lives to cherished values. But a speaker who purports to increase understanding, whether as a primary or an ancillary purpose, should be expected to meet several fundamental criteria.

Criteria for Evaluating Speeches That Increase Understanding

Four general criteria are especially important for evaluating speeches that seek to increase understanding. Failure to satisfy any of these four will seriously restrict the speaker's communication of information.

1.   Is the information communicated accurately, completely, and with unity?

Because genuine understanding by an audience is the speaker's goal, an *accurate, complete,* and *unified* view of the subject must be presented. Wilson, Arnold, and Wertheimer have expressed this criterion in this way:

> The tests that listeners apply when talk seems intended to be predominantly informative are these: (1) Is the information *accurate?* Listeners want information that is true to fact in both detail and proportion. (2) Is the information sufficiently *complete?* Does the speaker cover the *whole* subject adequately? (3) Is the information *unified?* We want information that "hangs together" to form a whole of some sort. If we're to understand a wheel, we must understand not just that there are a hub, some spokes, and a rim, but we must understand also how their arrangement in relation to one another enables the wheel to *turn.* Speakers trying to inform need to pay special attention to how facets of the explained subject "fit together" to form or create the explained thing as a totality. If an explanation meets the three tests we have just given, listeners experience the satisfaction of "having been informed."[2]

Given a specific body of knowledge to impart, a speaker must select those items of information that an audience must have to gain understanding. These items must then be arranged in a unified sequence and expressed in an undistorted manner.

---

[2] John F. Wilson, Carroll C. Arnold, and Wertheimer, Molly, *Public Speaking as a Liberal Art,* 6th ed. (Boston: Allyn and Bacon, 1990), pp. 190–191.

2.   Does the speaker make the information meaningful for the audience?

It is not enough that speakers know the essential components of a truth. In seeking to increase understanding for a particular audience at a particular time, they must transform their perceptions of facts and concepts into symbols that evoke understanding in those who listen. Even a highly motivated audience may lack the substantive, linguistic, and conceptual skills essential to understanding an idea presented in its pure form. Speakers must be faithful to both the integrity of the truth they seek to impart and to the demands of the particular audience they address.

These demands need not be incompatible, as an example will demonstrate. Let us assume that you wish to clarify the reasoning processes of induction and deduction to an audience of laborers who have come to your campus. You know that *induction* is a method of systematic investigation that seeks to discover, analyze, and explain specific instances or facts in order to determine the existence of a general law embracing them, whereas *deduction* is a process by which a particular conclusion about an instance is drawn from the application of a general law. In appraising your audience, you recognize that, although these terms are meaningful to you, they represent an unfamiliar level of conceptual abstraction to your audience. The rhetorical problem is clear; the solution is not.

In 1866, Thomas Henry Huxley faced exactly the same problem. The rhetorical choices that he made in explaining these processes to a group of English workingmen in his speech entitled "The Method of Scientific Investigation" are demonstrated in the following paragraphs.

> Suppose you go into a fruiterer's shop, wanting an apple—you take one up, and, on biting, you find it is sour; you look at it, and see that it is hard and green. You take another one and that too is hard, green, and sour. The shopman offers you a third; but, before biting it, you examine it, and find that it is hard and green, and you immediately say that you will not have it, as it must be sour, like those you have already tried.
>
> Nothing can be more simple than that, you think; but if you will take the trouble to analyze and trace out into its logical elements what has been done by the mind, you will be greatly surprised. In the first place, you have performed the operation of induction. You found that, in two experiences, hardness and greenness in apples went together with sourness. It was so in the first case and it was confirmed by the second. True, it is a very small basis, but still it is enough to make an induction from; you generalize the facts, and you expect to find sourness in apples where you get hardness and greenness. You found upon that a general law, that all hard and green apples are sour; and that, so far as it goes, is a perfect induction. Well, having got your natural law in this way, when you are offered another apple which you find is hard and green, you say, "All hard and green apples are sour; this apple is hard and green, therefore this apple is sour." That train of reasoning is what logicians call a syllogism and has all its various parts and terms—

its major premise, its minor premise, and its conclusion. And, by the help of further reasoning, which, if drawn out, would have to be exhibited in two or three other syllogisms, you arrive at your final determination. "I will not have that apple." So that, you see, you have, in the first place, established a law by induction, and reasoned out the special conclusion of the particular case.

In this instance, Huxley chose to impart only a very basic understanding of the processes of induction and deduction by showing them to be inherent in a commonplace happening familiar to the workers who comprised his audience. He chose not to treat the subtleties of form and fallacy. Did he compromise the integrity of the truth in order to win popular understanding? Most critics think not. Although he simplified these processes, he did not misrepresent them. His illustration accurately portrays their essential nature. And it is complete in the sense of comprehensively demonstrating the specific purpose of the speech: to show that "there is not one here who has not in the course of the day had occasion to set in motion a complex train of reasoning of the very same kind, though differing of course in degree, as that which a scientific man goes through in tracing the causes of natural phenomena." Finally, his speech possesses unity in providing a systematic development through which the listener may gain a clear grasp of the total meaning.

In giving meaning to the knowledge that he wished to present, Huxley chose to move from a simple illustration to a complex generalization, to develop a common understanding of a process before attaching labels to it, and to use periodic summations of what had been discussed. Martin Luther King, in his speech "Love, Law, and Civil Disobedience," utilized definition to amplify the various meanings of the concept of love. Other speakers have used restatement and repetition, clarity of organization, factual and hypothetical examples, synonyms and negation, comparison and contrast, analogies and statistics, description and narration, photographs and films, blackboards and diagrams, questions and answers, meaningful gestures and movement, and varied patterns of rate and pitch.

3. Does the speaker create audience interest in the information being presented?

Because understanding is the goal of the speech designed to increase understanding, the speaker must create in the audience a reason for concentrating on the information that is being transmitted. Creating this interest is not always easy. Often the speaker must explain technical, detailed, and abstract concepts to an apathetic audience. In seeking to do so, the speaker can capitalize on the interest factors in content, language, and delivery. *Concrete* and specific terms and illustrations have more interest value for most listeners than vague generalities or abstract concepts. *Conflict* in the form of disagreements, threats, clashes, and antagonisms capture and hold an audience's attention. *Suspense* and *curiosity* in building to a climax, anticipating a conclusion, or asking intriguing questions can be used. Description or narration focusing on activity and movement capitalizes on *action*. The new, unusual, or unexpected reflect the *novelty* factor. On the other hand, listeners are also interested in things that are "close to home" and *familiar*. When carefully and appropriately used, *humor* may increase interest while explaining or highlighting a main point.

As a study of the choices that one speaker made, let us again return to Huxley's illustration. In appraising his audience, Huxley realized that, for average English workingmen of his time, the scientific method represented an esoteric construct of little interest or significance to all but the disciples of science. By making his individual audience member "you," the chief participant in his illustration, by choosing a familiar environment as the setting, and by selecting such suspense words as "suppose" and "you will be greatly surprised" as major transitional devices, he gave to his material a sense of vitality, realism, suspense, and urgency that it did not naturally possess. Huxley chose a hypothetical illustration for this purpose; others have selected metaphors, narratives, comparisons, contrasts, real and figurative analogies, and specific examples. Thus, a speaker who is inventive need not worry about losing the audience even when an unusual or difficult subject is involved.

4.   Does the speaker show the audience that the information is important?

Beyond presenting information that is accurate, complete, unified, meaningful, and interesting, speakers must also get their audiences to feel that they should make such knowledge a permanent part of their storehouse of data. In order to do so, speakers might clarify the relation of the information to the wants and goals of their audiences. They might point out ways in which the information can be used or applied, where this new knowledge fits within the context of information already considered worthwhile by the audience, and, if appropriate, where and how the audience can obtain additional information on the subject.

Given the vast array of information that may be communicated, the critic has a right to question the quality of the information that the speaker chooses to present. Student speakers often err by selecting speech topics that are trivial and lacking in real information value. Gruner, Logue, Freshley, and Huseman, in *Speech Communnication in Society*, recall

> . . . a dreadful speech by a young man who spoke on and demonstrated how to use two simple types of can openers, one being the elementary "church key" type for opening beverage cans. Disappointed by his low grade he compained, "Well, the speech *did* contain information, didn't it?" The instructor replied: "Not for this audience; I'm sure they already know how to open cans." The instructor's reply could be paraphrased: "You instructed no one."[3]

---

[3] Charles R. Gruner, Cal M. Logue, Dwight L. Freshley, and Richard C. Huseman, *Speech Communication in Society* (Boston: Allyn and Bacon, Inc., 1972), p. 179.

An effective speech of this form presents information that is worth having to an audience that lacks such knowledge.

Conclusion

Increasing understanding is one of the primary and ancillary functions that speeches serve. When speakers try to fulfill this purpose, they must be aware of the constraints that govern their speech behavior. They must choose information that is worth knowing. They must present the information with *accuracy, completeness,* and *unity.* They must be aware of the demands that varied audiences impose on the choices they make in giving *meaning, interest,* and *importance* to a body of knowledge. In other words, they must be faithful to the integrity of their perception of truth while adapting to the demands of their audiences.

For Further Reading

Allen, R. R., and Ray E. McKerrow. *The Pragmatics of Public Communication.* 3rd ed. Kendall-Hunt Publishing Company, 1985. Chapter 7 discusses the nature, types and development of speeches to inform.

Hart, Roderick P.; Friedrich, Gustav W.; and Brooks, William D. *Public Communication.* 2nd ed. Harper and Row, 1983. Chapter 5 is devoted to reducing the complexity of information.

Lucas, Stephen. *The Art of Public Speaking.* 5th ed., McGraw-Hill, 1995. Chapter 14 presents guidelines for speaking to inform about objects, processes, events, and concepts.

Netter, Gwyn. *Explanations.* McGraw-Hill, 1970. Chapters 2–6 explore the main variations of explanation used in discourse: definitional, empathetic, scientific, and ideological.

Osborn, Michael, and Osborn, Suzanne. *Public Speaking.* 2nd ed. Houghton Mifflin, 1991. Chapter 12 examines the functions, types, and structure of speeches to increase understanding.

Rowan, Katherine. "A New Pedagogy for Explanatory Public Speaking," *Communication Education,* 44 (July 1995): 236–250.

Verderber, Rudolph F. *The Challenge of Effective Speaking.* 8th ed. Wadsworth, 1991. Chapters 8–12 examine demonstration, description, definition, and reporting.

Walter, Otis M. *Speaking to Inform and Persuade.* 2nd ed. Macmillan, 1982. Chapters 2–4 present an extremely useful discussion of imparting knowledge, including selection of main ideas and use of supporting material.

An American Prisoner of War in South Vietnam

James N. Rowe

For more than five years Major James N. Rowe was a prisoner of the Viet Cong. He was captured by the enemy when he was a Special Forces advisor in 1963 and was held prisoner in the Mekong region and the U Minh Forest. He devised a cover story about himself that kept the enemy from executing him, a fate which befell several others imprisoned with him. His cover story held up until 1968, when the enemy found out he had lied. Major Rowe felt that they received a biographical sketch with complete information about him and his family from the Peace and Justice Loving Friends of the National Liberation Front in America. This information put him on the list for execution. But on December 31, 1968, circumstances conspired that allowed Major Rowe to escape. A heavy American air strike shook up the guards. One of the Viet Cong groups panicked when United States gunships came into the area, and Major Rowe took advantage of the confusion. He was picked up by an American helicopter pilot who almost mistook him for a member of the enemy because he was wearing the pajama-like garb of the Viet Cong. The beard that Major Rowe had grown during his imprisonment permitted the helicopter pilot to identify him as an American a second before pulling the trigger.

Major Rowe delivered his speech at the U.S. Army General Staff and Command College at Leavenworth, Kansas. The audience consisted primarily of students of the college—mostly majors and lieutenant colonels of the American Army, some Navy and Air Force personnel, and a significant number of Allied officers attending the college. [More information about Major Rowe's experiences can be found in his book, *Five Years to Freedom* (Boston: Little, Brown, 1971).]

This speech by Major Rowe is a personal narrative used to impart knowledge about Viet Cong prison camps and what an American prisoner of war lives through. In assessing the speech you will thus want to ask how well Major Rowe tells his story. Does he make effective use of suspense? Imagery? Action? Anecdotes? Is he able to organize his nar-

---

✝This speech is printed by permission of Major James N. Rowe.

rative effectively so it can easily be followed? How well does he draw increased understanding with general application from his story?

Major Rowe delivered this address extemporaneously and used no notes. The manuscript you are about to read is a transcript of an audiotape recording. The extemporaneous style of Major Rowe is thus very apparent. What difficulties do you encounter in reading a speech with genuine oral style? You may want to discuss the statement "Good speeches don't read well."

On April 21, 1989, Col. "Nick" Rowe was assassinated by communist terrorists on the streets of Manila, the Philippines.

---

1   The American prisoners of war are particularly close to those of us in the military, because the prisoners of war are members of the military. It could be any one of us, and I was one of those prisoners of war. I am Major Nick Rowe; I spent 62 months as a prisoner of the Viet Cong in South Vietnam. The issue of the prisoners of war has come to the forefront in our nation; and in bringing this issue to the forefront, we have found that it's not that American people don't remember, or that they don't care, it's that most of the people in our country don't know. And those of us who have come out feel that we have a particular duty, because we are speaking for 1,600 men who have no voices. So this afternoon I would like to bring you some insight into the prison camps and some insight into what an American prisoner of war lives through.

2   I was a Special Forces advisor in 1963 in Phuoc Hoa. I was in a camp approximately in this area and I was captured very near there in October of 1963. Shortly after capture, I was moved down in the Mekong region; I stayed in this region until January of 1965, when I was moved into the U Minh Forest. I stayed in the U Minh Forest from January 1965 through December of 1968, when I escaped. The camp I was held in was on canal 21 and canal 6. I was approximately fourteen kilometers from our old district capital. I was that close to Americans, and yet they couldn't get to me nor could I get to them. This is the most frustrating thing about being an American prisoner in South Vietnam.

3   The conditions that an American lives under are those that are structured by his captors, and there are several new aspects of captivity. It is not the Hogan's Heroes concept that many people have, because in South Vietnam and in North Vietnam, we found that an American prisoner of war is not a military prisoner, he is a political prisoner; and the Communists are dealing with American prisoners of war based on the Pavlovian theory—stimuli and response— the manipulation of human behavior. These are parameters that we have never dealt with before and are not prepared to deal with. The American prisoners

find themselves being manipulated and being made more pliable by the Communists using principles that we have read about in Koestler's *Darkness at Noon*, perhaps in *1984;* these types of things that are never reality. But in prison camps in South Vietnam and in North Vietnam and in Laos, it is reality. An American prisoner of war has two main purposes for the Communists. First of all, propaganda; because in an age of ideological conflict, the most important thing is political opinion, and formation of political opinion, and this is done through propaganda. What more effective source do the Communists have for propaganda than an American prisoner of war? Through coercion, manipulation, or force, to cause that man to condemn our society, our government, our actions throughout the world; and then, as a representative of our system of government and our society, for him to confess to crimes against humanity. Think of the impact of this propaganda in either a Communist or nonCommunist country when contrasted with the same propaganda coming from a Communist source.

4   The second purpose of an American prisoner of war is that when the Communists finally do decide to negotiate, what better blue chip do they have to lay down on the table than an American prisoner of war, trading American lives for political gain—this is why they take an American prisoner of war. When I was captured, there were three of us, two of us Special Forces and one MAAG

Major James N. Rowe pays a courtesy call on President Nixon at the White House. Major Rowe escaped from the Viet Cong on 12/31/68 after five years of captivity.

Photo courtesy of Bettman Archive

advisor, who were with a strike force company when we were overrun; all three of us were wounded and were taken prisoners. The other strike force wounded were shot by the VC. And yet an American was of value. In captivity we found, first of all, that we were political prisoners. We weren't military prisoners. This was typified during the initial interrogations. I was one of the first American officers captured in the Mekong Delta, and they really didn't know what to do with us. The first cadre who came in were hampered by the decided lack of ability to speak English, so they brought in a journalist-by-trade who spoke English, and used him as an interrogator. They had an S-2 who stayed across the canal from our camp in a cadre hut, and he was responsible for the interrogation. But since he couldn't speak English, he would write his questions down in Vietnamese, give them to this journalist, the interpreter, who would then translate them into English and come down to my cage. I was in the low-rent district right behind the camp, about thirty meters behind the camp, and he would come down and would sit down and ask me the questions. Anything I said he would write down verbatim. Then he would take the answers back and translate them from his Vietnamese-English dictionary back into Vietnamese to take to the S-2. Well, the first thing I discovered there was that he could deal with a large number of American prisoners, because the S-2 is in one place with the interpreter doing the legwork for him. And he got nothing for it.

5   About four to five weeks, six weeks, seven weeks, and the S-2 got upset, but he was apparently prevented from doing any more than threatening us. And when this little interpreter would come down and threaten, he would say, "I can kill you, I can torture you, I can do anything I want"; then he'd wince. So we knew he wasn't really serious; and I decided after a period of time, that since he had so much flexibility, it would be better to try and see if anything could be done to play with him, I had him come down one day, and I said, "Well, all right, Plato, I am ready to talk." We had nicknames for all of them, and he was very philosophical, so we nicknamed him Plato. I said, "All right, Plato, I am ready to talk." He beamed, pulled out extra paper and a new ballpoint pen, and sat down. I gave him four pages on the theory of laminar flow. This was to include calculus, integrated differential. I gave him pressure formulas—the weights, dams, storm gutters—the aerodynamic principles of air flow. I almost failed mechanical fluids at West Point, so it wasn't really that good anyway, but he copied it down verbatim. Everything I said he copied down, checking on spelling, and he took it back to his hut, and spent the next five days translating it from English into Vietnamese, coming down every day to check on the formulas and things like that; and I said, "Drive on, Plato, you are in good shape." Well, when he finished, he had a great volume, almost like *Khrushchev Remembers*. He took all of this great volume of paper over to the S-2. The enemy are

very stoic individuals, and although I was thirty meters behind the camp, I soon heard screams from the S-2's hut. Not more than two minutes later, here came Plato scurrying down this little log walk with the S-2 right behind him. Obviously, the S-2 found out in a very short period of time what Plato had been doing, and it had erased his ability to deal with other American prisoners. Had the S-2 had the ability to deal with me as he wished, there wouldn't have been a tree high enough in the area for him to string me up to. But, I was a political prisoner, and the political cadre said no. Interrogation is secondary, indoctrination is primary. If they lose you through interrogation, they lose you for indoctrination; and so that was when we established what was of primary importance.

6   In dealing with an American prisoner of war their philosophy is that you can take any man and if you control the physical, you do not necessarily control that man; but if you can control and manipulate his mind, you will control the physical and the man. So this is what their target is, not necessarily physical torture, because they realize that indiscriminate physical torture can alienate a man, and once you have done that, he identifies you with the enemy, and you will never indoctrinate him. They will use physical torture, but they use it only to amplify the mental pressure. We found that a bruise will heal, a broken bone will heal, a wound will heal, but if they push you over the line mentally, or they break your spirit, then you are not coming back. That was the big battle. And that was what we had not been prepared for.

7   One of the first things that came up, and I will bring this up here because it is very important to members of the military, was the Code of Conduct. The Code of Conduct to me was a series of pictures in an orderly room. I had read them, I had gotten the T.I. and E. classes on Code of Conduct; it really wasn't that clear. I knew that I was supposed to give my name, my rank, my serial number, my date of birth, and then I thought I was supposed to shut up. This is the way it usually comes down to the troops. But this is a fallacy, because if you don't know the Code of Conduct when you're captured, the Communists will teach it to you. Because they teach our Code of Conduct to their cadre. And then they tell you while you're there, go ahead and follow it, but you will die if you do. They'll let you make your own decisions. What they are doing here is one of the first steps in breaking down a man's will to resist, because generally speaking, an individual feels if he goes beyond name, rank, serial number, and date of birth, he is a traitor. I know I felt it right at first. And this is the first question that comes up in a man's mind. What about the Big Four? How long do I last? Well, you hang onto the Big Four as long as you can, but the next line says, "I will evade answering further questions to the best of my ability." It does give you credit for having basic intelligence. And this is what a man does. Fortu-

nately, I went to West Point, and they teach you ambiguity; this is one of the things that really comes in handy. When you get a B.S. degree from West Point, that is exactly what it is. I liked English up there, and that is where they teach you to say the same thing 25 different ways. So this is what the American is doing. He is hedging, working for a way to get around, or get under, or get through. But if an individual goes in thinking, if I break from name, rank, serial number, and date of birth, I am a traitor, the first thing they are going to do is instill a guilt complex into him that will beat him into the ground. I know, because we had an individual who felt, initially, that anything beyond name, rank, serial number, and date of birth, was a violation of a punitive article of the uniform code of military justice. Now, this is where a man feels, all right, I have broken; and then they say, "Well, you have broken once, you are going to be punished, you might as well go all the way." Once they've got their finger in that crack, you're in trouble. And they teach our Code of Conduct as a punitive article, if you don't know it before you go in, find out about it now and find out exactly what it is. Because they are going to tell you and they are going to try to convince you that it is a punitive article, once you violate anything, once you go beyond name, rank, serial number, and date of birth, you have violated the Code of Conduct and you are going to be punished. Then they have their foot in the door. And they say, "Drive on, because you are going to be punished anyway. Why not get out sooner and go home?" This is the thing that a person has to be aware of. Remember that the code says, "I will make no statements disloyal to my country, its allies, or detrimental to their cause." And that's the thing that you have to remember. But as far as name, rank, serial number, and date of birth, you hold it as long as you can, but they are going to move you off of it at one point or another. They have developed all types of evasive techniques. We are training our people now, finally, to include a calculated breakdown, where you plan ahead what you are going to say, and then you dole it out a little bit at a time over an extended period, buying time to escape.

8   The other thing I used is a cover story; and in this case, I realized I wasn't the bravest person, so I decided to devise something which would allow me to say, "I don't know," rather than "I can't tell you" or "I won't tell you." So, I employed first of all the old artillery kiss formula, keep it simple, stupid. Then I built a cover story that would allow me to say, "I don't know"; and in that cover story, I graduated from the United States Armed Forces Institute in Washington, D.C., as an engineer; I went there for four years, and gave them three years of service back. It was 1963 and I was ready to go be a civil engineer. Since I studied engineering, I was assigned to the Adjutant General. I went to Fort Belvoir afterward, and studied bridge building and house building and road building, and then I went to civilian seminars throughout the nation, again en-

gineering subjects; finally I was assigned to a Special Forces attachment because of my outstanding capabilities as an engineer, and because they needed civil affairs project people. So this was my cover story which allowed me over the period of time to tell them, "I don't know," to a great volume of things, and to hide behind it.

9   So, what they are trying to do initially is find out who is this person that they have, what are his capabilities? And they come out with a very neat form, it is entitled, "Red Cross Index Data Card"; the first thing it says, military information: name, rank, serial number, and date of birth. And you think, great, that is what it is supposed to be. But they have a heavy dotted line; under it, it says, "Who did you train with in the United States, what was your unit in the United States, when did you come to Vietnam, who did you come with, how did you come, when did you land, where did you serve in Vietnam, what operations did you go on?" They want to know your educational background, your political background, your religious background; they want to know your mother, your father, your wife, your children; educational, religious, and political backgrounds for all of them; your hobbies and your sports. Then they give you four sheets of paper and they want a short biographical sketch. Now they are going to try and build a picture of this American. And they've taken American prisoners of war from Korea, from North Vietnam, and from South Vietnam. They try to fit these people into some sort of category, based on their background, the psychological category if you will, and this is column A. They've got different categories; column B is different environmental situations of the stimuli that have been applied to these different groups of Americans. In column 3 are the reactions they have gotten from them. So if they get a new man and they can categorize him, then they just look to column 3 to find out what they want him to do, and then they come back to column 2 to find out what they have to do to him to get him to do it. This again is stimuli and response.

10   Now, in the camp, the physical conditions in South Vietnam with the Viet Cong are primitive. I was in the U Minh Forest, the camps were temporary at best. You had two to three feet of standing water during the rainy season; in the dry season it sank out, and you were hunting for drinking water. We had two meals of rice a day, and generally we got salt and nuoc mam with them. We did get infrequent fish from the guards, but always the castoff that the guards didn't want. If we got greens, it was maybe one meal's worth every two or three months. Immediately vitamin deficiency and malnutrition were a problem. This is a thing you are going to fight the whole way through. And you are fighting on two sides. You are fighting a physical survival, and you are fighting for mental survival. The physical survival is just staying alive. We found that we had to eat a quart pan of rice each meal, two meals a day, just to stay alive. We

found that if we could put down everything we had, and I think the most difficult thing initially was the nuoc mam. It is high in protein value, but the VC don't have that much money to spend on nuoc mam. You don't get Saigon nuoc mam. Theirs is called ten-meter nuoc mam. You can smell it within ten meters, and it is either repulsive or inedible, depending on how long you have been there. But this was the type of thing you are eating for nutritional value, and not for taste. So you are fighting on that side.

11   Disease, this is always present. Dysentery, beri-beri, hepatitis, jaundice, lac—which is a fungus infection, I had all those while I was in. I had about 85 percent of my body covered with lac. And you find that depending on your political attitude, there is either very little medication or no medication.

12   This is another thing which was disturbing, as if your political attitude determines whether you will get medication and what your treatment will be. And you are either reactionary or progressive, or somewhere in between. You find that it is not a military type thing, it is purely political. And again, we are not prepared for this. The Geneva Convention, international law, the VC say, we don't recognize them. The only law you are subjected to is our law. And if you ever want to go home, you are going to have to be a good POW, and it is based upon your good attitude and behavior as prisoner and your repentance of your past misdeeds. That last one is a hooker, because that is a confession. So they set up perimeters, and they set up this dirty little world that they keep you in; then they throw the mental pressure on top of this.

13   Indoctrination, this is where they take an individual's beliefs, and his faiths, and his loyalties, and they challenge them, because they have to break all of these before they can influence him. This is where thought correction comes in, because thought correction is nothing more than creating confusion and doubt in a man's mind and filling the void that follows with answers to the questions that you have created for him. If you will take a man as an island, with little bridges running to the mainland, and his faiths, his beliefs, his loyalties, his ethics, his standards, are all these little bridges that link him to something, to his place in the universe. If they can cut these, then they are going to turn that man inside himself, and they are going to make him fight himself. And that's exactly what they want him to do. Because as soon as you compromise one of your beliefs, as soon as you compromise one of your loyalties, just to survive, then you are condemning yourself for it. That is exactly what they want. Because this is the pressure that doesn't stop. Physical torture, as soon as they stop it, you've got relief. But mental torture is something that will last 24 hours a day, and you do it to yourself.

14   One of the most vital things that came up was when men in the camp were asked, "Do you have a wife, do you have a family?" A couple of them answered, "Yes, we've got wives, we've got families." And the first thing that was asked was, "Do you think of your wife very often, do you think of your children, do you think of your family?" In an off-hand manner, we would respond, "Well, yah, we do, we are concerned, but we can't do anything about it." Then the guard would walk off. It didn't bother the individual for a couple of days, but pretty soon he started to think, and he began to wonder, "Is my wife all right, are my children all right, do they have enough money, are they sick, are they provided for?" and this was beginning to bother them, because they didn't know. Then the guard came down, and a little bit later, he would toss in another one; he would say, "How long does it take a woman in the United States to get a divorce after her husband is missing in action? Would your wife do this?" And of course, the immediate comment was, "No sweat. Not with my wife. She is going to hang in tight." Then he goes back to his cage at night, where he is by himself, and he lays there in that mosquito net, and he starts to think, and they give you plenty of time to think, and he begins to wonder, "Will she? What is it? What's the story? What's happening back there?" And he doesn't know. Next they go one step further, after he is going up the wall over these two questions, maybe a week later, he will come back, and he will say, "What is this we hear about immorality in your country? We read much about immorality. Do you know what your wife is doing?" And again, the first answer that comes out of the prisoner's mouth is what he believes, "My wife is straight, there's no problem." But then he goes back to his cage at night, and he begins to wonder: "I've been gone four years, I've been gone three years, what is happening back there?" You talk about frustration and anxiety, this is what does it to a man. This is a very subtle thumbscrew that they put on his mind, and then he tightens it down. And they don't even have to touch him. Because he doesn't know and he is in a prison camp. Now this works constantly. There is no getting away from these, and these are just everyday things.

15   Then you have the threats, and you find that anxiety comes in. When Plato said, "I can kill you, I can torture you, I can do anything I want," it really didn't mean anything. But in 1965, they moved us into the U Minh Forest and we met Mr. Hi. Mr. Hi was a political cadre, he was in charge of indoctrination, interrogation, and proselytizing of the enemy troops. He was a professor of English in Saigon before he joined the Revolution. We called him Mafia, and he fitted his name. Because when Mafia said I can kill you, I can torture you, I can do anything I want, he meant it. We met him in March 1965, Captain Humbert "Rock" Vercase and I both failed the initial interrogation indoctrination, we both went to punishment camps. I stayed in a starvation camp for six months, Rocky Vercase was executed in September of 1965. That was Mafia's lesson. When he said I can kill you, I can torture you, I can do anything I want, he meant it. And

that was a lesson to all the American POW's. It was an entirely new ballgame. Here was a political cadre who was in charge of our lives; he could take us and he could do anything he wanted to with us. This is a hard lesson to learn. This was the new concept beginning in 1965, and this is what exists now.

16   The threat of violence, the anticipation of violence, the anxiety that goes with it, sometimes, in fact most of the time, is far more devastating than what follows. This is what they are doing. They'll take a man and they'll threaten and then they will watch him run himself up and down the ladder worrying about what is going to happen to him. This is the thing—when they get hold of your emotions, and they can run them up and down the scale like a yoyo; then they've got you ricocheting off the wall; and this is exactly what they want. Because now they've got you fighting on both fronts. They've got you fighting to stay physically alive, and they've got you fighting to maintain your sanity. At that point you're becoming pliable. Because they're dangling this carrot in front of you that says, "Comply, and go home." And they toss in a few extras. One of the cadre told me in 1968, "Merely because the war ends is no reason for you to go home. If your attitude is not correct, you may rest here after the war." And ties that in with something he said a few months before, "We are here to tell you the truth of the situation today, and if you do not believe us, we will tell you tomorrow. And if you do not believe us tomorrow, we will tell you the day after, and the day after, until one day, if you don't die first, you'll believe us, and then you can go home." And so you have that carrot dangling in front of you which is "Going Home," and that is something you really want to do, because the environment is so oppressive that you want to get out of it, and yet what he is telling you is that there is no way out except our way.

17   Well, there is a way, initially, and that's escape, but that's hard. I tried three times and failed, and a fourth time it took a B-52 strike, and Cobras and light observation helicopters to get me out, which is a rotten way to do it, but it worked. But this is the only other way an American has out at the immediate time. The people in the prison camps in North Vietnam are not so fortunate. Like Bob Frishman said one time, "You know, even if you do get out of the camp, where does a round-eye go in downtown Hanoi wearing striped pajamas?" So this is one thing that the prisoners in North Vietnam don't even have to hope for. The prisoners in South Vietnam have this to look forward to, if they are strong enough to do it. But generally speaking, you are kept so physically weak that you can't. Yet you keep trying. So you are closed in on from all sides, and they seem to give you the only way out. But to take their way means you are going to compromise everything you believe in.

18   Now there have been individuals who have done this without really believing it, just going along to get out. The cases are very few, and I think the

Communists have found that the Americans are probably the most insincere group of people they have ever come in contact with. The only thing is when a man comes out, if this has actually happened, when he finds that freedom is something of a hollow thing, because he has given more to get that freedom than it was worth. He's got to live with himself the rest of his life. This is one thing people have to think about. I found, for myself, that under this pressure, you find that there is a tight, hard little core inside of everybody, and it is basically faith, a person with a faith in God. This is something they can't challenge, because they don't believe in God. You find that if you can attach your belief to something far above and beyond this dirty little world they've got you in, then you have an opportunity to remove yourself from it. Their understanding of faith or of God is purely ritual and dogma. They've studied our ritual. For instance, every Christmas, they'd come down, like Mafia would come down, and he gave me a candle. He said, "According to our policy, the Front respects the religious beliefs of the POW. Take this candle, go to your net, and burn it for Midnight Mass." And I said, "Look, Mafia, I'm a Protestant, I've already had my little service, and I really don't need a candle, I don't have Midnight Mass." He stuck the candle out and said, "Take it to your net and burn it, we respect your religious beliefs." So I took the candle, I went to my net, and I burned it, for a couple of minutes. This is what they understand about religion. But you find it's a very personal and a very simple communication between one man and his God. And that's all it requires. This is essential, because it removes you from this imprisonment. And you find, I think more importantly, that the Communists have stripped you of everything that identifies you. They strip you of your rank, your position, your money, of status, anything which allows you to identify yourself with material means, to identify yourself as a human being. They are trying to dehumanize you; you might as well be a handful of mud that they pick up off the ground. But faith in God is something that identifies you far more clearly than anything material that we have right now. Once you establish that, then you'll never lose your identity.

19   The second thing was faith in our country and faith in our government. And this they did attack very well. Initially, their Communist propaganda sources were not really effective because it was a Vietnamese writing for American consumption. When Radio Hanoi, the Radio Liberation, and all their bulletins and papers came across, they were using Webster's 1933. The words were either obsolete or obsolescent. I had to look some of them up when I got home to find out what they meant. What they are sending out is things that you will not accept because they are so far out. Like we lost 3,247 aircraft over North Vietnam, which includes five B-52's and three F-111A's. And they said one of the F-111A's was shot down by a girls' militia unit in Haiphong. So we read that

and said, "Okay, fine, that's great." The next thing they came up with was that we lost more tanks and artillery than we actually had in Vietnam. Another one they came up with, two of the ones that I really liked, they said that the VC platoon in the Delta had defeated a South Korean company in hand-to-hand combat. I read through that and I sort of scratched my head on that one. The next thing they came up with was during the Tet offensive in 1968, a VC girls' militia squad in Hue, they were called the Twelve Daughters of the Perfume River, which flows through Hue, had defeated a Marine batallion. The first thing I asked the cadre was, "Well, was this hand-to-hand combat, too?" But you know, we read this, and it really didn't affect us.

20   But then, in 1966 and '67, they started dropping all their sources, and we started getting the Congressional Record, magazines, newspapers, articles from the United States. This is what really turned out to be the greatest morale-breaker in the camp. The fact that we were sitting here defending our country and our government and our system, not only against the Communist political cadre, but against individuals right within our own government. And it is difficult to defend yourself when somebody in your own government is calling you an aggressor. This was the greatest weapon that they had. I think this was the thing that was most devastating to my morale personally, because there was no way that I could contest it. This was coming from my country. How do you explain dissent to Communist cadre who have never had the right to dissent in their whole lives? It was something they couldn't understand. And yet even in this context one of the cadre said, "Very soon the people in your country will decide that your coming to Vietnam was a mistake. And at that time those of you who have died here will have died a useless death. And those who lead the Revolution in your country will be the heroes and the saviors. Why should you rot in a jungle prison camp when you can return to your home, join the Revolution, repent of your crimes, and live with your family?" And you sit there and you say, "Why?" And then you begin to evaluate; and I found that no matter how many negatives they came up with, on our side, we always had more positives than the system that they were advocating. And there was always a chance for change within our system, whereas in the system they offered there was no chance for change. We got everything about the demonstrations, the riots, and the anti-war movement. I looked at the groups, the photographs of the college students carry VC flags, the American flags being desecrated, and the one thing I thought of was, well, what if these people did this in Czechoslovakia, or Hungary, or Communist China? And I thought, "Thank God they are in the United States and they've got the right to do it." But it was disturbing to me, because nobody wants to die for nothing.

21   The other thing that came up was a faith in the other American POWs. You find that these are the only friends you've got. The communist cadre are going to try to convince you that they are your friends, but you learn rapidly that all they are doing is exploiting you, they're using you as a tool. When you see an American prisoner giving up his meager ration of fish, just so another American who is sick can have a little bit more to eat, that is sacrifice. Because when you don't have anything and you give it up, or you have very little and you give it up, then you're hurting yourself, and that is true sacrifice. That's what I saw in the prison camp.

22   So those were the three things that I found were a sort of a basis for survival in this environment that's structured to break you down. The one thing they're finding out is that the American prisoners are first of all physically tougher than they ever expected. They read our society as materialistic, as being soft, as being apathetic, and yet they're finding that once they put these prisoners in this situation, and it's a battlefield just like any other, except it's more terrifying because you're fighting in the mind, they are finding that the American prisoners are hanging on. Everybody who has come out has said the same thing—there's three faiths, and these are the three things that stand strong. But the thing is, how long can these people hold up? In my camp, there were eight of us total over the five-year period. Contrary to the VC claims for humanitarian treatment, in my camp alone, out of eight of us, three died of starvation and disease, one was executed, three were released, one of whom was dying, and I escaped before I was executed. This is actuality. This is the fact contrasted with the promise.

23   Since my wife and I have been around the country, the one thing that civilians are asking is "Why doesn't the military do something for its own people? Why don't they do something to help those men?" We're starting. We just got a letter from Fort Knox the other day in Fort Campbell, and both of them are starting a Concern for POW drive; the whole posts are turning out. This is the type of thing that needs to be done, because it could be any one of us, and it could be any one of the military families of men on this post. I had one individual that told me on one occasion, "Why should we do it, when we've got too much other to do, the Red Cross, the Officers' Wives' Club, the various things that we have to do?" and the only thing I could think of was "Just pray to God that your husband doesn't get captured some day, and you have to ask somebody else for help." I think this is the saddest commentary, that the families and loved ones of these men have to go out and seek help, not only from the military community, but from the civilian community, for their husbands, and their fathers. This is to me something that needs to be changed, and it's not so much that the people don't care, it is just that most people don't know.

24   I'm thankful for the opportunity I had to come today, to perhaps enlighten you a little bit as to what does happen inside the camps. Thank you.

Take a Test Drive on the Information Superhighway: Unmasking the Jargon

Carl S. Ledbetter, Jr.

Carl S. Ledbetter, Jr., while President of Consumer Products at AT&T, delivered this speech at the Town Hall of Los Angeles on May 17, 1995. The Town Hall has, for more than half a century, been southern California's leading public issues forum. Because of its reputation for excellence, Town Hall attracts leaders in government, industry, and the arts and sciences from throughout the world. Town Hall's General Meetings are normally held at luncheon venues attended by leaders from across the professions who value dialogue on contemporary issues.

Recognizing that many members of his audience might feel uncomfortable with high technology nomenclature and concepts, Mr. Ledbetter promises to "unmask the jargon and hyperbole" that are often used in discussions of the Information Superhighway. To further allay the concern of audience members that they might not be able to comprehend his message, the speaker asks for "a show of hands" of those present who think they already know what the Information Superhighway is all about. Additionally, a videotape shows excerpts from a survey on the streets of New York City revealing that "the average person doesn't have a clue about the Information Superhighway." What effect are these strategies likely to have had on his listeners?

In seeking to increase understanding, especially when the subject is complex and difficult, it is important that the speaker clarify his or her meanings through the use of such expository devices as comparisons, definitions, and examples. Identify the types of devices employed in this speech. Which type is used to greatest advantage? When explaining technical or detailed concepts to an audience, it is also important to

✝Carl S. Ledbetter, Jr., "Take a Test Drive on the Information Superhighway: Unmasking the Jargon," July 1, 1995, pp. 565-569. Reprinted with permission of *Vital Speeches of the Day* and the author.

make the information interesting. What means does the speaker use to invite audience interest in the Information Superhighway? Finally, in order that an audience may value the information provided, a speaker is well-advised to demonstrate that the information being presented is important and worthwhile. How does Mr. Ledbetter demonstrate the value of information related to the "I-way"? (Note: Mr. Ledbetter is no longer with AT&T. He is currently CEO of Hybrid Networks of California.)

---

1 Good afternoon. My topic today—information technology—could be a little indigestible coming right after lunch, so I'll make it as palatable for you as I can. Let's ease into it by talking about the technology of another time.

2 I was born in a small town in Kansas, long enough ago so that any kind of modern technology was pretty rare, and long enough ago so that we still had the quaint practice of holding town meetings. I remember one of those meetings at which the main subject was the terrible indignity our town had suffered recently at the hands of a neighboring town. It was even smaller than ours, and clearly less prestigious, but it had stolen a march on us by purchasing a brand-new high-falutin' rheostat-controlled electric chandelier for its town hall. And they were embarrassing us all over the county by talking up their advanced status, and our backwardness.

3 So the debate that day was about whether or not we should allocate the money—nearly a third of the town's whole budget for the year—to buy our own rheostat-controlled electric chandelier. There were good arguments advanced on both sides of the issue, some thinking that to buy this new electric gadget would be an unnecessary waste of money that could be better spent on fixing the leak in the water tower, others insisting that it was intolerable to continue to exist in the humiliating situation of being thought inferior to those bumpkins down the road.

4 Finally, the mayor called the question. "Before we vote on this momentous matter," he said, "I would like to know one final thing. Is there anyone in town who actually knows how to play one of these rheostat-controlled electric chandeliers?"

5 We have one of those chandelier technologies in this era, too, and by now, most of you have heard the "All-Digital, Simultaneous, Real-Time, Interactive, Broadband, Multimedia, Information Superhighway Blues," and you are probably wondering if you can ever learn to play it on your harmonica. I'm going to try to help you in the next few minutes with some facts about just what this new Information Superhighway is, what it offers you as individuals and as civic and business leaders, and, most important, why you should take an active

interest in its development. I'll also do it in a way that seeks to unmask the jargon and hyperbole that surround most discussions of this topic.

6   Let's begin with a show of hands from those of you who think you already know what the Information Superhighway is, and where you can find the nearest on-ramp. Don't feel bad if your hand isn't up. You're not alone. A great many people have heard about the Information Superhighway, but very few know what it is, or where it is, or even if it is. AT&T recently ran an informal survey on the streets in New York City that illustrates this point. We have some excerpts of the survey on a brief video.

7   That video makes two significant points. The first is that you should be wary of the answer when you ask New Yorkers for directions. The second is that the average person doesn't have a clue about the Information Superhighway. And there's a good reason for this: "When you get there, there's no there there." The Information Superhighway doesn't exist.

8   This Information Superhighway, which increasingly is called by the shortened name, the I-way, has form only as a virtual concept. You've probably heard about virtual concepts in high technology—like virtual reality.

9   In keeping with the spirit of this talk today I'm going to define in plain English the word "virtual," and some of the other specialized argot of the high technology industry to strip aside the techno-babble and lay bare the true meaning of this gibberish.

10   "Virtual" is an adjective we use in the industry when we're talking about something we can't quite get a fix on. But we do know that it can't dance and it's too fat to fly. So it is with the I-way. Today it has no fixed design, no overarching plan, no defining blueprint, no timetable for completion. It's not about computers, or telephones, or TV, or cable with 500 channels, or video-on-demand, or satellites, or fiber optics, or PCS wireless frequencies, or any other single form of information or method of transmission. It's about all of them.

11   But it's also about communicating simply, and cheaply, and with benefits far richer than the ability to summon *Forrest Gump* at the click of a button. The I-way is still a "vision thing," and a confusing one at that. You won't see it completely realized in this century.

12   This is not to say that the I-way is developing entirely haphazardly. A number of companies in the information and entertainment industries have very definite ideas about how this I-way should evolve. But the last word on the subject will not belong, and should not belong, to these companies or to this industry.

13   The final say will belong to the customer, because, ultimately, the I-way, as it becomes real, will adapt to the demands and expectations that people have for advanced information services.

14   Those of you who are dying to take a spin on the I-way have probably already used the sections of it that are in place today. An ordinary telephone, or a personal computer with a modem, will get you to the on-ramp.

15   Fax machines, broadcast television and radio, cable TV, satellite and wireless networks, direct broadcast TV, and on-line computer networks will also be part of the I-way.

16   So will repositories of information—like libraries, newspapers, magazines, and databases for everything from airline schedules to the prices of stocks and bonds. In addition, a whole host of live information will be available on the I-way—information that goes by the awkward-sounding name *content*—and includes real-time movies, video images, and all the individual pieces of information in those various databases.

17   Here's an example to help make it all clear: There's already a rancher in Texas who hangs pagers around the necks of his cows while they're out grazing and has them trained to come in from the pasture when he beeps them.

18   Think of the I-way as the road that carries that paging signal to the cows to induce them to transport their *content*—the stuff that cows are full of—back to the barn. (The milk, not the manure.)

19   All of these elements of the I-way exist today, but separately. The goal of the I-way is to bind those elements into a National Information Infrastructure, the sum total of resources that will allow Americans to share all forms of information, anytime, anywhere, with each other and with people around the world.

20   The National Information Infrastructure is the Emerald City of Oz. The I-way is the Yellow Brick Road that gets you there. And what will we find when we finally do reach this Emerald City?

21   We are promised the wizardry of all-digital, simultaneous, real-time, interactive, broadband multimedia.

22   I'll have to get back to some definitions to keep my promise to demystify this jargon. Let's start with "National Information Infrastructure." That means pork for every state. This is the only kind of infrastructure ever invented for which the construction workers are politicians.

23   "Multimedia" means more than one medium—a fancy way of saying "Talkies"—movies with sound. Multimedia means mixing voice, video, image, and data in a single communications system.

24   It's the difference between the records we played as teenagers, which we could only listen to, and the music videos our kids listen to and watch.

25   "Interactive" means the communication is two-way. Telephone calls are interactive. You talk, the person you called talks—back and forth, and simultaneously—which means both parties can talk at once without cutting off the signal to the other speaker. Television and radio are not interactive—they are broadcast media. You can talk back to Rush Limbaugh if you want, but he won't hear you—and that is a technology fact, not a statement about his attitude.

26   "Real-time" means right now—with no delay. Real-time means live rather than taped, in-the-moment rather than after-the-fact, a conversation you conduct face-to-face or on the phone at normal pace and tempo rather than through a series of messages left on the refrigerator or answering machine to be picked up later.

27   What does "digital" mean? In surveys of consumers we've discovered that they think it means "high-quality." That perception is driven by the very much improved sound quality of digital audio compact discs—CDs—over older technologies like records and tapes. And although there are some important quality improvements which digital technologies induce, the real difference is in how the information is carried and presented.

28   Communications are handled as either digital information or as what we call analog, which is the other kind of representation.

29   I want everybody to look at his or her watch. If your watch is digital it's 12:57:36. But if your watch is analog the little hand is on the one and the big hand is nearly straight up, so it's almost one o'clock. Digital information can be more precise, it can be handled more reliably and consistently by our information systems and network, and importantly, it can be protected from corruption and eavesdropping more easily, and can be corrected more readily if some of it is damaged or lost.

30   Broadband describes signal carrying capacity. Like a wide multi-lane freeway—think of Interstate 5—broadband technology can carry lots of information. We say it has lots of band-width. Narrowband is a smaller-capacity capability, like a narrow country road. Both of these kinds of roads are necessary and good. In particular, broadband is not always better than narrowband—think what it would be like to have the driveway of your house opening into I-10, or a narrow two-lane country road providing the only access to LAX. The bandwidth which is best is that which is scaled to the size of the task.

31   If you had to drive your son's basketball team to a game, you could get them there in one trip in your station wagon. That's narrowband. But suppose it was your daughter's entire Little League team. For that, you'd need a team bus or a caravan. That's broadband.

32   Bandwidth is measured in megahertz or in megabits per second. Megahertz has nothing to do with what the Los Angeles Lakers did to the Seattle Supersonics. A megahertz is a million cycles per second.

33   Telephone conversations are narrowband—4 kilohertz, the equivalent of eight thousand bits of data per second. That sounds like a lot, and in a way

it is—it's enough to carry the crisp, clear sound of voice on telephone wires—the station wagon of telecommunications.

34   Full-motion video, like cable TV, requires considerably more data, so it's broadband. The bit rate for TV-quality video is 114 million bits per second. That calls for a team bus, the coax cable—the one with the sharp little wire in the center that screws into the back of your TV set.

35   Right now, you probably have a TV in the family room, a fax and maybe a PC in your home office, telephones in several places around the house, and an answering machine wherever it's most convenient. If you want to check your telephone messages, you go to the answering machine.

36   If you find a call you want to return, you pick up the telephone. If you want to check your e-mail or cruise the Internet for information or entertainment, you boot up the computer. And if you want the local news and weather, you turn on the TV or radio to a broadcast already in progress and hope you haven't missed anything. And you may even send a fax or page your spouse from your home.

37   The Information Superhighway will eventually enable you to combine those services in one device, not six, and you'll be able to make this technology adapt to your schedule rather than the other way around. In addition, you'll be able to order movies on demand through your TV—no running out to the video store only to find out that the one you want isn't in stock. You'll get scheduled TV programs when *you* want them. If you miss Dan Rather and Connie Chung fighting on the evening news at six, you'll be able to recall it at eight, or nine, or whenever it's convenient, and you won't have to program your VCR to record it.

38   You will be able to bring up educational programs and town bulletin boards. You'll be able to order sports and theater tickets, do home shopping, and conduct your banking from the comfort of your couch, all by using a remote control device like the one you use to change channels on your TV set.

39   You'll be able to get local traffic and weather reports on demand, the west coast baseball scores, the winning lottery number, your personal horoscope, and the answers to your crossword puzzle.

40   You'll be able to use your PC to place phone calls: pop up your personal phone directory on the PC, select the number you want to call, click the mouse, and it will dial your phone.

41   Let's turn that around. Instead of a screen with a phone attached, you'll have a phone with a screen attached, and be able to use the same process: touch a key in your personal directory, bring up a number on the screen, press "dial" and it's done. You'll also be able to pick up names and addresses through a national directory assistance service and have the information displayed on your screen to dial with a single button.

42   And eventually you will have true video telephony—a telephone with full-motion video quality. And by the way, "full-motion" means no flickering or fuzziness—at least the quality of standard TV.

43   But the I-way promises more than convenience and entertainment. It promises real value in information exchange. Research hubs in education could give local schools access to information they might not be able to afford themselves. A student working on a paper at Centennial High School would be able to call up the full annotated text of Shakespeare's *Hamlet* from the New York Public Library, or maybe just the Cliff Notes. In medicine, a doctor in Sacramento could have a patient's x-rays and CAT-scans analyzed by specialists at UCLA, in real time, so the patient can have a diagnosis and treatment plan right now.

44   Multimedia services—especially those involving image and video—require handling great amounts of digitized information. Moving and managing this information calls for special technology—advanced communications systems that can ship and route large volumes of signals quickly and reliably. We have this now in the digital, fiber optic long distance networks operated by AT&T and other companies.

45   Optical fibers can carry vast amounts of data at the speed of light. A research director at AT&T Bell Laboratories once calculated that a cable consisting of ten strands of optical fiber could transmit the entire contents of the Library of Congress across the United States in one second. And that was ten years ago.

46   The capacity of fiber systems has been doubling every year since then. One pair of hair-thin glass fibers can now carry 53,000 phone calls simultaneously. Fiber optic systems now in service carry the equivalent of close to one million calls simultaneously.

47   We have not only the technology needed to transport all these voice calls, but also the switching to route them to customers' homes quickly, easily and dependably. That element of the I-way is up and running. Other elements are still in the works.

48   One of the under-developed elements is the local loop, the line closest to the customer's home. Delivering information to the customer's street is one thing: getting it inside the house is another. The difficulty is a lot like the long-carry problem when the moving van can't get up your narrow driveway. When that happens they have to carry everything all the way in from the curb one piece at a time. In communications we can do this to some extent with existing technology by compressing signals to make them smaller—to squeeze them through a phone line. But the average home is not yet equipped to accept real-time interactive multimedia services. A number of companies, in a number of industries, are working on that problem.

49   Cable TV companies, for example, already have high-capacity access to the home, but they lack the switching system—the roadway network, the map, and the traffic-control system—needed to send specific information to a certain house, and only there. Telephone companies have the switching systems, but lack the high-capacity access—the big wide driveway—the coax cable to the house. This seems like a natural opportunity for the two industries to partner, but so far, efforts to marry the two have failed at the altar, although we make and break engagements frequently. It's getting so you're as likely to read about these partnerships in the gossip pages as in the business section. Another option is for the cable companies to build their own switching networks, and some of them have talked about this. But it will take years.

50   Pacific Bell, which has the switching, is now building the access using technology from AT&T. Last year the company broke ground on a fiber optic network that will deliver interactive multimedia throughout California, coming to your neighborhood no later than the year 2010. Pacific Telesis doesn't want to wait that long. It plans to acquire a wireless cable company so it can offer video services to 5 million customers in your area by the end of 1996, but this might require spectrum that hasn't been allocated yet and technical breakthroughs that haven't happened yet, so we'll see.

51   The entertainment industry is also seeking access. The Walt Disney Company plans to partner with three regional Bell companies to distribute entertainment and interactive programming over telephone lines. But even that will take at least five years.

52   This is not happening overnight.

53   And once the I-way does get inside the home we come to another important consideration. It's the problem of the "First Foot" of the I-way—the devices or appliances in your house that actually deliver the services. There's some question as to what these devices will be. Will they look like the PC, the TV, or the telephone?

54   Some contend that the PC is the only logical choice. Eckhard Pfeiffer, the president of Compaq Computer, believes the PC will ultimately emerge as the primary delivery system. The argument is that while more than 90 percent of American homes have access to cable TV, none are wired for interactive services. On the other hand, nearly a third of American homes—some 30 million—already own PCs with more than enough power to handle interactive services.

55   But how many of these homes actually use their PCs as the on-ramp to the developing I-way?

56   Only a third of these PCs—about 10 million of them—have a modem to connect them to on-line services. About half of these—five or six million today—actually subscribe to an on-line service. And only about half of those—around 3 million—log on more than twice a month after the trial period. Let's get real here—there are twice as many people as that in the U.S. who still use rotary telephones.

57   PC penetration will grow. Make no mistake about that. But it will grow more slowly than the hype suggests.

58   I just don't think the average consumer is going to invest $3,000 in a 60-MHz, Pentium-based, 8 megabyte machine with a 540 megabyte hard drive, a CD ROM, Sound Blaster, SVGA monitor, and a set of operating manuals for which a stand of prime timber gave its life just so they can cruise the chat rooms or alt.pets.cats on the Internet.

59   It's not going to happen that way. It's too expensive. More than that, it frightens people. In a survey conducted by Apple Computer, 85 percent of respondents said computers terrified them. The prospect of dealing with a computer that won't behave is daunting.

60   And let's face it—PCs just don't behave yet. And I don't mean just for the 85 percent of those who are terrified by computers. I'm in the other 15 percent. In fact, I'm about six sigma out on the skew.

61   I've been using computers for 28 years and have done just about everything you can do with them. I have six computers in my house, and an ethernet in the walls, three gigabytes of hard disk storage, more than 8,000 floppy diskettes, three laser printers, four CD ROMs, and every gadget and software package my family can find a way to install.

62   But when I describe the intolerance of users for the complexity of these systems I am describing me, as well as my mother, who won't have a computer in her house. I just won't put up with the fact that I can't install a new software package without having the whole system crash because an Interrupt Request or Terminate and State Resident conflict.

63   PCs have a long way to go to reach the level of simplicity, reliability, dependability and capability we all want as users.

64   Let me contrast that problem with the ease of using the telephone network.

65   When was the last time you got an "Unrecoverable Operating System Error" on your phone—or had your phone seize up during the middle of a conversation? You don't need an autoexec.bat or config.sys or win.ini to use a telephone. You don't need an instruction manual, and the phone doesn't go down even when the power goes out in your house.

66   Ed McCracken, the head of Silicon Graphics, believes that the 85 percent who are terrified by the PC will turn to the television set. Don't worry about its ability to handle interactive services—the capabilities now being built into High Definition TVs will make them more powerful than any PC. So goes the argument. Perhaps, but Americans will not go into a buying frenzy to add another TV set to the house. That will take time, especially if they have to learn to program it.

67   An evil word, programming. Ninety-five percent of the VCRs in the world have the 12:00 blinking. We just don't program these things. The directions are too complicated.

68   I am with Calvin of the *Calvin and Hobbes* cartoon by Bill Watterson: "Instructions are for wimps." The only kind of instruction manual I'm willing to tolerate anymore is the one on the back of those Wet-Naps they give you to wipe your hands with when you're on a long airplane trip. If you turn one of those over you can read the entire set of directions. They say: "Instructions for use: Open and Use."

69   So if it's going to be TVs, we'll have to make them simple. Whatever we need on the Information Superhighway we should be able to get it on our TV with one click of a button, and no manual. And certainly no programming.

70   We at AT&T don't believe that any company, any industry can decide which device is best. That choice properly belongs to the customer. So we've developed what we call a three-screen strategy that will let the user display information on a TV, a PC, or a telephone with a built-in-screen—or a mixture of the three—whichever is most convenient.

71   We also believe that whichever device the customer chooses, it must be simple to use. Complexity is the reason 85 percent of the populace fear the PC. Simplicity is the reason 100 percent have no trouble operating the world's largest and most complex computer—the worldwide telephone switching network.

72   Telephone customers can place a call virtually anywhere in the world in less time than it takes to heat leftovers in the microwave, and they don't need to understand the dynamics of electronic switching or alternate routing to do it. All it takes is a simple, 12-button touch-tone keypad. The only excuse for high technology is to make things simple.

73   We need to build simplicity into the I-way if we expect it to realize the full potential of the services it can offer. What will those services look like? I can't guess, but we are already looking at a preview. *The New York Times* operates a 900 number that charges frustrated crossword puzzlers 75 cents a minute to find the answer to 34 down—what's a four-letter word for "Bantu language."

74 Thousands of people call that 900 number every week. I'm one of them, and I know it costs me $3.75 a week on average to finish the puzzle. Instead, the I-way will someday allow you to display the puzzle on your TV, highlight the clue you need, and have the screen fill in "Zulu" at 34 down.

75 The New York State Lottery Commission has a 900 number that charges 79 cents a call to learn the winning number in the Lotto. Eighteen million people call that number every year. Think about that. New York State makes an extra $14 million dollars on the lottery just for telling people they didn't win a few hours earlier than they can find out for free by listening to the news or reading the paper.

76 What this tells us is that for consumers convenience is a commodity, and people will gladly pay for it. The I-way will create thousands of new services to supply that convenience. It will get services directly to customers instantly when they want it.

77 What those services will be depends largely upon the imagination and initiative of service providers. The customer will make the final decision on what travels along that highway—not the service provider or the network provider, not AT&T, the FCC or Pacific Bell. And that's as it should be.

78 The final step is to ensure that those services are available to anyone at reasonable cost. The only way to achieve that is through open access and full competition. Currently cable TV and local telephone companies remain monopolies that control the price and content of the services they supply.

79 The local telephone companies now want the freedom to compete in the long distance market so they can become major players in providing interactive multimedia services. The Congress will probably give them this freedom in the next couple of years, and we think that is a good idea as long as it's done correctly, and "there's the rub."

80 Even while the local telephone companies champion competition in long distance service, they still want to maintain control over final access to the customer. It you want to deal with their customers, you do so on their terms, and those terms are costly.

81 Since the Bell System was divested in 1984 and long distance service became competitive, long distance costs have gone down 66 percent. But local service costs have gone up 14 percent over the same period, and more than that, 45 cents of every long distance dollar actually goes to the local phone company in what are called access charges. If you think of the telephone network as an analog of the transportation system, it is as if a handful of taxicab companies control the only access to the nation's airports from your homes and offices—no private cars, buses, or limos allowed—and the price of every airline ticket includes a special taxi access charge which amounts to 45 percent of your entire airfare. Now the taxicab companies want to go into the air carrier business. Terrific! Let's just not let them do it until we allow buses and private cars into the airport.

82   We don't want to see this gatekeeper role perpetuated. Allowing local companies to control access and pricing for the connection to your home without competition would frustrate the benefits of the free market, both to service providers and their customers, and would drive up the cost of services. It could easily lead to a nation of information haves and have nots, those who can afford access to basic information services and those who are effectively excluded by price.

83   Vice President Al Gore, addressing this issue in a recent article on the Information Superhighway, said:

> "When competition replaces regulation, consumers will have more choice, better service, and much lower prices."

84   So let's bring on the Information Superhighway, with all its promise and with full competition and no gatekeeper. But let's not get turned off by all the hype and techno gibberish we hear about it.

85   When that high-falutin' rheostat-controlled electric chandelier finally arrived at our town hall, no one had a hard time learning how to play it.

86   When the All-Digital Simultaneous, Real-Time, Interactive, Broadband, Multimedia Information Superhighway Blues finally arrives at your home, I think you'll find it's not that hard to play, either.

INHERITING THE EARTH:
LOUIS FARRAKHAN AND THE NATION OF ISLAM

Ian M. Rolland

For many Americans, the essential elements of the Islamic faith remain a mystery. An even larger enigma, however, is understanding the key spokesman for the Nation of Islam, Louis Farrakhan. On February 3, 1995, Ian M. Rolland spoke to the Quest Club of Fort Wayne, Indiana

---

+Ian M. Rolland, "Inheriting the Earth: Louis Farrakhan and the Nation of Islam," April 1, 1995, pp. 376-380. Reprinted with permission of *Vital Speeches of the Day* and the author.

with the general purpose of informing his audience about the Nation of Islam and Louis Farrakhan.

Ian Rolland is Chairman and CEO of the Lincoln National Insurance Corporation based in Fort Wayne. Educated at Depauw University and the University of Michigan, Rolland, a native of Fort Wayne, has been with Lincoln National since 1956. The Quest Club is an eighty-five year old luncheon organization that meets twice a month to hear presentation by members on historical, cultural, and political topics. Over one hundred of the leading civic and business leaders in Fort Wayne are members of the Quest Club.

Rolland begins his lengthy presentation with a clear "common ground" statement for his audience (1) that is reinforced with an engaging rhetorical question (2) While Rolland promises a focus on Farrakhan, his internal preview (3) suggests that listeners need to be first introduced to the larger "cast of characters" that created the Nation of Islam. Once established, does Rolland maintain this dramatic metaphor as a structural device throughout the presentation? How helpful are his internal summaries and transition devices (20, 28, 47, 61, 94) in this speech?

Following an historical summary of Islamic theology and its transition to America (4-14), Rolland provides biographical descriptions of W.D. Farad Muhammad, Elijah Muhammad, Malcolm X, and Warith Deen Mohammed (38-60). Rolland is careful at the beginning to compare and contrast how Elijah Muhammad's teachings differed from traditional "mainstream Islam" (30–36). In addition, Rolland offers his audience colorful personal insights about each of these key individuals (44, 46, 58).

Karlyn Kohrs Campbell observes in the second edition of *The Rhetorical Act* (Belmont, California: Wadsworth, 1996) that "chronological organization argues that this topic . . . is best understood in terms of how it develops or unfolds through time, or that you cannot achieve a goal without following a certain sequence" (p.249). Does Rolland achieve his goal with the historical narrative presented? Are all the distorical details he includes interesting and meaningful?

Over half-way through the speech, Rolland finally begins his discussion of Louis Farrakhan (62-63). Following a biographical sketch of Farrakhan (68-73) Rolland confronts the more controversial aspects of the Nation of Islam leader. Are the statements made by Rolland "fair" regarding the claim that Farrakhan is a "racist or a 'hatemonger' (33, 75-79)?" How do you evaluate Rolland's brief use of irony (56)? Has Rolland, with his final references to a public opinion poll on Farrakhan's influence (96-98), been objective and "balanced" with his choice of information presented?

After reading Rolland's speech, were misconceptions that you had about the Nation of Islam or Louis Farrakhan clarified? What additional information could Rolland have presented that would have increased your understanding of this organization and its leaders?

---

1   After 200 years as a nation, America still fights an internal battle with racism, a widening gulf between the haves and have-nots, deterioration of the inner cities and the lives of those who live there.

2   The man you just saw—Louis Farrakhan—has an answer. It's an answer that has been repeated to thousands of black Americans since the early 1930s. And, while we might not always like what we hear, the real question is this: is his message worth listening to?

3   Today, you're going to hear about Louis Farrakhan. But you're also going to hear about a whole cast of characters preceding Farrakhan's rise as a leader of the Nation of Islam. They include:

- W.D. Farad Muhammad, a mysterious door-to-door silk peddler who founded the movement.
- Elijah Muhammad, who succeeded Farad as head of the group and over the next four decades built it into national power.
- Warith Deen Mohammed, Elijah's son, who was named to head the organization upon his father's death 20 years ago.
- And Malcolm X, perhaps the best known and most influential of all.

4   While different in many respects, each man had one goal in common: to recognize the anger and explain the disenfranchisement of black people— poor and middle class alike—while instilling group identity, self-respect and hope. The Nation of Islam addresses the issues of religion, racism, economic exclusion, drug abuse and destruction of the traditional family.

5   Both black people and white people should listen to what Farrakhan is saying. Blacks because he speaks to them—whites because he speaks AGAINST them—and both because his assessment of the world, whether right or wrong, can force us to more closely examine our own.

6   To understand the Nation of Islam, we first have to look at Islam itself.

7   Islam is the youngest of the three great monotheistic religions, but it has grown to 1.16 billion adherents worldwide—nearly a fourth of everyone alive today. The number of people who call themselves Muslims is second only to Christianity.

8   By definition, a Muslim is someone who has surrendered his or her whole being to God. Anyone can be accepted as a Muslim who professes that "there is no god but Allah, and Mohammed is his messenger."

9   Muslims are generally expected to adhere to the "Five Pillars" of the faith: Profession that there is no god but Allah, prayer five times a day, fasting during Ram-a-DON, almsgiving, and pilgrimage to Mecca, if the person is physically and financially able to make the trek.

10   Today, Islam is thought to be the fastest growing religion in the U.S., though it is difficult to find statistically valid numbers. Immigration and census figures from 1980—as well as estimates of the number of African-American Muslims in America—indicate that the number of Muslims living here was about 3.3 million at the time, or one and a half percent of the population. That would make Islam the third largest religion in the United States—after Judaism, with 3 percent of the population and Christianity, with 55 percent.

11   It's likely that this number rose to at least 4 million by 1986. If that rate holds steady, the number of Muslims in the United States in the next five years will have nearly doubled over the 1980 estimate, and could pass Judaism as the country's second largest faith.

12   Part of this growth can be attributed to the liberalization of immigration policies in the 1960s. But growth of Islam among indigenous African-Americans skyrocketed for another reason—Malcolm X. The Nation of Islam's spokesman during the 1950s and early 1960s, Malcolm X's eloquence and message of hope struck a chord with many black people who had grown impatient with the pace of civil rights.

13   Today, nearly one in three American Muslims are what were once generically referred to as "Black Muslims." And Malcolm X deserves much of the credit.

14   Still, Islam has a longer history in America than its recent growth might suggest. As many as one-fifth of the slaves brought to America were educated in some of the principles of Islam. And we know that slaves from West Africa and the Sudan practiced the religion secretly in both North and South America during slavery. Louis Farrakhan, in promoting

---

Ian M. Rolland, Chairman and CEO of the Lincoln National Insurance Corporation, Fort Wayne, Indiana

the need for black people to identify more closely with their origins, often uses this point to claim Islam is the natural religion of African-Americans.

15   In the black community, Islam has fulfilled a variety of needs. It spread as a religion, a vehicle of protest and as a means of self-identity. Conversion to Islam fit the separatist "nation-within-a-nation" school of thought that insisted blacks had a claim to America because it was built on the blood and labor of their ancestors.

16   As Islam spread in the black community, the non-orthodoxy of many Muslim groups became obvious, drawing criticism from more mainstream Muslims. The focus of these new groups was to give *poor* blacks especially—but also others—an identity apart from a system and society that was oppressive.

17   Islam gave many disenfranchised African-Americans a right that they felt Christianity did not give—the right to fight back against the oppressor. While the Koran forbids aggressive warfare, it allows Muslims to use force to rectify the injustices of others.

18   Islam also lent a structure to daily living and fostered development of communities based on collective needs, adherence to a strong moral code, respect for women and the family, authority for men and economic self-sufficiency.

19   Today, at least 17 distinct groups of African-American Muslims exists. Among those is Louis Farrakhan's Nation of Islam, with an estimated membership of anywhere from 20,000 to 100,000. The largest group, estimated at 1 million members, is led by Warith Deen Mohammed—son of Nation of Islam's former leader, Elijah Muhammad.

20   So where does the Nation of Islam fit within the context of Islam in general? Well, I think we have to start at the beginning. And in the beginning, was W.D. Farad Muhammad.

21   Farad founded the Nation of Islam in 1930. A silk peddler working the poor neighborhoods of Detroit, Farad gained converts during his door-to-door sales calls. He said he was an Arab born in Mecca, but his claim has never been substantiated. His origins—and his disappearance in 1934—remain clouded in mystery.

22   Farad built a following through stories of his homeland, which he said was also the original homeland of American black people. His ministry began with gentle cautions against eating certain foods and stories about how people in the homeland preserved their health. As people asked to hear more, he gradually introduced religious concepts and doctrine about the origin of black people in Asia and Africa. Eventually, his teachings became diatribes against Christianity and "blue-eyed devils."

23   When Farad vanished without a trace—apparently even the police were mystified—his teachings were advanced by his closest associate, Elijah Muhammad, who would rule the Nation of Islam for the next 41 years.

24   Elijah Muhammad was born in rural Georgia as Elijah Poole. His impression of race relations was formed early when, as a small boy walking through the woods, he stumbled upon the lynching of a black man by two whites. Elijah hid in the bushes as the man was beaten, then hanged from a nearby tree.

25   Maybe it was that image that helped him overcome a third-grade education, a hostile press, and an unsympathetic economic system. In any case, Elijah Muhammad built an admirable business operation and a significant religious movement that drew thousands of African-Americans between the 1950s and the 1970s.

26   Revered as god-like by some and a king by others, his teachings appealed to many blacks looking for meaning in their lives. The Nation of Islam's political and ideological appeal owed to its claims to Islam, black supremacy and the unity of black people against the white man.

27   Muhammad's Nation of Islam owed a debt to two movements of the early 1900s: The Moorish Science Temple established by Noble Drew Ali and the International Negro Improvement Movement of Marcus Garvey. But Elijah Muhammad's impact was more than the sum of those parts. He was the father of a social and political movement that to this day forces mainstream leaders to sit up and take notice.

28   In a minute, I'm going to discuss some of Elijah's religious teachings—some of them will sound quite strange. But before I do, it's important to note that his primary mission was not religious conversion. His main goal was to develop a group solidarity that could become strong enough to overcome oppression by whites.

29   To quote from one Muslim minister, the aim was to get "the white man's foot off my neck, his hand out of my pocket and his carcass off my back."

30   Consequently, Elijah Muhammad's teachings differed widely from mainstream Islam. In fact, many questioned whether it was Islam at all. Muhammad did not stress fulfillment of any of the five pillars, and his ministers relied more on the Bible than the Koran. While most Muslim organizations have been more or less egalitarian, the Nation of Islam was extremely hierarchal and its leadership centralized.

31   Muhammad taught that Farad, the Nation's founder, was God incarnate. He interpreted his OWN role as that of divine messenger, and espoused a doctrine both mythical and practical in his teachings:

32   According to Muhammad, blacks belong to the tribe of Shabazz, which came from space 66 trillion years ago. The white race was created 6,000 years ago by a black scientist named Yakub. Yakub, through genetic manipulation, created a number of races that were lighter, weaker and genetically inferior to the black man.

33   The lowest of this order is the Caucasian. The white man turned out to be a liar and a murderer—Elijah Muhammad called them white devils—but according to Elijah, Allah allowed the Caucasian to dominate the world as a test for the black race. This, by the way, is a theme that lived on in the sermons of Louis Farrakhan and which has contributed to his label as a racist.

34   Elijah Muhammad also taught that blacks are Allah's chosen people and will inherit the earth. White people—and Muhammad often specified Jews—are anxious to impede black people from achieving success. He believed the way out of repression wasn't integration, but self-sufficiency and separation.

35   Muhammad gave black people an identity apart from the existing "system." He reminded them that they were not Americans, but members of an "Asiatic nation from the tribe of Shabazz." New members were required to write a letter to him asking for permission to discard the "slave name" given to them by the white man by taking the last name "X."

36   Elijah Muhammad's success was built on his ability to instill pride of self and race, an emphasis on personal responsibility and morality, respect for the family, and abstinence from drugs, alcohol and pork.

37   These teachings drew substantial numbers of followers over the years, although it is difficult to pinpoint just how many. Elijah Muhammad once put the number at several hundred thousand, but his son, Warith, has said active membership never exceeded 10,000.

38   In building this movement, Elijah made use of a
   — Strong charismatic and centralized leadership.
   — He also designed a well organized militia, called the Fruit of Islam, which consisted of former servicemen. The Fruit of Islam was charged with the duty of protecting the community, the temples, and other institutions.

39   It was also accused of many misdeeds, including the assassination of Malcolm X. But in recent times there have been relatively few problems, despite the organization's continued high visibility.

40   Elijah Muhammad built a well-run, profitable business organization that comprised, among other things, a bank, a publishing facility, a fish import company, temples, apartment complexes and various small businesses. In all, the Nation's assets grew to an estimated $80 million to $100 million.

41   These businesses provided jobs for hundreds of people in the inner cities. Elijah Muhammad's former attorney estimates that the fish import business alone did $27 million to $30 million a year in trade and had cornered the distribution system at the time of Elijah's death in 1975.

42 In addition, Elijah established institutions originally called Universities of Islam, which continue to run a highly disciplined system of education. These schools are now called Sister Clara Muhammad schools after his wife.

43 And he established a national network of temples including some in the West Indies that continue to be very well organized under the direction of their ministers.

44 Stop for a minute and think about what Elijah Muhammad actually did. Over 41 years, a sharecropper's son with little education took a small, local, religious sect begun by a door-to-door salesman and transformed it into a nationwide, multi-million dollar organization that affected the lives of thousands of people.

45 Maybe it's not too surprising, then, that the mysticism that grew out of this movement during this time eventually attached to Elijah himself.

46 For example, many of his followers believe Elijah is still alive, and Louis Farrakhan has said that he did not physically die. Farrakhan tells of a vision in which he was beamed aboard a UFO. This craft docked in the Motherplane—a plane-like object a half-mile in diameter. And inside, Farrakhan heard Elijah speak, telling him that Ronald Reagan had met with the Joint Chiefs of Staff to plan a war against Libya. With that information, Farrakhan warned Libyan officials of an impending attack.

47 Elijah owed his success to his knowledge of the U.S. economic and political system, his business savvy, his charisma, and commitment to his cause. But he didn't build his organization all by himself, he had help. And his greatest help came from Malcolm X.

48 During the 1950s and early 1960s the Nation of Islam was, in the public mind, synonymous with the name Malcolm X. Until he left the organization, Malcolm X was its greatest success story, a former prison convict who became an internationally-known activist and political figure.

49 Elijah Muhammad's national spokesman until 1964, Malcolm X may be better known than any other member of the Nation of Islam. His detractors at the time criticized him for taking the spotlight from Elijah Muhammad, but he is credited for recruiting thousands of people into the organization.

50 His break with the Nation of Islam was precipitated by his move toward orthodox Islam and by his discovery that Elijah Muhammad had been involved in a number of extramarital affairs. He was assassinated in a Harlem dance hall in 1965 while speaking to followers, seven months after leaving the organization.

51   Some have blamed Malcolm X's assassination on the man who now leads the group—Louis Farrakhan. You probably read or heard about the arrest last month of one of Malcolm X's daughters, Qubilah Shabazz, on charges that she tried to hire someone to kill Farrakhan. She was four years old and in the room when her father was killed, and her mother—Betty Shabazz—has said publicly that she thinks Farrakhan had something to do with the assassination.

52   Farrakhan, in turn, has said that his public condemnation of Malcolm X probably contributed to the atmosphere that resulted in the assassination. However, he denies any direct role in the killing.

53   In the years after Malcolm X, Elijah Muhammad and the Nation of Islam took a quieter public posture.

54   Finally, in 1975—10 years after Malcolm X's assassination—Elijah Muhammad died. Shortly before his death, the ailing Muhammad named his successor—his son, Warith Deen Mohammed.

55   Ironically, Warith Deen had been expelled from the organization several times for speaking against his father's teachings. But Elijah gave his son one more chance, "rehabilitating" him on his deathbed, and naming him heir to the Nation.

56   If Elijah *is* still alive, you have to believe he regrets his decision.

57   Warith Deen's style contrasted sharply with that of his father. Like Malcolm X, Warith Deen was drawn to a more orthodox form of Islam, and he gradually decentralized the power structure his father had designed and gave less attention to the business side of the movement. Only a year after his father's death, Warith Deen declared that Elijah was not a prophet and consequently started to replace the theology of the Nation with orthodox Islam.

58   He also changed the spelling of his last name—instead of spelling it M-U-H-A-M-M-A-D, he changed it to M-O-H-A-M-M-E-D. In addition, he renamed his organization the World Community of Al-Islam in the West. Temples became mosques, ministers imams, and the islamic rituals began to be observed.

59   Leadership stopped preaching the race-tinged ideology that identified white people as devils, relaxed strict discipline and disbanded the Fruit of Islam militia. In 1980, the name changed finally from the World Community of Al-Islam to the American Muslim Mission.

60   Despite—or perhaps because of—his break with his father's teachings, Warith Deen's organization has grown to become the largest African American Muslim organization. While that in itself is a notable achievement, Warith Deen is notable for another reason. Without him, most of us probably would never have heard of Louis Farrakhan.

61 I want to take just a few seconds here to recap. There are so many people who are part of the story, that it's difficult to keep them straight. First there was Farad Muhammad, a door-to-door salesman who founded the organization. Elijah Muhammad took over when Farad disappeared in 1934, and Malcolm X was his national spokesman during the '50s and early '60s. Elijah's son, Warith Deen was placed at the top when Elijah died in 1975.

62 Now comes Farrakhan, who succeeded Malcolm as minister of the Nation's Harlem temple. When Warith Deen began to distance the group from his father's teachings, Farrakhan was horrified. He broke away, claiming for himself and other hard core followers of Elijah Muhammad the designation "Nation of Islam."

63 Farrakhan's group is just one of four now claiming to be the true Nation of Islam, but it is the largest and has the highest profile.

64 His numbers of followers is estimated at 20,000 on the low end to as many as 100,000—perhaps more than the Nation had at the time of Elijah Muhammad's death, but not nearly the estimated 1 million members of Warith's American Muslim Mission.

65 Oratorically gifted and passionate about his goals, Farrakhan is one of the most popular speakers on black college campuses today. He typically draws 15,000 to 20,000 people to his lectures, but attracted 60,000 to a speech he gave in Atlanta in 1992. In doing so, he outdrew the opening game of the World Series, taking place about a mile away.

66 Farrakhan can speak for two hours or more without the apparent use of notes, mesmerizing audiences with his alternate use of gravity and humor, compassion and anger, fact and hyperbole. He easily covers a huge range of subjects in his lectures.

67 The need for strong families, black economic empowerment, education, morality, the media, self-worth, and the white conspiracy against blacks are all common themes.

68 Farrakhan was born Louis Eugene Walcott in the Bronx in 1933. His mother was a West Indian domestic worker who raised him Episcopalian. His family moved to Boston, where he graduated from Latin High School with honors. He spent two years at college in North Carolina, where he also ran track.

69 But he loved music most of all. He became an accomplished violinist and, as a teenager, appeared on Ted Mack's Original Amateur Hour. In the 1950s he became a nightclub singer billed as "The Charmer," singing calypso songs and playing the violin.

70 He became aware of the Nation of Islam at a convention in Chicago. He later visited the Nation's temple in Harlem, where he heard Malcolm X speak. He decided to join and became Louis X.

71   Because Elijah Muhammad forbade members from being entertainers, Farrakhan abandoned his career. Some say he rejected a movie deal later signed by Harry Belafonte.

72   Farrakhan became Elijah Muhammad's minister of Temple 11 in Boston, while raising a family of nine children. He later went to New York, but was moved to Chicago by Warith Mohammed after his father's death.

73   Farrakhan has continued to run the Nation of Islam from Chicago. When Warith Muhammad's organization later filed bankruptcy, Farrakhan's organization bought Elijah's old flagship temple in Chicago and renamed it Mosque Maryam.

74   Outside his organization, Farrakhan is widely viewed as a racist, not only for some of his own public remarks but also for those made by his predecessors and contemporary aides. You may have heard about Khallid Abdul Muhammad, whom Farrakhan demoted last year after complaints about the reference to Jews as "bloodsuckers" and for insensitive comments about the Holocaust.

75   Farrakhan has denied that he is a racist or a "hate-monger," tagging Jews and other whites as hypocrites for criticizing *him* while they perpetuate racism against blacks.

76   In fairness to Farrakhan, a reading of his published speeches between 1984 and 1989 reveals much scapegoating, but little evidence of outright hate against anybody—nowhere does he advocate violence against any group. He often takes great pains to distinguish between hate of actions and hate of people, and in recent years has toned down what could be construed as racist language. Even some mainstream religious leaders say Farrakhan's remarks have been distorted by the media or taken out of context.

77   However, it is true that Farrakhan often blames Jews—sometimes without explaining his reasons—for many of the problems of African-Americans. His remarks can be inflammatory, such as calling Judaism "a gutter religion." And the Nation's natural affinity for Arab Muslims puts it at odds with Zionist causes, which many Jews interpret as anti-Semitic.

78   His disdain for homosexuals also remains clear. And in 1990 he accused whites of manufacuring AIDS and deliberately spreading it among blacks.

79   He doesn't allow white people to worship in his mosques, and he tolerates other members of the Nation who have little inhibition against expressing clearly racist beliefs. So, while Farrakhan may not be the seething hate-monger some would have the public believe, he hasn't done much to change his image as a bigot.

80   Despite all this, Farrakhan's harshest language—as well as his greatest encouragement—is reserved for his own audiences.

81   He tells his followers they feed white prejudice by allowing their communitites to deteriorate—through teen pregnancies, drugs, violence, lack of respect for each other and lack of faith in God. He tells them they bear much of the blame for the way they are viewed and that they can't wait for the current system to bring them out of oppression—they must do it themselves.

82   His solution? A separate society based on Nation of Islam values and a black economic base in which African Americans become producers, not just consumers.

83   Farrakhan's lectures and sermons have strong religious components, and he uses the Bible and Koran almost equally in arguing his points. He's been known to preach Easter sermons on the need for renewal, and his home temple is Mosque Maryam—named for the mother of Jesus.

84   Taken by themselves, his pro-family, anti-drug arguments could come from any number of conservative religious figures or politicians. Unlike some of those conservative Christian leaders, however, Farrakhan actually appointed a woman as one of his ministers.

85   Farrakhan sounds quite mainstream at times, depending on the subject he is addressing.

86   Farrakhan says black people are God's chosen people, but that they have been "sleeping" while Allah allowed white people to dominate. He uses Biblical interpretation to prove this claim: The bondage of the Jews by the Egyptians, he says, is not historical fact but prophetic allegory—the Jews of the Bible weren't really the Jews of ancient times, but the blacks of today. Just as Moses was said to have led his people out of slavery, the time is at hand in which black people will be victorious over their white oppressors.

87   Farrakhan does not call himself a prophet—Mohammed of Arabia was, as Islam teaches, the last of the prophets—but he believes he is divinely chosen to bring his message to a black nation.

88   While Farrakhan has continued many of the traditional teachings of Elijah Muhammad, he has never shown the business acumen Elijah Muhammad demonstrated. It is not for lack of effort.

89   His regrouped Fruit of Islam militia is sometimes feared by outsiders, yet credited with cleaning up several inner city housing complexes that contracted with the group to eradicate drugs and violence. Despite some failures, in many cases these programs have made a significant impact in reducing drug trafficking and violence where they operate.

90   His success in other business areas has been limited. In 1985, he launched a new line of health and beauty-aid products made by POWER—People Organized and Working for Economic Rebirth.

91   While five black-owned companies had promised to make POWER products under the Clean 'N Fresh brand name, they later withdrew, reportedly for fear of alienating Jewish distributors.

92   Farrakhan persuaded Libyan leader Mo-Mar Khaddafi to lend POWER $5 million interest free. But distribution in high crime areas proved difficult because residents were reluctant to open their doors to solicitors and salespeople were afraid to go into those areas.

93   So the business side of Farrakhan's organization is struggling. While disappointed, Farrakhan has remained steadfast—never losing sight of his mission.

94   Farrakhan sees himself as Elijah Muhammad's heir: a messenger from God, sent to help African-American people take their rightful place as Allah's chosen people. His sentiments hit home with many in the black community in need of structure in their lives, unity with other blacks, inspiration for the future and who see no chance that the current power structure will ever meet their needs.

95   Farrakhan's biggest stumbling block to broader acceptance has been his refusal to compromise his beliefs, which many view as racist or unforgiving. His inability to shed this image has left him unable to bridge important gulfs between his organization and other black organizations who see his potential but shun the baggage that he brings.

96   While he is able to command large groups to hear his speeches, it is difficult to gauge how much influence he has in the general population. A *New York Times* poll last year showed that most blacks reject the notion that Farrakhan and the Nation of Islam represent their views, but they do share some of his racial beliefs. For example, only 15 percent said he and his organization represent the views of most blacks in America, but 40 percent said they agree that most Jews are against progress by blacks.

97   Sixty-six percent say most whites feel they are superior to blacks, and thrity-two percent said most whites want to keep blacks down.

98   Finally, twenty-three percent said they agree with Farrakhan that the government deliberately makes drugs easily available in poor black neighborhoods in order to harm black people.

99   From this standpoint, it appears he has the ears—and possibly the hearts—of many who cannot be formally counted as members of the Nation of Islam.

Chapter Four

Speeches That Affirm Propositions of Fact

Matters of fact . . . are very stubborn things.

Matthew Tindal

The Nature and Importance of Speeches That Affirm Propositions of Fact

There are instances of discourse when a speaker tries to prove to the satisfaction of an audience that a proposition of fact is, in reality, true. While the preceding chapter was concerned with the art of interpreting established knowledge or original inquiry for the *enlightenment of an audience,* the present chapter is devoted to the principles involved in *establishing an alleged truth in order to win agreement.* Earlier, the primary task for the speaker was to help an audience understand an event, process, concept, or inquiry; in this chapter, the speaker's efforts are directed toward seeking approval of the "facts" that are presented. In the previous speech form, the speaker might publicly analyze, "What is the present state of space exploration?"; in this chapter, the speaker seeks to gain acceptance of a conclusion: "The American program of space exploration is without military significance."

The social environments that produce speeches affirming factual propositions are diverse. A district attorney may seek to establish the guilt of a labor leader charged with misuse of union funds. The president of a liberal arts college may try to convince the board of regents that faculty salaries are not equal to those of competing schools. A state legislator may attempt to prove to his or her constituency that the condition of state highways will deter expansion of the tourist industry. While in certain instances the affirmation of a proposition of fact is the sole purpose of a persuasive speech, at other times a speaker may affirm a fact as a means of affirming a value, creating concern for a problem, or gaining acceptance for a course of action. On the whole, matters of fact are more commonly argued in relation to one of those ends than they are as separate entities.

In the quotation opening this chapter, Matthew Tindal expresses an awareness that matters of fact are not self-evident. In the common vernacular, the term *fact* connotes an incontrovertible truth. Thus the novitiate to the advocate's art seeks to stifle further argument by asserting, "It's a fact"—by which it is meant, "It is uncontestable truth." But "Matters of fact . . . are very stubborn things." Were all facts self-evident, there would be no such thing as a proposition of fact because the term *proposition* implies a statement about an unsettled or controversial state of affairs.

What, then, is a proposition of fact? A proposition of fact may be defined as a statement (a sentence with assertive content) that may be affirmed or denied through tests of *existence, occurrence,* or *causality.* The fact in question may concern an individual, an event, a process, a condition, a concept, or even a policy. Whatever the fact to be judged, however, the advocate is primarily interested in gaining listener acceptance that something was, is, or will be true. Consider these examples:

Proposition A: The Great Depression was caused by excessive speculation on the stock market.

Proposition B: *The Japanese attack on Pearl Harbor was precipitated by United States fail-ure to provide military safeguards.*

Proposition C: *The sightings of flying saucers are real events.*

Proposition D: *Marijuana smoking is harmless.*

Proposition E: *The nuclear family as we know it will utlimately become obsolete.*

Proposition F: *The absence of the player reserve clause will ultimately cause the demise of major league baseball.*

Although these six propositions differ substantially in subject matter, they are all legitimate factual propositions. Propositions A and B concern matters of past causality. Propositions C and D concern matters of present existence and causality. Propositions E and F concern matters of future occurrence and future causality respectively.

Whatever the subject matter and tense of a factual proposition, its proposer is interested in gaining audience acceptance of an alleged truth. The following section identifies the criteria that are especially relevant for evaluating speeches that affirm propositions of fact.

Criteria for Evaluating Speeches That Affirm Propositions of Fact

Because propositions of fact treat supposedly verifiable or predictable phenomena, the tests of speeches affirming such propositions are strongly concerned with the logical sufficiency of the affirmation.

1.   Has the speaker adequately assessed the proof requirements of the factual proposition?

Implicit in a proposition of fact is the assumption that there are reasonable criteria with which to judge the truth of alleged events, states of being, causal relationships, and so on. Proof requirements are often field dependent; that is, they differ from one area of knowledge or profession to another. For example, the affirmation of a proposition of medical fact may require that standards on the observation and clinical diagnosis of patients be met. The affirmation of a proposition of historical fact, on the other hand, may require that standards relevant to sound historical research be met. Lawyers, behavioral scientists, chemists, mathematicians, and astronomers have all devised standards by which certain types of phenomena are to be judged. When talking to a specialized group about a specialized topic, the speaker can expect that the proposition will be judged by the special proof requirements established by that profession as a modus operandi.

In the world of ordinary discourse, the criteria by which propositions of fact are judged are less well defined and less rigorous. However, even the popular proposition of fact demands that the speaker employ responsible standards of assessment. If popular speakers fail to support their assertions or if they support them with emotional appeals and shallow truisms, they will be criticized for their faulty interpretation of the responsible proof requirements of their propositions. Enlightened lay critics do not excuse the maxims and pseudo-arguments of modern mass media advertisements even though they are aware of the logical permissiveness of the American consuming public.

2.   Has the speaker offered acceptable arguments in support of the proposition of fact?

Given that a speaker demonstrates awareness of the general proof requirements of a particular factual proposition, the next question to be raised is "Has the speaker offered relevant arguments—reasons for belief—in support of the proposition of fact?" Imagine, for example, that a district attorney seeks to affirm the proposition that "a labor leader is guilty of misusing union funds." Imagine, further, that our barrister has recognized that the particular proof demands that must be met are those of the bar rather than the public forum. We may then question whether the arguments that are selected support the conclusion that the labor leader is guilty of misusing union funds. We might expect, for example, that it would be argued that (1) the labor leader in question did spend union funds on nonunion activities, (2) legal precedence makes the misuse of union funds a criminal offense, and (3) the expenditure of the funds in question is classifiable as a misuse in light of legal precedence. Should our lawyer fail to offer any of these arguments or should irrelevant nonlegal arguments be offered in their place, we may deny that a convincing case in support of the proposition has been made.

In the world of everyday discourse, the specific argument or arguments necessary for the establishment of a factual proposition are largely dependent on the criteria of sufficiency employed by the listener/critic receiving the argument. As an enlightened critic the listener should consider the possible reasons that make the argument advanced questionable. Assume, for instance, the following argument:

Proposition (claim):   Capital punishment is not an effective deterrent to crime.

Reason (justification):   The states that have capital punishment have more serious crimes than the states that do not have capital punishment.

Will you accept this argument? What possible exceptions or reservations to this argument might you legitimately raise? Should you note that there are serious differences between the states that have capital punishment and those that do not, you are well on your way to discrediting the argument. Should you know that the capital-punishment states are highly populated urban areas, while the noncapital-punishment states are essentially rural and less populous, you may raise one important reservation to the argument. Should you know that the states with capital punishment have a higher incidence of poverty, unemployment, and racial antagonism, you may raise another serious reservation.

Thus, in evaluating an argument, the critic must ask whether there is cause to question the sufficiency of it. If there are reasonable reservations and if the speaker has failed to refute them, the argument may be denied.

3.   Has the speaker provided adequate evidence in support of arguments?

In some fields of argument, the nature of adequate evidence is carefully specified. For example, the rules of evidence of the American bar are rather carefully specified. In the courtroom, there are rules governing the admissibility and inadmissibility of evidence. Historians, scientists, and behavioral scientists also have some clear notion of what constitutes sound evidence and what does not.

However, in the world of ordinary discourse, evidential requirements are less well known and less well defined. Perhaps the most distinctive characteristic of ordinary arguments on propositions of fact is the reliance of the speaker upon secondary information and uncontrolled, unsystematic observation. Thus, the popular speaker often bases arguments on the *testimony* of others, well-known or verifiable *specific instances,* and *statistical data.* Sometimes speakers use a *literal analogy* or describe a *cause-effect relationship.*

In using *testimony*, the speaker draws evidence from the statements of others. One interesting example of testimonial evidence occurred in the championship debate at the National College Debate Tournament at West Point in 1960. John Raser of San Diego State College sought to prove that "Eventually the public and the nation always get their way in national policy." Having stated what he hoped to prove Mr. Raser went on to say:

> Now that sounds like a strong statement, but I've got more than a few people who tell me it's true. . . . I'd first like to turn to Robert H. Jackson, the former Supreme Court Justice, who should know if anyone does. He said, in *Vital Speeches* in October 1953, that "The practical play of the forces of politics is such that judicial power has often delayed but never permanently delayed the persistent will of substantial majorities." In other words, the majority always gets its way. Let's turn to some more support. Professor Jack W. Peltason, University of Illinois . . . [in] his book *The Federal Courts and the Political Processes*, states, "In almost every decision in which the judges have imposed a check on Congress in the name of the Constitution, in one way or another Congress eventually has done what the judges told them they could not do and should not do." . . . Let's turn to further support of

this idea that judges can't really thwart national policy. James MacGregor Burns, and the same man, Jack Walter Peltason, told us that, in their joint effort, *Government by the People*, published in 1954, "Judges have no armies or police to execute their laws; they have no authority to levy taxes to support their activities. In the long run they must adapt themselves to the nature and demands of government by the people." Now what do we draw from this? Simply that the Supreme Court does not thwart national policy because always eventually the policies which the people apparently want and always the policies which Congress endorses eventually are put into effect.

In this example, a college debater uses three pieces of testimony to support his point, In evaluating a speaker's use of testimony, the critical listener should employ some of the popular tests of testimonial evidence: (1) Was the source of the testimony in a position to observe? (2) Was the source of the testimony competent to observe? (3) Was the source of the testimony biased? (4) Was the source of the testimony qualified? (5) Was the source of the testimony consistent with other sources and with himself or herself on previous occasions? and (6) Is the testimony sufficiently recent?

In using *specific instances* as evidence, the speaker provides well-known or verifiable examples that demonstrate the truth of the proposition or of a claim leading to the proposition. An excellent example of the use of specific instances can be found in a speech delivered by Richard Nixon well before his catastrophic involvement in the Watergate affair. As vice president under Dwight Eisenhower, Nixon visited Russia, and during his stay there delivered an important "Address to the Russian People." In an effort to prove that United States efforts to assure peace had been thwarted by the Soviet government, Nixon effectively drew upon a series of specific instances.

> . . . It is possible that many of you listening to me are not aware of the positive programs the United States has proposed which were designed to contribute to peace. Let me tell you about just a few of them and what happened to them:
>
> We had a monopoly on the atomic bomb when on June 14, 1946, we submitted the Baruch plan for international control of atomic energy. What happened? It was rejected by the USSR.
>
> At the Summit Conference in Geneva on July 21, 1955, President Eisenhower made his offer of open skies aerial inspection. What happened? It was rejected by the USSR.
>
> On May 1, 1958, the United States offered an Arctic aerial inspection plan to protect both nations from surprise attack. What happened? It was rejected by the USSR. I realize that your government has indicated reasons for its rejection of each of these proposals. I do not list these proposals for the purpose of warming over past history but simply to demonstrate the initiative our government has taken to reduce tensions and to find peaceful solutions for differences between us.

An equally good example of the use of specific instances occurs in a speech by Phyllis Jones Springen on "The Dimensions of the Oppression of Women."

> An infuriating example of unequal pay for equal work concerned a New Jersey manufacturer. Their chief financial officer was a woman paid $9,000 a year. When she left, they had to pay a man $20,000 a year to do her job. When he left they hired another woman at $9,000. When she left, they hired a man at $18,000. According to the recruiter, they were all good at the job.

In evaluating specific instances used as evidence in support of factual propositions, the critic should raise such questions as these: (1) Was a sufficient number of instances presented? (2) Were the instances presented typical instances? and (3) Are there any negative instances that should be accounted for?

In using *statistical data*, the speaker draws evidence from studies that have surveyed large numbers of cases and reported data numerically. In a speech, Charles Schalliol seeks to demonstrate that "The increasing size of our metropolitan areas is compounding our air pollution problem" by citing relevant statistics.

> Since 1940, our population has grown by 50,000,000, the use of energy had quadrupled, disposable income has increased 60%—yet—our air supply remains the same. In such a setting air pollution is a murderer. According to Edward Parkhurst, a noted health authority, death rates are "consistently higher in the central cities of 50,000 and over than in places under 10,000 and in rural areas in nonmetropolitan districts." The Census Bureau further establishes that life expectancy is three years greater in the rural states than in the urban states.

In evaluating a speaker's use of statistics, the enlightened critic asks: (1) Do these statistics come from a reliable source? (2) Are these statistics based on a reliable sample? (3) Were these statistics accurately and completely reported? and (4) Are they presented in a meaningful form?

In demonstrating a *literal analogy*, the speaker typically compares two things or instances that belong to the same category or classification (two nations, people, corporations, etc.) to show that because the two actually are similar in several major relevant elements, something known to exist in the first instance probably exists (or will exist) in the second. You might contend, for example, that because England and the United States are similar in language, general economic system, and general political system, and because so-called "socialized medicine" is working in Great Britain, it probably would work in the United States. In evaluating the soundness of a speaker's literal analogy, the critic could ask some of the standard questions: (1) Are the known elements of both actually similar enough? (2) Are the known similarities actually relevant to the issue-at-hand? (3) Are significant relevant differences ignored? (4) Does the element assumed to exist in the first instance but unknown in the second actually exist in the first? (5) Do essential points of similarity outweigh essential points of difference?

In asserting a *cause-effect relationship*, the speaker contends that one factor (or set of factors) directly contributes to the occurrence of another factor (or set of factors); in some sense the first causes (or will cause) the second. As a variation, a given effect or circumstance is described as the result of a certain cause. Sometimes use of words such as "because," "due to," or "if . . . then" can alert us to possible cause-effect arguments. Jenkin Lloyd Jones, in a speech titled "Let's Bring Back Dad: A Solid Value System," suggests a number of cause-effect relationships, including the following. At one point he describes "neo-Socialist" university professors who are "hostile" to the free enterprise business system "because they have never had any experience with it." At another point he asks concerning some Black families, "Why are our ghetto societies in such chaos? Because the man walks off when it gets tough." Jones concludes the speech by predicting a cause-effect relationship:

> . . . If enough American dads were to resolve to become partisan dads, unashamed to hold moral standards, willing to take the time to communicate values, then the chances of raising a new generation that would live in the agony of social chaos, or worse yet, lose their liberties for generations yet to come, will be substantially diminished.

To assess the soundness of any asserted cause-effect relationship, the critic could inquire: (1) Might there be multiple causes, several significant contributing and interrelated influences, rather than just the one asserted? (2) Might there be a chain or sequence of causal factors to consider, not just the asserted one as the immediate cause? (3) Is the speaker confusing a causal connection either with *chronology* (one thing simply happened after another) or with *correlation* (two things vary together in predictable ways, but *both* may be the effects of some unknown cause)? (4) Might there be additional positive or negative effects to consider other than the single effect identified? (5) Can the asserted cause-effect relationship be supported by evidence such as scientific studies, expert testimony, or other factual examples of the relationship?

Conclusion

In certain instances of persuasive discourse, speakers seek to prove to the satisfaction of their audiences that given propositions of fact are really true. When evaluating such speeches, the critic should consider *whether the speaker has adequately assessed the proof requirements of the factual proposition, whether acceptable arguments in support of the proposition of fact have been offered, and whether adequate evidence in support of the argument has been provided.*

For Further Reading

Cooper, Martha. *Analyzing Public Discourse.* Waveland Press, 1988. Chapter 3 examines issues of fact, value, and policy and Chapter 6 discusses standards for sound evidence and reasoning.

Gronbeck, Bruce, et al. *Principles and Types of Speech Communication.* Scott, Foresman/Little, Brown, 1990. Chapter 7 on finding and using supporting materials discusses specific instances, illustrations, statistics, and testimony. Chapter 17 on organization and critical thinking discusses claims of fact, value, and policy and explores the nature and evaluation of evidence and reasoning.

Lucas, Stephen E. *The Art of Public Speaking.* 5th ed., McGraw-Hill, 1995. Chapter 7 discusses supporting ideas with examples, statistics, and testimony. Chapter 9 examines questions of fact, value, and policy in persuasion and the use of evidence and reasoning.

Osborn, Michael, and Osborn, Suzanne. *Public Speaking.* 2nd ed. Houghton Mifflin, 1991. Chapter 6 explains the use of supporting materials such as facts, testimony, examples, and narrative. Chapter 14 discusses evidence, proof, and sound argument.

Rieke, Richard D., and Sillars, Malcolm O. *Argumentation and the Decision Making Process.* 2nd ed. Wiley, 1984. Chapter 5 examines use of factual instances, statistics, and expert testimony and notes the field-dependent nature of some standards for sound argument.

Toulmin, Stephen, Rieke, Richard, and Janik, Allan. *An Introduction to Reasoning.* 2nd ed. Macmillan, 1984. This book presents a framework for analyzing the soundness of arguments and stresses that criteria for sound evidence vary among fields of discourse such as law, science, the arts, and business.

Warnick, Barbara, and Inch, Edward S. *Critical Thinking and Communication: The Use of Reason in Argument.* 2nd ed. Macmillan, 1994. Chapters 3–5 discuss claims of fact, value, and policy and types of evidence and reasoning.

WOMEN IN THE MARKETPLACE: HAVE WOMEN IN JOURNALISM MADE A DIFFERENCE?

Joan Konner

Joan Konner, Dean of the Columbia University School of Journalism, delivered this speech at the New Jersey Press Women's Association Luncheon, Paterson, New Jersey, May 5, 1990. The speaker achieves considerable interest value through personal anecdotes. The introduction, for example, is highly personal, and then after Konner states her topic to the audience (3) and gives a few examples of historic women pioneers in journalism (5), she returns to a fairly lengthy personal anecdote (7–18). Discuss what the possible impact is in terms of interest and credibility of the speaker's personal involvement. You may want to take time to review theoretical thoughts concerning personal involvement in public address. Is it possible that since the speaker herself is dean of a nationally known school of journalism she enacts her basic proposition so as to give a kind of credibility to her argument? What is meant by rhetorical enactment of the argument?

Konner makes heavy use of examples in developing her thesis that women in journalism have made a difference. How effective is this in establishing factual credibility? The speech is also interesting in that the speaker argues that a shift in values supports her basic proposition. Once more, we have an issue of causality. As a minimum, causality arguments must seem plausible, if not probable or certain. What is your critical evaluation of the causality in this instance?

---

1   Good afternoon. Thank you very much for inviting me. I am pleased to have the chance to address the New Jersey Press Women's Association for several reasons. One, I grew up in New Jersey. Paterson is my hometown. My children and my grandchildren still live here. My first job was in New Jersey in the Bergen *Record,* where I enjoyed one of the best jobs in this business . . . and the New Jersey Press Women's Association was, I believe, at least in part, responsi-

---

+This speech is reprinted from *Vital Speeches of the Day,* September 15, 1990, pp. 726–728.

ble for the opportunity I was given at the *Record* so early in my professional life. I had worked at the newspaper only a short time when you gave me my first award in this business for a feature story I wrote for the Women's Page.

2   Shortly thereafter I became assistant editorial page editor, and an editorial writer and columnist, working for the best boss—teacher, mentor, friend—I ever had in this business, Bill Caldwell. I always credited the award with helping to call attention to my work. The award was a silver plate. I still have it. Also, it was second prize, so I always tried harder. I thanked you then, but I'm pleased to have the opportunity to thank you again today.

3   I'm going to talk about: "Have Women in Journalism Made a Difference?" Actually, that title isn't quite right. It should be: "Are Women in Journalism Today Making a Difference?" but for those of you who were drawn here by the first title, the short speech is "Yes."

4   There have been great women journalists since the beginning, and their work has, indeed, made a difference.

5   Margaret Fuller, Leonel Campbell O'Bryan aka "Polly Pry", Elizabeth Cochrane Seaman aka "Nellie Bly", Anne O'Hare McCormick, Dorothy Thompson, and others. They were pioneers and we all have benefitted from their accomplishments.

6   The slice of this subject I'd like to consider today is the impact of increased numbers in all media as a result of the most recent chapter in the women's struggle for equality, in our society, in our time.

7   I'll start with an anecdote. It goes back to the late 60s or early 70s. It must have been that one of my children was ill that day because it was a weekday and I was home.

8   I always tried to follow a piece of advice I picked up when I was a student at the Columbia Graduate School of Journalism. The school had a ritual for the women students in the class at the end of the school year. A panel of women journalists was invited to discuss how to manage home and career.

9   One of the panelists, if I recall correctly, was Betsy Wade of the New York *Times,* who advised:

> When you're sick, go to work, because when your children are sick, you're going to have to stay home and you can't be absent for both.

10   Such was the balancing act of women who worked in the newsroom at the time, and I'm not sure that it's much changed today.

11   In any case, I was home, and I was watching a morning program on WNBC-TV where I worked at the time as a documentary producer.

12   Barbara Walters was the host and the program was called "For Women Only." About a year later, the name was changed to "Not For Women Only," one of the early achievements of the women's movement.

13   The guest on the program that day was Clare Booth Luce, and they were talking about the time Mrs. Luce served in Congress.

14   Mrs. Luce said it was the worst experience of her professional life, and further, she thought that women would never become a strong presence in Congress.

15   "Why?" Barbara Walters asked.

16   Mrs. Luce replied, "because women do not have the instinct for the jugular, and men do."

17   Barbara Walters replied: "We'll learn."

18   I remember thinking that wasn't the point at all. We weren't supposed to be trying to become like men. We were supposed to be trying to get into the decision-making roles so that we could change the way business is done to the advantage of both sexes. What's the point of women getting into the positions of power if, in the process, we have to turn ourselves into killers, psychologically, at least, with an instinct for the jugular? Aren't those killer values the ones we are trying to change?

19   That's still the question today when we ask: Are women in journalism, especially now that there are more of us, some of us in positions of leadership, making a difference? Given the impact of the media in shaping our social, political, and economic life, are we seeing changes not only in numbers in the newsrooms, but in the agenda and priorities of society?

20   I suggest the answer is "yes," but it is only beginning.

21   Here is one recent example, a story reported on the front page of The New York *Times* on Sunday, March 25, 1990.

22   The *Times* reported on an article in another newspaper, the Des Moines, Iowa, *Register*, written by the editor, Geneva Overholser. Ms. Overholser wrote that by withholding the names of victims of rape, the press did more than protect their privacy. It also compounded the stigma, and she urged that victims of rape speak out and identify themselves.

23   "As long as rape is deemed unspeakable—and is therefore not fully and honestly spoken of—the public outrage will be muted as well," she wrote.

24   Nancy Ziegenmeyer, a rape victim, read the article and shortly afterward decided to tell her story publicly. What followed was a five-part front-page series reporting the experience in graphic detail in defiance of journalistic tradition. The series still sparks debate about rape and journalistic propriety.

25   The *Times* wasn't the only one to report on the *Register's* series. Subsequently an episode of ABC's "Nightline" was devoted to it, and that was followed by an entire editorial page of *USA Today* carrying several columns, not only opinion about the coverage of Nancy Zeigenmayer's story but another column giving a graphic account of a rape told in the first person by a senior editor of that newspaper who also identified herself by name—Karen Jurgensen. The headline was: "I was another nameless victim." The ripple effect, in which the courage of one woman editor begins to have an impact on the handling of a serious issue in other news media. You probably know the most often quoted definition of news: It comes from the editor who said: "News is what I say it is." In these cases, the editorial sensibility, and judgment, of a woman editor was different, the published story was different, and it is producing a change. There are other examples, some just that obvious, and others much subtler.

26 But before I go on with anecdotal evidence about changes of sensibility in the news, let's look at some statistics: I have seen some of this association's communications.

27 You are clearly following the documentary evidence about numbers of women employed in the newsroom. But I'd like to review just a few because despite some good news, the situation is still discouraging. In television, where statistics can be seen in the flesh: The number of female network correspondents increased by only six percent from 1975 to 1989. In 1974, women reported 9.9 percent of the stories on network news. In 1984, they accounted for 10.2 percent. In February 1989 women were responsible for 15.7 percent, according to a study conducted by the Communications Consortium for a conference on "Women, Men and Media" held last year.

28 The print statistics don't look much better. In March '89, women accounted for 27 percent of the front page bylines in 10 major American newspapers. *USA Today* was at the top. The New York *Times* was at the bottom.

29 Clearly, there is an upward trend, but slow. And when you consider that women comprise 52 percent of the population and that more than half of today's journalism students are female, the disproportion is considerable. Salary statistics reinforce the finding.

30 When you get to management ranks, the percentages dwindle to near imperceptibility. As of 1989, females constituted just three percent of television station presidents and vice presidents, six percent of newspaper publishers and 8 percent of radio presidents and vice presidents. Women hold about 25 percent of middle management jobs. The prediction that once we got in we would work our way to the top hasn't yet come true.

31 But let's look at how far we've come. Take television again: Some of the stories seem funny now . . . almost. Pauline Frederick, for example, became the first female full-time network correspondent for NBC in 1953. The story goes that she was reluctant to accept an assignment to cover the candidates' wives at the 1948 political conventions for television because she didn't know what to wear, and there was no one to tell her how to do her makeup. She ended up doing her own and the wives, too.

32   The FCC started requiring affirmative action plans for women to be filed with license renewal applications in 1971—the forced entry into a male-dominated establishment which was met with a good deal of resistance.

33   In 1974 Susan Peterson arrived to take up her assignment as a correspondent at the London Bureau of CBS and found her desk near the door next to the receptionist. Her male colleagues all had offices.

34   Before women could become members of the National Press Club, they were allowed in for important speeches but they had to sit in the balcony, and the rules permitted questions to be asked only from the floor.

35   Few male assignment editors were willing to take the risk of sending the first woman out to cover a priority hard news story. Those who did were pleasantly surpised. A 1971 story in *Newsweek* drew attention to a new breed of reporters, "tough young women" like Gloria Rojas, Pia Lindstrom and the 25-year-old Connie Chung "who can cover hard news on an equal basis with men." In that same story Reuven Frank of NBC said:

> I have a strong feeling that audiences are less prepared to accept news from a woman's voice than from a man's.

36   Flash forward from there to 1976 when Barbara Walters gets the first million dollar contract to move to ABC from NBC . . . Reuven Frank gets his comeuppance.

37   1981: Christine Craft sues Metromedia and wins a half a million dollars because she was demoted for being too old, too unattractive, and not deferential enough to men.

38   1989: Diane Sawyer goes from CBS to ABC for $1.6 million; Connie Chung goes from NBC to CBS for between 6 and 7 hundred thousand. Mary Alice Williams goes from CNN to NBC for $500 thousand.

39   But stars, salaries, and statistics alone do not tell the story.

40   We shouldn't mistake quantity for quality, and the quieter history includes the accomplishments of many women off-camera in television newsrooms as well as many more in newspapers and magazines throughout the country. For one, the remarkable *Ms.* magazine, which legitimized women's issues by producing a serious magazine about them. It no doubt can take the credit for the greater seriousness of women's magazines in general, and for leading the way to the changing definition of news generally—the inclusion of domestic and workplace issues like battered wives, child abuse, and maternity leave, in so-called hard-news; values and quality of life stories; stories about

children, health, education, social trends, community, and the environment—not only on the front page, but on every page and on television news as well.

41   Last fall the Columbia Journalism School Alumni chose the topic "Is News Getting Too Soft?" for its annual fall meeting. The subject, and the title, were picked by one of the men. Of course. "Hard" and "soft" are terms only a man would have invented. It goes with the sports metaphor of most news. Who's winning? Who's losing? In politics, business, culture. Who's up? Who's down? If you're winning, you're "hard" news. If you're losing, you're a "soft" feature for the inside pages.

42   I didn't know exactly what the title—"Is News Getting Too Soft"—meant. It turned out there was concern about changes brought about by different perspectives in the newsrooms—from women and minorities—that are beginning to alter the definition of news.

43   Soma Golden, national editor for The New York *Times,* an alumna of our School, gave her analysis of the change in the front page of her paper. On a given day in 1959 there were 18 stories, all hard news. On the same day in 1969, there were 23 stories, again all hard news. By 1979, the format had changed so there were fewer stories, but even so, what was called "new" news stories made it to the front page along with hard news. In 1989, the trend continued with as many as three "new" news stories mingled with dateline news. A new story was a series on care of the elderly or Public School 94 in the Bronx or an analysis of social trends. The position of these stories in The *Times* tells us that the distinction between soft news and hard news is blurring.

44   Is this happening because there are more women in the newsrooms?

45   Probably, but who knows? Clearly a shift of values and priorities is taking place.

46   Are women better equipped to cover this "new" news? It is possible we are. The psychologist Carol Gilligan, in her book, "In A Different Voice," described a difference between the moral development of men and women.

47   Women, she says, develop an ethic of care, an empathy based on their identification with the primary parent, usually the mother. Women define themselves in terms of relationship and responsibility.

48   Men develop an ethic of justice as they separate from the mother. They define themselves in terms of difference, position and hierarchy. If we accept this, then I think we can assume the responsibility that comes with our capacity to adopt a broader perspective and show the human, caring side of the news.

49   The feminine sensibility is growing everywhere in our culture today—in literature, in art, in history, politics, and the media. It coincides with concerns about the environment, a growing awareness of Mother Earth, as our life support system. There is talk of the Saia principle, of world view that says we are all part of one living body. We find the principle expressed in the mythology of the Goddess, in which there is also a revival of interest today. The Goddess was worshipped for thousands of years in agrarian, egalitarian societies in which there was a love of life, of nature and beauty.

50   There seems at this time to be a greater hunger in the American culture for the values of the goddess—the values of life, generation, and creation. There seems to be a growing reverence for nature, for a collective spirit, and relationship based on the awareness of the interconnectedness of life. We are becoming more concerned that our competitive Western culture that developed along the lines of the Darwinian principle of the survival of the fittest may have been a life-supporting pattern for one period of human evolution but it may no longer be a life supporting pattern for another—this one. Human intelligence creates systems to protect human life. Today those very systems are threatening it— industrial development which threatens the environment; nuclear weapons that threaten all of life. In such a world, those with a wider perspective and greater awareness are turning out to be the fittest.

51   We are coming around a bend, and we realize there is a need for other values, values of collaboration, community, care. These are the values that used to belong to the private sphere of home and family. But we are beginning to see these values in the workplace and in public life as well. One hypothesis is that women, as they succeed in the marketplace, retain what is valuable from what used to be considered the domestic sphere and bring that wider perspective into view. It does seem some of us—women and men—have had enough of the instinct for the jugular. I think that women in positions of power—in politics, public service, and the media—are helping to make that difference.

A BLACK PRESIDENT: WHEN?

Carl B. Stokes

In 1967 Democrat Carl B. Stokes was elected to a two year term as mayor of Cleveland, Ohio. Thus he became the first African-American elected mayor of a major U.S. city. After a second term, he did not seek re-election. In the 1970s he worked as a TV anchor in New York City.

+Carl B. Stokes, "Racial Equality and Appreciation of Diversity in Our Urban Communities: How Far Have We Come? A Black President: When?" April 1, 1993, pp. 357–361. Reprinted with permission of *Vital Speeches of the Day*.

You may find his autobiography, *Promises of Power* (1973), of interest. When he died, April 4, 1996 of throat cancer at age 68, he was serving as U.S. ambassador to the Seychelles Islands which are a British possession northeast of Madagascar in the Indian Ocean.

On February 19, 1993, while serving as a judge of the Cleveland Municipal Court, Carl Stokes presented this speech at a luncheon forum of the Columbus, Ohio, Metropolitan Club. This organization promotes free speech and fair debate by sponsoring weekly forums on a broad range of current political, cultural, civic, and international issues. Spirited question-and-answer periods typically follow a speaker's presentation. Columbus Metropolitan Club members represent such fields as government, law, finance, health care, real estate, marketing, and public relations, but the weekly forums also are open to the general public.

Carl Stokes clearly is arguing a proposition of future fact—of future occurrence: An African-American will be elected President of the United States "in the near future," perhaps "within the next 20 years" (3, 45, 55). At the beginning of the speech, he forecasts the theme he will develop at length through factual examples and specific instances (4-5).

Over half of the speech (largely the first half) is Stokes' personal narrative of his first-hand experience with significant events (7-36). The narrative embodies extensive use of specific instances for factual support. This narrative captures and sustains audience attention. We all like to hear captivating stories, especially when they reflect personal emotions (23), depict the overcoming of obstacles (14-15, 17-18, 29, 32), and reflect elements of tension, opposition, and tragedy (20, 24-31). Stokes also narrates the story of Cleveland and his experiences as mayor as a "microcosm" of broader national issues, problems, and progress (6, 39). His story is to be taken as illustrative of and evidence for his larger points.

In the last third of the speech, Stokes employs a roughly chronological history of examples of African-American political progress to demonstrate a factual trend that supports his prediction (45). Some of the examples are more fully developed as a sort of landmark event (40-42, 44, 47-49). How adequately does Stokes demonstrate the significance of these landmark events? Some specific instances are used to prove that racism in America is practiced inconsistently (50-53, 56). At various points in the speech, Stokes uses a quick, tight-knit, cumulative listing of examples to strengthen an argument (33, 35, 38, 39) or to summarize previous instances (54).

It is clear, then, that throughout the speech Stokes employs examples and instances as his major type of evidence. How might you apply the test questions for reasonable use of specific instances to Stokes' usage? (1) Was a sufficient number of instances presented? (2) Were the instances presented typical instances? (3) Are there any negative (contradictory, inconsistent) instances that should have been mentioned or accounted for?

As might be expected, Stokes also employs a cause-effect argument implied in such words as "compounded" and "making" (33) and employs statistical data (17, 18, 43). Where appropriate apply the tests for soundness of cause-effect argument and for statistical evidence. Note, too, how Stokes uses parallel phrasing ("It means that . . . ") to sharpen his conclusion (56).

One final question remains. Based on Carl Stokes' arguments and evidence, do you believe that an African-American will be elected President in the near future of approximately twenty years? Why?

---

1   Twenty-five years ago, people told me that a black man could not be elected mayor of a major American city—particularly if the population of that city was majority white. I asked them "why not." They told me "because its never been done." I did it.

2   Today, the question tantalizing our nation, is when, if ever, the United States will elect an African American as its President. It seems to me that the discussion of the election of a black president is not "if" or "when," but "who." "When" is necessarily subordinate to and conditioned upon the unique persona of "who" will be that maker of history.

3   But there is no question in my mind that there will be an African American elected President of the United States. And it could easily occur within the next twenty years.

4   One hundred thirty years ago, the ratification of the Thirteenth Amendment began a remarkable political odyssey for the black people of this country. From an enslaved people, they have become an integral component in the election of Governors, Senators, and Presidents—as President Clinton and former President John F. Kennedy would attest.

5   And with the passage of the 1965 Voters Rights Act, they have projected themselves into every elective and appointed office in the land—with the only exception being that of the presidency and vice-presidency of the nation.

6   Cleveland, Ohio, which I was once honored to serve as its mayor, is a microcosm of that latter development.

7   Many years ago, 26 to be exact, there was international media and public reaction to my being elected as Mayor of Cleveland. I was delighted, happy, and gratified.

8   But seemingly ignored by everyone was that the year I was elected, 1967, Edward Brooke had been serving as a member of the U.S. Senate for almost five years—the first black to be elected to that body in this century.

9   And Brooke's election to the U.S. Senate followed his state-wide election as Attorney General of the Commonwealth of Massachusetts. That despite there being only a 3 percent black population in Massachusetts; that Brooke was a Republican in a largely Democrat-leaning state; and that he was in an interracial marriage in a heavily Catholic, European-Ethnic state. Lots of traditional reasons there that he not be elected. But he was.

10   Brooke's election as a state official and then to the Senate was not lost on me as I was planning my own race for the mayoralty of my city—63 percent white, almost all of them conservative Eastern European ethnics. In fact, his experiences helped convince me that I could win, although there were some major differences in that Brooke's candidacy for the U.S. Senate did not excite the same fears from a white constituency that mine did for mayor.

11   A U.S. Senator, though powerful, exercises no direct control over his constituency. He is physically removed in Washington, his vote one of many. But the mayor lives "down the street," he has authority over the police (white), he spends the city tax dollar, and he decides when and where the snow is going to be plowed or not plowed. Those fears had to be frontally faced by me and allayed in the campaign. And they were.

12   I had long studied the ethnic political history of Massachusetts, Connecticut and New York. I understood that the visible color difference added a problem that the immigrant groups didn't have. But the ever-increasing numbers of black people in my and other central cities, coupled with the "white-flight," was creating the same demographic opportunities for a black person to seize City Hall, as had occurred for an Italian, LaGuardia, an Irishman, Hague, and the Polish mayor, Cermak in their era.

13   The task was to maximize my black vote, get as many white votes as I could, and to minimize white-fear reactions that would cause a majority voter turn-out for my white opponent. It would have been easier had my opponent been less accomplished.

14   Seth Taft, my Republican opponent, was the grandson of President and former U.S. Chief Justice William Howard Taft. My grandfather was born into slavery in 1859 in the state of Georgia. Taft had been educated at private Ivy League schools, graduated from Yale Law School, and was a partner in the eighth largest law firm in the U.S.

15   I attended public schools, spent a year at all-black West Virginia State College, earned my law degree from Cleveland Marshall Law School, and was a single-practitioner with my brother.

16   We had a hard-fought but clean campaign. Taft knew that he was going to benefit from much of the white vote solely because he was white—or that I was black. But not once did he make that appeal. Correspondingly, I made no appeal to the black voter on the basis of race—obviously, I knew that the black people also were not blind. So, to the extent such things are possible, Taft and I had a clean campaign—certainly one that was free of any overt racial appeal. He and I were friends before that campaign, during the campaign, and remain friends to this day. The problem after winning the election was: how to govern.

17   It was not easy. Cleveland had been identified in national surveys as second only to Chicago in racial segregation. The population of 800,000 was balkanized into 33 wards—23 white and 10 black. The mayoralty term of two years was legislated insecurity. The federal government had cut off urban renewal funds due to shortcomings by the prior administration. There was no political organization in the city: the two daily newspapers had been credited over the previous 40 years with having elected mayors. Neither paper had a black person serving in an editorial or policy-making position. There were no black anchor people on the three local television stations and no black political reporters.

18   I was a black man elected to run a majority-white city with a national reputation for racism; with white people in control of the city council, the various media, and all of the business, financial, and commercial institutions. And with a 93 percent white police force. The odds of success were dramatically short from the outset.

19   But had it not been for one fatal mishap, Cleveland would have been a national role model for cities, and a microcosmic view of a black presidency.

20   The middle 1960s was a time of great national turmoil. Students throughout the nation were taking over university facilities and violently protesting the Viet Nam War. Dr. King and his followers were under attack in Illinois and Tennessee as they made their shift from civil rights to fighting racism in the labor unions, in residential housing, and other areas of economic concern. Rioting and looting had become commonplace in all the major cities. The mainly white police forces were at swords-point with the black communities. The Kerner Commission came out with its finding that America was fast becoming two societies: One white and one black, separate and unequal. Unemployment and inflation were on the increase and the resultant economic insecurity was causing short tempers nationally.

21   Then, as though all of these national tensions had come to one focus in Cleveland's neighborhood of Glenville, white police and a group of young black nationalists, both sides armed with rifles, shot it out. Three policemen were killed and nine suffered permanently disabling wounds. Seven of the young black men were killed. The worst nightmare of any mayor, had actually happened only ten months into my first term.

22   The news came to me over a police radio in my car, just as we were pulling away from my home to go to the Glenville area where we'd learned shortly before that there was a potential of trouble. "One policeman is down and still being hit by rifle fire . . ." the dispatcher's voice said. Seconds later he added that one civilian "was down" from police fire after fleeing from the house from which the nationalists were firing. The "Glenville Shoot-out" was underway.

23   I sat unmoving in the back seat of my car listening to the broadcast. There was not need now for me to go to the area. The war that both groups had wanted, was on. Tears of frustration and helplessness rolled down my cheeks as I sat there, miles away from the scene, powerless to stop those damn fools whose mutual hatreds were killing each other—and the hopes of a city. I then became angry, and cursed out loud, because I knew that this armed conflict would shut down all our delicately-crafted plans for integrated housing, affirmative action in jobs, and cooperation from a majority-white city council.

24   No one had to tell me, at that instant, that all of the worst fears of the white people had actually happened: their white police were under attack from black men. I also knew that, as the black mayor, I would be personally blamed for the tragedy. I understood that the police were viewed by many of my white constituents as their "line of defense" against "them," the black people. And now—without regard as to how the battle began, or who shot first, the white perception would be that it would never have happened if a black man had not been mayor.

25   And that is what happened. The radio talk shows were jammed with hate calls, now that it was "acceptable" for the white bigots to surface and to attack and blame the black mayor. Vitriolic letters to the editor from white readers and op-ed criticisms followed in all the local papers. Every taxi driver had his or her own personal insight as to how and what happened.

26   And the rumors escalated to the certainty that I had personally armed the militants and dispatched them to their war with the police.

27   But Glenville wasn't over the next morning. We still had to bury the dead, and visit the wounded. Store windows had to be boarded up and fires extinguished from the local reaction to the small war. And a decision had to be made as to how to avoid a repeat of the previous nights violence. There was anger in the streets among other young black nationalists about their colleagues who had been killed the night before. And the white policemen were distraught with anger over the officers who had fallen. Both sides were vowing revenge.

28   I made the decision that the best way to avoid the almost certain armed conflict, and loss of lives, was to withdraw all white police officers from the Glenville area. I had arrived at that conclusion after a day-long consultation with dozens of black community leaders. To keep the peace that night, I assigned all of our black city police officers to the area accompanied by black deputy sheriffs, and supplemented them with a corp of 500 black community leaders — ministers, athletes, gang leaders, school teachers, Boy Scout leaders, and other activists.

29   It worked. No shots were fired that night. No lives were lost. The following night, and thereafter, the regularly assigned white police officers were returned to the area, together with members of the national guard, and, with tempers having cooled, there were no more covert incidents. The bloodshed had ended.

30   But the political damage was deep and proved to not be reversible. A major, innovative public-private sector program that depended upon and had been receiving funding from the business community, dried up. The racial lines in the city council hardened, and the passage of any legislation of significance became the occasion for confrontation and obstruction that had no relation to the subject of the bill.

31   Any hope of softening the long-established racial divisions in the city was over. The bright promise of the partnership of a young, black mayor and a majority white city population, being able to fashion new ways of racial cooperation, was not to be.

32   Nonetheless, I was reelected in 1969, by a wider margin and with more white votes than in my first election.

33   However, the local problems I have described were being sorely compounded by our national problems. In 1967 it had seemed that the cities could be turned around. But by 1970, in the early months of my second term, the national economy had worsened, and we were headed for even more problems than before. Local governments' lack of resources, the revolt against taxes, the high crime rate, the seemingly inexorable slide of housing, bridges and highways into decay and deterioration, the continued flight from the cities by even the marginally affluent, the increasing unemployment and labor problems — all these things were making cities virtually unmanageable.

34   It became clear to me and other big-city mayors who had been the cutting-edge in battling the urban crisis, that the nation no longer had the will to commit the resources and priorities that the problems of major central cities demanded.

35 The time for activist mayors committed to achieving change and reform had passed. Most of us were unwilling to be overseers whose function would be to preside over the absolute demise of neighborhoods; increased social and physical sicknesses from drugs; new and old diseases and little or no health care; a renewal of rioting in the streets; soaring crime rates; the rise of an underclass highlighted by generational welfare; dysfunctional public school systems; the flow of jobs to the suburbs; increased infant mortality; the city infrastructure falling apart; the middle-class gone; and the poor battling the poor for anything left in deserted downtowns, vacant office buildings, and vandalized and empty former factories.

36 Over half of the mayors elected between 1960 and 1970, did not run for reelection. New York City's activist mayor, John Lindsay, announced his retirement. Boston's mayor, Kevin White, Mayor Tommy Delasandro of Baltimore, and I met and decided that we would make a "statement" by the three of us jointly announcing that we would not stand for reelection. A few days later, White recanted, saying that he "could not imagine life not being mayor." Delesandro and I were left to go it alone. On April 16, 1971, I announced that I would not run again for mayor and my retirement from politics.

37 During my years at city hall, the local and national black political scene changed dramatically. Following my tenure, the acknowledged, most powerful politician in Cleveland during fifteen years in which the city had three white mayors, was a black man, George Forbes, the President of City Council.

38 The current mayor, Michael White, is black. And so is the elected county prosecutor, the president and superintendent of the public school system, and a member of Congress, Louis Stokes, my older brother. Other black men and women head the metropolitan housing authority, the community college, the state's lottery commission, and one of America's oldest and most prestigious philanthropic organizations, the Cleveland foundation.

39 Without many Americans being overly conscious of it, that pattern of black political participation is being replicated nationwide. California's Speaker of the House of Representatives, Willie Brown, has dictated and/or manipulated that state's policies for over a decade. Other black men have led their legislatures in New Jersey and Pennsylvania. California and Colorado have elected black Lieutenant Governors. The southern states of Mississippi, Georgia, and Alabama have elected black men and women to offices ranging form mayor, congressperson, and county commissioners, to that old citadel of power in southern communities: The Sheriff.

40 The centerpiece of this non-violent, political revolution is, of course, Douglas Wilder, the elected Governor of the Commonwealth of Virginia. A black man.

41   In 1661, while still a colony, Virginia was the first to pass statutory recognition of slavery. And its unremitting struggle against the Union as the oldest of the Confederate states is a matter of history. Yet, in 1986, Doug Wilder was elected its Lieutenant Governor, and in 1990, the over 85 percent white population of Virginia elected Wilder their Governor over his white opponent, the elected Attorney General.

42   What a feat. This country had quietly gone from slavery in 1865, to the election of a black man in 1990 to the chief executive officer of one of its fifty states.

43   In the interim, over 300 black men and women have been elected mayor of their cities—indeed, the six largest cities in our nation have been led by African American mayors; the number of black congresspersons has ballooned from none in 1990, to 40 today, many of them chairs of major committees; most state legislatures have black members occupying varying degrees of power; the school boards and city councils in every large city are led or dominated by their black elected members; several states have black officials elected state-wide; the police chiefs of most of the largest industrial cities are black; black judges, elected and appointed, are serving from the municipal level to the highest state courts, and in the Federal district and appellate courts, and the U.S. Supreme Court; and the current Chairman of the Joint Chiefs of Staff of the U.S. military forces is a black man, General Colin Powell.

44   General Powell's current position as head of the military is of great significance to one of my generation. When I was in the U.S. Army from 1945 to 1947, there were only a few black lieutenants, almost no captains, black majors or colonels, and with the exception of Benjamin O. Davis, Sr., generals were not to be thought of. We were totally segregated in our living quarters and training facilities. We were generally denied the opportunity to serve in combat, and relegated to driving trucks. Today, 45 years later, the boss of all the armed services, an African American, General Colin Powell.

45   It is the totality of these events in American history that support the thesis of an African American President in the near future.

46   In the preliminaries to last year's presidential election, there was serious talk among Republicans about replacing Vice-President Quayle with General Powell. There was even talk among Democrats of drafting Powell. It wasn't done, by either party. But not because it was considered any longer to be unthinkable. Several of the recognized, political-savvy news columnists and commentators speculated on the positives Powell could bring to the vice-presidential slot — especially after Operation Desert Storm. In politics, once that an idea becomes realistic and pragmatic, its just a question of time before one or the other political party uses it.

47   In 1967, the conventional political wisdom was that I could not be elected mayor. The black and white voters of Cleveland proved them wrong. In the 1988 Democratic primaries, over a six months period, the white and black voters in states from Maine to Colorado, chose Jesse Jackson over four of his five white opponents. In a campaign that began with derision from many national columnists and commentators, Jackson was the surviving candidate against the ultimate nominee, Michael Dukakis, and garnered over 6 million votes.

48   As you read the results in the various state primary votes, Jackson won some primaries, and consistently ran second and third in others. The significance, of course, is that everyone in America — those who voted for him, and those who didn't — knew that he was a black man. In those primary elections, white voters had a choice of five other seasoned, capable, and responsible candidates — all white. But a consistent, sizable number of white voters from states throughout the union, knowingly cast their ballot for the black man over most of his counterparts. Their votes stamped him, indelibly, as being the best-qualified — regardless of his being black!

49   An equally telling realization late in the 1988 primaries that Jackson had become a serious, potential winner of the Democratic nomination, was the public conversion of Sam Donaldson and his fellow television political reporters, from derision and scorn, early on, to subsequent heated discussions of whether Jackson or Dukakis would get the necessary electoral votes to win the Democratic nomination.

50   Racial bias, prejudice and discrimination are institutionalized in our nation. But a consistent feature of racism is its inconsistency.

51   There is no other way to explain Massachusetts electing a black Republican to be its state law enforcement official, and then being elected as its United States Senator, while black candidates in Boston were being rejected out-of-hand by white voters in their campaigns for city council.

52   Again it is the inconsistency of racism that helps explain last year's election of Illinois', and America's, first African American woman to the United States Senate.

53   Carol Mosley-Braun, a resident of Chicago, the most segregated city in the nation, defeated a white, well-financed Republican, in a two-person race, white against black, in a state renowned for its down-state conservatism, and some Ku Klux Klan activity. Nonetheless, white Illinoisans voted for Braun over a perfectly acceptable and qualified white male.

54   This black woman has now been elected to the second-highest office in our land. Wilder presides over one of our fifty states. Willie Brown still heads the legislative body of our most populous and diverse state. And Colin Powell is directing the U.S. armed forces in the United Nations' historically unprecedented humanitarian excursion in Somalia.

55 It therefore takes no leap of faith, nor convoluted reasoning, to project that an African American can and will be elected President of the United States in the near future. African Americans already have been accorded electoral approval at all but the highest level in our country.

56 This does not mean that racial bias and prejudice is not existent in the political market place. It means that racial animosities are not uniform and not universally employed. It means that more often than noticed, American's acknowledged racism, is well off-set by a fundamental decency in a nation still molding the kind of democracy it wants to be. It means that there is a framework in this country within which the individual can cause the system to respond to his or her appeal to the best that is in us. It means that the opportunity to rise to one's level is a fact; that the precept that "all men are created equal" had credence when viewed from the realities of those who have succeeded; and that the democratic principles on which this nation was formed, continue to evolve and expand and to fulfill the promise of a Democracy that has yet to reach full bloom.

HUMAN RESOURCE MANAGEMENT ISSUES IN THE '90S

Christine D. Keen

One of the most frequently heard terms in American business in the past decade has been human resource management, for many think that proper management of human resources is the key to an effective business enterprise. It is thus that the Society for Human Resource Management, consisting of human resource, personnel, and industrial relations executives, attempts to promote the advancement of human resource management. In this vein, Christine D. Keen, Issues Manager for the Society for Human Resource Management, delivered the following address to its National Conference at Atlanta, Georgia, June 25, 1990.

+This speech is reprinted by permission from *Vital Speeches of the Day*, October 1, 1990, pp. 752–754.

This tightly organized, factual prediction speech, which begins with a quotation from Yogi Berra and ends with one from Shoshana Zuboff, consists of two sections, the first being devoted to three predictions about today's Baby Boomers (1–24) and the second consisting of four scenarios for the changing times (25–33). A speaker wishing to predict must make the predictions seem both plausible and probable. To do this the speaker must look to present trends that seem to be deviating from the past and discern those trends that are the most likely to develop. Examine how Keen uses data from the present to support her predictions. Are all her predictions sufficiently developed to be both plausible and probable? Can you offer different predictions and different scenarios? Of what use are such attempts at predictions?

---

1   When asked about an upcoming series, Yogi Berra supposedly once said, "I try never to make predictions, especially about the future." But I've never been very good about following commonly accepted wisdom, so that's exactly what I'm going to do. I'm going to chance some predictions about how the workplace may change over the next 10 or 15 years.

2   Let me start by asking you a question: how many of you were born sometime between 1946 and 1964? You're the Baby Boom generation, and during the '90s the work force and the work place will come to be dominated by the Baby Boomers—demographically, hierarchically, and psychologically. The Boomers already make up 55 percent of the work force, but during the '90s they will be moving into senior management. They will be policy-setters, and their attitudes and philosophies will govern the workplace.

3   I think we could see three broad trends developing over the next ten years which have, at their root, the differences between the Baby Boomers and the generation which preceded them.

4   First, we are seeing a shift toward putting more importance on family relationships and less on work. During the '70s and '80s the Boomers deferred marriage and children in order to develop their careers. They were ambitious and worked long and hard. But the restructurings of the last several years have taught them an important lesson: you cannot rely on your job as your source of self-validation. If all you've got is your career, when you lose your job, you lose your sense of self.

5   Consequently, the Boomers are now shifting from "In Search of Excellence" to "in search of meaning." They are seeking non-career avenues of self fulfillment, including family relationships, volunteer work and the personal growth movement. Not too surprisingly, the birth rate is rising again: last year there were more babies born in the U.S. than in any year for the past 25. The fertility rate went up 2 percent, which means, in layman's terms, women are having more children.

6   And perhaps even more revealing, we are starting to hear more comments—from men and women—like "unless I'm inventing a cure for AIDS or something, my work is not worth missing my kids grow up." Or "I married you for you, not for your paycheck." Don't get caught in the trap of thinking this is just a "women's thing." Men may not articulate it, but a recent study of employees at Fortune 500 companies showed men were three times as likely to cite children as a reason for leaving a position as women were.

7   During the '90s we may see parents—male and female—scaling back their devotion to their jobs or dropping out of the traditional 9 to 5 work force entirely.

8   Where are they going to go? This brings me to my second broad trend: the emergence of the independent work force.

9   We are moving toward a point when we may have individual contracts with each of our employees. Employees may, in fact, become more akin to independent contractors, negotiating schedules, responsibilities, and rates of pay. We are already seeing a trickle-down effect, for example, from the severance contracts we gave senior executives in the '80s—more middle managers are now insisting on similar written guarantees.

10   Likewise, many companies are broadening their experiments with flextime. A hospital in Dallas, for example, is using a "work three, get one free" approach to recruiting nurses. The nurses work nine months a year, get to choose any three months they would like off, and have benefits for a full year. (This approach has, by the way, increased employment inquiries by 100 percent.)

11   Meanwhile, some European companies are taking the flextime approach to its logical conclusion. Whereas flextime generally lets you choose which 8 hours a day you want to work, and the compressed work week lets you choose which 40 hours a week you want to work (say, four 10 hour days), European companies are pioneering the flexyear: an employee chooses which 2000 or so hours he or she wants to work during the year.

12   The computer, the modem and the fax machine are allowing employees to choose not just when but where they work.

13   Further, the independent employee wants to determine his or her compensation package—not just the money, but the benefits. Flexible or cafeteria benefit plans have, in part, appealed to this desire. The '90s, though, could go in one of two opposite directions: a smorgasbord of mandated and optional benefits or no benefits at all.

14   Congress is actively interested in the possibility of taxing the value of employee benefits as income. Already, tuition assistance benefits are taxed in many cases, and the new child care bill awaiting President Bush's signature contains a provision taxing the value of employer-provided child care benefits for couples with a household income of $70,000 or more. Are benefits going to be an effective recruiting tool if their value is taxed. Perhaps companies would be wiser to get rid of their benefits entirely and compensate employees with more cash—after all, that's more the way we compensate consultants and independent contractors in the first place.

15   Further, the movement toward an independent work force may be accelerated by the Boomers' emphasis on independence and self-reliance. More outplaced middle managers are choosing to chuck corporate life entirely and go into business for themselves than ever before. Half of a recent graduating class of MBAs said they expect to work for themselves one day. Moonlighting is at its highest level in 30 years. Two factors will be feeding the entrepreneurial urge of the independent employee during the '90s; career plateaus and inheritance.

16   The Boomers are plateauing earlier than the previous generation. This is true for a couple of reasons: (1) there are more Boomers and fewer middle management positions for them to aspire to, and (2) much of the job growth over the last 15 years has been in small firms which often do not have the well-developed corporate ladder larger firms might. Second, in another 10 years the Boomers are expected to have more of the necessary capital to invest in their own businesses—not because of any saving they did, but because they will have inherited their parents' considerable assets.

17   How are you going to respond to the challenges and opportunities posed by the independent work force?

18   My third broad trend for the '90s and beyond is a complete redefinition of employment rights and responsibilities.

19   The Boomers do not share their parents attitudes about the role of business in society. "Big business" still carries a negative connotation. This generation doesn't think twice about targeting the deep pockets of business if they think they've been wronged. And they think they've been wronged a lot.

20   The Boomers tend to believe they should not have to waive their Constitutional rights in order to make a living. They believe in rights to privacy, due process, and freedom of speech in the workplace. They believe employees should not be fired without a good reason. They believe in meritocracy—the best should be rewarded without regard for age, gender, race, position, or seniority.

21   The ramifications of these attitudes will reverberate throughout the workplace. We can reasonably expect more concern about testing, for example. Polygraphs are all but gone, and there is movement afoot to ban psychological testing as well. Drug testing is still a thorny subject, and genetic testing could be a powder keg in the '90s.

22   We can also expect more erosion of employment-at-will doctrine. We may see more whistleblowing and more challenges to separation agreement waivers.

23   We will definitely see a call for a more equitable sharing of the benefits and burdens of the company's success and failure. That means linking pay more clearly with individual performance. It may mean generous severance compensation if the termination is not related to performance. It could even mean demands for reform of exorbitant CEO pay packages.

24   These three trends—the renewed emphasis on family, the independent work force and the redefinition of rights and responsibilities—may apply to some but certainly not all of your work force during the '90s. I'd like to sketch very quickly for you four other scenarios to watch for during the '90s.

25   First, the official bilingual or multilingual workplace. Immigration levels are at their highest levels this century, and for most of these immigrants, English is a second language—if they know it at all. We may see the development of a bilingual or multilingual workplace out of necessity or out of government intervention.

26   At Digital Equipment Corp.'s Boston plant, for example, 350 employees speak 19 different languages. Company announcements are printed in English, Chinese, French, Spanish, Portuguese, Vietnamese and Haitian Creole. Other companies are finding they need to teach employees English or teach managers Spanish.

27   Some people apparently feel employers are not reacting to this problem quickly enough on their own. A new law in Iowa requires all business to hire interpreters if 10 percent or more of their workplace speaks no English. This is the first law I am aware of which requires accommodation of a language handicap.

28   In the second scenario, tuition assistance for dependents becomes to the late '90s what child care was to the mid '80s. Tuition has been outpacing inflation for the last 10 years, and federal support for financial aid has halved since 1980. The leading edge of the baby boomlet—the children of the Baby Boomers—will be 13 this year. It was the birth of these same children which turned child care into a political issue and ushered in employer-provided child care benefits.

29   The Boomers have high expectations of their kids. Eighty-six percent expect their kids to go to college. Yet only 54 percent are saving for it. As was the case with child care, employers could be asked to come up with the rest.

30   In the third scenario, employers may step up dramatically their importation of skilled workers because the domestic work force cannot meet the demands for quantity or quality. Canada, for example, which currently has a higher national unemployment rate than the U.S., could be one pool to tap in the '90s (Canadians tend to be well educated, speak English, and free movement of labor may be encouraged by the U.S.-Canada free trade agreement.)

31   Finally, we may see a resurgence of unions during the '90s. Organized labor has spent much of the last decade reinventing itself to appeal to a changing work force. They have been successful in capitalizing on mainstream family issues such as health care, child care, parental leave and housing affordability. Unions have a rising approval rating among the general public, particularly among younger people, and have a rising rate of victory in union elections.

32   Women, minorities, immigrants, service sector workers and even white collar workers are being targeted by organized labor in an attempt to reach out to pockets of the work force which do not typically join unions. Employers should not be too sure that their work force is immune to the charms of a repositioned labor movement, particularly if workers feel their interests are at odds with management's—and evidence is that feeling is growing.

33   Issues for the '90s—the good, the bad and the ugly. How things develop over the next 10 years depends in large part on how we respond today. I read a quote from Shoshana Zuboff, a Harvard business school professor, a few months ago: "The future creeps in on small feet." Here at SHRM we are trying to not only track the footprints; we're trying to help you head them off.

Chapter Five

Speeches That Affirm Propositions of Value

> *Values are the light by which we see our world; they are the bases of our choices; they help determine which problems, causes, and solutions we believe are important; they give our civilizations their distinctive hues. . . . Therefore, we must understand how to analyze values and how to persuade others to accept them if we are to make intelligent speeches.*
>
> *Otis M. Walter and Robert L. Scott*

The Nature and Importance of Speeches That Affirm Propositions of Value

The centrality of values to human existence and to the communication process is acknowledged by Richard M. Weaver, a rhetorical theorist and critic, and by Kenneth Boulding, social critic and economist. In his *The Ethics of Rhetoric*, Weaver contends, "It is the nature of the conscious life of man to revolve around some concept of value. So true is this that when the concept is withdrawn, or when it is forced into conflict with another concept, the human being suffers an almost intolerable sense of being lost." Boulding, in *The Image*, argues:

> . . . The value scales of any individual or organization are perhaps the most important single element determining the effect of the messages it receives on its image of the world. If a message is perceived that is neither good nor bad it may have little or no effect on the image. If it is perceived as bad or hostile to the image which is held, there will be resistance to accepting it.

On the other hand, when a message reinforces a value that is cherished, auditors are likely to be receptive to the position being advanced.

During the past three decades, values have been very much in conflict in American society. Activists have questioned war as a legitimate method of resolving international disputes, poverty as a necessary consequent of a complex economic order, and civil obedience as an unquestioned obligation of responsible citizenship. Americans of all ages have become more compellingly aware of their own values. Some have sought to translate new values into working political and economic practices. Others, threatened by the aggressiveness of reformers, have reasserted their own traditional values as the appropriate way for civilized community life. Hopefully this continuing dialogue about values will meet Richard Weaver's test of public discourse in its finer moments: " . . . Rhetoric at its truest seeks to perfect men by showing them better versions of themselves, links in that chain extending up toward the ideal. . . ."

Not all propositions of value, however, concern the crucial issues of modern social existence. While some speakers affirm propositions related to war or peace, prosperity or poverty, and human love or bigotry, others affirm propositions of value related to artistic excellence, academic achievement, or even, via the mass media, the taste of colas and toothpastes. Propositions of value pervade all facets of human life.

Recall that in Chapter 2 a value was defined as a conception of "The Good" or "The Desirable" which functions sometimes as a goal motivating our behavior and sometimes as a standard for evaluating means to achieve ends. You may wish to reread the comments in that chapter explaining the line of critical analysis that asked: "To what degree do the speaker's ideas harmonize with the audience's relevant values?"

Sometimes speakers urge adoption of a new value, or adoption of a new perspective through redefining an old value. Some speakers aim to reinforce and reenergize audience commitment to values already held. Often speakers offer their value judgment of something (such as a book, film, play, or speech) as valid for audience belief. On occasion a speaker must defend his or her character and reputation against criticism. Such a speech of personal defense aims at refuting negative value judgments concerning the speaker's honesty, integrity, ethics, morals, and public responsibility.

Speakers also affirm values in speeches not primarily devoted to values. A speaker presenting information to enhance audience understanding will show that the information is valuable because it is relevant and useful. To generate listener concern about a problem, a speaker must show that the situation threatens or violates basic relevant audience values. To secure audience acceptance of a policy as a solution to a problem, a speaker must show that the policy is consistent with or enhances central audience values. And, contrary to the popular notion, "facts" do not "speak for themselves." *Humans* present and interpret matters agreed upon as factual in light of their own related values.

Whatever the particular proposition of value, the advocate seeks listener agreement that something meets or does not meet a specific value standard. Unlike the proposition of fact, which is affirmed or denied through tests of existence, occurrence, or causality, the proposition of value is affirmed through tests of *goodness* or *quality*. A value standard may be applied to an individual, an event, an object, a way of life, a process, a condition, or even to another value. Consider the following examples:

Proposition A: Modern art is rubbish.

Proposition B: Sexual chastity before marriage is an outmoded value.

Proposition C: Winston Churchill was a great man.

Proposition D: War is immoral.

Proposition E: A speaker who uses primarily emotional appeals is unethical.

Proposition F: Civil disobedience always is bad.

Proposition G: President Reagan was irresponsible in his handling of the Iran-Contra Affair.

These propositions of value differ in subject matter being valued or devalued. However, each affirms or denies something measured against standards rooted in listener values. Like all propositions of value, those noted above include a word or words that imply a value dimension—"is rubbish," "is an outmoded value" "was a great man," "is immoral," "is unethical," "is bad," "was irresponsible." Because the meanings associated with such evaluative terms are deeply rooted, saturated with emotion, and wrapped in tradition, the task of the advocate seeking to affirm a proposition of value frequently is an incredibly difficult one. And equally difficult is the task of judging such speeches.

Criteria for Evaluating Speeches That Affirm Propositions of Value

1. **Has the speaker demonstrated or is it assumed by the audience that he or she is a person of high credibility with respect to the proposition being advocated?**

When the speaker leaves the realm of empirically verifiable fact and enters the realm of culturally-based and often abstractly-defined values, the assessment by listeners becomes increasingly dependent on their perceptions of the speaker's expertness and trustworthiness. In stressing the potency of speaker ethos, Aristotle wrote: "As a rule we trust men of probity more and more quickly about things in general, while on points outside the realm of exact knowledge, where opinion is divided, we trust them absolutely."

Listeners tend to believe statements about values and value judgments made by speakers they admire and respect. But different audiences and cultures value different qualities in speakers. A college professor of economics arguing that American advertising is unethical may be considered an expert by an audience of high school sophomores, a starry-eyed idealist by an audience of business people, and an extreme liberal by an audience of college Young Republicans.

Although most communication scholars agree that the speaker who is considered by an audience as highly credible has an advantage over the speaker whose ethos is low, they do not always agree on the exact factors determining speaker prestige. In *Principles of Speaking,* for example, Hance, Ralph, and Wiksell list *competence,* which "grows out of a combination of mental ability, know-how, intelligence, understanding, experience with the subject, and knowledge"; *good character,* which is "made up of honesty, integrity, sincerity, fairness, and similar qualities that meet the standards of listeners"; and *good will,* which "consists of friendliness, likeableness, rapport, warmth, and being 'in' with the audience." In *The Art of Persuasion,* Minnick includes confidence and poise, physical energy, sincerity and conviction, mental alertness, intelligence and knowledge, fairness and justice, self-discipline, even temper and restraint, sympathy and understanding, decisiveness, dynamism, and similarity to audience values and beliefs. For further discussion of the importance of source credibility, you may want to read again in chapter 2 the line of critical inquiry which asked: "To what degree is the speaker perceived as a highly credible source on the subject?"

Among the questions you may wish to ask about the advocate of a proposition of value are these: Is the speaker a person who embodies the qualities of character, intelligence, and experience most admired by the audience? Does the speaker's life demonstrate commitment to the value she or he advocates or applies? Does the speaker have the training and experience to qualify for making the value judgment expressed?

2. Has the speaker advanced acceptable criteria for the assessment of the proposition of value?

The criteria for assessing a proposition of value differ from those for assessing a proposition of fact. The criteria for the latter are essentially empirical or quasi-empirical, whereas those for the former are steeped in feelings and related values. For example, consider the following proposition:

Proposition of fact: *Capital punishment is not an effective deterrent to crime.*

Proposition of value: Capital punishment is morally bad.

In the first case, widely accepted criteria for judgment involve tests of empirical reality. Has capital punishment led to a reduction in serious crimes in states where it has been tried? Do states with capital punishment have lower rates of serious crimes than equivalent states that do not have capital punishment? Have carefully controlled, systematic studies demonstrated that potential criminals consider the consequences of their crimes before committing them? In the second instance, the criteria for judgment are rooted in earlier value commitments. Is the taking of human life, for whatever cause, contrary to values fundamental to the Judeo-Christian ethic, to human decency, or to communal life?

In attempting to gain acceptance of a proposition of value, a speaker has a number of rhetorical options available for stressing the appropriateness of his or her value criteria. The speaker can show that the value standards used or values advocated are consistent with other values already held by the audience. The speaker might show that the value advocated has produced desirable consequences in the past when adhered to; this involves using *another* value standard to demonstrate "desirability." Sometimes speakers use examples and testimony to show that "good" persons generally have accepted the advocated value and "bad" or less desirable persons have rejected it. Or the value being advocated may be *contrasted* with its undesirable opposite (disvalue) or with a less desirable value. And some speakers offer to an audience a *hierarchy* of values by verbally indicating that the value advocated or defended is *better than* other specific values. Finally, a speaker might argue that socially undesirable consequences will result from continued adherence to old, out-moded values.

Speakers need not fail when their value judgments run counter to the values of the audience. When in 1932 Franklin D. Roosevelt spoke to San Francisco's Commonwealth Club, a group of businessmen with conservative economic values, he began with a careful historical review of the values that had produced industrial America. Then he pointed out that these values had served the nation well but were no longer consistent with our best national interest. In 1886, Southerner Henry W. Grady, in an address to members of the New England Society, sought to erase their long-standing hostility toward the South by praising the spirit of Lincoln and by urging commitment to national values rather than to regional loyalties. Admittedly persuading about values is a complex task, but it is one that a perceptive and sensitive speaker can accomplish to some degree.

In evaluating a speech affirming a proposition of value, the enlightened listener must carefully consider the criteria for judgment that he or she is being asked to accept. Is the value advocated for acceptance or application clearly and exactly specified? Does the speaker demonstrate that the value is reasonable and relevant for the subject at hand? Is the value or value judgment only asserted or implied without clear and reasonable support or demonstration? To what degree do the value appeals serve a legitimate function of promoting social cohesion, of reinforcing audience commitment to ideas they already believe? With what degree of appropriateness are the consequences of commitment to the values clarified? To what degree do the value appeals serve as substitutes, as pseudoproof, for the factuality of an assertion? To what degree do the value appeals divert attention from more fundamental, pressing, or controversial matters? To what degree do the value appeals seem to promote, intentionally or not, unreflective stimulus-response reactions when the occasion demands reflective judgment?

3.   Has the speaker presented a fair view of what is being evaluated?

It should be apparent that a speaker may be eminently qualified to judge and may have acceptable criteria of judgment in mind and yet may have a distorted view of what is being judged. Propositions of value usually are emotion-laden and a speaker's bias may impair her or his ability to depict fairly the object being judged.

Propositions of value often depend on the previous acceptance or establishment of a proposition of fact. Thus the critic must consider whether the advocate has met adequate criteria for the assessment of fact that portrays what the advocate is judging. Should the speaker be intersted in evaluating an event, we first must be assured that the event has been portrayed accurately. Similarly, should the speaker wish to assign a value to a work of art, a belief, an individual, an institution, an action, or another value, we should inquire about the accuracy with which the object being judged is described. Faced with an object described in two-valued, either-or, no-middle-ground terms, the critical listener must consider whether such a description is accurate and adequate for the situation.

Conclusion

The climate of public debate in America during the late 20th Century reflects "an unwillingness, if not a psychological inability, to make and defend judgments of better and worse." Emmanuel Mesthene, a professor of philosophy, elaborates on his view by condemning the widespread hesitancy to "argue a position or justify an action on the basis of judgments of relative worth, whether of morality, of art, of individuals, or of institutions." To what extent do you agree with his contentions? Are value judgments or advocacy of values far too rare in contemporary public discourse?

No matter how frequently we are exposed to value-oriented messages, and because values play such an important role in decisions related to individual and social well-being, the enlightened listener/critic must consider carefully the evaluative messages received each day. In assessing speeches that affirm propositions of value, the critic should consider (1) *whether the speaker is a person of high credibility with respect to the proposition being advocated,* (2) *whether the speaker has advanced acceptable criteria for the assessment of the proposition,* and (3) *whether the speaker has presented a fair view of what is being evaluated.*

For Further Reading

Andersen, Kenneth E. *Persuasion.* 2nd ed. Allyn and Bacon, 1978. Chapter 11 probes the influence of a persuader's credibility.

Condon, John C., and Yousef, Fathi S. *An Introduction to Intercultural Communication.* Bobbs-Merrill, 1975. Chapters 3 and 4 examine the functioning of values in various non-American cultures and between different cultures.

Bradley, Bert E. *Speech Communication: The Credibility of Ideas.* 6th ed. Wm. C. Brown, 1991. Chapter 6 examines the elements of speaker credibility: competence, trustworthiness, similarity, attraction, and sincerity.

Ehninger, Douglas, and Hauser, Gerard. "Communication of Values." In Carroll Arnold and John Bowers, eds. *Handbook of Rhetorical and Communication Theory.* Allyn and Bacon, 1984, Chapter 4.

Fisher, Walter R. "Toward a Logic of Good Reasons." *Quarterly Journal of Speech,* December 1978, 376–384.

Harrell, Jackson; Ware, B. L.; and Linkugel, Wil A. "Failure of Apology in American Politics: Nixon on Watergate." *Speech Monographs,* November 1975, 245–61. Analyzes Nixon's first two Watergate speeches from the perspective of the bases of political authority and the theory of apology.

McEdwards, Mary G. "American Values: Circa 1920–1970." *Quarterly Journal of Speech,* April 1971, pp. 173–80. Illustrates how basic American values have remained relatively constant.

Mesthene, Emmanuel G. "On the Importance of Judging Between Better or Worse." *National Forum,* LXIX (Summer 1979): 4–8.

Rieke, Richard D., and Sillars, Malcolm O. *Argumentation and the Decision Making Process.* 2nd ed. Scott, Foresman, 1984, Chapter 6. After explaining the nature of values, the authors describe in detail six traditional and nontraditional American value systems.

Rokeach, Milton. *The Nature of Human Values.* Macmillan, 1970. A theoretical discussion of what values are and an empirical description of major contemporary American value commitments.

Sillars, Malcolm O. *Messages, Meanings, and Culture: Approaches to Communication Criticism.* Harper/Collins, 1991. Chapter 7 considers criticism of values in discourse.

Walter, Otis M. *Speaking Intelligently.* Macmillan, 1976, pp. 131–49, 228–30. The author focuses on the functioning of values in public discourse aimed at problem-solving.

Walter, Otis M., and Scott, Robert L. *Thinking and Speaking.* 5th ed. Macmillan, 1984. Pages 95–97 survey some contemporary American values and Chapter 10 discusses persuading about values.

Ware, B. L., and Linkugel, Wil A. "They Spoke in Defense of Themselves: On the Generic Criticism of Apologia." *Quarterly Journal of Speech.* October 1973, 273–83. Examines the rhetorical strategies and tactics available to speakers in defending their personal character against negative value judgments.

Warnick, Barbara, and Inch, Edward S. *Critical Thinking and Communication: The Use of Reason in Argument.* 2nd ed. Macmillan, 1994. Chapter 9 discusses advocating and opposing value propositions.

Weaver, Richard M. *The Ethics of Rhetoric.* Regnery, 1953, Chapter 9. Weaver's discussion of "ultimate terms" in the rhetoric of the era illuminates the persuasive potency of values and disvalues as they appear in the form of societal "god terms" and "devil terms."

For the World to Live, 'Europe' Must Die

Russell Means

In the Summer of 1980, Russell Means, a member of the Ogala Lakota tribe, of the Sioux nation, addressed several thousand people during the Black Hills International Survival Gathering held on the Pine Ridge Reservation in South Dakota. This meeting was held to protest the pollution and exploitation of American Indian lands throughout the West. For most of those in his audience, Means' ethos, his level of source credibility, would be extremely high. Their perceptions of his personal qualities, such as expertness and trustworthiness, would be very positive. He co-founded the activist American Indian Movement (AIM). He organized activist groups in cities and on reservations. He played a major role in the protest occupation of Wounded Knee, South Dakota, in the Spring of 1973. In the course of his various activities, he has been injured, shot, and jailed. Although now he downplays his leadership role (par. 46), his audience would listen carefully to his advice because of their high esteem for him as a leader.

The central issue, according to Means, is the clash between two antagonistic value systems, between two opposite world views—the European and the traditional American Indian tribal. A revolution in value commitments is needed, and he offers a persuasive definition of what we should mean by the label "revolution" (par. 21, 23, 33–34).

An attack on the European-American value system comprises the bulk of Means' address. He pinpoints some of the values he feels are central to the European mind-set; step-by-step logical thinking (7): mechanical image of nature and humans (8); material gain (10); scientific despiritualization of nature and humans (11); and arrogant elevation of humans above other animate and inanimate things (29–30). The values of progress, development, victory, and freedom, all highly prized in the European cultural view, Means depicts as actually undesirable, as disvalues (12).

One major strategy used by Means to undermine European values is to describe the dangerous consequences of following such values

---

+Reprinted with permission from *Mother Jones* magazine, December, 1980, pp. 24–38.

(11–12, 24, 18–19, 25–26). Assess the soundness of the cause-effect reasoning he uses to make such arguments. Means contends very specifically that Marxism is only a different version of the European cultural tradition and, as such, is just as flawed as capitalism or Christianity (21–23, 27). As another rhetorical strategy he itemizes objectionable groups and individuals who embody the undesirable European values (38).

To a lesser extent, Means discusses a few of the specific values central to the traditional American Indian world view: the universe as complex and spiritual (7); "being" a good person (10); and the interrelation of all humans and facets of nature (29–31, 40). To what degree would the speech have been strengthened by a more complete discussion of the values central to the Indian world view? Might Means' audience already have understood and assumed the validity of some key values not discussed? Means mentions a few groups that seem to embody the praiseworthy tribal value system (39). The labels Means chooses heightens the stark contrast between the antagonistic value stances: "death culture" (41) versus "correct peoples" (32). Means' fundamental belief is that the strength to resist and overturn Europeanization flows from commitment to traditional American Indian tribal values (5, 34).

In December 1985, along with other members of the New American Indian Movement, Means went to Nicaragua to join Indians native to Nicaragua in fighting that country's Marxist Sandinista government (*Chicago Tribune,* December 28, 1985, Sec. 1, p. 3). Means argued that the Marxist government could not deal fairly with Nicaraguan Indians because "Marxists are racists."

For an analysis of the broad historical and cultural context within which Means advocates Native American values, see Richard Morris and Philip Wander, "Native American Rhetoric: Dancing in the Shadows of the Ghost Dance," *Quarterly Journal of Speech,* 76 (May 1990): 164–191. The clash of the Lakota and European cultures and value systems in the late 1800s in the American West is depicted vividly in the 1990 academy award film, "Dances With Wolves," produced by, directed by, and starring Kevin Costner.

---

1   The only possible opening for a statement of this kind is that I detest writing. The process itself epitomizes the European concept of "legitimate" thinking; what is written has an importance that is denied the spoken. My culture, the Lakota culture, has an oral tradition, so I ordinarily reject writing. It is one

of the white world's ways of destroying the cultures of non-European peoples, the imposing of an abstraction over the spoken relationship of a people.

2   So what you read here is not what I've written. It's what I've said and someone else has written down. I will allow this because it seems that the only way to communicate with the white world is through the dead dry leaves of a book. I don't really care whether my words reach whites or not. They have already demonstrated through their history that they cannot hear, cannot see; they can only read (of course, there are exceptions, but the exceptions only prove the rule). I'm more concerned with American Indian people, students and others, who have begun to be absorbed into the white world through universities and other institutions. But even then it's a marginal sort of concern. It's very possible to grow into a red face with a white mind; and if that's a person's individual choice, so be it, but I have no use for them. This is part of the process of cultural genocide being waged by Europeans against American Indian peoples today. My concern is with those American Indians who choose to resist this genocide, but who may be confused as to how to proceed.

3   (You notice I use the term *American Indian* rather than *Native American* or *Native indigenous people* or *Amerindian* when referring to my people. There has been some controversy about such terms, and frankly, at this point, I find it absurd. Primarily it seems that *American Indian* is being rejected as European in origin—which is true. But *all* of the above terms are European in origin; the only non-European way is to speak of Lakota—or, more precisely, of Oglala, Brulé, etc.—and of the Diné, the Miccosukee and all the rest of the several hundred correct tribal names).

4   (There is also some confusion about the word *Indian*, a mistaken belief that it refers somehow to the country, India. When Columbus washed up on the beach in the Caribbean, he was not looking for a country called India. Europeans were calling that country Hindustan in 1492. Look it up on the old maps. Columbus called the tribal people he met "Indio," from the Italian *in dio*, meaning "in God.")

5   It takes a strong effort on the part of each American Indian *not* to become Europeanized. The strength for this effort can only come from the traditional ways, the traditional values that our elders retain. It must come from the hoop, the four directions, the relations; it cannot come from the pages of a book or a thousand books. No European can ever teach a Lakota to be Lakota, a Hopi to be Hopi. A master's degree in "Indian Studies" or in "education" or in anything else cannot make a person into a human being or provide knowledge into the traditional ways. It can only make you into a mental European, an outsider.

6   I should be clear about something here, because there seems to be some confusion about it. When I speak of Europeans or mental Europeans, I'm not al-

lowing for false distinctions. I'm not saying that on the one hand there are the by-products of a few thousand years of genocidal, reactionary, European intellectual development which is bad; and on the other hand there is some new revolutionary intellectual development which is good. I'm referring here to the so-called theories of Marxism and anarchism and "leftism" in general. I don't believe these theories can be separated from the rest of the European intellectual tradition. It's really just the same old song.

7   The process began much earlier. Newton, for example, "revolutionized" physics and the so-called natural sciences by reducing the physical universe to a linear mathematical equation. Descartes did the same thing with culture. John Locke did it with politics, and Adam Smith did it with economics. Each one of these "thinkers" took a piece of the spirituality of human existence and converted it into a code, an abstraction. They picked up where Christianity ended; they "secularized" Christian religion, as the "scholars" like to say—and in doing so they made Europe more able and ready to act as an expansionist culture. Each of these intellectual revolutions served to abstract the European mentality even further, to remove the wonderful complexity and spirituality from the universe and replace it with a logical sequence: one, two, three, Answer!

8   This is what has come to be termed "efficiency" in the European mind. Whatever is mechanical is perfect; whatever seems to work at the moment—that is, proves the mechanical model to be the right one—is considered correct, even when it is clearly untrue. This is why "truth" changes so fast in the European mind; the answers which result from such a process are only stop-gaps, only temporary, and must be continuously discarded in favor of new stop-gaps which support the mechanical models and keep them (the models) alive.

9   Hegel and Marx were heirs to the thinking of Newton, Descartes, Locke, and Smith. Hegel finished the process of secularizing theology—and that is put in his own terms—he secularized the religious thinking through which Europe understood the universe. Then Marx put Hegel's philosophy in terms of "materialism," which is to say that Marx despiritualized Hegel's work altogether. Again, this is in Marx' own terms. And this is now seen as the future revolutionary potential of Europe. Europeans may see this as revolutionary, but American Indians see it simply as still more of that same old European conflict between *being* and *gaining*. The intellectual roots of a new Marxist form of European imperialism lie in Marx'—and his followers'—links to the tradition of Newton, Hegel, and the others.

10   *Being* is a spiritual proposition. *Gaining* is a material act. Traditionally, American Indians have always attempted to *be* the best people they could. Part of that spiritual process was and is to give away wealth, to discard wealth in order *not* to gain. Material gain is an indicator of false status among traditional

people, while it is "proof that the system works" to Europeans. Clearly, there are two completely opposing views at issue here, and Marxism is very far over to the other side from the American Indian view. But let's look at a major implication of this; it is not merely an intellectual debate.

11   The European materialist tradition of despiritualizing the universe is very similar to the mental process which goes into dehumanizing another person. And who seems more expert at dehumanizing other people? And why? Soldiers who have seen a lot of combat learn to do this to the enemy before going back into combat. Murderers do it before going out to commit murder. Nazi SS guards did it to concentration camp inmates. Cops do it. Corporation leaders do it to the workers they send into uranium mines and steel mills. Politicians do it to everyone in sight. And what the process has in common for each group doing the dehumanizing is that it makes it all right to kill and otherwise destroy other people. One of the Christian commandments says. "Thou shalt not kill," at least not humans so the trick is to mentally convert the victims into nonhumans. Then you can proclaim violation of your own commandment as a virtue.

12   In terms of the despiritualization of the universe, the mental process works so that it becomes virtuous to destroy the planet. Terms like *progress* and *development* are used as cover words here, the way *victory* and *freedom* are used to justify butchery in the dehumanization process. For example, a real-estate speculator may refer to "developing" a parcel of ground by opening a gravel quarry; *development* here means total, permanent destruction, with the earth itself removed. But European logic has *gained* a few tons of gravel with which more land can be "developed" through the construction of road beds. Ultimately, the whole universe is open—in the European view—to this sort of insanity.

13   Most important here, perhaps, is the fact that Europeans feel no sense of loss in all this. After all, their philosophers have despiritualized reality, so there is no satisfaction (for them) to be gained in simply observing the wonder of a mountain or a lake or a people *in being*. No, satisfaction is measured in terms of gaining material. So the mountain becomes gravel, and the lake becomes coolant for a factory, and the people are rounded up for processing through the indoctrination mills Europeans like to call schools.

14   But each new piece of that "progress" ups the ante out in the real world. Take fuel for the industrial machine as an example. Little more than two centuries ago, nearly everyone used wood—a replenishable, natural item—as fuel for the very human needs of cooking and staying warm. Along came the Industrial Revolution and coal became the dominant fuel, as production became the social imperative for Europe. Pollution began to become a problem in the cities, and the earth was ripped open to provide coal whereas wood had al-

ways simply been gathered or harvested at no great expense to the environment. Later, oil became the major fuel, as the technology of production was perfected through a series of scientific "revolutions." Pollution increased dramatically, and nobody yet knows what the environmental costs of pumping all that oil out of the ground will really be in the long run. Now there's an "energy crisis," and uranium is becoming the dominant fuel.

15   Capitalists, at least, can be relied upon to develop uranium as fuel only at the rate at which they can show a good profit. That's their ethic, and maybe that will buy some time. Marxists, on the other hand, can be relied upon to develop uranium fuel as rapidly as possible simply because it's the most "efficient" production fuel available. That's *their* ethics, and I fail to see where it's preferable. Like I said, Marxism is right smack in the middle of the European tradition. It's the same old song.

16   There's a rule of thumb which can be applied here. You cannot judge the real nature of a European revolutionary doctrine on the basis of the changes it proposes to make within the European power structure and society. You can only judge it by the effects it will have on non-European peoples. This is because every revolution in European history has served to reinforce Europe's tendencies and abilities to export destruction to other peoples, other cultures, and the environment itself. I defy anyone to point out an example where this is not true.

17   So now we, as American Indian people, are asked to believe that "new" European revolutionary doctrine such as Marxism will reverse the negative effects of European history on us. European power relations are to be adjusted once again, and that's supposed to make things better for all of us. But what does this really mean?

18   Right now, today, we who live on the Pine Ridge Reservation are living in what white society has designated a "National Sacrifice Area." What this means is that we have a lot of uranium deposits here, and white culture (not us) needs this uranium as energy production material. The cheapest, most efficient way for industry to extract and deal with the processing of this uranium is to dump the waste by-products right here at the digging sites. Right here where we live. This waste is radioactive and will make the entire region uninhabitable forever. This is considered by industry, and by the white society that created this industry, to be an "acceptable" price to pay for energy resource development. Along the way they also plan to drain the water table under this part of South Dakota as part of the industrial process, so the region becomes doubly uninhabitable. The same sort of thing is happening down in the land of the Navajo and Hopi, up in the land of the Northern Cheyenne and Crow, and elsewhere. Thirty percent of the coal in the West and half of the uranium deposits

in the U.S. have been found to lie under reservation land, so there is no way this can be called a minor issue.

19   We are resisting being turned into a National Sacrifice Area. We are resisting being turned into a national sacrifice people. The costs of this industrial process are not acceptable to us. It is genocide to dig uranium here and drain the water table—no more, no less.

20   Now let's suppose that in our resistance to extermination we begin to seek allies (we have). Let's suppose further that we were to take revolutionary Marxism at its word: that it intends nothing less than the complete overthrow of the European capitalist order which has presented this threat to our very existence. This would seem to be a natural alliance for American Indian people to enter into. After all, as the Marxists say, it is the capitalists who set us up to be a national sacrifice. This is true as far as it goes.

21   But, as I've tried to point out, this "truth" is very deceptive. Revolutionary Marxism is committed to even further perpetuation and perfection of the very industrial process which is destroying us all. It offers only to "redistribute" the results—the money, maybe—of this industrialization to a wider section of the population. It offers to take wealth from the capitalists and pass it around; but in order to do so, Marxism must maintain the industrial system. Once again the power relations within European society will have to be altered, but once again the effects upon American Indian peoples here and non-Europeans elsewhere will remain the same. This is much the same as when power was redistributed from the church to private business during the so-called bourgeois revolution. European society changed a bit, at least superficially, but its conduct toward non-Europeans continued as before. You can see what the American Revolution of 1776 did for American Indians. It's the same old song.

22   Revolutionary Marxism, like industrial society in other forms, seeks to "rationalize" all people in relation to industry—maximum industry, maximum production. It is a materialist doctrine that despises the American Indian spiritual tradition, our cultures, our lifeways. Marx himself called us "precapitalists" and "primitive." *Precapitalist* simply means that, in his view, we would eventually discover capitalism and become capitalists; we have always been economically retarded in Marxist terms. The only manner in which American Indian people could participate in a Marxist revolution would be to join the industrial system, to become factory workers, or "proletarians" as Marx called them. The man was very clear about the fact that his revolution could occur only through the struggle of the proletariat, that the existence of a massive industrial system is a precondition of a successful Marxist society.

23   I think there's a problem with language here. Christians, capitalists, Marxists. All of them have been revolutionary in their own minds, but none of them really mean revolution. What they really mean is a continuation. They do what they do in order that European culture can continue to exist and develop according to its needs.

24 So, in order for us to *really* join forces with Marxism, we American Indians would have to accept the national sacrifice of our homeland; we would have to commit cultural suicide and become industrialized and Europeanized.

25 At this point, I've got to stop and ask myself whether I'm being too harsh. Marxism has something of a history. Does this history bear out my observations? I look to the process of industrialization in the Soviet Union since 1920 and I see that these Marxists have done what it took the English Industrial Revolution 300 years to do; and the Marxists did it in 60 years. I see that the territory of the USSR used to contain a number of tribal peoples and that they have been crushed to make way for the factories. The Soviets refer to this as "The National Question," the question of whether the tribal peoples had the right to exist as peoples; and they decided the tribal peoples were an acceptable sacrifice to industrial needs. I look to China and I see the same thing. I look to Vietnam and I see Marxists imposing an industrial order and rooting out the indigenous tribal mountain people.

26 I hear a leading Soviet scientist saying that when uranium is exhausted, *then* alternatives will be found. I see the Vietnamese taking over a nuclear power plant abandoned by the U.S. military. Have they dismantled and destroyed it? No, they are using it. I see China exploding nuclear bombs, developing uranium reactors and preparing a space program in order to colonize and exploit the planets the same as the Europeans colonized and exploited this hemisphere. It's the same old song, but maybe with a faster tempo this time.

27 The statement of the Soviet scientist is very interesting. Does he know what this alternative energy source will be? No, he simply has faith. Science will find a way. I hear revolutionary Marxists saying that the destruction of the environment, pollution, and radiation will all be controlled. And I see them act upon their words. Do they know *how* these things will be controlled? No, they simply have faith. Science will find a way. Industrialization is fine and necessary. How do they know this? Faith. Science will find a way. Faith of this sort has always been known in Europe as religion. Science has become the new European religion for both capitalists and Marxists; they are truly inseparable, they are part and parcel of the same culture. So, in both theory and practice, Marxism demands that non-European peoples give up their values, their traditions, their cultural existence altogether. We will all be industrialized science addicts in a Marxist society.

28 I do not believe that capitalism itself is really responsible for the situation in which American Indians have been declared a national sacrifice. No, it is the European tradition; European culture itself is responsible. Marxism is just the latest continuation of this tradition, not a solution to it. To ally with Marxism is to ally with the very same forces that declare us an acceptable cost.

29   There is another way. There is the traditional Lakota way and the ways of the other American Indian peoples. It is the way that knows that humans do not have the right to degrade Mother Earth, that there are forces beyond anything the European mind has conceived, that humans must be in harmony with *all* relations or the relations will eventually eliminate the disharmony. A lopsided emphasis on humans by humans—the Europeans' arrogance of acting as though they were beyond the nature of all related things—can only result in a total disharmony and a readjustment which cuts arrogant humans down to size, gives them a taste of that reality beyond their grasp or control and restores the harmony. There is no need for a revolutionary theory to bring this about; it's beyond human control. The nature peoples of this planet know this and so they do not theorize about it. Theory is an abstract; our knowledge is real.

30   Distilled to its basic terms, European faith—including the new faith in science—equals a belief that man is God. Europe has always sought a Messiah, whether that be the man Jesus Christ or the man Karl Marx or the man Albert Einstein. American Indians know this to be totally absurd. Humans are the weakest of all creatures, so weak that other creatures are willing to give up their flesh that we may live. Humans are able to survive only through the exercise of rationality since they lack the abilities of other creatures to gain food through the use of fang and claw.

31   But rationality is a curse since it can cause humans to forget the natural order of things in ways other creatures do not. A wolf never forgets his or her place in the natural order. American Indians can. Europeans almost always do. We pray our thanks to the deer, our relations, for allowing us their flesh to eat; Europeans simply take the flesh for granted and consider the deer inferior. After all, Europeans consider themselves godlike in their rationalism and science. God is the Supreme Being; all else *must* be inferior.

32   All European tradition, Marxism included, has conspired to defy the natural order of things. Mother Earth has been abused, the powers have been abused, and this cannot go on forever. No theory can alter that simple fact. Mother Earth will retaliate, the whole environment will retaliate, and the abusers will be eliminated. Things come full circle, back to where they started. *That's* revolution. And that's a prophecy of my people, of the Hopi people, and of other correct peoples.

33   American Indians have been trying to explain this to Europeans for centuries. But, as I said earlier, Europeans have proven themselves unable to hear. The natural order will win out, and the offenders will die out, the way

deer die when they offend the harmony by overpopulating a given region. It's only a matter of time until what Europeans call "a major catastrophe of global proportions" will occur. It is the role of American Indian peoples, the role of all natural beings, to survive. A part of our survival is to resist. We resist not to overthrow a government or to take political power but because it is natural to resist extermination, to survive. We don't want power over white institutions; we want white institutions to disappear. *That's* revolution.

34   American Indians are still in touch with these realities—the prophecies, the traditions of our ancestors. We learn from the elders, from nature, from the powers. And when the catastrophe is over, we American Indian peoples will still be here to inhabit the hemisphere. I don't care if it's only a handful living high in the Andes. American Indian people will survive; harmony will be reestablished. *That's* revolution.

35   At this point, perhaps I should be very clear about another matter, one which should already be clear as a result of what I've said. But confusion breeds easily these days, so I want to hammer home this point. When I use the term *European,* I'm not referring to a skin color or a particular genetic structure. What I'm referring to is a mind-set, a world view that is a product of the development of European culture. People are not genetically encoded to hold this outlook; they are *acculturated* to hold it. The same is true for American Indians or for the members of any other culture.

36   It is possible for an American Indian to share European values, a European world view. We have a term for these people; we call them "apples"—red on the outside (genetics) and white on the inside (their values). Other groups have similar terms: Blacks have their "oreos"; Hispanos have "coconuts" and so on. And, as I said before, there *are* exceptions to the white norm: people who are white on the outside, but not white inside. I'm not sure what term should be applied to them other than "human beings."

37   What I'm putting out here is not a racial proposition but a cultural proposition. Those who ultimately advocate and defend the realities of European culture and its industrialism are my enemies. Those who resist it, who struggle against it, are my allies, the allies of American Indian people. And I don't give a damn what their skin color happens to be. *Caucasian* is the white term for the white race; *European* is an outlook I oppose.

38   The Vietnamese Communists are not exactly what you might consider genetic Caucasians, but they are now functioning as mental Europeans. The same holds true for Chinese Communists, for Japanese capitalists or Bantu Catholics or Peter "MacDollar" down at the Navajo Reservation or Dickie Wilson up here at Pine Ridge. There is no racism involved in this, just an acknowledgment of the mind and spirit that make up culture.

39   In Marxist terms I suppose I'm a "cultural nationalist." I work first with my people, the traditional Lakota people, because we hold a common world view and share an immediate struggle. Beyond this, I work with other traditional American Indian peoples, again because of a certain commonality in world view and form of struggle. Beyond that, I work with anyone who has experienced the colonial oppression of Europe and who resists its cultural and industrial totality. Obviously, this includes genetic Caucasians who struggle to resist the dominant norms of European culture. The Irish and the Basques come immediately to mind, but there are many others.

40   I work primarily with my own people, with my own community. Other people who hold non-European perspectives should do the same. I believe in the slogan, "Trust your brother's vision," although I'd like to add sisters into the bargain. I trust the community and the culturally based vision of all the races that naturally resist industrialization and human extinction. Clearly, individual whites can share in this, given only that they have reached the awareness that continuation of the industrial imperatives of Europe is not a vision, but species suicide. White is one of the sacred colors of the Lakota people—red, yellow, white and black. The four directions. The four seasons. The four periods of life and aging. The four races of humanity. Mix red, yellow, white, and black together and you get brown, the color of the fifth race. this is a natural ordering of things. It therefore seems natural to me to work with all races, each with its own special meaning, identity, and message.

41   But there is a peculiar behavior among most Caucasians. As soon as I become critical of Europe and its impact on other cultures, they become defensive. They begin to defend themselves. But I'm not attacking them personally; I'm attacking Europe. In personalizing my observations on Europe they are personalizing European culture, identifying themselves with it. By defending themselves in *this* context, they are ultimately defending the death culture. This is a confusion which must be overcome, and it must be overcome in a hurry. None of us have energy to waste in such false struggles.

42   Caucasians have a more positive vision to offer humanity than European culture. I believe this. But in order to attain this vision it is necessary for Caucasians to step outside European culture—alongside the rest of humanity— to see Europe for what it is and what it does.

43   To cling to capitalism and Marxism and all the other "isms" is simply to remain within European culture. There is no avoiding this basic fact. As a fact, this constitutes a choice. Understand that the choice is based on culture, not race. Understand that to choose European cluture and industrialism is to choose to be my enemy. And understand that the choice is yours, not mine.

44   This leads me back to address those American Indians who are drifting through the universities, the city slums, and other European institutions. If you are there to learn to resist the oppressor in accordance with your traditional ways, so be it. I don't know how you manage to combine the two, but perhaps you will succeed. But retain your sense of reality. Beware of coming to believe the white world now offers solutions to the problems it confronts us with. Beware, too, of allowing the words of native people to be twisted to the advantage of our enemies. Europe invented the practice of turning words around on themselves. You need only look to the treaties between American Indian peoples and various European governments to know that this is true. Draw your strength from who you are.

45   A culture which regularly confuses revolution with continuation, which confuses science and religion, which confuses revolt with resistance, has nothing helpful to teach you and nothing to offer you as a way of life. Europeans have long since lost all touch with reality, if ever they were in touch with it. Feel sorry for them if you need to, but be comfortable with who you are as American Indians.

46   So, I suppose to conclude this, I should state clearly that leading anyone toward Marxism is the last thing on my mind. Marxism is as alien to my culture as capitalism and Christianity are. In fact, I can say I don't think I'm trying to lead anyone toward anything. To some extent I tried to be a "leader," in the sense that the white media like to use that term, when the American Indian Movement was a young organization. This was a result of a confusion I no longer have. You cannot be everything to everyone. I do not propose to be used in such a fashion by my enemies; I am not a leader. I *am* an Oglala Kalota patriot. That is all I want and all I need to be. And I am very comfortable with who I am.

TEACHING VALUES IN PUBLIC SCHOOLS

Mario M. Cuomo

A lawyer by profession and Democrat by party, Mario M. Cuomo was elected Governor of New York in 1982 and re-elected to four-year terms in 1986 and 1990. He was defeated in 1994. Cuomo is a political liberal and a Roman Catholic and has advocated controversial po-

+The text of this speech was provided by Governor Cuomo's office in Albany, New York.

sitions against the death penalty and against government restrictions on abortion. On March 4, 1987 the Long Island newspaper, *Newsday,* sponsored an Education Symposium held at the State University of New York College at Old Westbury. In his address at the symposium, Governor Cuomo argued his view on another controversial topic—whether and what values should be taught in public schools.

In a broad sense this speech is about a policy—a course of action—and Cuomo does mention suggestions for implementing the policy. However, it seems clear that his main purpose is not to detail a comprehensive plan for implementing the policy. Rather his focus is on the necessity for reaching agreement about what values should be taught (par. 48). Primarily Cuomo advocates adoption of a specific system of values (27). At length he itemizes and explains these values (29–33). How clearly does he explain the values? Are there any of these values that you believe should *not* be taught in public schools? Why?

As a prelude to identifying the specific values he advocates, Cuomo uses two strategies to predispose the audience toward their adoption. He stresses the desirable consequences of living by these values when he contends that the nation has made progress when citizens have remembered and adhered to the values (11). In contrast, he stresses the undesirable consequences of not following these values. At length he accumulates a list of overwhelming problems facing Americans—problems which implicitly reflect people who never learned or have rejected the values (13–18).

Cuomo further justifies the values in two ways. First, they are rooted in revered founding documents of America (5, 28) and they derive from the Greco-Roman, Judeo-Christian, Western cultural tradition (34–36, 45). Second, they represent a consensus of the core values of American life and form the basis of "our nation's conscience" (27–28, 38).

Where and how adequately do you find Cuomo refuting the idea that public schools can be or should be value-neutral? Where and for what purpose does he associate the desirable values with revered persons? What rhetorical functions are served by the clusters of questions throughout the speech (5–6, 15–18, 49)? For what apparent purpose and how well does Cuomo use personal narrative and dialogue (19–21)? Finally, how perceptive and realistic is Cuomo's recognition of the complexity and difficulty of the subject? (4, 7–10, 49–50).

1   Thank you, Mr. Johnson. Chief Judge Wachtler; Regent Matteoni; Dr. Pettigrew; Steve Isenberg; Sam Ruinsky; Charlotte Frank; Dr. Mondschein; Judge Forest; ladies and gentlemen.

2   First, let me commend Newsday for sponsoring this symposium on the occasion of two most important events—the bicentennial of the Constitution and the celebration of the Year of the Reader.

3   Second, let me say that the format of this morning's program puts me in an unenviable position. Although the Constitution is a subject I study and talk about with relish, and although the gift of literacy that I was given by PS 50 in South Jamaica is one I regard with immense gratitude, you've already heard those topics treated by Chief Judge Wachtler, Louise Matteoni and the other distinguished panel members—people much better equipped than I to discuss them.

4   Instead, then, of trying to expand on what the panelists have already said so well, let me suggest another direction in which their words on the Constitution and on literacy may lead us. It's a direction into territory that's already been explored and charted but is, nevertheless, somewhat perilous—with few sure footholds or reliable signposts and much disputed land.

5   It's the whole question of teaching values in public schools. When, finally, we use our gift of freedom to make ourselves all as literate as we should be, when we are all able to read and understand the Constitution—and the Declaration of Independence and the Federalist Papers and all the documents that order us and describe us as a people—what ultimate ideas will we find in them? What values, norms, and codes of conduct will they teach us?

6   Should we then, having found them, try to teach any of these values to children in our public schools? If so which? Or should we avoid even trying to teach any at all, for fear that we may encourage the teaching of religions, or specific orthodoxies, that will threaten our most precious gift of all . . . our freedom.

7   Difficult questions. Exactly the kind we politicians

New York Governor Mario Cuomo drives home a point during his keynote address at the 1984 Democratic National Convention.

like to avoid. But I believe they are so important it would be wrong to neglect them.

8   Let me add quickly that the very idea that anyone my age should purport to talk about values—let alone teach them to our children—is a personally difficult one. How can anyone of my generation, the generation largely in control of things in recent years, talk about values and try to teach lessons that we seemed to have learned so imperfectly ourselves?

9   How could we—who have so often done the wrong thing to one another—tell students that it is *their* duty to use all that they have been given to make a better world? We who did so much to pollute and poison the environment? We who allowed drugs to become so widely available that they are now one of the most menacing threats to the future of this generation? Isn't it hypocritical?

10   Mark Twain made the same point . . . a little more gently; "To be good and virtuous," he said, "is a noble thing, but to *teach* others to be good and virtuous is nobler still—and much, much easier." That's good. Because if, as I fear, we have little right to hold ourselves out as examples, still I believe we have an obligation to try, at least, to teach the values on which our nation was founded.

11   We know that despite our personal failures, when this nation *has* remembered and acted upon those basic values, we have made progress and thrived as a people. Despite Howard Beach, Queens, and Forsyth County, Georgia, the civil rights of all citizens are more respected today than they were two decades ago. Despite some of the failures in our schools, education *is* more widely available today than ever in our history. Despite lingering discrimination, women are closer today than ever before to occupying the place they deserve in our society.

12   These are all embodiments of strong basic values on which this nation is built. I believe we must point that out to our youth. And I believe they would welcome that instruction. They need it.

13   Today's children are confronted with more complexity, more distractions, more psychological pressures, more temptations than we were. Every night prime-time television assails them with mindless sit-coms and soap operas that present ostentatious materialism and unrelenting self-gratification as the only goals worth pursuing; confronts them with "action" shows in which vigilantism is portrayed as the answer to crime, and macho heroes who live by a code of violence are glorified; with videos that demean women and make a mockery of gentleness.

14   There's another syndrome involving children today—one my generation hardly knew—that is even more menacing—and can be deadly: drugs. The statistics on the self-inflicted madness of drug abuse are frightening—hospital

emergency rooms crowded; treatment centers overwhelmed; more and more victims, many of them adolescents and even pre-adolescents; a rising death toll. And the drug epidemic is only one aspect of a broader *syndrome of self-destructive activity* involving our youth: the steady rise in alcoholism and other forms of reckless abuse of their own minds and bodies . . . even teenage suicide.

15   Add to these a disgraceful school drop-out rate, and the confusing wave of adolescent pregnancy, and we're left with profoundly disturbing, fundamental questions: Have we cared enough about what happens to our children? What is it that we believe in, that we value? What *are* we teaching them? Are we sure enough about our own values to convince youngsters to live *for* something, to believe in themselves, in the significance of their own lives? To believe in believing? If so, how do we go about doing it? How do we stop the madness?

16   And there are more questions—What do we do about Aids? If in fact it is now threatening a wider and wider part of our population, do individuals have the right to engage in personal expressions of intimacy that threaten themselves with perhaps deadly illness . . . and threaten those beyond them? Is it time to surrender privacy in the name of public safety? Can a surrogate mother "own" the child she carries from an implanted seed by agreement with a man and woman who understand that she was merely hosting *their* fetus?

17   Is the Governor from a western state right to raise a question as to whether we are trying too hard to keep people alive for too long because society can't afford the costs? How do we decide if life is worth living in a society where the technology needed to make it happen is available only to the super-rich?

18   What should be the test for opening Shoreham [nuclear reactor]—economic necessity? A new chance for economic growth? The threat to health and life? How much of a threat? How important is one life? Who should decide? By what rules? By what *values?*

19   These are powerful questions that can hit one with great force. It happened to me not long ago, in a New York City schoolyard. I was there to talk to a couple of hundred ninth and tenth graders about the dangers and madness of using crack. I spoke about the beauty of life, the opportunities in their future, and the threat to all their hopes and dreams that drugs posed.

20   After I'd finished, I asked them if what I'd said made sense to them. Most of them nodded. One didn't. A boy, maybe fifteen—with a chipped front tooth who looked at me with his head half-cocked to the side, his face impassive but his skepticism showing through quite clearly. "Didn't you agree with me?" I said. "That your life is too precious to give away to drugs?" "I'm not sure," he answered. "The stuff you said sounded good but I don't really know.

I'm not sure what my life is for, why we're here. I really don't understand it." I was stunned by his answer. By its simplicity. By its staggering profundity. I was at a loss. I told him he was awfully bright to be thinking about those kinds of questions, and that a lot of what life was about was looking for answers to those questions. And that if he did that with his whole mind and his heart, he'd never be sorry, and he'd discover all sorts of wonderful things as he searched. But that if he started looking for answers in three minute drug highs, all he'd ever do was cripple his searching and all he'd ever be was sorry.

21   I don't think I reached him. And I didn't leave those questions behind when I left the schoolyard. They have followed me ever since that afternoon. And they've followed me here this morning. . . . That boy's need to be told and to somehow understand that his life—and everyone's—is good. And precious. And full of purpose. That he has value. And that we have values.

22   So, setting aside the personal tentativeness I have about speaking of values, let me tell you what I think. Ideally, the primary and best source for instruction in values is the family. There are other sources. Churches and synagogues, youth organizations and community groups—all of these can project a strong sense of values as well.

23   But it's clear that today we need more. And I believe it's clear we need to turn to our public schools. Of course, schools cannot—alone—counter the messages and pressures that bombard children. It's too much to ask teachers to do single combat with all of those influences. But if schools can't be expected to do it all, they have proven in the past to be one of the best ways we have for exposing youth to the ideals and traditions—intellectual, ethical, moral—that form our common heritage.

24   Actually, asking whether schools should teach values may be the wrong question. The truth probably is that they do it, *inevitably*, whether formally or informally, deliberately or inadvertently.

25   Even when schools try to be totally silent on the question of ethics, of morals—their silence is *not* a neutral lesson. Silence teaches! Silence teaches that the choice between good and evil is not important; the difference between right and wrong, not significant; the difference between being a good or a bad citizen inconsequential. That's a very real kind of instruction.

26   Given that, it seems to me that at the very least, schools should work to make young people aware that *some* standards of virtue and decency do exist. I believe that can be done without teaching a specific religion or philosophy or instilling someone else's orthodoxy. Not easily, but nonetheless it can be done appropriately and effectively.

27   We can begin with the recognition that whether formally taught or not, at the core of every society is a set of moral values, a code of behavior, a

credo. That has been so throughout history. Even here in our uniquely free society where diversity of belief is protected and cherished, there is a rough—but clear—national understanding of what is right and wrong, what is allowed and what is forbidden, what we are entitled to and what we owe.

28   We can find much of that consensus in the original documents that defined us as a people. The Declaration of Independence and the Constitution reflect values at the core of American life . . . values implicit in the concept of ordered liberty, to which the founders of our nation mutually pledged their lives, their fortunes, their sacred honor . . . and our nation's future.

29   What are those values? Here are some: An awareness of the profound ways in which we are all equal; reverence for the individual rights that issue from that equality—the rights of others as well as our own; a sense of the importance of working for a good greater than our individual goals—a common good; a respect for our system of laws, which so majestically balances individual rights and that common good; and, finally, a love for this place, America, that has dared to try to be true to these revolutionary insights and principles.

30   Now, these are real, tangible, specific values. And we can teach them to our young specifically. We can show them that: *equality, individual rights, the common good,* (or community, what I prefer to call "family,") *the rule of law,* and *love of country* aren't just pat phrases to be wheeled out and paraded on national holidays. They are some of the realities on which our national life was founded. On which we have flourished. And on which America's future will be built.

31   As we study these values—and explicate them—it becomes clear that for all the genius and daring of their ideas and actions, America's founders did not invent these basic principles.

32   In drafting this magnificent new chapter in the history of government, they drew from a deep well of wisdom and history, from philosophical, cultural, and religious traditions that stretched back thousands of years . . . traditions that yielded other values on which our own great civic values are based. Traditions that were supposed to shape us and guide us in our coming together as a nation. They include: a sense of personal worth; the importance of each individual person; the protection of one's self and others from all forms of degradation or abuse. We can call these values *dignity* and *integrity.* There are others. Real and specific values. Like: *compassion, service,* and *love of knowledge.*

33   These values are not just sweet abstractions. Nice generalities. They are not inert ethical entities, but dynamic ways of understanding human nature and purpose—ways that men and women have struggled for centuries to define and develop. As are the companion values of *responsibility* and *accountability*—the limitations on freedom created by the rights of others—and *the need for discipline and order.*

34   These are things that have been taught in places for centuries. They have guided much of the progress in this civilization. They can be formally taught again. When the great thinkers of the Greek city-states first made explicit the dignity inherent in our nature as human beings, their insights were as startling and unsettling to the Mediterranean world of their day as gene-splicing is to ours.

35   Integrity isn't something that an ancient philosopher simply stumbled over on his way to work one day. It is the fruit of a tradition of learning that produced the Book of Exodus and the Psalms. It is an idea that Virgil and Cicero, Aquinas and Thomas Jefferson grappled with . . . refining and expanding it.

36   The development of the idea that we should love our neighbors as ourselves—the golden rule used by the great philosophers to teach compassion and service—has been as crucial to the course of human history as the splitting of the atom.

37   And basic to all these achievements has been a respect for knowledge— at best a *love* of knowledge—a sense of wonder and excitement for the human enterprise. A sense of delight that comes from understanding what you didn't understand before, from stripping away some of life's mystery, unravelling some of the reasons for things. If there is anything that is the mark of a successful school—and of a successful society and civilization—it is the presence of that electric sense of wonder on which all our knowledge has been built.

38   Not all these values are written explicitly into our laws. But they are part of the consensus—sometimes spoken, sometimes unspoken—that underlies our nation's conscience. They all continue to play a crucial role in how we live, how we conceive of ourselves and of others, what we cherish, and even how we construct our hopes and ambitions.

39   To recollect these things and to recall our history, is a helpful reaffirmation of the existence of the essential understanding of values in this nation. And to do it explicitly by making a list of shared values is an exercise I recommend to teachers and school boards and community groups.

40   But simply making a list is not enough. If we're serious about it, if we really believe that a life lived according to our code of values is a more fulfilled, more fully human life, then we must find concrete ways to teach values in our schools.

41   The obvious experts on that are those among us who are teachers and education professionals. In many instances they have been doing it, and doing it well, for years. Our own Regents have included values components in the curricula they have already produced. What we need to do *now* is elaborate and expand their experience and the efforts of the other professionals.

42   Our educators remind us that a school should be a place where students have a pervasive exposure to the best we're capable of; where they learn self-esteem because they're treated as individuals with their own special dignity; where they begin to see that a community works best when each individual—their peers and those in authority—respect the rights of others, and that their actions have an effect on the community.

43   A school should be a place where students learn, as well, the necessity of discipline. Where they come to appreciate more fully that success—in the classroom, in the gym, or on the athletic field—requires self-control, practice, some measure of denying oneself immediate gratification . . . training that gradually corrects weaknesses and perfects strengths.

44   How can we accomplish all of this? To a non-professional like myself, some broad ideas occur. We know that the curriculum—especially in areas like History, Science and Literature—can be an effective instrument for transmitting values.

45   History can teach students that no man, no woman is an island . . . no people, no country either. It can teach them to see events as connected, to realize that the world is ever-changing and evolving but that the best—and the worst—of human instincts are constant. Students can be taught that our own nation's history—and our state's—is more than a jumble of dates and events. It's a continuous story built on outrageous dreams in millions of men and women—early settlers and wave after wave of those who came later—many in steerage or in chains—and who fought and struggled to make the dream they believed in come true for their children and those who would come after them. A real life struggle in which men and women gave all their talents—and sometimes their lives—to uphold freedom and equality. To eradicate racism and discrimination. To preserve the Union and the rule of law. To expand opportunity. And throughout this entire history, properly taught, it will be clear that this progress was largely guided and propelled by the values I speak of today. So teaching history *well* is a good way to teach values.

46   And we can derive powerful instruction from biography and autobiography—in all their forms. Children need heroes. We all do. We can all benefit from reading Carl Sandburg's life of Lincoln, or Dumas Malone's life of Jefferson. *A Man For All Seasons*, the dramatization of Thomas More's life; the *Diary of Anne Frank*; the monumental achievements of Eleanor Roosevelt or of Martin Luther King, Jr.—all these, and many others, can teach us about integrity and courage and steadfastness. We can learn from people admired for their willingness to devote their lives to serving others. If our teachers will point it out, literature can teach children that they're not the first ones in the world to experience fear or disappointment, failure or sorrow. It can teach them the great nobility we are capable of, at our best. And it can show them, especially as they develop intellectually, how difficult it sometimes is to resolve the conflicts among values. How patriotism doesn't always require us to march lock-step to the same drummer. How integrity can mean standing alone.

47   Beyond the curriculum, schools should offer students opportunities to apply the values we say we share. Real opportunities to serve the community and its people—younger students and older residents, the sick, the homebound, anyone in need of the help students can provide, if given the chance. There are all sorts of community organizations that will provide them the opportunity. We should get them involved. It is a common experience of people who volunteer their services that they get out of the experience more than they put in. For adolescents, particularly, one benefit may be a new sense of self-esteem . . . a new understanding of the idea of community.

48   Others are more competent than I to suggest all the specific ways to teach values. My point is that we need to be clearer about what we believe and what we value. We must overcome any reluctance to teach our values from every public pulpit, especially in our public schools. Not just talk about them, but teach them. And that work will involve everyone—the Board of Regents, school boards, teachers, administrators, parents, public officials, all the people of this state. Where it's not being done it should be. Where it's being done we should continue to do it . . . and do it better.

49   If we do all these things—if we identify our basic values and teach them throughout the curriculum of our public schools—will it answer all the hard questions? Will it make a difference? Where it counts, in the lives of our children? Would it have made a difference to the boy in the schoolyard? Will it convince some youngsters that they are too good, too valuable—that they have too much to contribute to our society—to throw it all away by using drugs? Will it keep some from committing suicide? Will we see a decline in the drop-out rate, in teenage pregnancy? Will there be diminished violence and vandalism in the schools?

50   No one can say for sure. Perhaps our efforts won't make a difference. But I believe that, unless we try, we are conceding—in full view of our children—that there are forces whose evil power and sweep are too great to be met by instruction in values or by a summons to dignity and self-respect. I don't believe such a concession to hopelessness is one any of us wants to make. It would be an abdication of our responsibility as parents, as teachers, as public officials. We must value responsibility more than that.

51   And, we know, our responsibility cannot end with mere exhortation. Hard as it is to teach values, we know there are other basic needs which, if not met, make instruction too difficult. We have to invest more intelligently and more generously in our schools and our teachers. We must remember that a child who comes to school malnourished will not learn well. That lessons in self-love can be too hard to teach to a child who is abused at home. That lessons in civility will ring hollow to students who wage a daily struggle merely to survive the violence of the streets. That without the prospect of a job or of the chance to go to college if they choose, students won't be sufficiently motivated to succeed.

52   In the end, the best lesson in values is the example we give as individuals and as a society. What we do to give this generation of students—all of them—the same opportunities that most of us were given, the same chance to be everything they can be. For me as a child, that work began at home, with my parents. With momma and poppa and church and rules, and discipline learned from the hard end of a broom. But for me and probably most of you—and millions like us—it was continued and reaffirmed, fleshed out and fortified in public school.

53   I believe we need that help from our public schools today more than ever. It may be the most important thing our schools can do. I believe that as we teach literacy, we must teach the values that have made us a special people in the 200 years since we were joined together by the miracle of our Constitution.

54   Thank you for having me.

THE TEACHING OF VALUES IN THE PUBLIC SCHOOLS

Phyllis Schlafly

By chance, less than four months after Mario Cuomo presented his speech on teaching values in public schools, Phyllis Schlafly also addressed the same topic. On June 26, 1987 she spoke at a conference sponsored by the Office of Legal Services of the New York City Board of Education and held at the Pocono Manor Conference Center in Pennsylvania.

A nationally prominent political conservative, Mrs. Schlafly organized the STOP ERA movement in the early 1970s against the Equal Rights Constitutional Amendment. In 1975 she founded the Eagle Forum

+The text of this speech was provided by Phyllis Schlafly's office and is reprinted with her permission.

which absorbed STOP ERA and undertook persuasive efforts on a broad spectrum of current issues. She earned her B.A. from Washington University of St. Louis, her M.A. from Harvard University, and her J.D. degree from Washington University Law School. A syndicated columnist and radio commentator, she is author of 12 books including *A Choice Not An Echo, The Power of the Positive Woman, Kissinger on the Couch,* and *Child Abuse in the Classroom.*

To an audience for whom her views probably were in a minority (par. 1), Phyllis Schlafly overtly attempts to clarify and strengthen her credibility—the audience's perception of such personal qualities as expertness, trustworthiness, and sincerity (2, 8–9, 16). Assess the appropriateness and probable successfulness of her approach. Also evaluate how adequately she justifies her basic premise that "anybody who spends the taxpayers' money simply has to put up with citizen surveillance" (6).

While not wanting to *impose* her religious and moral values on the public schools (2), she *defends* the constitutional right of parent and child not to have their religious and moral values attacked, belittled, and deemed irrelevant in public schools (17, 32). To underscore her argument, she offers two clear summaries—one internal (20) and one concluding (33).

Unlike Mario Cuomo who itemized the values he advocated, the values that Phyllis Schlafly advocates for adoption are imbedded in her arguments and often phrased in antithetical style where the preferred values are contrasted with disvalues or violations of values (11, 12). Among Schlafly's preferred values are: basic skills; facts; knowledge based on the great books and classics; knowledge of what society judges illegal (21); God's moral law (17); traditional family structure (24–26); and equality of treatment under the law (19, 22, 32). What other preferred values can you identify? Among the disvalues or violations of values that she attacks are: education as group therapy (11); teaching moral dilemmas that undercut religious and family values (12); "mischief-making" between parent and child (23, 26); and moral relativism (20, 23, 33).

Phyllis Schlafly's extensive use of examples and illustrations strongly invites evaluation by the rhetorical critic (8–9, 14–17, 19–31). She uses examples to attack the alleged value-free, value-neutral procedures of the Values Clarification educational method (15, 17). She employs questions to reinforce her conclusions from the examples

(24–26). Consider how adequately she reassures the audience that her examples are typical or representative of many others that exist (14–16, 29).

Assess the question-and-answer period that followed the speech (35–45). To what degree and in what ways did her answers strengthen or weaken her position? Why might it have been desirable or undesirable for her to introduce the tests of truth, health, legality, and constitutionality explicitly in her speech rather than waiting for the answer period (38, 44)? Where do you believe she significantly clarified a view that actually was unclear in the speech?

Finally, compare Phyllis Schlafly's speech with the previous one by Mario Cuomo. What potential common ground, if any, appears to exist between their views? With which of the values advocated by Cuomo might Schlafly agree or disagree? Why? With what premises or positions of Schlafly might Cuomo agree or disagree? Why? Explore other points of comparison and constrast between the two speeches.

---

1   I thank the sponsors of this meeting for presenting a balanced program, and I thank you for your willingness to hear another side of the issue.

2   First, it's important to know what frame of reference I am coming from. I am not part of the religious right or a fundamentalist group trying to impose my religion on public school children. I come from a state where prayer was banned from the public schools at the time of World War I, and I am not seeking to put it back in. I am not an enemy of public schools. I had a very happy public school experience. I certainly believe in education. I come from a family where the women and men have been college graduates for more than a century. I wanted college so much that, having no money, I worked my own way through college without any aid of any type, in a grimy night job, 48 hours a week. My husband and I have financed six children through 38 years of university education at seven secular universities. So, indeed, I care about education.

3   The three lawsuits pertaining to public school textbooks that have been in the Federal Courts this year (*Smith v. Board of School Commissioners of Mobil County, Mozert v. Hawkins County Board of Education,* and *Edwards v. Aguillard*) are symptomatic of two movements which are current in our society. On the one hand, we have those people who seem to believe that the public school child is a captive of the administrators of the public schools, and that the schools can do anything they want with the children, pretty much as though they were guinea pigs. Those people seem to think that, if parents presume to interfere with or criticize curriculum, they can be called troublemakers, mischief-makers, censors, bigots—the whole host of epithets spun out by the American Civil Liberties Union and People for the American Way.

4   On the other hand, there are those of us who believe that, since the children—and they are minor *children* in public schools—are a captive audience under compulsory school laws, the authority figure must be limited and restricted by two other factors.

5   First is the power and rights of the parents. It is good constitutional law in our nation that the parents are the primary educators of their children. They have the right to safeguard the religion, the morals, the attitudes, the values, and the family privacy of their children.

6   Secondly, the schools are subject to the taxpayers and the citizens of our nation. I come from the frame of reference that anybody who spends the taxpayers' money simply has to put up with citizen surveillance. The President has to put up with it. The Congressmen have to put up with it. The state legislators have to put up with it. And teachers, school administrators and librarians have to put up with it. This is one of the penalties of being able to spend the taxpayers' money. Those who don't like other citizens looking over their shoulders and second-guessing their judgment should really go into some other line of work where they're not spending the taxpayers' money. So, we find it very distressing when schools resent parents and citizens looking over their shoulders.

7   Forty years ago it was not necessary to identify these different categories or types of rights because the public schools had a very high reputation in our land. I can remember that 40 years ago, when conservative speakers made some critical remarks about public schools, they were literally hooted down. Public schools then enjoyed a high reputation like the Post Office. They were sacred cows. Nobody could attack them and get by with it.

8   That public confidence, frankly, is no longer there. Let me explain one reason why it's no longer there. Thirty-two years ago, I was ready to enter my first child in public school, thinking that the first task of the school was to teach the child to read. We now know that there are at least 23 million illiterates in this country, adults who have been through the public schools and didn't learn how to read.

9   Well, 32 years ago when my first child was ready to start school, I discovered that the public schools didn't teach children to read. They only taught them to memorize a few words by guessing at them from the picture on the page. That is why I kept all my six children out of school until I taught them to read at home—so that they would be good readers, and so they would not be six of the 23 million functional illiterates in our country today. This is not a matter of Secular Humanism or morals, or affluence versus poverty, or anything else. No public school in my area taught children how to read. Schools only taught word guessing, which was a cheat on the taxpayers and on the children. We see the results today.

10   Thirty-two years ago I didn't know anybody else who taught her own child. Today there are about a million parents doing that because they feel cheated by the public schools.

11   In the mid-1970s something else came into the schools to use up the hours that could not be spent in reading the great books and the classics, which formerly children were able to do. This new element was best summarized and described by Senator Sam Hayakawa, who was a university president before he became a United States Senator. He called it a "heresy" in public school education. He said that, instead of teaching children knowledge and basic skills, the purpose of education has become group therapy. That's the best way to describe what has happened in the schools.

12   In public school classrooms, children are required to discuss feelings and emotions and attitudes. They are confronted with all sorts of moral dilemmas, instead of being given the facts and the knowledge they need. As a result, Hayakawa was a major promoter of a federal law passed in 1978 called the Protection of Pupil Rights Amendment, which said that schools should not give psychological testing or treatment to public school children on subjects that include family privacy, sexual and other personal matters, without the prior written consent of their parents. The purpose of this law was to prevent the schools from engaging in psychological probing, invasion of privacy, or manipulation of values.

13   The education establishment was so powerful that no regulations were issued on this law until 1984. But the parents were discovering what was happening to their children, and they didn't like it. They discovered that these psychological manipulations in the classroom constituted a continuing attack on their religion, on their morals, on their family, and even on parents. We believe that the continuing attack is so gross as to rise to the level of a violation of the First Amendment rights of parents and their children.

14   What happened is best illustrated by the classic lifeboat game presented in Sidney Simon's book on Values Clarification, and probably used in every school in this country. I had a reporter tell me that she had some variation of it at every level of elementary and secondary education. This is the game where the child is taught that ten people are in a sinking lifeboat, and the child must throw five of them out to drown. What five will you kill? Will it be the senior citizen, or the policeman, or the pregnant woman, or the college co-ed, or the black militant, or whoever? You pick *which* you will kill.

15   This "game" is played widely, in many variations—the fallout shelter, the kidney machine, starting a new race, and so forth. To explain what's wrong about this game, we have the example of the child who answered the lifeboat problem by saying, "Jesus brought another boat, and nobody had to drown." That child was creative but she got an "F" on her paper. That explains what values clarification does. It is not value neutral in any shape or form. It is a direct attack on the religion and the values of those of us who believe that God created us, and that it is not up to the child to play God and decide who lives and who dies.

16   The curriculum is filled with these moral dilemmas. The reason we know about so many of them is that, in 1984, the Department of Education conducted hearings across the country, where parents could come and describe what had happened to their own children. Those hearings had no press, but you can read much of the testimony in my book called *Child Abuse in the Classroom.* They are the authentic testimonies of parents. They told how the children were given such moral dilemmas as: stand up in class and give a good example of when it's okay to lie; write a paper on when it's all right to steal; discuss which kind of drugs you will take, how much and how many.

17   These moral dilemmas never tell the child that anything is wrong. The child is taken through all the areas of sex, with obscene descriptions, discussions, role-playing, and other psychological manipulations in the classroom. You can call this secular humanism, you can call it situation ethics, you can call it group therapy, you can call it psychological manipulation, you can call it counseling. You can call it no-name. But whatever it is, it is pervasive in the public schools, and it is a direct attack on the First Amendment rights of those who believe that God created us and that He created a moral law that we should obey. There's nothing neutral about the way values clarification is taught. The option that we should abide by God's law is never offered.

18   The Alabama textbook case (*Smith v. Board of School Commissioners of Mobile County*) finally brought out of the closet a situation that has been going on for 15 to 20 years, without media coverage or public attention. A previous speaker said how surprised he was to discover that home economics is about sex. Well, if you've been reading the textbooks, you would have known that. And that is why parents are so upset.

19   The issue in the Alabama textbook case was, simply, does the child who believes in God have the same rights in the public school classroom as the atheist?

20   In the 1985 case of *Wallace V. Jaffree,* the Supreme Court held that little atheist Jaffree had the right to be in the public school classroom and not be embarrassed when his peers said a prayer or spoke about God. In the Alabama textbook case, the U.S. District Court decision simply gave the child who believes in God the same rights as the atheist (but that decision was overturned

by the U.S. Court of Appeals). I believe that the child has a right to be in the public school classroom, and not have his religion, his morals, or his family, belittled or harassed, or told that they are irrelevant, or be presented with moral dilemmas which tell him that he can personally decide what is moral or legal.

21   We hear about teaching the child to make decisions. Of course, the child, if accosted by the drug peddler, must make a choice whether to buy or not. But it is so wrong to tell the child in class that he is capable of making a choice on an issue which the law has already decided. The schools should teach that the law has already decided that illegal drugs are bad and that he must not take drugs.

22   Since the First Amendment seems to prohibit the public schools from teaching a belief in God and His moral commandments, the school must also not be permitted to teach that there *isn't* any God, that God did *not* create the world, or that God did *not* give us His moral commandments.

23   If you look at what was involved in the textbooks in the Alabama case, you'll find textbooks saying that "what is right or wrong depends more on your own judgment than on what someone tells you to do." That's a direct attack on religion. One book tells the teacher to design a bulletin board showing conflicting values held by young people and their parents. This is mischief-making between the child and his parents.

24   Another textbook teaches that a family is a group of people who live together. That's not what a family is. A family starts with a marriage between a man and a woman. We find one textbook telling a child that, "in democratic families, every member has a voice in running the family, and parents and teenagers should decide together about curfews, study time, chores, allowances, and use of the car." Where does anybody get the idea that the school can tell the child that he's got a right to decide when he uses the car?

25   Here's another one. "Steps in decision-making can apply to something so simple as buying a new pair of shoes. They can also be applied to more complex decisions which involve religious preferences, use of alcohol, tobacco, and drugs." Where did anyone get the idea that schools can teach children that the family should be democratic and that children should participate in making such decisions?

26   Here's a quotation from another Alabama textbook: "In the past, families were often like dictatorships. One person, or two, made all the decisions." Is that mischief-making? You bet it's mischief-making.

27   Here's a quotation from another textbook: "People who have strong prejudices are called bigots. Bigots are devoted to their own church, party, or belief." That really puts your parents down, doesn't it!

28   Another textbook seems to say that it's okay if people want to experience parenthood without marrying. A long passage from another textbook says that divorce is an acceptable way of solving a problem. Then it calls on the class to role-play the circumstances that might lead the child to choose a divorce. The school has no right to attack the morals of children by telling them that divorce is acceptable.

29   Actually, the Alabama school textbooks are probably pretty mild compared to a lot of others we find around the rest of the country. In Seattle we found a textbook which said that promiscuity should not be labeled good or bad, that premarital sexual intercourse is acceptable for both men and women, that morality is individual—it's what you think it is, that homosexuality is okay, that prostitution should be legalized, that it is not deviant for teenagers to watch others performing sex acts through binoculars or windows, that alternatives to traditional marriage such as group sex and open marriage are okay, and then asks the child if he'd like to join such a group.

30   It took 18 months and finally some TV cameras, to get the curriculum committee to say the school would replace that textbook. It had been the textbook in a mandatory course in the Seattle public school system from 1978 to 1987.

31   Your New York City School Board video, "Sex, Drugs and AIDS," has been so controversial in New York that it is now being revised. But the original version has now gone all over the country. It blows my mind to think that anybody could believe it is constitutional to present a video in the public school classroom teaching children that fornication and sodomy are acceptable behavior so long as you use condoms, and telling them that homosexuality is all right, which is exactly what that video does. It is hard to believe that anybody could approve such an evil video for use in the public school classroom. The video is a direct attack on the First Amendment rights of those who believe that fornication and sodomy are wrong.

32   We want the same rights for people who believe in God and His commandments as the atheist has already established. Whatever you call it, this no-name ideology, it all boils down to an attack on religion, a war on parental rights, and a betrayal of trust. What a terrible thing it is to indicate, imply or even tell children that sexual intercourse, outside marriage, with males or females, of the same sex or the opposite sex, is okay and socially acceptable! Yet, that is widely taught in the public schools across the country.

33   The general attitude of most public school administrators, when parents make objections is: If you don't like it, take your child out and send him to a private school. That is not an acceptable answer. Our position is that the child who believes in God and His commandments has a right to be in the public school classroom without having his religion, his morals, and his family degraded, belittled, subjected to "clarification" or role-playing, or subjected to any of the psychological dilemmas that are presented by authority figures, who tell them in every possible way, overtly and indirectly, that there is no right or wrong answer, that anything the little fifth grader decides will be perfectly all right.

34   While the public schools, with their great battery of lawyers, may be able to win in the courts, and the media are clearly on their side, these cases are not increasing respect for the public schools. These cases have brought into public debate issues which should have been debated for the last 20 years.

35   **Question:** Whose morality are we going to be teaching in the public schools, and do you recognize that your personal morality may not be the morality of a majority of the other citizens in that community, and what would be the mechanism that you would establish in order to decide what morality should be taught in school?

36   **Mrs. Schlafly:** I think you heard me say I wasn't trying to impose my morality on the schools, and there wasn't anything in my remarks that could have possibly led you to believe that I'm trying to do that. I feel that the public schools can teach consensual values as indicated by the laws in this country. For example, it is a crime to lie, steal, cheat, kill, destroy property. It is against the law, in at least half the states, to engage in fornication or sodomy. At the very least, the public schools can teach that you should not do things which are illegal. Unfortunately, that is generally not done in the drug education courses. I've examined hundreds of these drug ed courses. They teach the child that we're in a drug society, that everybody takes drugs, that it's simply a question of how many you take and which kind, that it's up to you, little child, to make your own decision. This is called "critical thinking" or "decision-making skills," but they don't tell children that drugs are wrong. I see no problem with teaching children that acts are wrong when they are illegal. Schools are now telling children that smoking is not preferable. In the sex courses, schools are definitely teaching that it is wrong to have a baby, but they are not teaching that fornication is wrong. Now, there's no constitutional difference between teaching that it's wrong to have a baby and teaching that sex with unmarried teenagers is wrong. So, my answer to that question is that, if schools would simply teach the criminal law version of morality in this country, we would go a long way toward promoting civil order.

37   **Question:** In regard to AIDS education, what do we do? Do we live in the real world or do we live in a world of what should be?

38   **Mrs. Schlafly:** Anything taught about AIDS should meet four tests. It should be true, it should be healthy, it should be legal, and it should be consti-

tutional. If any public schools teach a child that sex with condoms is safe or healthy, they are telling them something that is not true. Just wait for the lawsuits that are going to come! Sex for teenagers is unhealthy for many reasons of which AIDS is only one. As I pointed out earlier, fornication and sodomy are illegal in about half the states. I believe it is unconstitutional to teach sex-with-condoms because the children who come from homes where they believe that premarital sex is wrong have a constitutional right to be in the public school and not have that belief diminished, harassed, or taught that something that they believe is immoral is socially acceptable. The schools have an obligation to teach only that which is true, healthy, legal and constitutional.

39   Dr. C. Everett Koop told the *Village Voice* that he has already discussed sodomy with his gifted nine-year-old grandson. If he wants to do that, that is his privilege, but he has no right to discuss sodomy with our nine-year-old children or grandchildren. That's what the New York video does, and that's what some people are trying to do all over this country. We should get this teaching out of the public school classroom because it isn't legal, it isn't constitutional, and it certainly isn't healthy.

40   **Question:** Is the remedy, then, for a parent to be able to bar a curriculum, or do you suggest a more restrained approach that a parent should have the right to opt his child out of a program?

41   **Mrs. Schlafly:** A parent should not have to opt his child out of the public school classroom. The child has a right to be in the public school classroom without being embarrassed by some teacher describing how to use condoms and how to engage in sex, or role-playing what to do when you get pregnant with an illegitimate baby, or discussing conflicts with your father or your mother. The child has a right to be in the public school classroom and not be subjected to that type of teaching by an authority figure.

42   **Question:** 85% of public school parents in a nationwide poll indicated that the public schools should teach a family living/sex education course. How can you deny these parents who want such a program in the schools?

43   **Mrs. Schlafly:** The 85% doesn't impress me at all because all Gallup and Harris polls say that at least 85% of the American people want prayer in the public schools. But the Supreme Court has said no. The atheist child not only has a right not to pray, he has a right to silence everybody else in the classroom. So, when we're talking about religion or attacks on religion, the one person, apparently, can silence the rest. As I said, those who believe in God and His moral law, including about sex, have a right to be in the public school classroom without having an authority figure telling them that fornication is acceptable behavior. Whether 85% want sex education becomes totally irrelevant because I see it as an unconstitutional attack on the First Amendment rights on those

who believe that discussed behaviors are wrong. Those parents who want to give their children contraceptives, that's their privilege, but the public school shouldn't do it.

44   My answer is that schools cannot appear to give social acceptance or authority acceptance to a behavior which is contrary to the faith and morals of a number of children. Whatever the school teaches must be true, healthy, legal, and constitutional.

45   You can make the same argument about drugs. Maybe half of your children are on drugs, but certainly we don't set up a room to pass out clean needles and tell them how to avoid some of the consequences. That isn't the way to teach. We should start by telling them that illegal drugs are bad and wrong and you shouldn't take them or they might kill you. The whole subject can be approached as a health measure. Furthermore, schools ought to teach that the consequences of sex fall twice as heavily on girls as on boys. The morals are the same, but the consequences are very different. It's contrary to feminist ideology to teach children that there's any difference between boys and girls. But little girls ought to be taught about the terrible price that girls pay in terms of the side effects of contraceptives, of abortion and its trauma, venereal diseases, the poverty, the cervical cancer, the emotional and psychological trauma. In all those ways, the girl pays twice as much.

A JUST WAR

George Bush

Prior to the start of the war with Iraq on January 16, 1991, many "advocates and opponents of war resorted—at least implicitly—to the distinctions and categories of just-war thinking" (*Newsweek*, February 11, 1991, p. 47). On January 28, 1991, in an address to over 1000 delegates at the conservative National Religious Broadcasters annual conference in Washington, D.C., President George Bush explicitly and at length employed the "just war" doctrine to defend American and coalition military action. He advocates the value judgment that the war with

---

✝The text of this speech is reprinted from *Weekly Compilation of Presidential Documents*, 27 (February 4, 1991): 87–89.

Iraq "is a just war" (par. 8, 22) and he applies the traditional value criteria for such a war.

President Bush is speaking to a friendly audience (2, 4) and he reinforces values (3) and policy positions that he and the audience share (5–6). As he begins his argument, he employs antithetical phrasing to underscore the moral conflict involved and he describes the roots of the just war doctrine in Greco-Roman philosophy and Christian theology (8). A morally just war, the doctrine holds, should be waged only: (1) for a morally just cause; (2) when approved by a legitimate authority; (3) as a last resort when all peaceful alternatives have been exhausted; (4) when the good achieved outweighs the bad side-effects; (5) when the war is waged with just means; and (6) when there is a reasonable chance for success.

To develop his contention that the war with Iraq is a noble and just cause, Bush discusses the purposes and motivations of American military action (9–10, 13). Toward the end of the speech, he uses a quotation from Abraham Lincoln to stress again the morality of the cause (24). The President then cites twelve United Nations resolutions and the united agreement of twenty-eight nations from six continents to show that the war is approved by legitimate authority (11–12).

Bush employs a compact summary of statistics and examples to demonstrate that peaceful diplomatic efforts have been exhausted. (14–15). In contrast, in his speech to the nation on January 16 announcing the start of the war, the thrust of his argument focuses not only on exhausted diplomatic efforts but also on the failure of economic and political sanctions against Iraq. In fact the tone of that speech is very pragmatic and his rationale is not at all placed in the context of a morally just war. Bush's speech on January 16 stresses pragmatic necessity—circumstances now dictate that we have no choice but to go to war with Iraq. Why might the President have used a primarily pragmatic justification in announcing the war and a full-blown moral argument here?

That the greater good of thwarting the threat posed by Saddam Hussein can be achieved through just means with minimal bad side-effects is a contention developed through Bush's pledge to minimize casualties, act humanely, and "avoid hurting the innocent" (16–17). Finally, Bush argues that there is a reasonable chance of success—that victory can be achieved—by pledging that it will be a relatively short and decisive war (not another Vietnam) and by reminding the audience of the high quality of America's military forces (18–19).

In what ways and to what extent do you agree or disagree that Bush proved his value judgment that the war with Iraq was a morally just war? Also consider the role in war rhetoric throughout American history of what critic Robert Ivie terms "images of savagery"—images of "cunning but otherwise irrational enemies who are driven to circumvent all the restraints of international law and of human principles in order to impose their will on others." (See Robert L. Ivie, "Images of Savagery in American Justifications for War," *Communication Monographs*, 47 (November 1980): 279–294; also see Ivie, "Presidential Motives for War," *Quarterly Journal of Speech*, 60 (October 1974): 337–345.) What rhetorical functions in this speech might be served by such images as "naked aggression"; "the rape, the pillage, the plunder"; "wanton, barbaric bombing of civilian areas"; and "indiscriminate use" (9, 13–14, 17)? Also see David E. Decosse, *But Was It Just? Reflections on the Morality of the Persian Gulf War* (New York: Doubleday, 1992); Kathleen M. German, "Invoking the Glorious War: Framing the Persian Gulf Conflict Through Directive Language," *Southern Communication Journal*, 60 (Summer 1995): 292–302.

This speech by President Bush to the National Religious Broadcasters was given on the morning of January 28 and was covered live only by the CNN television network. On the evening of the next day, January 29, 1991, via major network television and radio coverage, President Bush presented the annual State of the Union message to the nation. In his lengthy State of the Union speech on both domestic and international topics, Bush does indirectly and implicitly touch on some of the standards for a just war but does not explicitly and clearly apply the just war criteria. In place of the tone of morality pervading the January 28 speech, there remains in the State of the Union address a simple summary alluding to the more complex argument of the previous day: "Our cause is just. Our cause is moral. Our cause is right." The morning hour and the coverage only on CNN severely limited the exposure of the general citizenry to the explicit just war argument of Bush's January 28 speech. Why might the President have decided not to use the same explicit and overtly developed just war argument in his State of the Union address to the nation the next night?

---

1   Thank you, President Rose, thank you, sir, and Executive Director Gustavson—all. First, let me salute your leadership of the NRB: Billy Graham and Jerry Falwell, Pat Robertson, James Dobson, Chuck Colson; and FCC Commissioners: Sikes and Duggan and James Quello.

2 This marks the fifth time that I've addressed the annual convention of the National Religious Broadcasters. And once again, let me say it is, for both Barbara and me, an honor to be back here.

3 Let me begin by congratulating you on your theme of declaring His glory to all nations. It's a theme eclipsing denominations and which reflects many of the eternal teachings in the Scripture. I speak, of course, of the teachings which uphold moral values like tolerance, compassion, faith, and courage. They remind us that while God can live without man, man cannot live without God. His love and His justice inspire in us a yearning for faith and a compassion for the weak and oppressed, as well as the courage and conviction to oppose tyranny and injustice.

4 And I'm very grateful for that resolution that has just been read prior to my speaking here.

5 Matthew also reminds us in these times that the meek shall inherit the Earth. At home, these values imbue the policies which you and I support. Like me, you endorse adoption, not abortion. And last year you helped ensure that the options of religious-based child care will not be restricted or eliminated by the Federal Government.

6 And I commend your concern, your heartfelt concern, on behalf of Americans with disabilities, and your belief that students who go to school to nourish their minds should also be allowed to nourish their souls. And I have not lessened my commitment to restoring voluntary prayer in our schools.

7 These actions can make America a kinder and gentler place because they reaffirm the values that I spoke of earlier, values that must be central to the lives of every individual and the life of every nation. The clergyman Richard Cecil once said, "There are two classes of

George Bush in the campaign for the 1980 Republican presidential nomination. Photo used with permission of SIPA PRESS/Art Resource, NY.

the wise: the men who serve God because they have found Him, and the men who seek Him because they have not found Him yet." Abroad, as in America, our task is to serve and seek wisely through the policies we pursue.

8   Nowhere is this more true than in the Persian Gulf where—despite protestations of Saddam Hussein—it is not Iraq against the United States, it's the regime of Saddam Hussein against the rest of the world. Saddam tried to cast this conflict as a religious war, but it has nothing to do with religion per se. It has, on the other hand, everything to do with what religion embodies: good versus evil, right versus wrong, human dignity and freedom versus tyranny and oppression. The war in the Gulf is not a Christian war, a Jewish war, or a Moslem war; it is a just war. And it is a war with which good will prevail. We're told that the principles of a just war originated with classical Greek and Roman philosophers like Plato and Cicero. And later they were expounded by such Christian theologians as Ambrose, Augustine, Thomas Aquinas.

9   The first principle of a just war is that it support a just cause. Our cause could not be more noble. We seek Iraq's withdrawal from Kuwait—completely, immediately, and without condition; the restoration of Kuwait's legitimate government; and the security and stability of the Gulf. We will see that Kuwait once again is free, that the nightmare of Iraq's occupation has ended, and that naked aggression will not be rewarded.

10   We seek nothing for ourselves. As I have said, U.S. forces will leave as soon as their mission is over, as soon as they are no longer needed or desired. And let me add, we do not seek the destruction of Iraq. We have respect for the people of Iraq, for the importance of Iraq in the region. We do not want a country so destabilized that Iraq itself could be a target for aggression.

11   But a just war must also be declared by legitimate authority. Operation Desert Storm is supported by unprecedented United Nations solidarity, the principle of collective self-defense, 12 Security Council resolutions, and in the Gulf, 28 nations from 6 continents united, resolute that we will not waver and that Saddam's aggression will not stand.

12   I salute the aid—economic and military—from countries who have joined in this unprecedented effort, whose courage and sacrifice have inspired the world. We're not going it alone, but believe me, we are going to see it through.

13   Every war—every war—is fought for a reason. But a just war is fought for the right reasons, for moral, not selfish reasons. Let me take a moment to tell you a story, a tragic story, about a family whose two sons, 18 and 19, reportedly refused to lower the Kuwaiti flag in front of their home. For this crime, they were executed by the Iraqis. Then, unbelievably, their parents were asked to pay the price of the bullets used to kill them.

14   Some ask whether it's moral to use force to stop the rape, the pillage, the plunder of Kuwait. And my answer: Extraordinary diplomatic efforts having been exhausted to resolve the matter peacefully, then the use of force is moral.

15   A just war must be a last resort. As I have often said, we did not want war. But you all know the verse from Ecclesiastes—there is "a time for peace, a time for war." From August 2, 1990—last summer, August 2d—to January 15, 1991—166 days—we tried to resolve this conflict. Secretary of State Jim Baker made an extraordinary effort to achieve peace: more than 200 meetings with foreign dignitaries; 10 diplomatic missions; 6 congressional appearances; over 103,000 miles traveled to talk with, among others, members of the United Nations, the Arab League, and the European Community. And sadly, Saddam Hussein rejected out of hand every overture made by the United States and by other countries as well. He made this just war an inevitable war.

16   We all know that war never comes easy or cheap. War is never without the loss of innocent life. And that is war's greatest tragedy. But when a war must be fought for the greater good, it is our gravest obligation to conduct a war in proportion to the threat. And that is why we must act reasonably, humanely, and make every effort possible to keep casualties to a minimum. And we've done so. I'm very proud of our military in achieving this end.

17   From the very first day of the war, the allies have waged war against Saddam's military. We are doing everything possible, believe me, to avoid hurting the innocent. Saddam's response: wanton, barbaric bombing of civilian areas. America and her allies value life. We pray that Saddam Hussein will see reason. To date, his indiscriminate use of those Scud missiles—nothing more than weapons of terror, they can offer no military advantage—weapons of terror—it outraged the world what he has done.

18   The price of war is always high. And so, it must never, ever, be undertaken without total commitment to a successful outcome. It is only justified when victory can be achieved. I have pledged that this will not be another Vietnam. And let me reassure you here today, it won't be another Vietnam.

19   We are fortunate, we are very fortunate, to have in this crisis the finest armed forces ever assembled, an all-volunteer force, joined by courageous allies. And we will prevail because we have the finest soldiers, sailors, airmen, marines, and coastguardsmen that any nation has ever had.

20   But above all, we will prevail because of the support of the American people, armed with a trust in God and in the principles that make men free— people like each of you in this room. I salute Voice of Hope's live radio programming for U.S. and allied troops in the Gulf, and your Operation Desert Prayer, and worship services for our troops held by among others, the man who over a week ago led a wonderful prayer service at Fort Myer over here across the river in Virginia, the Reverend Billy Graham.

21   America has always been a religious nation, perhaps never more than now. Just look at the last several weeks—churches, synagogues, mosques reporting record attendance at services; chapels packed during working hours as Americans stop in for a moment or two. Why? To pray for peace. And I know— of course, I know—that some disagree with the course that I've taken, and I have no bitterness in my heart about that at all, no anger. I am convinced that we are doing the right thing. And tolerance is a virtue, not a vice.

22   But with the support and prayers of so many, there can be no question in the minds of our soldiers or in the minds of our enemy about what Americans think. We know that this is a just war. And we know that, God willing, this is a war we will win. But most of all, we know that ours would not be the land of the free if it were not also the home of the brave. No one wanted war less than I did. No one is more determined to seize from battle the real peace that can offer hope, that can create a new world order.

23   When this war is over, the United States, its credibility and its reliability restored, will have a key leadership role in helping to bring peace to the rest of the Middle East. And I have been honored to serve as President of this great nation for 2 years now and believe more than ever that one cannot be America's President without trust in God. I cannot imagine a world, a life, without the presence of the One through whom all things are possible.

24   During the darkest days of the Civil War, a man we revere not merely for what he did but what he was, was asked whether he thought the Lord was on his side. And said Abraham Lincoln: "My concern is not whether God is on our side, but whether we are on God's side." My fellow Americans, I firmly believe in my heart of hearts that times will soon be on the side of peace because the world is overwhelmingly on the side of God.

25   Thank you for this occasion. And may God bless our great country. And please remember all of our coalition's armed forces in your prayers. Thank you, and God bless you.

Joy in Our Times

Georgie Anne Geyer

Georgie Anne Geyer is an internationally respected foreign correspondent and syndicated news columnist. She has regularly appeared
as a panelist or questioner on such television news programs as Washington Week in Review and Meet the Press. In 1983 she published her
autobiography, *Buying the Night Flight.* On May 7, 1989 Geyer delivered this address at the annual commencement ceremonies of Saint
Mary-of-the Woods College, a small Roman Catholic liberal arts college
for women located in the Indiana town of the same name.

The typical commencement speech has earned a reputation for
dullness, triteness, and irrelevance. But this need not be the case. Creative and sensitive commencement speakers genuinely can praise, inspire, and challenge the graduates rather than bore them with irrelevant
examples, cliché phrases, stereotyped images, and sleep-inducing plat-
itudes. Among the expectations that an audience may hold concerning
speeches that honor graduates for completion of a course of study are
the following. (1) Praise for the individual and collective achievements
of the class. (2) A call to use the knowledge and skill they have acquired
in innovative, humane, and socially worthy ways. (3) Description of the
significant challenges, problems, or opportunities facing the graduates;
this may include criticism of existing societal conditions or forces.
(4) Creative interweaving of realism and idealism—of telling it like it is
and envisioning how it ought to be. (5) Reinforcement of commitment
to values already held by the audience; or perhaps more often advocacy
of a set of values to be adopted by the audience in preference to less desirable (but more currently popular) values.

Clearly Georgie Anne Geyer advocates adoption of a value (joy)
and its components (risk-taking; historical and personal perspective; appropriate timing; wise choices; and love). These values are contrasted
to pervasive but less desirable values such as selfishness, isolated individualism, and desperate approval of others (paragraphs 3, 4, 8, 14, 20).
What assessment could you make of her speech in light of the other four

✝Reprinted with permission from *Vital Speeches of the Day,* August 15, 1989, pp. 666–668.

commonly held audience expectations for a good commencement speech?

How adequately does Geyer clarify and justify the values that she advocates? Processes of definition are central to her persuasive effort. Among her definitional techniques are dictionary meaning, descriptive explanation, and negation (5); she also uses personal examples (11–12) and identification of elements that foster joy (15, 17, 21, 23, 28). Geyer's use of narration—of stories and illustrations—is so widespread as to strongly invite, indeed demand, the attention both of the audience and the rhetorical critic (1–2, 12–13, 16, 19, 22, 24–26). How clear, relevant, and effective are the stories she tells?

Speaker credibility is a vital factor in speeches that propose a value judgment or advocate adoption of values. In addition to the positive reputation that Geyer probably had with her audience prior to the speech, assess the appropriateness and effectiveness of sections of her speech that function to reinforce that high credibility (10, 24–26). Also consider what rhetorical functions are served—what communicative work is done—by such stylistic resources as antithesis (5, 7, 18), alliteration (28, 29), parallel structure (10, 30), and questions (4, 9, 14).

---

1   Three months ago, I walked into my condominium in downtown Washington and happened to see the great Russian/American conductor, Mstislav Rostropovich, standing at our front desk. We are proud that he lives there. He is always a man filled with life and spirit, but this day he had the most marked look of pure joy on his face that I had ever had the . . . well . . . joy of seeing.

2   After greeting me, he stood for a few minutes at the desk and repeated several times, as if in sheer wonder, "Last night, I conducted 250 cellists. . . . Last night, I conducted 250 cellists. . . ." Ladies and gentlemen, at that moment I knew that I had seen as close to a beatific joy as I have ever seen, next to certain pictures of Christ. For I discovered then that this great musician, who is a cellist, had conducted at the world conference of 5,000 cellists!

3   That magical moment—that blessed moment—made me think of our younger generation today—of your generation—and I wondered if any of them, of you, would understand that kind of joy. For when I go around to schools—and to the very best and most serious schools—what even our best young people ask me is things like, "Miss Geyer, what are they looking for out there?" In short, in place of that inner joy of Rostropovich's which knew his love for his music and for his cello, many young people of your generation instead

are looking and waiting for some elusive and fickle "someone" out there to tell them what they are.

4 "What are they looking for out there?" That is one phrase that will warn you if you let it of what NOT to be thinking, even in today's often treacherous world. Some others? "How can I get ahead? What's in it for me? Let's get him." And, "How can I stop being bored? What company can I take over today? How much will I make? What's in it for me?"

5 Let us, for a moment, consider "Joy." My dictionary says that it is the emotion excited by the acquisition or expectation of good." I like that. Not the acquisition of things, or of power, or of a handsome husband, or of importance of position, but of good. It is right action, rather than merely the paltry fruit of any action. It is the magical and mystical act of discovering and finally knowing the God-given talents and the artistry that is inside yourself and nurturing and expressing them rather than trying vainly to find out what "society," whatever that is, fashionably at that moment, wants. Aristotle said that happiness is an activity that is "in accordance with virtue." Vince Lombardi, more in tune with our times, said that "happiness is winning." Donald Trump carried it to the zenith of our times' senselessness and anomie, saying that it's not "whether you win or lose, it's winning."

6 Let me say right off that I think the search for joy—and, remember, that only in America is the "pursuit of happiness" assured in the very Constitution itself—is very difficult for all Americans, young and old, today. Dr. Joseph Plummber, an authority on values, recently put out a study listing profound changes in our basic American values. He found that more people in the developed Western nations were seeking self-actualization rather than security or traditionally defined success. He found a self-fulfillment ethic, individualized definitions of success, a growing sense of limits . . . .

7 Now, this is all right so long as it is associated with principles, with "good," and with the courage to carry it through, for, as Churchill said, "Courage is the most important virtue, because it GUARANTEES all the rest." Instead, I see many Americans terrified by risk, thinking apparently that a life without risk really IS possible. We see the mother who drank half a bottle of Jim Beam whiskey every day during her pregnancy and is suing the company because her poor child is deformed. I see a remarkable amount of lack of joy, of gamesplaying instead of principle and of cases where the grand principle of equality has been debased to no more than equality of appetite.

8 And I see the warning of Alexis de Tocqueville about excessive individualism being realized. Two centuries ago the brilliant Frenchman warned of the democracy that he so admired that it held within it the seeds of its own demise. "Not only does democracy make every man forget his ancestors," he

wrote, "but hides his descendants and separates his contemporaries from him; it throws him back forever upon himself alone and threatens in the end to confine him entirely within the solitude of his heart." That isolation, ladies and gentlemen, graduates and friends, is not democracy but a perverted democracy that looks to others desperately for approval, that looks not to a work one loves but to a lottery and to chance for succor, and that creates a person afraid to take the joy to live in one's time, and equally incapable of living fully either in one's own self—or in community, for the common good.

9   Amidst all the good we have in our country, our churches and our lives, nevertheless today I also find this wanting. Where is joy? What is joy? Permit me to muse, modestly, on what I have learned through living an unorthodox life, about joy.

10   So I was the first woman foreign correspondent and syndicated columnist in our time. So I had to break ground and sometimes face barriers put up against me. So I lost a number of fiances because of my love for understanding other countries, because of my liking for hotels and plane rides across the Red Seas of the world. So one of them once said in irk, "Gee Gee, the most beautiful words in the world to you are not, 'I love you' but 'Room Service, Please.' "

11   That meant that everybody was always and is still asking me, "Didn't you feel bitter about it?" I have thought about that. Bitter? It never crossed my mind to be bitter. I was having so much fun, I was so filled with spirit and joy, I thanked God every day for the very privilege of being able to know everyone in the world and for being able to do this work I so loved. And if the Sisters of Providence will forgive me a wicked aside, I will add that the one thing your enemies can never forgive you is, not money, not even success, but having so much fun in life!

12   My joys were often the little things: Interviewing a Khomeini or a Castro, Sadat or a Duarte, yes, those were good professionally, and afterwards I felt a great sense of satisfaction for breaking through . . . But I would often experience pure joy in odd and unexpected places . . . Sitting at breakfast in Chile and quietly observing people and feeling so privileged to be there . . . being able to bring some message of truth about the world to my own people, something they didn't know . . . seeing an election in a war-torn El Salvador and watching the poor people dare everyone to go to vote . . . seeing Russia return to its own conscience—the inner conscience that was always there, waiting—as Gorbachev frees the Russian people these very days, before our eyes. . . .

13   I remember special messages that warmed me tremendously, like when I interviewed the late great Archbishop Oscar Romero of El Salvador in 1979. At one point, I asked this man, who seemed just to radiate goodness,

whether it would not have been easier to have stayed out of all the fights for social justice he had entered? And his simple but profound words: "Well, I could
have just stayed in the Archbishop's palace, but that would not have been very
EASY, would it?" It rang so very true. It would have been immeasurably harder,
just as it will be immeasurably harder for you, if you choose to live a life without the components of joy.

14   But—what are those components? And why are they so hard to come
by in our "fun-loving . . . non risk taking . . . gamesplaying . . . world?"

15   —RISK TAKING. First and very important, being able to feel joy involves risk taking, and I do not mean juggling monies around frenziedly in the
stock market. It means risking your popularity by taking a genuinely unpopu-
lar stand, risking your life to do what it is that YOU want to do in life. Risks are
going to be there anyway. It's just street sense to take them on your terms, not
theirs. In warfare, it is called being on the offensive. In life, it is called embracing life with all your heart.

16   Along these lines, I recall one spring day seven years ago when I was
going to Central America—again. I just had a gut feeling that I did not want to
go to El Salvador, because there had been so much fighting there. Usually I
don't obey fearful feelings, having found that they pass and are not really accurate, but this time I did. So I took the plane to Nicaragua, and that week nothing at all happened in Salvador—and when I got to the Managua airport, I was
standing second in line to pass through to the center of the airport . . . and the
airport was blown up! I never try to second-guess fate again after that!

17   —PERSPECTIVE. What, you may ask, does perspective have to do
with joy? Well, a whole lot!

18   Young people are always asking me how I "control" (a favorite word
of your generation) my interviews. And I always answer, "Knowing more than
they do." This is not, repeat not, a popular answer, but it is genuine and work-
able. I know history—so nothing surprises me. I know where things are, why
and where they will be. The perspective of history—of all human life—gives me
a terrifying confidence. Knowing the trajectory of mankind—its victories, its
sordid defeats, its searchings for God and for meaning—I cannot be a utopian,
which is dangerous anyway, but I also cannot be a pessimist. I see how far we
have come, I can take joy in what we can accomplish in our lifetimes, because I
know and understand the limits of what we can do.

19   Once I wrote a good friend, a Jesuit priest in Latin America, about
how discouraged I was about how Latin America was going and he wrote back
these very wise words, "Remember, Gee Gee, I am not responsible for the outcome, but I am responsible for my own fight." That's it. That's what I know.
And that very simple perspective allows one to have joy in what one IS able to

do and not to moan and mourn over not being able to do the impossible. Because we cannot be perfect, that does not mean we cannot be good.

20   Perspective comes at you from the funniest, most unexpected places. In Finland last fall, I went to see this fine artist, Bjorn Weckstrom, and he explained to me, as no one else quite has, how we have come to this point, where so many search not for deeper meaning or for joy but "to do something, just to be someone for a moment." "A hundred years ago," Bjorn said, "people were living in small communities. Everyone had an identity known by the whole village. The group created the morals, the rules . . . Even your name was taken from your father—you were 'son of . . .' Now the frames are eliminated. People are desperate, living in this super tribe. The village was an enormous security for people. In a way it gave people stability and a kind of harmony in life. The problem has been to create something new which would replace this . . . Before, it was enough to be recognized for what you do before the village. But now the borders of the tribe have been moving out. Now to be somebody you have to be on television. It is the problem of the identity of man today, the need to be someone even for a short moment. Even if man knows he's almost at the end of his rope. . . ." And, of course, the amorphous, unseen, cruelly judgmental audience of the TV is a harsh audience indeed, compared to the village—and the person never really knows, in this new audience, whether what he has done is good or not. And it really doesn't matter, for this audience more than likely has already long succumbed to the lowest value of the collective will.

21   —TIMING. Understanding the right time for an idea, for a painting, for doing something—it is critical. It is an instinct, it comes from within people in whom street sense has been blended blessedly with intellectual searching. It is critical for work and it is critical for personal relationships. Too often today, we want to rush work, rush relationships, become managing editor at 32, editor at 35 . . . And later, we wonder where we have been, or whether we've been anywhere at all.

22   I talked with a young man the other day, who happened to be a fundamentalist Christian. He spoke of how important the three years before marriage to his wife had been, when they were not making love. "We got to know each other in a way at that time that we could never have known otherwise," he told me. "When you go to bed too soon, you lose all kinds of precious levels of the development of a relationship." He was so right. The Bible has a lot about this. "There is a time to . . . and a time . . ."

23   —CHOICES. I have found through life that a truly joyful person is willing to make choices on the basis of what he knows, then stick with them, and change them if he must. It is a terribly unjoyful life, not to be able to make choices, not to have the inner confidence.

24   That recalls the most interesting evening I had, four years ago, when I was asked to drive the late Clair Booth Luce to a dinner party. I was delighted, for here was one of the truly great women of our time, a woman who had done just about everything. . . . Mrs. Luce was not, repeat not, a woman you contradicted or, as I soon found out, even questioned. As soon as she got in the car, she was throwing very pointed and brilliant one-liners at me. She obviously had a message for me. In fact, she repeated it several times.

25   "You did it right." she said. "You spent 20 years doing what you do best." When I tried to remonstrate with this woman who had been ambassador, playwright, journalist, novelist, wife, mother, she disdained the suggestion. "No," she said, "I could have been a great playwright, I could have been a great playwright. . . ."

26   I am not suggesting that Mrs. Luce was right. Personally, I feel deeply what I have had to give up for what I wanted most. I am suggesting that wise people at different times in their lives realize that we all make choices, even when we think we are not making them; so, again, it is better to embrace them than to run from them. I dedicate that story to our noble older women graduates here today, who I know have had to make many, many choices and are still courageously making them, as their presence here attests.

27   And think, women of my generation—think of what we have seen! We have seen the first age when women have sought to define THEMSELVES! All through history, men have defined us. Finally, we are taking responsibility for ourselves! Easy? How could it be easy. And yet, we have finally arrived at trying to know and understand the ultimate political relationship, which is the ecstatic but endlessly bedeviling relationship between men and women and we have finally arrived at the moment, as the poet Louise Bogan puts it so beautifully, of women giving back to the world "half of its soul." Which brings me to . . .

28   —LOVE. Finally, love! There is really only one thing that I know to tell you graduates—only one thing—and that is to FOLLOW WHAT YOU LOVE! Follow it intellectually! Follow it sensuously! Follow it with generosity and nobility toward your fellow man! Don't deign to ask what "they" are looking for out there. Ask what you have inside. I was blessed—I was blessed because I knew what I loved—writing, my countries, being a courier between cultures—and I had dogged determination to follow it. Doing what you love, whether it is having children, working in a profession, being a nun, being a journalist, is all encompassing, all engrossing, it is like a very great love affair occurring every day. It is principle and creation, you know why you are here, your personal life and your professional life is all one. It is not fun, not games, not winning or losing, not making money or having your 15 minutes on television; it is what no one can ever, ever take away from you, it is . . . pure joy.

29   In closing, I would like to ask you just to look around you today . . . to relish and preserve in your mind's eye and your memory this treasured moment at this quintessentially beautiful school.

30   Never again will you graduates be at this pure moment of your existence, when all the roads are open to you. Perhaps never again will you have friends and comrades, and teachers and sisters, as pure in their friendship because no one is yet what he or she is going to become. Never again probably will your families be quite so specially proud of you.

31   So, seize the moment joyfully. Follow not your interests, which change, but what you are and what you love, which will and should not change. And always remember these golden days.

32   God bless you all, and may the gods of the winds and the seas be with you on your voyage. Thank you.

CARING FOR CREATION: RELIGION AND ECOLOGY

Russell E. Train

As Chairman of the World Wildlife Fund and Conservation Foundation, Russell Train represents an organization with over 300,000 members—an organization that seeks to protect the biological resources on which human well-being depends. On May 18, 1990 Train presented this address at the closing session of the North American Conference on Religion and Ecology held in Washington, D.C. As is true of other speeches in this anthology, this speech legitimately could be evaluated from several critical viewpoints. It could, as discussed in Chapter 6, be analyzed primarily as attempting to create concern for environmental problems (paragraphs 12–14).

In our view, however, this speech primarily advocates propositions of value—it offers value judgments and advocates adoption of certain desirable values in contrast to less desirable values. After stressing that organized religion generally has been oblivious to and silent on envi-

---

✦This speech is reprinted with permission from *Vital Speeches of the Day*, August 15, 1990, pp. 664–666.

ronmental issues (3–4) and illustrating possible cooperative efforts (6), Train argues both early and late in the speech that organized religion should be the primary vehicle for instilling environmental values in people (4, 19, 22). He criticizes the value priorities imbedded in the Roman Catholic Church's birth control policies for contributing to ecological problems (11–12). Note his use of alliteration—the repetition of the same initial sound, usually a consonant, in a series of words in proximity. Often used to make an idea more memorable or to associate several positive or negative ideas, here alliteration stimulates negative associations (degrade, deface, desecrate, destroy). Train urges organized religion to readjust its value priorities to show equal concern for human and ecological issues (16). Very overtly he advocates specific values to be taught by organized religion (19) and he encourages adoption of them by describing the positive consequences of holding those values (20).

A key strategy in advocating his values and value judgments is the emphasis through diverse techniques in the interrelation and interdependence of human welfare and environmental welfare (15, 16). He develops the "web of life" metaphor (7) and presents creative twists on two common phrases: "facts of life" (9) and "right to life" (15). Train overtly employs representative examples (9—"their number could be almost infinite") and he accumulates a lengthy list of examples to underscore the massiveness of the threats to the environment (10).

Finally, consider the role of speaker credibility in this address. In what ways might some of his statements (2, 7) strengthen or weaken his credibility with his audience?

---

1   It is a privilege to address this closing event of the Conference on Caring for Creation on the subject of "Religion and the Environment." Following so many splendid speakers, it is highly doubtful that I will offer you anything very original. Anyway, someone has said that "the only secret of being original is not to reveal your sources."

2   I am neither a theologian nor a philosopher. For a good many years of my life, I was a relatively active layman in the Episcopal Church here in Washington, although something of a "backslider" in more recent years. It may have some significance that my absence from regular attendance at Sunday services dates back almost exactly to the time my wife and I purchased a farm on the Eastern Shore of Maryland. Suddenly, my weekends no longer included formal religious observance in church but instead were filled with the enjoyment of

fields and woods and water, the presence of wildlife, the rhythm of the seasons. And for the past 30 years I have been part of the environmental movement, both in government and in the private sector.

3   During much of this time, I have been puzzled—to say the least—by what has seemed to me the almost total obliviousness of organized religion toward the environment. It has been nothing less than extraordinary. Here we have had one of the most fundamental concerns to agitate human society within living memory—certainly in North America and Europe and increasingly around the globe. Here we have issues that go to the heart of the human condition, to the quality of human life, even to humanity's ultimate survival. Here we have problems that can be said to threaten the very integrity of Creation. And yet the churches and other institutions of organized religion have largely ignored the whole subject.

4   Of course, a number of thoughtful persons have over the past twenty years or so explored the interrelationship of religion and the environment, of human spirituality and nature. However, until recently, organized religion has remained largely silent and on the sidelines. Yet our churches, synagogues, temples, and mosques should be a principal vehicle for instilling environmental values in our planet's people. And, believe me, it is very much a matter of values.

5   To be fair, I must point out that the organized environmental movement has on its side largely ignored the potentially central role that religion can have in bringing about a new harmony between man and nature. Hopefully, an active partnership is now arising between the environmental and religious communities. This conference will help build that partnership.

6   It was in 1986 that the World Wide Fund for Nature (formerly called the World Wildlife Fund and still so called in the United States and Canada) brought together at Assisi representatives of the five major religions of the world—Christian, Jewish, Moslem, Hindu and Buddhist—to explore the development of a single, unified statement of religious responsibility toward nature. As you know, while a single statement did not prove practical at that time, each religion did its own statement consonant with its own beliefs and traditions, and these have been published in the *Assisi Declarations*. The Assisi experience was an exciting one, and it has been highly influential in bringing different religious groups to address their responsibility toward nature. In 1988, Pope John Paul II and the Dalai Lama met in Rome to discuss issues of "world peace, spiritual values, and protection of the earth's natural environment." A number of other initiatives have and are occurring, and I will not try to enumerate them here. At long last, religion seems to be awakening to the environment. I am delighted on this occasion to acknowledge that our honored guest,

H.R.H. The Duke of Edinburgh, was the principal moving force in bringing about Assisi and its continued follow-up.

7   I said earlier that I am neither a theologian nor a philosopher. Nor am I a scientist. Yet I know that our human life, its quality and its very existence, are totally dependent upon the natural systems of the Earth—the air, the water, the soils, the extraordinary diversity of plant and animal life—systems all driven by the energy of the sun. We could not exist without the support of these natural systems. Nor could any of the other forms of life with which we share the Earth. These are facts over which it seems to me there can be no argument. We are all part of a living community that is mutually dependent. All life exists in an infinitely complex set of interrelationships—truly a "web of life"—that we disturb at our peril.

8   We depend upon the air to supply us with oxygen we must breathe—oxygen that in turn is produced by the microorganisms in the surface of the ocean and by the vegetative cover of the land, particularly its tropical forests, often referred to as the "lungs of the planet." We depend for our sustenance on the productivity of the soil, whose fertility is in turn sustained by the nitrogen-fixing ability of soil bacteria. The humus essential to productive soils is of course the product of the work of other bacteria, beetles, worms, and such. (Size is clearly no measure of the importance of one's role in the planetary scheme. In fact, it is truly the little things that run the world!) Our grains and other crops, our orchards, and much of the world's forests depend for pollination and, thus, their continued existence upon insects, birds, and bats among other mammals—often highly specialized to serve the needs of a particular species of plant. The most valuable fruit crop of southeast Asia is *durian,* a $100 million-a-year crop, and it is pollinated entirely by bats. Birds and bats are responsible for eliminatng a high proportion of the world's destructive insects and weed seeds—far more than all the insecticides and herbicides we apply. Only last week, I read a news report that in Pakistan a species of owl, considered there a bird of ill omen, is responsible for controlling the rats and mice that would otherwise destroy a large part of the grain crop. A majority of our North American bird species, which provide us with such valuable (and free) services, migrate to Mexico and farther south in the winter. A number of these species are in substantial decline because of the destruction of the tropical forests on which they depend for winter habitat. And, of course, it is on the tropical forests that the entire planet depends for much of the production of oxygen and much of the sequestration of carbon which together in turn help maintain the life-sustaining quality of the global atmosphere.

9   These are a few examples—and their number could be almost infinite—to illustrate the dependence of human and other life on the natural sys-

tems of the Earth as well as the intricate interdependence of the living community as a whole. I feel it is important to be explicit about such examples because our increasingly urban population tends to take human self-sufficiency for granted and lives in almost total ignorance of the true "facts of life."

10   Given the historic tendency of the human race to put its own self-interest ahead of everything else and usually to measure that self-interest in the near term rather than the long term, it is probably not surprising that the natural systems of the Earth are under such dire threat today. You are no doubt familiar with the litany of environmental threats. A partial one would include the destruction of tropical forests, the loss of productive soils, the spread of deserts, declining supplies of fresh water, the depletion of ocean fisheries, the pervasive pollution of air, land and water, the accelerating extinction of species, the likelihood of global warming, and the depletion of the life-protecting stratospheric ozone layer. It should be pointed out that, in the case of stratospheric ozone depletion, which could have a catastrophic impact on life on Earth, the cause is purely and simply human technology—our refrigerants, air conditioners, fire extinguishers, spray propellants, etc. Finally, overarching all the other environmental threats, of course, is the burgeoning human population. And here again we clearly have no one to blame but ourselves, and here it is not so much our technology as the lack of its use.

11   As critical and seemingly intractable as environmental problems are today with 5.3 billion people on the face of the Earth, these problems will be compounded exponentially as we move inevitably to 11.3 billion and very likely to 14 billion by the end of the next century. And yet, Pope John Paul is reported to have declared last week in Mexico:

> If the possibility of conceiving a child is artifically eliminated in the conjugal act, couples shut themselves off from God and oppose His will.

12   Personally, I find it difficult to accept that it is the will of God that humanity should degrade, deface, desecrate, and ultimately, perhaps, destroy His Creation on Earth. Yet that is the course on which we are embarked. Almost every significant threat to the environment is contributed to and compounded by human numbers. Moreover, whatever other adverse impacts on the natural environment may result from the growth in sheer human numbers, such growth is necessarily accompanied by a reduction in space for other species, in the opportunity for other forms of life. Natural ecosystems do not have the capacity to absorb infinite numbers of species.

13   To me, the most grievous assault on the Earth's environment is the destruction of species—both plant and animal. It is the destruction of life itself, life which has evolved over hundreds of millions of years into a diversity of forms that stagger the imagination, life of a beauty and complexity that fill one with awe and wonder, life in which the Creation is surely manifest.

14   Some scientists today estimate that there are up to 30 million species of life on the Earth. Twenty to 30 percent of these are projected to vanish forever over the next very few years due in large part to human action and especially to the destruction of tropical forests. The eminent biologist, E. O. Wilson, has said: "The sin our descendants are least likely to forgive us is the loss of biological diversity."

15   We hear much today about the "right to life" and the phrase as normally employed seems to extend only to human life, as if the rest of life is somehow irrelevant. I have tried to develop the point that human life cannot exist in isolation from other forms of life, that our existence is, in fact, dependent upon those other forms of life. We are, indeed, part of a community of life and our apparent dominance as a species should not be permitted to obscure that fact. Putting it bluntly, anthropocentrism is simply irrational. And yet that is the thrust of much of our traditional religious thought and teaching, particularly in the West.

16   I do not suggest that the Christian church abandon its concern for humanity but that it give at least equal time to the rest of God's Creation and do so not as a concern that is separate and apart, but as one that recognizes that the welfare of any part, including the human part, is inseparable from the welfare of the whole; that it is the community as a whole for which we must necessarily care. We really have no other option in this regard. If we truly care for the human condition, then we must necessarily care for the rest of Creation on which humanity's well-being and even existence so clearly depend.

17   It is not enough in my mind to say that we should act as good stewards of the Earth. Stewardship suggests that we have a management responsibility and that smacks too much to me of the same anthropocentrism that has gotten us into trouble in the first place. After all, the planet got along very well indeed for a very long time without our managerial assistance. Indeed, you might say that the Earth has been a far better steward of the human race than vice versa. If the living community of the Earth operated on a democratic basis, I have no doubt the other members would quickly vote us out.

18   There is no doubt that humanity is now the dominant species on the Earth although there is no assurance that this is a permanent status. After all, *homo sapiens* has only been here about 250,000 years, a blink of the eye in evolutionary terms. Humanity today holds the fate of most other life in its hands, a reality that is awesome and should be humbling. Unfortunately, we are more apt to feel such power a mark of our success. I am afraid we have our values pretty much backwards in this regard.

19   And here it is, it seems to me, that the church should define its special role in environmental matters. In my own experience, family, school, and church were the principal transmitters of values in my early life. The church will seldom have the expertise and, thus, the credibility to involve itself in the increasingly technical and complex debates over environmental issues, whether involving clean air, toxic wastes, tropical forests, etc., but it does have the credibility and the historic mission of articulating and teaching values to society. The church should assume a major responsibility for teaching that we humans, individually and collectively, are part of the living community of the Earth that nurtures and sustains us; that humanity as well as all life depends for its very being upon the healthy functioning of the natural systems of the Earth; that all living things, including humans, are interdependent; that we have the duty, collectively and individually, to care for God's Creation and that in it lie all the creative possibilities for life now and in the future. These are precepts that could provide the substance for an Eleventh Commandment: Thou shalt cherish and care for the Earth and all within it.

20   Of course, adoption of such a set of values would require a fundamental change in the way we look at the world around us and at our relationship with it. Such values would be decidedly human values, not self-centered but providing positive guidelines for creative human outreach to the world and all within it. Such values would provide a logical framework within which human society can address the entire range of environmental problems facing the planet. And these values would provide the essential spiritual energy for effective action to address these problems.

21   And so it seems to me that the major challenge to religion as it addresses the environment is to give leadership to human understanding and acceptance of these essentially ecological values. It should do so in the curriculum of its seminaries, in the liturgy of its services, in its preaching from the pulpit, and in its teaching of the young. I suspect that a contributing factor in the failure of religion up to now to address these matters is that the clergy has not felt at home with them. Basic courses in ecology should be required in the seminaries and, as a matter of fact, throughout our education system. After all, ecology is nothing more than Creation at work.

22   Over the past twenty years, we have seen concern for environmental values institutionalized throughout much of our society—in government at all levels, in business, in the professions, in international agencies, in citizen environmental action, among other areas. It is now high time for the oldest human institutions of all, our religions, to make concern for nature—Caring for Creation—a central part of their doctrine and practice. I firmly believe that doing so could help revitalize society's commitment to religion, particularly among the young, and would help establish these fundamental values on which the future of the Earth and of ourselves so clearly depends.

THE ENVIRONMENTAL MOVEMENT: A SKEPTICAL VIEW

Virginia I. Postrel

"To a large degree, however, green ideology is not about facts. It is about values, and the environmental movement is about enforcing those values through political action." This argument highlights the central theme developed by Virginia I. Postrel in her speech to the City Club of Cleveland on June 19, 1990. As editor of *Reason Magazine,* she addressed an audience of men and women in leadership roles in the businesses and industries of Cleveland. *Reason Magazine* is published by the Reason Foundation which has as its goal the promotion of individualist philosophy and free market economic principles.

In taking a "skeptical view," Postrel identifies and attacks the central value underlying the "green" ideology of most environmental activists (7, 14–15, 29). Stasis or sustainability is the core value in a static view of "an ecosystem that has reached an unchanging climax stage." The values that a speaker advocates or condemns should be presented accurately and fairly. To what degree do you believe Postrel does so? Note that she is sensitive to the complexity of ideologies (11–12) and wants to demystify the green ideology (9–10).

Postrel's major strategy in attacking the core value of the green ideology is presentation of multiple undesirable consequences of adhering to that value (17). Green values, she contends, typically are enforced through government policies—often a single prescribed solution (18, 29). Green ideology overemphasizes both a crisis mentality (26–28) and feelings of guilt/sin (31–32). In the name of simplicity, green ideology promotes regression rather than progress (35–37). And most undesirable

---

+This speech is reprinted with permission from *Vital Speeches of the Day,* September 15, 1990, pp. 729–732.

of all, green ideology leads to extreme and radical programs for remaking human nature (41–43, 47–48, 51–52). Note how effectively she uses alliteration to associate the environmental movement with a negative concept: "environmentalists tolerate totalitarians in their midst."

Postrel's extensive use of quotations invites evaluation by a rhetorical critic. What type of person does she typically quote? What persuasive functions do such quotations seem to serve? Evidence to prove a point? Illustration to clarify a point? Would you question her use of any of the quotations? If so, on what grounds?

Often through contrast and antithesis, Postrel advocates a desirable value system to guide concern for the environment (19–20, 49). Her ideology embodies individual choice in pollution control, a dynamic and growth-oriented view, governmental encouragement of innovation, and the "common" or "ordinary" desire for a cleaner world through "tradeoffs," but not at all costs (7, 50).

Compare Virginia Postrel's speech with the previous one by Russell Train. Explore the ways in which the value systems advocated by them may be similar or clearly in conflict. Would Postrel probably condemn the values advocated by Train (19)? Why? Would she probably categorize the World Wildlife Fund as representative of the green movement? Note her statement: "Grassroots activists criticize the 'Gang of 10,' the large, well-funded environmental groups."

---

1   On Earth Day, Henry Allen of The *Washington Post* published a pointed and amusing article. In it, he suggested that we've created a new image of Mother Nature:

> A sort of combination of Joan Crawford in *Mildred Pierce* and Mrs. Portnoy in *Portnoy's Complaint*, a disappointed, long-suffering martyr who makes us wish, at least for her sake, that we'd never been born.
>
> She weeps. She threatens, She nags. . . .
>
> She's a kvetch who makes us feel guilty for eating Big Macs, dumping paint thinner down the cellar sink, driving to work instead of riding the bus, and riding the bus instead of riding a bicycle. Then she makes us feel even guiltier for not feeling guilty enough.
>
> *Go ahead, use that deodorant, don't even think about me, God knows I'll be gone soon enough, I won't be here to see you get skin cancer when the ozone hole lets in the ultraviolet rays . . .*

2   I think all of us can see that Allen is on to something. There's a lot of truth in his picture of the new Mother Nature.

3   The question is, Where did this New Mother Nature come from? And how does this picture of nature affect—even warp—the way we deal with environmental issues?

4   Americans have historically been a can-do people, proud of our Yankee ingenuity. We believe in solving problems. Based on our history, you'd expect to see us tackling environmental problems the way John Todd took on sewage sludge.

5   Todd is an environmental biologist who became concerned about the toxic sludge that comes out of sewage plants. Based on his biological research, he realized that the sludge could be cleaned up by mixing it with certain microbes. The microbes would metabolize it and produce clean water. Todd now has a pilot plant in Providence, Rhode Island, and he estimates that such a system could handle all of that city's sludge with 120 acres of reaction tanks—a modest number.

6   Now, if you're like me, you think this is great. Here is a bona fide environmental problem. An ingenious man with an environmental conscience has come along, put his ingenuity and training to work, and *solved the problem.* But rather than applauding Todd's solution, many of his friends in the environmental movement have stopped speaking to him. "By discovering a solution to a man-made offense," writes Gregg Easterbrook in *The New Republic,* "he takes away an argument against growth."

7   Todd's practical environmentalism has run up against what I refer to as "green" ideology. This ideology is distinct from the common desire for a cleaner world—that's why it can lead people to condemn solutions like Todd's. It is also different from the traditional doctrines of either the left or the right: It combines elements from each with a values system of its own.

8   This green ideology underlies many of the environmentalist critiques and policy recommendations that we see today. Now, I'm not suggesting that environmentalists are engaged in some sort of grand conspiracy or are governed by some lockstep system of thought. What I *am* suggesting is that if you want to understand a political movement, it's a good idea to read its theorists and find out who its intellectual heroes are.

9   Green ideology is not mysterious. Anybody can go to the library and read the books that define it.

10   Green ideology is not some fringe theory cooked up in California. Like many important ideas in American history, it is largely imported from Britain and Germany. It is, increasingly, one of the most powerful forces in our culture. We may even adopt parts of it without realizing their origins. To be informed citizens, we ought to know something about it.

11   First of all, a caveat. Ideologies are messy. They tend to associate disparate ideas in unexpected ways. What's more, people who share the same general ideological viewpoint rarely agree on everything. No two conservatives or liberals or libertarians or even Marxists believe exactly the same thing. And political movements are almost always riven by internal conflict (you should read some of the things the abolitionists said about each other).

12   The environmental movement is no different. Purist greens who distrust political compromise berate Washington-based groups that lobby for legislation. The Green-Greens, who aren't leftist, attack the Red-Greens, who are. Grassroots activists criticize the "Gang of 10," the large, well-funded environmental groups.

13   And perhaps the biggest *philosophical* split is between "deep ecology" and other forms of environmentalism. Deep ecologists advocate a mystical view of the natural world as an end in itself, not made for human beings. They criticize traditional conservationism, as well as leftist "social ecology," for emphasizing the environment's value to people.

14   Most environmental activists—the rank and file—combine some of each outlook to create a personal viewpoint. They can do this because, deep down, the greens aren't as divided as they sometimes like to think.

15   Every ideology has a primary value or set of values at its core—liberty, equality, order, virtue, salvation. For greens, the core value is stasis, "sustainability" as they put it. The ideal is of an earth that doesn't change, that shows little or no effects of human activity. Greens take as their model of the ideal society the notion of an ecosystem that has reached an unchanging climax stage. "Limits to growth" is as much a description of how things *should* be as it is of how they are.

16   That is why there is no room in the green world for John Todd and his sewage-cleaning microbes. Todd hasn't sought to stop growth. He has found a way to live with it.

17   The static view has two effects on the general environmental movement: First, it leads environmentalists to advocate policies that will make growth hard on people, as a way of discouraging further development. Cutting off new supplies of water, outlawing new technologies, and banning new construction to increase the cost of housing are common policies. And, second, the static view leads environmentalists to misunderstand how real environmental problems can be solved.

18   Consider how we regulate air pollution. Since the 1977 Clean Air Act, Americans spend some $30 billion a year just to comply with the 1977 Clean Air

Act—with very little to show for it. Current policy dictates *specific technologies*— for example, smokestack scrubbers for coal-burning power plants. The plants can't just use cleaner coal. And cars have to have catalytic converters. If someone comes up with a cheaper or more efficient way to get the same result, the government says, Sorry. We've picked our one true technology. You can't sell yours.

19 Now, for decades economists have suggested that we take a different approach to regulating pollution. Set an overall allowable level, they say, then let companies decide how to achieve it. Let them buy and sell permits that regulate the amount of pollution they can emit: If you wanted to build a new plant, you'd have to buy some permits from somebody else who was closing their plant or reducing their pollution. The economy could grow without increasing the total amount of pollution. Companies would have to pay a price for the pollution they put out. And plant managers would have an economic incentive to adopt—or even develop from scratch—pollution-saving technologies.

20 Most environmentalists, however, hate, loath, and despise this whole idea. They call it a "license to pollute." Emissions trading treats pollution as a cost, a side effect to be controlled, rather than an outright evil, a sin. It allows growth. And it lets individual choice, not politics, determine exactly which technologies will be adopted to control pollution. It takes a *dynamic* view, rather than a static one. Over time, it assumes, people will come up with better and better ways to deal with pollution. And, it assumes, we ought to *encourage* those innovations.

21 People rarely adopt a new technology because it makes life worse. But nowadays we tend to pay more attention to the dangers or pollution from new technologies. We take the old technologies' disadvantages for granted. So, for example, we forget that the automobile actually made city life cleaner.

22 By creating a market for petroleum-derived gasoline, the car also encouraged the production of heating oil and natural gas—much cleaner fuels than the coal people used to use to heat homes and businesses. And, thanks to the automobile, cities no longer have to dispose of tons of horse manure every day.

23 Extrapolating from his own time, a British writer in 1885 described the future of London:

> It is a vast stagnant swamp, which no man dare enter, since death would be his inevitable fate. There exhales from this oozy mass so fatal a vapour that no animal can endure it. The black water bears a greenish-brown scum, which forever bubbles up from the putrid mud of the bottom.

24   Clearly, modern environmentalists have no monopoly on dire predictions of disaster. From this particular fate we were saved by the automobile.

25   A dynamic view sees the pluses of change as well as the minuses. And it appreciates how new, unforeseen technologies or social changes can allay current problems.

26   By contrast, the environmental movement has been built on crisis. Around the turn of the century, Americans were terrified of the growing lumber shortage. A 1908 New York *Times* headline read: "Hickory Disappearing, Supply of Wood Nears End—Much Wasted and There's No Substitute." Actually, as prices rose, the railroad—the major consumers of wood—did find substitutes. And more-efficient ways of using wood.

27   Meanwhile, however, Gifford Pinchot used the specter of a "timber shortage" to get the U.S. Forest Service started. There was, of course, no such shortage, unless you take the static view. And a growing number of both economists and environmental activists now see Pinchot's legacy of central planning and federally managed forest lands as an economic and enviromental disaster.

28   Contrary to the doomsayers, both past and present, people have a knack for innovating their way out of "crises"—if they have both the permission and the incentive to do so. So we find that people developed petroleum as whale oil became scarce, that farmers turn to drip irrigation as water prices rise, and that drivers bought fuel-efficient cars when gas prices went up.

29   To a large degree, however, green ideology is not about facts. It is about *values*, and the environmental movement is about enforcing those values through political action. Green politics, write British greens Jonathon Porritt and David Winner, "demands a wholly new ethic in which violent, plundering humankind abandons its destructive ways, recognizes its dependence on Planet Earth, and starts living on a more equal footing with the rest of nature. The danger lies not only in the odd maverick polluting factory, industry, or technology, but in the fundamental nature of our economic systems. It is industrialism itself—a 'super-ideology' embraced by socialist countries as well as by the capitalist West—which threatens us."

30   If we look around, we can see the effort to remake "violent, plundering humankind" in a number of current initiatives. Take recycling. On one level, it seems like common sense. Why waste resources? That's certainly true with aluminum, which takes huge amounts of electricity to make in the first place and very little energy to recycle. But then there's glass. Both making glass in the first place and melting it down for recycling take about the same amount of energy. The only other thing new glass takes is sand—and we have plenty of that.

Unless you're worried about an imminent sand crisis, there's little reason to re-cycle glass. It doesn't even take up much room in landfills.

31   But, of course, glass—like other forms of packaging—is convenient. Getting people to recycle it is a way of reminding them of the evils of material-ism and the folly of convenience. As Jeremy Rifkin's little booklet *The Green-house Crisis: 101 Ways to Save the Earth* advises shoppers: "Remember, if it's dis-posable and convenient, it probably contributes to the greenhouse effect." On a scientific level, this is ridiculous. But as a value statement it conveys a great deal. Convenient disposable products are the creations of an affluent, innova-tive, industrial society that responds to consumer demands. In a static, green world, we would forego incandescent lighting for fluorescent bulbs and clothes dryers for clothes lines. We would give up out-of-season fruits and vegetables, disposable diapers (of course), free-flowing shower heads, and other self-indul-gent pleasures.

32   If green ideology is guilt transformed into politics, we might wonder why people adopt it. Partly, I think green ideology appeals to many people's sense of frustration with modern life. Technology is too complicated, work too demanding, communication too instantaneous, information too abundant, the pace of life too fast. Stasis looks attractive, not only for nature but also for human beings.

33   E. F. Schumacher put it this way in *Small Is Beautiful*, a central work of green theory. "The pressure and strain of living," he wrote, "is very much less in, say, Burma than it is in the United States, in spite of the fact that the amount of labour-saving machinery used in the former country is only a minute frac-tion of the amount used in the latter."

34   Jeremy Rifkin describes the green coalition as "time rebels," who "argue that the pace of production and consumption should not exceed na-ture's ability to recycle wastes and renew basic resources. They argue that the tempo of social and economic life should be compatible with nature's time frame." Rifkin, therefore, can't stand computers. They go too fast.

35   To slow economy and society to the approved *adagio*, the greens have some fairly straightforward prescriptions: Restrict trade to the local area. Elim-inate markets where possible. End specialization. Anchor individuals in their "bioregions," local areas defined by their environmental characteristics. Shrink the population. Make life simple again, small, self-contained.

36   It is a vision that can be made remarkably appealing, for it plays on our desire for self-sufficiency, our longing for community, and our nostalgia for the agrarian past. We will go back to the land, back to the rhythms of seedtime and harvest, back to making our own clothes, our own furniture, our own tools.

Back to barnraisings and quilting bees. Back to a life we can understand without a string of Ph.D.s.

37   "In living in the world by his own will and skill, the stupidest peasant or tribesman is more competent than the most intelligent workers or technicians or intellectuals in a society of specialists," writes Wendell Berry, an agrarian admired by both greens and cultural conservatives. Berry is a fine writer; he chooses words carefully; he means what he says. We will go back to being peasants.

38   These are, of course, harsh words. And we aren't likely to wake up as subsistence farmers tomorrow. But an economy, like an ecology, is made up of intricate connections. Constantly tinkering with it—cutting off this new technology here, banning that product there—will have unintended consequences. And sometimes, one suspects, the consequences aren't all that unintended.

39   Take electricity. Environmentalists, of course, rule out nuclear power, regardless of the evidence of its safety. But then they say coal-powered plants can cause acid rain and pollution, so they're out, too. Oil-fired plants release greenhouse gases (and cost a bundle, too). Hydroelectric plants are no good because they disrupt the flow of rivers.

40   Solar photovoltaic cells have always been the great hope of the future. But making them requires lots of nasty chemicals, so we can expect solar cells to be banned around the time they become profitable. Pretty soon, you've eliminated every conceivable source of electricity. Then your only option is to dismantle your industry and live with less: the environmentalist warning of impending shortages becomes a self-fulfilling prophecy.

41   And, make no mistake about it, many environmentalists have a truly radical agenda. "It is a spiritual act to try to shut down DuPont," says Randall Hayes, director of the Rainforest Action Network. From the appealing ads his group runs to solicit donations to save the rainforests, you'd never guess he had that goal in mind.

42   And consider the remarkably frank book, *Whatever Happened to Ecology?*, by longtime environmental activist Stephanie Mills, recently published by Sierra Club Books. Mills garnered national attention in 1969, when she delivered a college commencement address entitled "The Future Is a Cruel Hoax" and declared she'd never have children. The book traces the evolution of the environmental movement and of her ideas since then. Today, she and her husband live on a farm in northern Michigan, where they pursue their bioregionalist ideal of "reinhabiting" the land by restoring some of its wildness and blocking future development. A journalist, not a theorist, Mills speaks not only for herself but for the intellectual movement of which she is a part. Her words are chilling:

We young moderns resort to elaborate means of getting physical experience. Yogic practice, fanatical running, bicycling, competitive sports, bodybuilding. All of these recreations are voluntary and may not cultivate the endurance necessary for the kind of labor required to dismantle industrial society and restore the Earth's productivity.

Are voluntary . . . the endurance necessary . . . the labor required . . . dismantle industrial society. The prose is pleasant, the notions it contains disturbing. She continues:

One summer afternoon a few days after a freak windstorm, I made a foray out to buy some toilet paper. (Every time I have to replenish the supply of this presumed necessity, I wonder what we're going to substitute for it when the trucks stop running.)

43 *When the trucks stop running.* There is a history of the future buried in those words, fodder for several science-fiction novels—but no explanation of when and why the trucks will stop. Or who will stop them.

44 People don't want to be peasants: The cities of the Third World teem with the evidence. And certainly, the typical subscriber to the *Utne Reader* (a sort of green *Reader's Digest* with a circulation of 200,000 after only six years of publication) doesn't envision a future of subsistence farming—much less the hunter-gatherer existence preferred by deep ecologists. More to the reader's taste is, no doubt, the cheery vision offered by Executive Editor Jay Walljasper.

It's 2009. Nuclear weapons have been dismantled. Green publications have huge circulations. Minneapolis has 11 newspapers and its own currency ("redeemable in trout, walleye, or wild rice"). Sidewalk cafés sell croissants and yogurt. A local ordinance decrees a 24-hour workweek. Cars are nearly nonexistent (a delegation from the "People's Independent Republic of Estonia" is in town to help design better ski trails for commuters). Citizens vote electronically. The shopping mall has become a nature preserve.

45 Walljasper is clearly having fun—after all, he puts Aretha Franklin's face on the $10 bill—and he doesn't consider any of the tough questions. Like how all those magazines and newspapers exist without printing plants or paper mills. How the Estonians got to town without airplanes or the fuel to run them (Jeremy Rifkin specifically names the Boeing 747 as the kind of product that can't be produced in the small-is-beautiful factories of the coming "entropic age.") How the chips to run the electronic voting got etched without chemicals. Where the chips were made. How a 24-hour workweek produced the sustained concentration needed to write software or the level of affluence that allows for restaurant croissants.

46   And, above all, Walljasper doesn't explain why after millennia of be-having otherwise, humans simply gave up wanting *stuff*. If the Walljasper of 2009 still overloads on reading material, why should we assume that people whose fancy runs toward fast food and polyester (or fast cars and silk) would be struck with a sudden attack of bioregionally approved tastes? How *exactly* did that shopping mall disappear?

47   "The root of the solution has to be so radical that it can scarcely be spo-ken of," says movie director and British green John Borrman. "We all have to be prepared to change the way we live and function and relate to the planet. In short, we need a transformation of the human spirit. If the human heart can be changed, then everything can be changed."

48   We have heard this somewhere before—in, for example, the promise of a "New Soviet Man." People are forever seeking to change the human heart, often with tragic results.

49   The greens want people to give up the idea that life can be better. They say "better" need not refer to material abundance, that we should just be con-tent with less. Stasis, they say, can satisfy our "vital needs." They may indeed convince some people to puruse a life of voluntary simplicity, and that is fine and good and just the thing a free society ought to allow. Stephanie Mills is wel-come to her organic farm.

50   But most of us do not want to give up 747s, or cars, or eyeglasses, or private washing machines, or tailored clothing, or even disposable diapers. The "debased human protoplasm" that Stephanie Mills holds in contempt for their delight in "clothes, food, sporting goods, electronics, building supplies, pets, baked goods, deli food, toys, tools, hardware, geegaws, jim-jams, and knick-knacks" will not happily relinquish the benefits of modern civilization. Many ordinary human beings would like a cleaner world. They are prepared to make sacrifices—*tradeoffs* is a better word—to get one. But ordinary human beings will not adopt the Buddha's life without desire, much as E. F. Schumacher might have ordained it.

51   At its extreme, green ideology expresses itself in utter contempt for humanity. Reviewing Bill McKibben's *The End of Nature* in the *Los Angeles Times*, National Park Service research biologist David M. Graber concluded with this stunning passage:

> Human happiness, and certainly human fecundity, are not as important as a wild and healthy planet. I know social scientists who remind me that people are part of nature, but it isn't true. Somewhere along the line—at about a billion years ago, maybe half that—we quit the contract and became a cancer. We have become a plague upon ourselves and upon the Earth. It is cosmically unlikely that the de-veloped world will choose to end its orgy of fossil-energy consumption, and the

Third World its suicidal consumption of landscape. Until such time as Homo sapiens should decide to rejoin nature, some of us can only hope for the right virus to come along.

52   It is hard to take such notions seriously without sounding like a bit of a kook yourself. But there they are—calmly expressed in the pages of a major, mainstream, Establishment newspaper by an employee of the federal government. When it is acceptable to say such things in polite intellectual company, when feel-good environmentalists tolerate the totalitarians in their midst, when sophisticates greet the likes of Graber with indulgent nods and smiles rather than arguments and outrage, we are one step farther down another bloody road to someone's imagined Eden.

53   Thank you.

THE ETHICS OF PROTEST: IS IT RIGHT TO DO WRONG?

Lee W. Baker

Lee W. Baker has had extensive public relations experience first in corporate managerial positions with Allis-Chalmers Co. and then as president of his own public relations firm in Milwaukee and later in Denver. He has maintained continued interest in ethical issues related to public relations specifically and to public discourse generally. He has served as an editorial board member for the *Journal of Mass Media Ethics.* You may want to read his book, *The Credibility Factor: Putting Ethics to Work in Public Relations* (1993).

On November 1, 1995 Lee Baker, then retired, addressed the monthly Business Ethics Forum at Trinity United Methodist Church in Denver, Colorado. The audience numbered 60-70 persons and his speech was followed by a lively question-and-answer period.

In his introduction, Baker establishes a positive relationship with his audience by citing instances familiar to most of them (1-2). Later he encourages this relationship by overtly inviting the audience to judge

✛Lee W. Baker, "The Ethics of Protest: Is it Right to Do Wrong?" February 1, 1966, pp. 252-255. Reprinted by permission from *Vital Speeches of the Day* and the author.

whether they agree with him (4, 15). Clearly Baker primarily focuses on propostions of value in the speech. He offers ethical judgments of various types of social protest tactics. He advocates a set of ethical standards to guide evaluation of protest tactics. At the outset, he makes careful distinctions before proceeding to his major arguments (3-4).

In the first half of the speech, Baker uses an extended illustration of the social protest tactics of animal rights activist groups such as PETA and ALF (4-10). This lengthy illustration allows him to reveal personal motivations (4), to dramatize the extremism of the tactics, to make vivid the range of tactics he condemns, and to criticize hypocrisy (4, 10). As a type of evidence, consider his example in paragraph 7: "A Michigan state police officer also has talked about what he called a 'real problem,' a string of hunter deaths in Michigan-Ohio-Indiana areas." Is Baker arguing by implication that these deaths were caused by animal rights protestors? If so, how reasonable is the evidence he offers?

In a major segment of the speech (11-17), Baker categorizes unethical protest tactics and presents them in an implied rank order from most unethical to least unethical. He highlights the categories by using verbal signposts to mark them (12, 13, 15, 16, 17). In this major segment, Baker continues to rely extensively on examples and specific instances both for proof and for clarification. To Baker's massive use of examples throughout the speech, apply the standard tests for reasonableness of specific instances: (1) Was a sufficient number of instances presented? (2) Were the instances presented representative of the type of instances being discussed? (3) Were there any negative or counter-instances omitted that need to be discussed?

Near the end of the speech, Baker advocates adoption of a specific set of values to guide our evaluations of the ethics of protest tactics. He outlines the standards (18-21) and then summarizes them (21). How do the numerous examples he presents earlier in the speech measure up to these ethical standards? Would his argument have been clearer if he had presented his ethical standards first and then applied them to his categories of unethical protest tactics? Baker's premise is that the ethical standards to be met by protestors "are the same accepted ethical standards—no higher or lower—as acknowledged by the other segments of society" (18). One scholar of social protest who disagrees with this premise is Steven Goldzwig in his article, "A Social Movement Perspective of Demagoguery: Achieving Symbolic Realignment," *Communication Studies,* 40 (Fall 1989): 202-228. Baker also contends that protestors must exhaust all available peaceful means before turning to illegal or extreme tactics. Do you agree? Why?

You may want to compare Baker's speech with one made on the same topic of social protest ethics in 1968 by Franklyn S. Haiman, "The Rhetoric of 1968: A Farewell to Rational Discourse," and reprinted in two sources: Wil A. Linkugel, R. R. Allen, and Richard L. Johannesen, *Contemporary American Speeches,* 4th ed. (Dubuque, IA: Kendall-Hunt, 1978), pp. 156-169; Richard L. Johannesen, *Ethics in Human Communication,* 2nd ed. (Prospect Heights, IL: Waveland Press, 1983), pp. 177-190. At what points would Baker and Haiman agree and at what points would they disagree? Whose analysis do you find most reasonable and why? On the ethics of social protest, also see Richard L. Johannesen, *Ethics in Human Communication,* 4th ed. (Waveland, 1996), pp. 90-96.

---

1   You've probably all watched or participated in protest actions. Their numbers surely reached a peak during the Vietnam War, when college campuses were alive with students challenging U. S. government leaders. In the Denver area, Rocky Flats has been the locale for many protesters; the Statehouse steps are a frequently-used stage; when President Clinton was here recently protesters marched outside the downtown hotel where a fundraising dinner was underway.

2   What do protesters want to paraphrase Dr. Freud's question? Well, they want you on their side, they want your support. To win you over, they use every form of communication and a variety of methods. You're familiar with many of the causes. Protesters may work through the democratic process, such as petitions to public officials and the ballot box, or take their causes to the public through picketing, parades, rallies, signs, handbills and paid ads; or directly to target representatives through angry confrontations. Sometimes, but not always, the protest group is a David challenging a Goliath, the little guy against the Establishment, which may be big business or big government, or established educational or religious institutions. In the West, such issues as cattle grazing and other uses of public lands, or those related to saving of endangered species and wetlands, or conservation of forests, fuel the causes. At times, protesters seem full of a holier-than-thou attitude, create the impression that everyone is out of step except them, that only their beliefs or credos are the right ones. They not only oppose beliefs counter to theirs, they make little room for the people who have them. Also, at times, it seems protesters are acting to satisfy desires for personal notoriety and attention as much or more than to spread the word about their issues.

3   Let me add that there are many good things about protests and their leaders. Many achieve their goals to bring about changes that benefit society and human lives. I hope I come across as selective as I focus on what to me are unethical protests. I'm not tarring all protests with an unethical brush or label.

4   My subject, "The Ethics of Protest," grew from early reactions to what I read and heard about the organization called People for the Ethical Treatment of Animals. I first became aware of PETA, to use the acronym, five or six years ago. I found that it then and since engaged in rather shocking protest activities for an organization that used the word "Ethical" in its title. You might presume from such usage that it shared a generally accepted view of ethical conduct and had an ethics record others would acclaim. Well, I found differently. See if you agree. After taking a look at People for the Ethical Treatment of Animals, I'll move on to an ethical examination of some other kinds of individual and group protests. As I do this, let me add, I'm commenting about the tactics of these individuals and organizations and not their issues. A discussion of issues, some highly explosive, might require several more of these meetings. Fair enough?

5   PETA is a nonprofit charity organization founded in 1980 to plead the cause of animal rights before policy-makers and the public. It particularly targets what it calls factory farm raising and slaughtering of animals for human consumption, and the use of animals in experimentation.

6   Here are a few protest activities conducted in the name of animal rights. A few months ago PETA's vegetarian campaign coordinator from the Washington headquarters was in Dever attempting to unload a truck full of manure in front of the Colorado Convention Center. She was protesting against the World Meat Congress that was meeting there. Signage on the side of the truck said, "Meat Stinks." Police arrested her before she completed the job. At a dog show, PETA protestors opened the cages of several of the show dogs and turned them loose; they also put anti-freeze in the water bowls of some cages. One of the protesters said, "A dead dog is better than a caged dog." Add to this such incidents as PETA protesters throwing paint or blood onto fur coats worn by women walking down the street. Or, consider this: A protester against the use of fashion furs appearing on David Letterman's show wearing leather shoes. This protester the day before had been arrested with others from PETA for vandalizing the offices of fashion designer Karl Lagerfeld, who uses fur. As part of its program, PETA makes claims found to be without substance. For instance, it says minks have their testicles electrocuted. The industry standard—said to be rigidly adhered to—is to euthanize the creatures by either carbon monoxide or lethal injection. That's the procedure used in animal shelters. Medical authori-

ties deny PETA claims of unnecessarily harsh treatment for animals in research. And they vouch for the need for animal experimentation to reveal valuable data in the development of medicines and health procedures. PETA terms guide dogs for the blind "akin to slavery."

7   There's another animal rights group, the Animal Liberation Front, that has been blamed for the firebombing of an animal-research lab at Michigan State University. Police reported an estimate of $200,000 in damages and the destroying of 30 years' worth of primary research data. A similar incident occurred at Washington State University a year earlier. There were grand jury indictments in Michigan against alleged perpetrators, whom I believe, are still at large. PETA issued a news release, said to have been provided by the ALF, on the disaster. A Michigan state police officer also has talked about what he called a "real problem," a string of hunter deaths in Michigan-Ohio-Indiana areas. Last year, the Animal Liberation Front planted incendiary devices in four downtown Chicago department stores.

8   A British journalist reports animal rightists placed incendiary bombs under cars of those whose work involves the use of animals, also 42 letter-bombs and 61 mousetraps, devices sent in parcels designed to slice off the fingers of whomever opens them. Another dimension in the fight for animal rights was provided by vegetarians who broke into the shop of a German butcher. They smashed equipment worth $21,000 and painted the message, "Meat is murder, animal killer," on the shop windows.

9   Subsequently, they slashed the butcher's tires and left a phone message, "Yesterday your store, tomorrow you."

10   These activities of animal rights proponents may have met their goal of grabbing the public's attention. But at what costs? In the flouting of high moral and ethical conduct they trampled on others' rights and inflicted harm.

11   The pattern of thinking that led me to have questions about PETA prompted me to look at the ethical aspects in protest actions of other groups that sought public understanding and even endorsement for their concerns and programs. I found numerous instances in which they too brought harm to citizens and portions of society. Here are a few of the ways. I've sorted them into several categories, but as I go through them you'll recognize that the instances often fit into more than one.

12   Number one. I reserve the top place on the chart of the most damaging kinds of protest for actions that endanger the lives of others. We're all familiar with the acts of zealous protestors that brought injuries to staff employees and the loss of lives at abortion clinics. Since 1993, at least five who work in abortion clinics—two doctors and three clinic staff members—have been killed. Save-the-forest protesters have driven spikes deep into trees in the northwest, en-

dangering the lives of lumbermen. New Orleans police had a two-day sickout to protest unresolved issues in contract negotiations with the city. (The right to collectively bargain was one of the issues.) A police department spokesman put the absences at more than 50 percent. On one shift 70 percent of the assigned officers stayed home. While there are no figures available on the negative effects to citizens' lives, can't we assume there were some? In 1970, during the height of the student protest against the Vietnam war, the Army Math Research Center at the University of Wisconsin in Madison was bombed. One student working there was killed, four others injured. Most of the contents, including a $1.5 million computer, were destroyed. Math research that was conducted there had nothing to do with military projects. We can include in this category the perpetrators of the Oklahoma City and World Trade Center bombings, and the Unabomber.

13   Second, as a category, are the protests that damage property and cut off income for individuals and employers. In a tiny town in Alabama last year, a fire believed to have been arson burned down a high school whose principal's stand against mixed-race dating had casued racial turmoil. The principal had threatened to cancel the school prom if interracial couples attended. The 25-year-old son of a protest leader, arrested for setting the fire, was acquitted just last week. While the identity of the protester who set the fire may never be known, the community suffered a real loss. In another kind of protest, there were the economic pressures applied by farm workers in California in the 1980s. They called on the public to boycott lettuce and grapes in the hope that reduced sales would help them gain concessions from the owners. Then there was the famous Alar case, in which a meticulously-conceived protest plan by the Natural Resources Defense Council swept apples from the bins of super markets and frightened families and school officials. Entertainment personalities led the chorus: Apples sprayed with Alar could cause cancer; children were most at risk. Mothers poured apple juice down sink drains. Apples were removed from school lunchrooms. Normalcy began to return when a joint announcement from the USDA, EPA and FDA declared apples safe. Meanwhile, apple growers lost $100 million and dozens of family-owned orchards went bankrupt.

14   Here's an unusual case from Germany. The Benetton Group, an Italian clothing manufacturer, ran ads with themes of human tragedy and suffering. Among photographs in its ads were a man's arm tattooed with the words "HIV positive," a dying AIDS patient, a war cemetery, an oil soaked seabird, children toiling in a South American sweat shop and the bloody uniform of a Croatian soldier. Benetton said the ads were designed to raise awareness about social issues. Licensees of many of its stores in Europe disagreed—as did cus-

tomers. They found them offensive, tasteless and insensitive, as did 84 percent of those responding to a German magazine poll. Customers at the four stores of one dealer joined the protest. They applied blood-red tape over his store windows to block out the Benetton name. At the center of the Xs formed by the tape was this message: "No more Benetton, because we condemn the scandalous advertising using misery, war, sickness and death." And they boycotted the stores. The merchant said the boycott cost him some $600,000 in lost sales. So he refused to pay Benetton that amount. However, a judge oredered him to pay the full bill plus interest.

15   I give third place for harm to the intimidation, coercion and harassment that stem from the fervor of protesters. Former Defense Secretary Robert McNamara said in his book published earlier this year that his vacation home near Snowmass, Colo., was a target for anti-war protesters who twice tried to burn it down in 1967. The FBI believed there were several attempts at arson at the house in later years. Blueprints of his home were found in a Berkeley, Calif., garage of the Symbionese Liberation Army after heiress-turned-revolutionary Patty Hearst was arrested for her work with the SLA. We know that physicians in Colorado and around the country who perform abortions have received death threats. Many have been stalked. Some doctors wear bullet-proof vests and helmets and have 24 hour security. A recent anti-abortion, pro-life strategy is the filing of malpractice suits against doctors, which harass them and intimidate their patients. In Denver, no clashes or damage to life or property occurred in the protests that led to the demise of the Columbus Day parade in 1992. But coercive pressures and threats by leaders of the American Indian Movement resulted in its cancellation by the Italian-American organizations. The decision was made in the interest of safety after a face-off between marchers and protesters shortly before the parade hour. The press reported a death threat against the man who would have been dressed as Columbus.

16   Next, protesters deprive others of their citizen rights. As Patrick Buchanan announced his candidacy for the Republican presidential nomination earlier this year in New Hampshire, four protesters leaped on the stage. They halted his speech with shouts and accused him of being a racist. Buchanan tusselled with one at the podium before they were hustled away by his supporters. Newt Gingrich had a similar experience in Chicago, where demonstrators protesting proposed Republican cuts in social programs forced him to stop speaking several times. In Georgia, Gingrich was met with such ardent protesters that the event he was attending had to be canceled. Speakers such as Buchanan and Gingrich have a First Amendment right to be heard. There have been instances in which protesters were so vociferous that police were called and, concerned about the safety of the speakers, said it would be best if they left. These instances illustrate what's called "the heckler's veto." If someones right to assemble and speak becomes shattered by hecklers, the First Amendment has been violated. It's the responsibility of the police to remove the protesting hecklers rather than urge the speakers to disperse under fire.

17   As a fifth category are protesters who cause inconvenience, disruption and unwanted bother in the lives of consumers and businesses. The effects are often hard to evaluate without more information about the circumstances. A couple of examples: Striking employees of Air France disrupted the schedules of international travelers by closing down the largest airport in Paris and partially shuttering another. Who knows if a passenger failed to arrive in time at the bedside of a dying family member? Or if the tardiness of a business representative forced a potential agreement to vanish? Lives of crew membres and ground forces surely were unnecessarily upset. And what was the loss to Air France? In Mexico City, dozens of masked men protested California's Proposition 187 that curbs benefits to illegal aliens by invading a McDonald's restaurant. They threw cash registers to the floor, smashed windows, overturned tables and spray-painted anti-American slogans. Fortunately, no customers were injured, though there may have been a case or two of indigestion caused by the excitement. At Rutgers University last February, 400 student protesters seeking the dismissal of the school's president descended on the gymnasium floor during half-time of a basketball game with the University of Massachusetts. They refused to budge and officials called off the remainder of the game—to the disappointment and frustration of the players and fans. Object of the protesters' wrath was a comment of the president they found to be a racial slur, made at a faculty meeting the previous November. Incidentally, the board of directors meeting three days later in a special session, open to the news media and broadcast live by CCN, voted to keep the president.

18   Each of these examples illustrates the lack of ethics in protest movements. What are the ethical standards that protesters should meet? They are the same accepted ethical standards—no higher or lower—as acknowledged by other segments of society. I know, someone out there may be asking, accepted by whom? Well, accepted by me for one, by you, I hope, by all who prize conduct based on high moral values. Here are components of those standards. First, fairness. Fairness is a key quality in ethical social behavior—fairness expressed as a matter of reciprocity. In order to receive fair treatment one should give fair treatment. Confucius, the Chinese philosopher and teacher, expressed it this way: "Do not do to others what you would not want others to do to you." The Golden Rule calls for a more positive stance, "Do unto others as you would have others do to you." Admittedly, the state of being fair can be subject to different meanings and definitions. But I think those precepts form the basis for

an objective definition. Do you agree with me that in the examples I've mentioned, there often was failure to observe fairness?

19   Observing respect is another basic ingredient in ethical conduct. Respect for the basic rights of others. Refusal to act in a manner that reduces or tramples on the rights of others. Respect for the law is also a basic. I cited numerous occasions in which protesters committed illegal acts. Some of you may say, sometimes protesters do need to take drastic action to get attention—and that this may mean breaking the law. But this reaction is most likely a cop out. Don't protesters sometimes travel the illegal route without exhausting all available peaceful means to get the attention and results they seek? Keep in mind that perhaps the largest protest in our country's history—until a few weeks ago—was the peaceful "I Have A Dream" march and rally of Martin Luther King, Jr., in Washington in 1963. That generated a tremendous wallop. Then, in October, we witnessed the even larger—and also peaceful—million men march.

20   Further, ethical individuals or organizations engaged in protests should be honest, should avoid misrepresentation of facts, lying, deceit and subterfuge, or manipulation. In a couple of earlier instances, we found protesters who made truth a victim. Another kind of case: A small group of protesters gather at their appointed spot, their placards at the ready. All is quiet until the television crews arrive and turn on their lights. Then the signs go up, the chanting starts, the leader shakes a fist at a distant target and tape depicting this spirited protest is ready for the evening news. As the lights go off, the protesters resume their relaxed mode.

21   And there's no place in protests for the activists to gloss over faulty conduct by saying, "The ends justify the means." Situational ethics and relativism have become too much accepted today as the platform for excusing questionable ethics. You may have trouble abiding by Immanuel Kant's moral imperative: What is right is right. All deception is morally wrong. He may seem too inflexible. Yet following as closely as possible his strict rules of moral conduct is preferable to reaching for the lowest possible level of ethics. Advancing the ethical standards of society requires that all must strive for what's right and what's fair, for mutal respect of rights, for honesty.

22   Protesters have no right to advance their cause with unethical methods and tactics. Though spurred by excess exuberance and fierce dedication, they shouldn't be so deluded that they believe they're entitled to unethical shortcuts. Those who disagree with or are neutral about the goals of a protest group have the right to their beliefs without being subject to pressure—economic, emotional or physical—from members of the movement. They should not feel impelled to restrict their movements or actions, including speech, because of fear churned by protesters.

23   Let's keep before us the outline of what's morally acceptable, the manner in which people of conscience and moral responsibility act, instead of looking for excuses to do wrong in the name of accomplishing what we believe is right.

THE NEW WORLD OF MEDICAL ETHICS: OUR DUTY LIES BOTH TO THE INDIVIDUAL AND THE POPULATION

Richard D. Lamm

"Governor Gloom" was the nickname earned by Richard D. Lamm during his terms as governor of Colorado (1974-1986). According to James S. Kunen (*People*, January 20, 1986, 46-50), Lamm's "typically apocalyptic speeches" won him a reputation as a doomsayer. Lamm sees himself in the role of an Old Testament prophet who warned of disaster unless people reformed their ways. Thus Lamm's speechmaking might be analyzed as illustrating the tradition of the American contemporary secular "jeremiad" (after the Old Testament prophet Jeremiah) as a form or genre of public discourse. See, for example, RIchard L. Johannesen, "The Jeremiad and Jenkin Lloyd Jones," *Communication Monographs*, 52 (June 1985): 156-171.

On March 27, 1984 Lamm captured national media attention when he made the following comment concerning the ethical and economic implications of high technology medicine that often permits costly and painful prolongation of our lives: "We've got a duty to die and get out of the way with all our machines and artificial hearts and everything else like that and let the other society, our kids, build a reasonable life." An excellent analysis of inaccurate news media coverage of his comment is Sue O'Brien, "The 'Duty to Die' Controversy: Taking Care with Health Care Reporting," in Philip Patterson and Lee Wilkins, eds., *Media*

✝ Richard D. Lamm, "New World of Medical Ethics: Our Duty Lies Both to the Individual and the Population," July 1, 1993, pp. 549-553. Reprinted by permission from *Vital Speeches of the Day* and the author.

Ethics: Issues and Cases, 2nd ed. (Dubuque, IA: Brown & Benchmark, 1994), pp. 31-33.

Author or co-author of three books, Lamm also is a lawyer and accountant. Since leaving the office of governor, Lamm has been Director of the Center for Public Policy and Contemporary Issues at the University of Denver. He presented the following speech on April 17, 1993 in San Francisco at the International Bioethics Institute during the Third Annual Congress of Healthcare Ethics and Ethics Committees.

This speech clearly argues a propostion of value. Lamm advocates adoption of a new set of values to guide medical ethics (3). And he itemizes for clarity the six new value orientations that he advocates (11, 18, 24, 30, 36, 46).

Lamm uses a variety of lines of argument to develop his central theme of necessary shift from individual-centered values to community-centered values (57-58). The old individual-oriented values, by themselves, are outmoded as norms for medical ethics (4-6). The new community-oriented values are contrasted with the old (27-28). He contends that there should be a balanced duty both to the individual and the community (32, 64). But also note that in other places he implies that the community values should be given some degree of priority in the hierarchy of values related to medical care (28, 54, 55). A book that explores the on-going tensions in American culture between individualism and community is Robert N. Bellah, et al., *Habits of the Heart: Individualism and Commitment in American Life* (1985).

A secondary theme is that economic resources available for medical care in this country are not unlimited (7, 28, 50-52). Lamm argues not only that maximum citizen access to medical care is vital but also that there must be rationing or prioritizing of economic resources for what is covered. Two analyses of the rationing of medical care are Daniel Callahan, *Setting Limits* (1987) and Robert Blank, *Rationing Medicine* (1988).

At strategic points Lamm employs statistics to support his analysis (6, 40, 43-44). But his most extensive use of evidence involves expert testimony (14, 16, 20-23, 34-35, 49-51). Considering the nature of his audience, how adequate are the statistics and testimony when judged by the tests of clarity, accuracy, relevance, recency, representativeness, and documentation of sources? For example, how well does he identify and present the qualifications and competency of the experts he quotes?

Lamm uses a variety of language resources to clarify and dramatize his points. He opens and concludes with parables—stories from ordinary life from which a moral message is extracted (1-2, 59). Although used few times, his literal analogies sharpen his points (19, 42). How well do his numerous uses of vivid metaphors function to clarify, reinforce, make memorable, or otherwise strengthen his statements (5, 9, 17, 32, 47-48, 57, 60-61)? Notable also is Lamm's use of antithesis—the phrasing of two opposing or competing items into sharp, terse contrast with one item of the pair given clear preference over the other (6, 7, 28, 39). In the conclusion of the speech, he employs one lengthy series of antitheses to summarize the necessary shifts in values and policy (62) and another lengthy series to underscore the need for early access and prevention more than later, more expensive, treatment and maintenance (63).

---

1   I should start with a parable. In the Christian tradition, there is the story about Saint Martin of Tours who in the Medieval Ages was riding his horse, alone and cold, through the deepening night toward the walled city which was his destination. Right outside the gate to the city, Saint Martin of Tours met a cold and starving beggar. In an act of charity that lives in Christian tradition, Saint Martin of Tours divided his cloak in half and gave that with half of his dinner to the cold and starving beggar. It was clearly the ethical and moral course to take. It has served as an example of Christian charity for centuries.

2   Yet Brecht, in his play "Mother Courage," raises the issue of what if, instead of one cold and starving beggar, there were 40. Or, if you like, 100. What then is the duty of an ethical and moral person? It obviously does not make any sense to divide one's cloak into 40 or a 100 painfully inadequate pieces. There is no reason to choose one among the many cold and starving beggars, and it is hard to solve this dilemma other than perhaps saying a prayer for them all as you ride past them into the city.

3   It is my passionate belief that this parable applies to the dilemma we are faced with in health care. There is a new set of realities with which we are confronted; and we must develop a new set of values and a new way of looking at health care if we are to resolve the implications of this brave new world of health care.

4   A whole new world has formed while we were busy inventing, developing, discovering, and innovating. A new world where our current and past values so agonizingly developed are no longer sustainable.

5   Ultimately, our health care ethics are tethered to the economic life support system of our economy. We cannot deliver medically what we do not earn economically. The arm bone of health care is connected to the backbone of the economy.

6 The medical values developed by the world's largest creditor nation with an economy that doubled every 30 years, with 9 percent of its citizens over 65, and modest biotechnology cannot now be sustained by the world's largest debtor nation that has already borrowed $4.3 trillion from its children and grandchildren, whose average worker has had no real growth in wages in 20 years; who has 12 percent of its population over the age of 65, and has incredibly expensive biotechnology.

7 No nation can long import more than it exports, borrow more than it earns, and spend medically what it does not produce economically.

8 Proust once observed that the real voyage of discovery lay not in discovering new worlds, but in seeing with new eyes.

9 I see a health care world where nothing we have done for the past 40 years has even dented the volcanic upward thrust of health care costs—a world of medical innovation that has become a fiscal black hole that threatens to bankrupt our children—a world where our medical miracles are fiscal failures.

10 Medical technology does *not* save us money, as a genre. "Cured" is a marvelous word, but it also means "alive to die later of something else." We have reduced mortality, but dramatically increased morbidity. Where we used to die inexpensively of the first or second disease, we now die expensively of the fifth or sixth disease having consumed far more resources. A new world has formed.

11 *Value Change No. 1:* Stop the egoism about the U.S. having "the finest health care system in the world."

12 It is often said, almost as a mantra, that the United States has the best health care system in the world. Whenever I hear this I am reminded of the historian who said that the 14th Century was a wonderful century, except for the Hundred Year War.

13 America has much to be proud of in its health care system; but like the rooster that knew the sun came up just to hear him crow, it overstates its case. Clearly, the United States has the most sophisticated and the best medical technology. I believe we have the best doctors. Yet, other industrialized countries have healthier people and lower health care costs. These countries deliver more health care services to more people more often, with less administrative hassle for substantially less money. Their doctors have more clinical freedom, and polls show both doctors and citizens in those countries are more satisfied.

14 As one of the most respected health care experts has found:

"In comparison with other major industrial countries, health care in the United States costs more per person and per unit of service, is less accessible to a large portion of its citizens, is provided at a more intensive level, and offers comparatively poor gross outcomes."

15   The test of a system is not the quality of its individual parts, but the effectiveness and efficiency of the total system. Like the man who knew seven languages, but had nothing to say in any of them—technical proficiency is not enough. You cannot have a good health care system without dedicated and brilliant doctors. Yet, dedicated and brilliant doctors are not enough to make a good health care system. A system can be flawed even if it is made up of individually spectacular parts. Clearly, the United States has a system which contains many specatcular parts. Yet, as society has come to recognize, the system contains two major flaws: 1. It leaves 35-37 million Americans uninsured, and an equal number underinsured; and 2. Cost.

16   The lack of access in America is well-known, but still worth repeating. We should take care we do not become hardened to these numbers. George Bernard Shaw once said, "The mark of a truly educated man (person) is to be moved deeply by statistics." In 1992, Louis Harris and Associates conducted a survey and found:

> —Approximately 23 million Americans needed medical care but did not get it in the last 12 months. Approximately 18 million could not get medical care for financial reasons.

> —Last year, 54 million people postponed care they thought they needed for financial reasons.

> —About 7 million Americans were denied health insurance because of a prior medical condition.

> —Nearly 22 million Americans said they themselves, or someone else in their family, or both, had been refused health care during the last year because they didn't have insurance or couldn't pay.

17   These figures are a national disgrace. They show that for all our technical proficiency, our system contains major flaws. The largest flaw is lack of access, and the access problem is the ugly stepchild of the problems with out-of-control costs. We must start to understand that these two flaws are not blemishes of an otherwise ethical delivery system—but fatal flaws that go to the heart of the system.

18   *Value Change No. 2:* Health care must be seen as a social good.

19   The first value issue involving access is to ascertain whether health care is a social good or a private commodity. It is important to first decide the context in which other decisions are made. Is health care a private commodity like a car or clothing? Or, is it a social good like education or a police department? I believe this is actually a question of community values.

20   I believe the hipbone of access is attached to the backbone of the values of our society. However, imperfect, we have a democracy which eventually responds to public will. The problem is that we are schizophrenic about health care—we want everybody to have everything, but we do not want anymore taxes and no more shifted costs. It we are to solve this problem of access, we shall have to form a new public consensus confirming that access is important. As Lawrence J. O'Connell, President & CEO of an ethics think tank, said:

> "All the talk from the campaign trail and the Oval Office is superficial. That is because it sidesteps the fact that before health care reform can succeed, we need to reexamine the fundamental societal values that gave birth to the health care system we have today."

21   Our values must recognize that today uninsured Americans clearly have access to poorer medicine and poorer health. Blendon finds:

> "Despite considerable amounts of uncompensated care provided by hospitals and physicians, Americans without health insurance face major barriers to the receipt of needed health services. Although they suffer from higher rates of ill health than the insurance population, the uninsured report fewer hospitalizations and fewer visits to a physician, shorter hospital stays, and fewer discretionary in-patient hospital treatments and tests, at higher costs. The uninsured also experience higher mortality rates when hospitalized than persons with health insurance coverage who have similar diagnoses."

22   The human toll was—and is—incredible though often unobserved. As John Kitzhaber has said:

> "Legislatures never had to confront the victims of silent rationing or be accountable for the very human consequences. It was like high level bombing where the crew never sees the faces of the people they are killing."

23   In light of the foregoing, modern health reforms state that health care is not a private good, but is a social good—and should be available to all. As Charles Dougherty has argued for universal access:

> "The argument is simple but powerful. Respect for the incalculably great value of each person creates a duty not only to refrain from destroying health . . . but also a duty to take reasonable steps to preserve and restore health by ensuring access to basic health care. Failing to act on this duty, by allowing lives to be shortened or diminished in quality because of lack of access to basic health care, expresses callow disregard for the dignity of human life."

24   *Value Change No. 3:* Access must go from a secondary value to a primary value.

25   Reinhard Priester, in a very thoughtful article, has stated:

"Since WWII, U.S. health policy has consistently subordinated access to other values, must notably to professional autonomy, patient autonomy, and consumer sovereignty."

26   This is consistent, says Priester, with other American values, for in our past and present, "individualism and personal autonomy have superseded community values in American society."

27   At least six values, focused on the individual, have had a major role in shaping our current health care system. These values have guided decisions of both individuals and policy makers in structuring our health care system. These values are:

1.   **Professional Independence: The importance of health professionals, especially physicians, to regulate their own work and to determine what is medically appropriate.**
2.   **Consumer Freedom: The importance of individuals to be able to choose their own insurance company, health organizations, and physicians.**
3.   **Patient Autonomy: The importance of individuals to be informed about their medical and surgical options and to accept or refuse the advice given.**
4.   **Patient Advocacy: The importance of health professionals to act in the best interest of their patients, not the hospital's, the insurance company's, or the community's.**
5.   **High Quality: The service of health professionals are expected to meet the highest standards of competence and compassion.**
6.   **Availability: The importance of having access to all (including the latest) that medicine and surgical technology has to offer.**

28   Priester suggests, given the new world of limited resources and unlimted demands, that we have to add four new values which put a priority on community good:

7.   **Resource Scarcity: There is a limit that can be spent on health and medical care if we wish not to undermine other important social needs.**
8.   **Universal Access: Society has a responsibility to provide access to all citizens regardless of income, job status, state of illness, and so forth.**
9.   **Personal Responsibility: Individual citizens have a responsibility to the community for staying well and keeping cost down.**

10. **Efficiency: The money spent on health care should help people stay well or get well. It should not be spent on needless administration or treatments that are not effective.**

29   Reforming the health care system will require that we consider these and other values which have given birth to the American health care system.

30   *Value Change No. 4:* We must start to value not only the individual, but also the whole society.

31   The bottom line of modern health care is that there is no bottom line. Modern men and women of medicine now have the capability to spend unlimited resources in heroic, and sometime vain attempts to extend life . . . Theoretically, one could now spend all of his or her available time and money in the pursuit of health.

32   Since health care is a public policy bottomless pit, we cannot build the new system looking only at the needs of the individual. We must never forget or abandon the individual, but we must look also at the needs of the entire population. There is an evolving new equation in this shift and it will come only after considerable ethical debate.

33   Using resources for one patient necessarily means that fewer resources will be available to treat others.

34   But it is coming. The Section on Health Care Systems of the American Hospital Association issued a report that found:

> Health care in the U.S. should be redesigned around the needs of the population, not the needs of providers. "Population" is a broader term than patient, which has been our concern. We should all commit to a health population as one fundamental objective, then organize ourselves to support that objective. The measure of our success should be health status, not full hospitals; manageable cost per capita, not profitability for thousands of separate provider units; value, not just cost control.

35   As Victor Fuchs has said: "The difference between what is beneficial for the indivdual and what is beneficial to the society as a whole is the key element in the current health care debate."

36   *Value Change No. 5:* In the new world of health care, reform for community hospitals will owe a duty to the community.

37   The same analysis applies to hospitals. In the United States, hospitals focus almost entirely on the patients *within* the hospital. There seems to be little awareness of—let alone, a sense of responsibility for—the community. A community should have geographical accountability. And, it would be considered unethical and wrong for community hospitals to make large profits, while other people in the community are going without needed medical services.

38   Related to the sin of gluttony is the sin of excess. What if Saint Martin of Tours had come by in a camper stuffed with donated food and found six starving beggars and did nothing. Just passed on by.

39   America has a new sin—the sin of excess in the face of need.

40   Half empty hospitals hire marketing people and run expensive advertising campaigns—to win market share from a neighboring half empty hospital who has hired a public relations firm and does expensive promotional spots on television—blocks away from women without prenatal care and children without vaccines. Half of the hospitals in Colorado are empty, filled with marketing people and advertising geniuses who are desperately trying to beat neighboring half empty hospitals.

41   In the new world of health care, spending money to advertise your hospital would be like taking your neighborhood crime protection money away to advertise your police department.

42   A hospital is a community asset—like a fire department. If there are too many, they should be closed; not advertised.

43   I am not here to criticize California. Colorado has 2.8 hospital beds per 1,000 people—53 percent are empty. We have 21 hospitals that do open heart surgery; many of them doing less than 50 a year (one a week), when 250 is the minimum number Medicare says is needed for proficiency.

44   California also has 2.8 hospital beds per 1,000 people. Southern California and Colorado have 2.8 hospital beds per 1,000 people. HMOs operate at 1.5 hospital beds per 1,000 enrollees. California has 118 open heart units and 400 MRI machines.

45   The most health producing ethical decision many Colorado hospitals could make is to close their doors or merge.

46   *Value Change No. 6:* You cannot say "yes" to new needs to health care, unless you also say "no."

47   There is a yin and yang to the issue of access: The issue is part expansion (people into the system) and part contraction (what is covered). We must expand the who and limit the what; we must give with one hand and take away with the other.

48   Access to health care could be a fiscal black hole into which we could pour unlimited societal resources. If we are going to grant universal access, we must put limits on what is covered. Health care is infinitely expandable.

49   It is estimated that in any given month:

"Approximately three-fourths of the population have an acute or chronic illness that leads to some action such as the restriction of activity or the taking of medication. Of these persons who report an illness during the month, approximately one-third seek medical consultation. Although, in general, illnesses that occur more dramatically or that cause greater discomfort or restriction of activity are more likely to lead to medical care, there is substantial overlap between the illnesses of treated and untreated persons."

50   While all politicians and many health care experts avoid the subject, increasingly society is recognizing a new world of limts:

"Plainly, a positive right of access must be a limited right. Society is obliged only to provide basic care, not everything that medicine can offer. Defining basic care sets the moral limits of what government must provide or subsidize."

51   David Hadorn observes:

"As costs continue to escalate out of cotrol, nothing is more certain than that an increasing number of patients will be forced to go without potentially life-extending or quality of life-enhancing treatments."

Preister further adds:

"While everyone ought to have access to health care this does not require univeral access to all potentially beneficial care. No society can afford to provide every service of potential benefit to everyone in need."

52   Thus, the easy part of the access question is arranging access. The hard part is defining "access to what" and figuring out how to pay for the new access.

53   A world of universal access is a world of choices and trade offs.

"Using resources for one patient necessarily means that fewer resources will be available to treat others."

54   We are thus left, in this new and strange world, with the task of deciding not what is "beneicial" to a patient (which is a medical decision), but what is "appropriate" or "cost effective" (which is a partly a social economic and a fairness decision). We shall have to balance quality of life with quantity of life, costs and benefits; preventive medicine versus curative medicine. We are, unfortunately but realistically, into prioritizing medicine. Medicine will never be the same.

55   Once we admit that we cannot pay for everything, we must ask ourselves not only what does a patient need, but how do we spend our resources to buy the maximum health for the largest number of citizens? This will inevitably impinge on a physician's judgement on what is the best medical treatment for an individual patient; when and where to admit patients to hospitals and when to discharge; under what conditions and symptoms are certain diagnostic or therapeutic procedures appropriate; and what prescriptions are appropriate under certain circumstances. It is the world of DRG writ large.

56   If the key to expansion of coverage is a matter of values so also the key to defining "appropriate" or "basic" healthcare is larely a matter of values. The access question shifts the question from *who* is covered to *what* is covered.

57   This is an ethical earthquake to existing medical values. Providers in America have been trained to monomaniacally focus only on the patient. In the new world of access:

> Providers should not do everything that may benefit an individual patient, since doing so may interfere with the ability of other patients to obtain basic services; rather, providers should treat each patient with a full range of resources as is compatible with treating patients yet to come.

58   The illusion of unlimited resources has been very counter productive for America. Once we admit that resources are limited, a whole new dialogue emerges. When we recognize that we cannot do everything we start to ask: What do we do to maximize the health of the community? Both individuals and the community are important, but the emphasis shifts from individual centered to community centered.

59   I end with another parable, but it is also a true story. Harvey Cushing, the famous surgeon and after whom the Cushing Lectures are named, made an international reputation in his allegiance to quality. He badgered his profession to a higher standard of self-effacement, railed against the debasement of clinical skills and overemphasis on research and pursuit of personal gain. We honor him to this day because those were, and remain, important points. Yet, Harvey Cushing served as a surgeon during World War I and at Ypres. Although the Allied mortality was as much as 50,000 soldiers a day, not counting the wounded, Cushing refused to operate on any more than two patients a day, arguing that to do so would have lowered his standard of care for his patients—a standard which made sense in one time became strikingly insensitive, and I suggest even unethical, in another when confronted with a different reality. The ethical claims for professional autonomy based on such standards of professional ethics has had the effect of supporting widespread distribution inequities. These inequitites are clearly a form of rationing that have been condoned implicitly by the professional ethics in the name of professional autonomy.

60   Many of the condemnations we hear today of perspective payment systems and how they will "ration" medicine contain a similar sense of unreality. The high standards are laudatory, but they should not be used as an excuse to not meet other pressing needs. High standards should never be used to make a problem worse. At some point, every ethical doctor has to lift their eyes from the patient in front of them and survey the needs of the whole battlefield.

61   America is right now at the beginning of a debate about the entire battlefield. Our system needs challenging. We have built up a health care system that better serves the needs of the providers than the public. We must substantially revamp our values and goals in health care.

62   We must move part of our existing emphasis:

Individual patient to population as a whole.

Acute care to chronic care.

Specialized care to primary care.

Institution based to ambulatory based.

Technology oriented to humanistically oriented.

Individual provider to team provider.

Cost unaware to cost aware.

Governed professionally to governed managerially.

63   We are spending millions of dollars on esoteric improvements at the margin in American medicine while spending pennies on the access problem where we could buy far more health. We give some people too much health care and others too little. We have money for Ecmo machines, but not prenatal care. We spend incredible amounts of money on kidney dialysis, but practically nothing on educating people to stop smoking and abusing alcohol. We have far too many MRI machines, but 30 percent of the women in America give birth without adequate prenatal care in their first trimester.

64   Our duty lies both to the individual and population; to the patient and to all citizens.. In a world of unconstrained demands and limited resources, we must adapt ourselves to the new world of medical ethics.

Chapter Six

Speeches That Create Concern for Problems

The speaker must awaken those who sleep or are indif-

ferent; he must help others see the unnoticed danger,

and understand it; he must direct us away from the false

and petty problems that set us off course.

Otis M. Walter and Robert L. Scott

The Nature and Importance of Speeches That Create Concern for Problems

Human existence in society gives rise to problems that threaten the perpetuation of the group and the welfare of its members. A problem might be described as a defect, difficulty, barrier, need, threat, state of dissatisfaction, or undesirable situation that people perceive as necessitating removal, rectification, or solution. The ability of groups and individuals to perceive and understand the nature and importance of the problems confronting them is one measure of a society's maturity and strength. If a society is unable to comprehend the significance of its problems, it has little chance of solving them.

Speakers often address audiences for the primary purpose of creating concern for problems. Whereas speeches advocating values are designed to develop value standards and value judgments in the minds of listeners, speeches trying to create concern for problems focus on specific social situations calling for remedial action. The mayor of a large city, for example, may seek to arouse public concern over the urban conditions that breed crime or riots. A sociologist may attempt to create concern for senior citizens on welfare. A politician may try to arouse sympathy for the plight of the American Indian.

Sometimes a speaker focuses on a problem as a prelude to advocating specific programs or policies as solutions for that problem. In any case, we face potential personal and public problems at virtually every turn: alcoholism, drug abuse, racial conflict, unemployment, suicide, pollution and abuse of the environment, violence as a way of life, discrimination against women, political deception, economic inflation, deceptive or harmful advertising, automobile accidents, and rising crime rates.

While the proposition of fact asserts that something is true or false and the proposition of value asserts that something has or lacks merit, the speech attempting to create concern for a problem asserts that specific social conditions should be perceived or defined as problems. Consider the following examples:

Proposition A: Racial unrest is Boston's most impelling community problem.

Proposition B: The unrestricted sale of firearms is cause for public alarm.

Proposition C: All parents should be concerned by the increased availability of hardcore pornography.

Proposition D: Student drug usage is a serious campus problem.

Proposition E: The depiction of violence on television programs oriented toward children merits public concern.

Proposition F: The increasing rate of traffic fatalities on Highway 12 warrants action by the state legislature.

Although the speech that creates concern for a problem usually depends on the affirmation of subsidiary propositions of fact and value, the basic purpose of such a speech is to invite attention to a problem needing solution.

Criteria for Evaluating Speeches That Create Concern for Problems

1. Has the speaker presented a compelling view of the nature of the problem?

The philosopher John Dewey emphasized the importance of this criterion when he wrote: "The essence of critical thinking is suspended judgement; and the essence of this suspense is inquiry to determine the nature of the problem before proceeding to attempts at its solution." To depict compellingly the nature of a problem, a speaker must prove that a certain state of affairs, a concrete set of circumstances, actually does exist. The nature is explained by focusing on the major elements of the problem and on its symptoms or outward manifestations.

Naturally a complete view of a problem includes a thorough exploration of the causes (the contributing influences) which combine to produce the state of affairs. Some problems are rooted in defective structures, personnel, or policies; other problems stem from inadequate goals, standards, and principles; still others derive from "outside" threats, opponents, or enemies. Remember, also, that social problems seldom are the result of a single cause. Rather, although one contributing factor may be described as the primary or the immediate cause, several contributing factors usually combine in primary-secondary and immediate-remote relationships. Finally, a compelling view often stems from describing the intensity and/or the widespread scope of the problem.

In exploring the nature of a problem, speakers may assume the role of social informant. When they do, the success of their speeches is governed, in part, by the same constraints imposed on speakers seeking to increase understanding. They must choose those supporting materials that best demonstrate the nature of the problem: analogy and illustration, expert testimony and factual example, description, definition, and narration. Their messages are subject to the same criteria suggested in Chapter 3: Is the information communicated accurately, completely, and with unity? Does the speaker make the information meaningful for the audience? Does the speaker create audience interest in the information presented? Has the speaker shown the audience that the information is important?

In a speech called "Mingled Blood," Ralph Zimmerman, a college student and a hemophiliac, chose to use definition and description to illuminate the nature of hemophilia:

What is this thing called hemophilia? Webster defines it as "a tendency, usually hereditary, to profuse bleeding even from slight wounds." Dr. Armand J. Quick, Professor of Biochemistry at Marquette University and a recognized world authority on this topic, defines it as "a prothrombin consumption time of 8 to 13 seconds." Normal time is 15 seconds. Now do you know what hemophilia is? . . .

What does it really mean to be a hemophiliac? The first indication comes in early childhood when a small scratch may bleed for hours. By the time the hemophiliac reaches school age, he begins to suffer from internal bleeding into muscles, joints, the stomach, the kidneys. This latter type is far more serious, for external wounds can usually be stopped in minutes with topical thromboplastin or a pressure bandage. But internal bleeding can be checked only by changes in the blood by means of transfusion or plasma injections. If internal bleeding into a muscle or joint goes unchecked repeatedly, muscle contraction and bone deformity inevitably result.

Along with increasing understanding about a problem, speakers also may affirm propositions of fact related to the problem. When speakers seek to prove propositions of fact in developing a compelling view of the problem, their efforts are subject to the same criteria suggested in Chapter 4: Has the speaker adequately assessed the proof requirements of the factual proposition? Has the speaker offered acceptable arguments in support of the proposition of fact? Has the speaker provided adequate evidence in support of the arguments?

2. Has the speaker shown the significance of the problem for the specific audience?

In addition to gaining an understanding of the nature of the problem, an audience must also be convinced that the problem has significance for them individually or collectively. Thus, value judgments must augment factual demonstrations. To demonstrate that juvenile delinquency is extensive, a factual state of affairs must be established. To demonstrate that juvenile delinquency poses a threat or is an undesirable situation, a judgment must be made in light of societal value standards. When a speaker affirms a proposition of value in showing the significance of a problem, the criteria suggested in Chapter 5 usually are relevant: Has the speaker demonstrated, or is it assumed by the audience, that he or she is a person of high credibility with respect to the proposition? Has the speaker advanced acceptable criteria for the assessment of the proposition? Has the speaker presented a fair view of what is being evaluated?

A problem is not really a problem to an audience until they perceive it as such. A situation may exist, and the audience even may know that it does, but in their eyes it remains nothing more than a lifeless fact until they view it as something that threatens or violates their interests and values. The members of an audience who have just been informed that many American Indians endure substandard economic, educational, and health conditions may greet this knowledge with indifference. Although they may accept the situation as actual, they have not perceived it as a problem for themselves, either as individuals or as members of society.

In the background of public debate on societal issues are values which, according to Robert B. Reich, in his book, *Tales of a New America* (Times Books, 1987, p. 6), often are unstated, disguised, or taken for granted. These values, typically embodied in narrative "morality tales," influence when we "declare a fact to be a problem, how policy choices are characterized, how the debate is framed." Reich emphasizes: "Public problems don't exist 'out there.' They are not discrete facts or pieces of data awaiting discovery. They are the consequences of our shared values. Without a set of common moral assumptions we would have no way of identifying or categorizing problems and their possible solutions." Clearly a problem is "created" for an audience through their own perceptual processes. An audience labels something as a problem only when they perceive a strong link between a situation (real or imagined) and their relevant basic values which they see as undermined or threatened by that situation. Speakers and listeners employ values as standards to "define" something as a problem.

What approaches could a speaker use to show the significance of a problem? Ralph Zimmerman concluded that for many listeners it is sufficient to show that the problem brings danger, degradation, or suffering to those who directly experience it. Thus he depicted hemophilia as a source of suffering for those afflicted by it:

> I remember the three long years when I couldn't even walk because repeated hemorrhages had twisted my ankles and knees to pretzel-like forms. I remember being pulled to school in a wagon while other boys rode their bikes, and being pushed to my table. I remember sitting in the dark empty classroom by myself during recess while the others went out in the sun to run and play. And I remember the first terrible day at the big high school when I came on crutches and built-up shoes carrying my books in a sack around my neck. . . . And how well I remember the endless pounding, squeezing pain. When you seemingly drown in your own perspiration, when your teeth ache and bombs explode back of your eyeballs; when darkness and light fuse into one hue of gray; when day becomes night and night becomes day—time stands still—and all that matters is that ugly pain.

Although the most hardened pragmatist might state that the problem is of little social importance because when Zimmerman spoke in 1955 there were only 20,000 to 40,000 hemophiliacs in the United States, most Americans, committed to the worth of the individual human, would agree with Zimmerman that "if society can keep a hemophiliac alive until after adolescence, society has saved a member."

Guided by the actual nature of the problem and by relevant standards of ethics, a speaker may choose from a variety of potential strategies to create audience concern. Here we present a few such strategies, some adapted from the writings of Otis

M. Walter. To show that the problem directly or indirectly harms the audience addressed (economically, socially, morally, physically) is an approach often used. Sometimes the problem is described as a unique, immediate, and pressing one demanding speedy recognition, diagnosis, and treatment; or it is described as an important contemporary manifestation of a timeless, continuing, larger problem always faced by humanity. Awareness of the problem may be emerging only gradually in the public consciousness and an audience might be urged to be in the vanguard of citizens concerned about it. On the other hand, the audience might be asked to join large numbers of fellow citizens who already recognize the problem.

Through use of historical examples, a speaker could argue that the failure of past societies to recognize the same or a similar problem caused them harm. Often this argument is embodied in an analogy to the decline and fall of the Roman Empire. The ways in which the problem contributes to or interacts with other societal problems could be demonstrated. If the problem is now in the embryonic stage, audiences could be warned that if it is not treated it will steadily worsen and perhaps become unsolvable. On occasion, a problem of concern for those affected takes on added significance when shown also to be working for the political or psychological advantage of our opponents or enemies. If the audience and the people harmed by the problem both have similar goals, values, needs, and fears, the audience could be made to feel that they might just as easily have experienced the problem themselves ("There but for the grace of God go I"). A speaker could show that the problem is acknowledged as vital by those whom the audience regards highly, such as public officials, statesmen, religious leaders, or experts on the subject.

The harmful economic, political, social, religious, or moral consequences of leaving the problem unsolved could be stressed. The problem could be shown as one of physical survival or security; or it could be shown as a problem threatening the enhancement or growth of the human spirit. A problem becomes of concern when it causes our society and its institutions to function at less than normal expected effectiveness. Sometimes the problem legitimately is described as stemming from conflict between an accepted but outmoded belief or value and existing circumstances. Finally, a speaker usually must secure audience perception of the problem as a high priority one—more crucial than most other problems faced by them or society.

Conclusion

In *Constructing the Political Spectacle*, Murray Edelman, a political scientist, reminds us: "Problems come into discourse and therefore into existence as reinforcements of ideologies, not simply because they are there or because they are important for wellbeing. They signify who are virtuous and useful and who are dangerous or inadequate, which actions will be rewarded and penalized." Problems, continues

Edelman, "constitute people as subjects with particular kinds of aspirations, self-concepts, and fears, and they create beliefs about the relative importance of events and objects." Edelman concludes that problems "are critical in determining who exercise authority and who accept it. They construct areas of immunity from concern because those areas are not seen as a problem."

In our society people often seek to generate concern about problems, both great and small. At certain times the speaker's sole purpose is to set the stage for private thought or public discussion. At other times the speaker seeks to arouse interest in a problem to prepare the audience for accepting a specific solution. In either case, the speaker must present *a compelling view of the nature of the problem* and *the reasons that it is significant for the particular audience.*

For Further Reading

Dewey, John. *How We Think*. D. C. Heath, 1910, pp. 72–74. Concisely explains the importance of understanding the nature of problems.

Edelman, Murray. *Constructing the Political Spectacle*. University of Chicago Press, 1988. Chapter 2 probes the symbolic construction and ideological bases of social problems.

Jensen, J. Vernon. *Argumentation: Reasoning in Communication*. Van Nostrand, 1981. Chapter 4 suggests potential lines of argument basic to presenting the nature of a problem.

Walter, Otis M., and Scott, Robert L. *Thinking and Speaking*. 5th ed. Macmillan, 1984. Chapters 6 and 7 focus on suggestions for persuading about problems and causes.

Walter, Otis M. *Speaking Intelligently*. Macmillan, 1976, Chapters 2, 3, 4, and pp. 216–21. An exploration of the nature of societal problems and causes of such problems, along with suggested strategies for persuading about problems and causes.

PESTICIDES SPEECH

César Chávez

Noted speakers—whether they are presidents of large corporations, heads of public service organizations, major government officials, or leaders of social movements—frequently are called upon to speak on the same general topic to numerous but varied audiences. Politicians during major campaigns often face the same demand. One approach such speakers sometimes take is to present a "generic" speech—a speech containing the same general information and arguments regardless of audience but with opportunities in the speech for a modest amount of concrete adaptation to each specific audience. For one discussion of such generic or "stock" political campaign speeches, see Judith S. Trent and Robert V. Friedenberg, *Political Campaign Communication* (Prager, 1983), pp. 171–177.

This speech by César Chávez is a generic speech. It contains standard or basic arguments on the topic suitable for diverse audiences and occasions with two places noted for specific audience adaptation: "insert names" (1) and "insert additional pitches" (18). There are no mentions in the text of the speech of a specific audience or occasion. The text simply is dated 1–9–90 and labeled as "Pesticides Speech for César Chávez." Other texts of speeches presented by Chávez provided by his office indicate specific audiences and occasions and some of the speeches make numerous adaptations to the audiences.

César Chávez was born in 1927 in Arizona and in 1962 in California founded the National Farm Workers Association (later called United Farm Workers of America). This was a labor union noted for its aggressive but nonviolent advocacy of the rights and safety of migrant farm workers. In numerous social protest efforts spanning four decades, Chávez often has utilized the pressure tactic of consumer boycott of the purchase of farm produce such as lettuce or grapes. Although in this speech he does urge adoption of a policy—the boycott of table grapes—and he does indicate its potential effectiveness (15–18), the bulk of the speech primarily aims at creating concern for a problem rather than de-

+The text of this speech was provided by President César Chávez's office at the national headquarters of the United Farm Workers of America.

scribing in detail a program of action. César Chávez died on April 23, 1993.

In presenting a compelling view of the problem, Chávez answers the question—Why grapes?—by demonstrating the scope of the problem. He employs statistics to show how widespread the problem is (4, 10) and argues that the problem threatens farm workers, their children, and consumers (5–6, 10). Statistics such as 800 percent and 1200 percent above normal index the intensity of the problem (8–9). Expert testimony is used in several places, including use of so-called "reluctant" testimony from grower and government sources (2, 6, 14). What are the causes of the problem? Chávez clearly identifies two: grape grower greed (2–3, 12, 18) and inaction and misaction by state and federal governments (12–14). For Chávez, government "is part of the problem."

Chávez attempts to generate audience concern for the problem by vividly depicting the danger, degradation, and suffering of people who directly experience the problem. First, he lists the general physical harms: "cancer, DNA mutations, and horrible birth defects" (6). Second, and at length, he "humanizes" the "technical" problem of pesticides with examples of real people and groups (7–11). Note his skillful use of alliteration to make his argument memorable: "*children* are dying . . . *slow, painful, cruel* deaths in towns called *cancer clusters*" (8) And note his use of parallel phrasing to summarize his point (11).

Of special interest to the rhetorical critic is Chávez's strategy of associating the pesticides and policies he condemns with so-called "devil terms" that carry intense negative force because they represent violations of fundamental human values. He establishes associations with nerve gas (6–World War I German use and use by Saddam Hussein against Kurds in Iraq in 1988); with agent orange (6–a chemical with harmful physical side-effects used to strip leaves from trees during the Vietnam War); with killing fields (10–allusion to the 1984 film of the same name that depicted mass slaughter of Cambodian civilians by Communist terrorists); and, sarcastically, with Idi Amin (Uganda's bloody dictator) and Adolph Hitler (13). How adequately and legitimately do you believe that he establishes these associations?

In what ways and to what degree might the lack in a generic speech of arguments and appeals specifically intended for a specific audience lessen Chávez's, or any speaker's, ability to create concern for the problem she or he describes? Here recall the discussion of the second suggested criterion for evaluating speeches that create concern for problems: Has the speaker shown the significance of the problem for the specific audience? In addition, are there any ethical issues involved in the use of generic speeches? If so, what might they be and on what grounds? For a brief analysis of Chávez's rhetoric during the 60s and 70s, see John C. Hammerback and Richard J. Jensen, "The Rhetorical Worlds of César Chávez and Reies Tierina," *Western Journal of Speech Communication*, 44 (Summer 1980): 166–176.

---

1   Thank you very much, I am truly honored to be able to speak with you. I would like to thank the many people who made this possible for their kindness and their hospitality. (insert names)

2   Decades ago, the chemical industry promised the growers that pesticides would create vast new wealth and bountiful harvests. Just recently, the experts learned what farm workers, and the truly organic farmers have known for years. The prestigious National Academy of Sciences recently concluded an exhaustive five-year study which showed that by using simple, effective organic farming techniques, *instead of pesticides*, the growers could make *more money*, produce *more crops*, and *protect the environment!*

3   Unfortunately, the growers are not listening. They continue to spray and inject hundreds of millions of pounds of herbicides, fungicides, and insecticides onto our foods.

4   Most of you know that the United Farm Workers have focussed our struggle against pesticides on table grapes. Many people ask me "Why grapes?" The World Resources Institute reported that over three hundred thousand farm workers are poisoned every year by pesticides. Over half of all reported pesticide-related illnesses involve the cultivation or harvesting of table grapes. They receive *more* restricted-use application permits, which allow growers to spray pesticides known to threaten humans, than *any* other fresh food crop. The General Accounting Office, which does research for the U.S. Congress, determined that 34 of the 76 types of pesticides used *legally* on grapes pose potential human health hazards and could *not be detected* by current multi-residue methods.

5   My friends, grapes are the most dangerous fruit in America. The pesticides sprayed on table grapes *are killing America's children*. These pesticides *soak* the fields, *drift* with the wind, *pollute* the water, and are *eaten* by unwitting consumers. These poisons are designed to kill life, and pose a very real threat to consumers and farm workers alike.

6   The fields are sprayed with pesticides like captan, a fungicide believed to cause cancer, DNA mutation, and horrible birth defects. Other poisons take a similar toll. Parathion and phosdrin are *"nerve gas"* types of insecticides, which

are believed to be responsible for the majority of farm worker poisonings in California. The growers spray sulphites, which can trigger asthmatic attacks, on the grapes. And even the growers own magazine, *The California Farmer*, admitted that growers were *illegally* using a very dangerous growth stimulator, called *Fix*, which is quite similar to *Agent Orange*, on the grapes.

7   This is a very technical problem, with very *human* victims. One young body, Felipe Franco, was born without arms or legs in the agricultural town of McFarland. His mother worked for the first three months of her pregnancy picking grapes in fields that were sprayed repeatedly with pesticides believed to cause birth defects.

8   My friends, the central valley of California is one of the wealthiest agricultural regions in the world. In its midst are clusters of children dying from cancer. The children who live in towns like McFarland are surrounded by the grape fields that employ their parents. The children contact the poisons when they play outside, when they drink the water, and when they hug their parents

Photo courtesy of Bettman Archive.

returning from the fields. *And the children are dying.* They are dying *slow, painful, cruel* deaths in towns called *cancer clusters*. In cancer clusters like McFarland, where the childhood cancer rate is *800 percent* above normal.

9   A few months ago, the parents of a brave little girl in the agricultural community of Earlimart came to the United Farm Workers to ask for our help. Their four year old daughter, Natalie Ramirez, has lost one kidney to cancer and is threatened with the loss of another. The Ramirez family knew about our protests in nearby McFarland and thought there might be a similar problem in their home town. Our union mem-

Farm labor leader César Chávez speaks to a group of supporters.

bers went door to door in Earlimart and found that the Ramirez family's worst fears were true. There are at least *four* other children suffering from cancer and similar diseases which the experts believe were caused by pesticides in the little town of Earlimart, a rate *1200 percent* above normal. In Earlimart, little Jimmy Caudillo died recently from leukemia at the age of three.

10   The grape vineyards of California have become America's Killing Fields. These *same* pesticides can be found on the grapes you buy in the store. Study after study, by the California Department of Food and Agriculture, by the Food and Drug Administration, and by objective newspapers, concluded that up to *54 percent* of the sampled grapes contained pesticide residues. Which pesticide did they find the most? *Captan,* the same carcinogenic fungicide that causes birth defects.

11   My friends, *the suffering must end. So many* children are dying, *so many* babies are born without limbs and vital organs, *so many* workers are dying in the fields.

12   The growers, and the supermarket owners, say that the government can *handle* the problem, can *protect* the workers, can *save* the children. It *should,* but it *won't.* You see, agribusiness is *big business.* It is a *sixteen billion* dollar industry in California alone. Agribusiness contributed very heavily to the successful campaign of republican governor George Deukmajian. He has rewarded the growers by turning the Agricultural Labor Relations Board into a tool for the growers, run by the growers. The governor even vetoed a bill that would have required growers to warn workers that they were entering recently sprayed fields! And only *one percent* of those growers who *are caught* violating pesticide laws were even fined in California.

13   President Bush is a long-time friend of agribusiness. During the last presidential campaign, George Bush ate grapes in a field just *75 miles* from the cemetery where little Jimmy Caudillo and other pesticide victims are buried, in order to show his support for the table grape industry. He recently gave a speech to the Farm Bureau, saying that it was up to the *growers* to restrain the use of dangerous pesticides.

That's like putting *Idi Amin,* or *Adolph Hitler,* in charge of promoting *peace* and *human rights.*

14   To show you what happens to pesticides supposedly under government control, I'd like to tell you more about captan. Testing to determine the acceptable tolerance levels of captan was done by Bio-Tech Laboratories, later found *guilty* of falsifying the data to the E.P.A. The tolerance level set was *ten times* the amount allowed in Canada. Later, government agencies tried to ban captan, but were mysteriously stopped several times. Finally, the government banned captan on 42 crops, but *not on grapes.* Even the General Accounting Of-

fice found that the government's pesticide testing is wholly inadequate. The government is *not* the answer, it is part of the problem.

15   If we are to protect farm workers, their children, and consumers, we must use *people power.* I have seen many boycotts succeed. The Reverend Martin Luther King Junior, who so generously supported our first fast, led the way with the bus boycott. And with *our* first boycott, we were able to get DDT, Aldrin, and Dieldrin banned, in our first contracts with grape growers. Now, even more urgently, we are trying to get deadly pesticides banned.

16   The growers and their allies have tried to stop us with *lies,* with *police,* with *intimidation,* with *public relations agencies,* and with *violence.* But *we cannot be stopped.* In our *life and death struggle* for justice, we have turned to the court of last resort: the American people.

17   At last we are winning. Many supermarket chains have stopped selling or advertising grapes. Millions of consumers are refusing to buy America's most dangerous fruit. Many courageous people have volunteered to help our cause or joined human chains of people who fast, who go without food for days, to support our struggle. As a result, *grape sales keep falling.* We have witnessed truckloads of grapes being dumped because no one would stoop low enough to buy them. As demand drops, so do prices and profits. This sort of economic pressure is the only language the growers understand.

18   We are winning, but there is still much work to be done. If we are going to beat the greed and power of the growers, we must work *together. Together,* we can end the suffering. *Together,* we can save the children. *Together,* we can bring justice to the killing fields. I hope that you will join our struggle, for it is *your* struggle too. The simple act of boycotting table grapes laced with pesticides is a powerful statement the growers understand. *Please, boycott table grapes.* For your safety, for the workers, *we must act,* and *act together.* (insert additional pitches)

19   Good night, and God bless you.

MEN AND WOMEN GETTING ALONG: THESE ARE TIMES THAT TRY MEN'S SOULS

Bernice R. Sandler

On March 26, 1991 Bernice Sandler spoke to several hundred students and faculty at Illinois State University in Normal, Illinois, at a meeting sponsored by the university's Women's Studies Program. Since 1971 Bernice Sandler has been Director of the Project on Status and Education of Women of the Association of American Colleges. Among the many awards received by Sandler are the Women Educators award for activism and the Anna Roe award from Harvard University. The Association of American Colleges promotes "humane and liberating learning," improves public understanding of the value of a liberal education, and explores issues affecting women in higher education.

In a style that relies on informal and colloquial language, Bernice Sandler creates audience concern for the problem of peer harassment on campuses of women by men, especially sexual harassment (6). Even before she identifies her specific topic, she alerts the audience to the difficulty of discussing such a sensitive topic (2–4). She employs a broad range of rhetorical resources to stimulate audience concern. Occasionally she places the problem in the broader context of peer harassment of ethnic groups and of gays and lesbians (5–6, 35). She defines the problem by discussing the range of its manifestations (7), by straightforward explanation (16), and by stressing the role of language choice in our definitions (40). In addition to respect, humaneness, and equality, what other values does she depict as being threatened or violated?

To illustrate the nature and scope of the problem, Sandler profusely employs examples (8–10, 17–18, 21–22, 25–28). Sometimes these examples stem from her personal experience (31–33, 39). In evaluating her use of examples, consider whether a sufficient number of examples was presented, whether the examples were typical instances, and whether there are counter-examples that should be taken into account. At one point she contends that "when things have a name, you know that they are not unusual occurrences, but that they happen often, in

---

✝The text of this speech was provided by Bernice Sandler.

many places at many times" (9). To what extent do you accept this argument as an index of the typicality or representativeness of examples?

In order to elaborate one important dimension of the problem, she often illustrates the differing perceptions of the same behavior held by women and men (11, 15, 18, 23–24, 35, 42). How effective would this approach probably be? Why? Another rhetorical resource used to support her analysis is statistics (13–14, 21, 24, 40). How adequately does she substantiate the source and credentials of the research "studies" she draws upon? Or does she seem to assume that the audience simply will rely on her own credibility and honesty? Sandler attempts to avoid overgeneralizations (11–12) and to draw careful distinctions (16). How adequately do you believe she does so?

As means of connecting the problem to the experience of her audience, she uses statistics (40), a hypothetical example (41), and a lengthy series of final questions that skillfully underscore the value choices facing the students, especially the men (46). Note particularly her adept use of "role reversal" examples to encourage men to empathize with the problem from the perspective of women (17, 19). A rhetorical critic immediately should note as important her extensive use throughout the speech of questions to provoke thought, as transitions or forecasts, or to underscore conclusions. How well do you believe she employs questions to serve these or other functions?

At length Bernice Sandler analyzes the major causes or "reasons" for the problem (36–42). And at various points she discusses the effects of the problem (12, 39, 43–45)—effects which in one way or another reflect devaluation or debasement of women. Consider how adequately she recognizes multiple and interrelated contributing causes, avoids confusing a causal connection with either chronology or correlation, recognizes both immediate causes and a chain or sequence of causes, explores major relevant effects, and employs sound evidence to support her arguments on causes and effects.

Finally, examine her strategy of dispelling sexual "myths" that unfortunately too often are used to justify sexual harassment (20, 21, 29–30). In what ways is this also an exploration of causes that contribute to the problem? And note that Sandler condemns the "it's just in fun" rationalization used as an excuse.

---

1 As everyone knows, the word "men" applies to women as well, and surely these are times that try women's souls as well. Since the days of Adam and Eve, men and women have had trouble getting along. Scholars—psychologists, sociologists, philosophers—indeed almost everyone has some opinion as to what the problems are. So when I venture into this territory, it is with some trepidation because everyone has opinions about what the problems are and what needs to be done, if anything.

2   I want to start off with a question. Do you remember when it was ok for the boys to tease the girls? People laughed—at least the boys laughed. The girls may have been uncomfortable, but nobody took this kind of teasing too seriously. In fact many people thought of it—some still do—as cute, as "boys will be boys," and as natural, normal, behavior.

3   Well, it is not okay anymore. And when big boys do it—men—in this institution or in the workplace, it may well be illegal in many instances. And so tonight, I'm going to talk about some of the negative aspects of men and women getting along. It is not an easy subject to talk about, and many of you may not like or agree with what you hear.

4   It's a subject that is hard for me to talk about, because most of the time I like to joke around, and it's hard for me to joke about this subject. But I hope you will listen and give some thought to this not only because it is important but also because it ultimately relates to what you want to get out of your college experience, and how you will relate to people who are not like you.

5   Ideally the college experience as a whole should help students not only acquire knowledge but also build skills and confidence, learn how to make good choices in life, and particularly how to handle differences, including those of race, class, gender and sexual orientation. All too often, colleges and universities fail in helping men and women meet the challenge of learning to get along. College is a lot more than just going to classes. The social learning that happens outside of the classroom is just as important as what happens inside. The wide range of experiences you have with friends and acquaintances is not only complementary but critical to what you will be learning in the next few years.

6   There is a darker side to campus life, often unnoticed, or if it is acknowledged, it is ignored or brushed off as "normal behavior." That darker side is peer harassment, whether it is men harassing women, men and women harassing gay and lesbian students, women harassing men, but particularly the harassment of women by men students, and that is what I'm going to be talking about tonight. That's the darker side of campus life: peer harassment. For too many students the relationships between men and women are not always positive. Too many women experience hostility, anger, and sometimes even violence from male students.

7   Peer harassment covers a wide range of behaviors. At one end of the scale, peer harassment consists of so-called teasing, sexual innuendos, even ob-

scenities—a sort of sexual bullying, both physical and verbal, often made in the guise of humor. At the other end, is explicit sexual harassment, up to and including sexual aggression, with rape as the most extreme form of peer harassment. Let me give you some examples, both serious and mild, of what I mean, although even mild ones can seriously affect a woman.

8   A woman raises something about women's issues in a class. The men in the class hiss and laugh at her. She is effectively silenced, even though theoretically in a classroom students are supposed to feel free to bring up any issues.

9   Here is another example. A lot of things happen in cafeterias. A group of men regularly sit at a table facing the cafeteria line. As the women go through the line the men loudly discuss the women's sexual attributes—size of breast and how she would act during intercourse—and then they hold up cards, rating each woman from 1 to 10. It's called "scoping", and when things have a name, you know that they are not unusual occurrences, but that they happen often, in many places at many times. Some women do not come to the cafeteria unless they can find a friend and pretend that they don't hear the men; other women skip meals altogether if the men are there.

10   Here is another example. A fraternity pledge approaches a woman student he has never seen before, and bites her on the breast, a practice called "sharking." And another. A group of men simultaneously expose themselves, or in another variation they simply surround a woman, demand that she bare her breasts, and do not allow her to leave the circle until she has done so.

11   I want to be sure that you all understand that not all men harass women students. And certainly not all women students experience this behavior. But just as certainly, on every campus, there are too many men treating women in ways that are disrespectful. That is an old-fashioned word, but I don't know what else to call this behavior, behavior that is invasive and can only be described as emotional and psychological harassment. Often however, the men do not describe their behavior this way. They are just having a good time. If a woman doesn't like it and she takes offense, the men probably say, "She just doesn't have a sense of humor." Yet to the woman, such behaviors can poison her college experience.

12   These behaviors are not universal; they don't occur all the time. And while men can also be harassed by women—that's the subject of another talk— not tonight—women are the majority of the peer harassment victims. What is interesting is that even though the women are harassed by men because they *are women*, not all women recognize these behaviors as harassment. Nevertheless, when these experiences occur again and again, and when they are either unnoticed, ignored by faculty and administrators, or even condoned by other students and some college officials, men and women alike receive the message that

women are not to be treated with respect—that women can be treated with disdain and it does not matter to anyone.

13   How much of a problem are we talking about? Well, there have been a few studies— not many—but from the best information we have, somewhere between 70–90 percent of women students have experienced some behavior from male students to which they reacted negatively. 70–90 percent! In contrast, sexual harassment of women students by faculty and staff has a far lower incidence. 20–30 percent of women undergraduates report some form of sexual harassment from someone in authority, with only two percent reporting actual threats or bribes for unwanted sexual activity.

14   Additionally, widespread harassment of women by fraternities has been documented on virtually every campus that has examined fraternity life in the last five years. There is also another group of men that are likely to harass women. Anyone want to guess? Yes. Athletes—and not the swimming team, not the golf team, but the football and basketball teams, occasionally rugby, wrestling, or lacrosse.

15   Much of peer harassment is sexual harassment. In general, sexual harassment involves unwanted sexual attention, and there are a lot of men who think that all women want this and are flattered by any kind of sexual attention, especially if a woman does not indicate any displeasure about the behavior. You see this at construction sites, where, when a woman walks by, the men show their "manliness" by hooting and hollering at her, but this happens elsewhere as well. Now why doesn't the woman indicate any displeasure? Why doesn't she just say "Hey guys, knock it off. I don't like this." Sometimes she thinks if she says anything like that the behavior will get worse. Her strategy is to ignore it because she really wants the behavior to stop; in contrast, his perception is that she must really like it because she didn't say anything.

16   All sexual attention is not sexual harassment. Certainly when men and women are together, sexual attraction is possible, and people will express that attraction. Sexual attention becomes harassment when it is persistent or unwanted or personal boundaries are crossed. What may be appropriate in a continuing relationship is inappropriate coming from a stranger or new acquaintance as in the following examples:

17   Inappropriate personal remarks such as comments about a woman, her body, or sexual activities. Comments such as "You've got great breasts" from a stranger are not perceived as compliments because they depersonalize women—they reduce women to being *only* a sexual object. Her breasts become the most important part of her and it ignores her individuality or humanity. If you are a male person, try to think how you might feel if the first thing someone said to you after being introduced—say, you're a swimming star at a swimming meet, and the first thing someone said when they met you was "you've got a great penis."

18   Unwanted touching or kissing. Women have had their breasts grabbed or have been hugged and kissed by people they did not know well, especially at parties. Sometimes people say that women "ask" for this behavior. "Look at the clothes she wore." This is a good example of how men's clothing and women's clothing are seen very differently. Now women wear clothing to be in style and for their self-esteem, but men, when they see women's clothing, often assume that she is looking for sex. She could be wearing tight pants or loose pants, lowcut clothes or a high neck, ruffles, short skirts, long skirts, short sleeves, long sleeves—indeed whatever a woman wears may be viewed by some men as a sexual invitation. A woman could be wearing an old burlap potato sack and there will be some guy who'll look at her and say "Wow—this is the sexiest potato sack I've ever seen and she obviously wants to have sex, and she obviously wants to have sex with me."

19   Interestingly, men's clothing does not communicate that at all. You're on a campus, and I'm sure you all have seen guys wearing jeans that are so tight that you can surely see the size and shape of the sexual apparatus. But a guy would be shocked if some woman—or man—came up to him and—grabbed—his penis, and when he said, "Hey what's going on here?" the person responded, "well, look at the way you're dressed. You're asking for it."

20   Women's clothing does not communicate a sexual invitation. It does communicate "I am a woman" but it doesn't give anyone else permission to grab or touch. It doesn't signal what a woman wants or what she will do. This is what I call the clothing myth and it essentially views sexual harassment, and to some extent rape, as an extension of biological drives. "She was so beautiful, I just couldn't help myself." It ignores the issue of power which I'll talk about later, but it also shifts the responsibility for the harassment or the rape to the victim. *She* is the one that is causing the men to harass her. It's her fault, not his. The women are causing the men to harass them.

21   Another example is persistent sexual attention. Asking a woman for a date or sex repeatedly, even if the woman has said no. Here we see the operation of another myth, that a woman says "no" when she really means "yes." So there is no way a woman can say "no," and many men feel it incumbent upon themselves to turn that "no" into a "yes." Someone did research on this and it turns out that most women have never said "no" when they meant "yes," and of the 15 or 20 percent that had said "no" when they meant "yes," almost all of these had said "no" when they meant "yes" only one time. So it is a relatively rare phenomenon for women to say "no" when they really mean "yes."

22   Another thing that happens are requests for sexual activity, such as men shouting obscene sexual invitations through an open dormitory window. This, like other forms of harassment, tells a woman that her individuality doesn't matter. She is being viewed only in terms of her sexuality.

23   Now, sometimes when sexual harassment or rape occurs, the man involved says, "well she asked for it." And when you ask questions about this, he usually refers to her clothing or her behavior. A woman smiled; he views it as a sexual invitation. A woman talked to him; and he views it as a sexual invitation. Indeed men often mistake a woman's friendliness as a sexual invitation.

24   Someone did a study on this. They taped several conversations of men and women talking to each other, and then showed the segments to a group of men and women and asked them to decide for each segment whether the woman was being friendly or was "coming on" to the guy. The women who view the video say for each segment, "she's being friendly, she's being friendly, she's being friendly." The men, in contrast, say "She's coming on to the guy, she wants to have sex with him, she's coming on strong." So we have a misperception here. Women are more likely to see friendliness and men are more likely to see sexual invitations. Think of how this affects the relationships between men and women.

25   Another example is a sexually demeaning climate, such as leaving pornographic materials in a woman's mailbox or in front of her dormitory door. Sometimes there are sexist posters or pictures or bumper stickers. At one fraternity party there was a poster on the door which said "No fat chicks allowed." Since 75% of young women believe that they are overweight, at least 75 percent of the women were offended.

26   Sexist graffiti can be on desks and walls, in library carrels or on cafeteria tables. Often the graffiti may also be racist or anti-semitic, or offensive to gays and lesbians. The graffiti can stay for years, often offending generations of students because most institutions ignore it. Syracuse University has one of the few programs to periodically examine the campus for graffiti and remove it. The only other example I know of graffiti being removed occurred at Brown University, where on the wall of the women's restrooms, women have begun to write the names of male students who have raped women students. These names are removed each day.

27   Let me give you an example of offensive graffiti. One university has a "free expression tunnel" which connects both sides of the campus which is divided by a railroad track. There is a painting of a Raggedy Ann doll, mutilated and bruised, with blood streaming between the doll's legs, and the statement, "I raped Raggedy Ann." What do women feel when they walk by this several times daily? And what do men feel as they see it? And is this the kind of free expression we should be encouraging?

28   Other examples of the chilly climate for women are wet T-shirt contests, activities focussing on women's sexuality, showing pornographic movies as fundraisers—that happens at a lot of campuses—or petty hostility toward women, such as throwing things at women, heckling women, pouring drinks over women's heads or inside their clothing. All of these give men and women a message—a message that women don't count except as sexual objects, that friendship with women is not possible, and that women are natural objects of scorn and derision.

29   Now a lot of these activities are seen as fun, and if someone doesn't think so, they are accused as having no sense of humor. That's the worst thing you can say about someone, no sense of humor.

30   Now humor is important, it can be used to relax people and lighten them up. But humor has other functions. It can also be used to enhance group solidarity, to define the outsider, in this case women, and to discuss subjects that are taboo. So rather than discuss gender and sexuality, we find it easier to joke about them instead. And it can also be used to express anxiety and anger and discomfort and resentment, in this case, against women.

31   I've become very interested in humor in recent years, especially when I noticed that all of the so-called locker-room jokes are demeaning to women. So I began to think there must be jokes demeaning to men and I began to seek out these jokes—not because I'm interested in demeaning men—some of my best friends are men—but because I'm curious about the uses of humor. I have been collecting for several years, and I must tell you, jokes demeaning men are quite rare—I have about ten, and some of these are variations on the others. I'm not talking about jokes which demean some men, such as Scotsmen and hillbilly men but jokes which demean men as a group.

32   And there is a difference between the jokes that demean men and the ones that demean women. The jokes that demean women demean them in all sorts of roles, activities, and behaviors. The jokes that demean men are very limited. They deal with sexual performance and size of the reproductive organ. I'm not sure what these differences mean, but they are interesting, and I also have to tell you that I can't yet tell these jokes in public. If you know of any and want to tell them to me, I'll be glad to add them to my collection.

33   A few years ago the first of my daughters got married, and I was very happy about the forthcoming marriage, I like the young man, etc. But as the time for the wedding approached, I found myself becoming more and more uncomfortable. I finally realized what it was. I, who had been a fairly likeable person, was about to become a mother-in-law, the kind of person who is often ridiculed in jokes. I could see that I was entering a dangerous stage of my life. And again I said, there are a lot of mother-in-law jokes ridiculing women, so where are the father-in-law jokes. I'm even offering a reward of $25 for a father-in-law joke, because I don't think there are any.

34   Now what do these jokes about women tell us? They tell us that there is anger against women, anxiety, and perhaps even fear. I don't understand all of the dynamics about mother-in-law jokes but probably the mother-in-law is a stand-in for anger against one's own mother, one's spouse, or all women.

35   Similarly racist humor, ethnic humor, jokes about JAPS (the Jewish America Princess), jokes about Black women or other ethnic women are not simple fun, for too often what passes for humor is humor at the expense of someone else. What the men see as friendly fun is often viewed by the women as harassment, even though they may not use that term to define it. The men are having a good time with each other. This is how they build solidarity with each other, by being nasty to women.

36   Now since most men are nice guys, what is going on here? People who might not heckle people of another race may have no difficulty in engaging in the same behavior if the object of their disrespect is female. Well, there are a lot of reasons why, and here are some of them.

37   At a very early age, boys learn to use girls as what the sociologists call a "negative reference group." In other words, the boys define themselves by comparing themselves favorably to girls, the lesser group, the females. After all, what is the worst thing you can call a little boy? A sissy—which says he is acting like a girl. By teasing girls a boy begins to feel good about himself—he is "better" than they are, and teasing them makes him feel like a "real boy." Moreover, by putting down girls and females he can get closer to his buddies. They can all put down the girls, and feel better and bigger than the girls. Harassment, and even sexual assault, can be, for many men, the way in which they show other men how "manly" they really are. We see this in its extreme in the case of gang rape, where psychologists have noted that the men are not raping for sexual reasons but are really raping for each other. This is how they show their friends how strong, how virile, how manly, how wonderful they are. This is how they strengthen the bond with their brothers. They need to be one of the boys and they find it difficult to go against the group. Harassment, whether it is gang rape or heckling women, is used by some men as a way to bond with their brothers.

38   For some men, harassment and sexual abuse expresses their need to show power over women. In that sense it is something like the bully syndrome—the men feel better and stronger by picking on someone they perceive as weaker than themselves, the women. Some men think primarily in stereotypes, so that

they may be uncomfortable with women who have minds of their own. Some men may be angry at feminism, or angry at a particular woman, or at all women in general. Harassment, after all, is simply a milder form of assault. It tells women that men can intimidate them at will.

39   Alcohol and drugs can play a role by lowering people's inhibitions and creating an atmosphere where hurtful and even violent behavior, even a gang rape, can be seen as amusing. Pornography, easily available on most campuses, often portrays situations in which women are weak and treated badly, where women enjoy rape, pain, and humiliation, where violence against women is often an integral part of the scenario. Violence toward women, whether in pornography, movies, music videos and TV, promotes a perception of women as outsiders, as people who are less than human, as people who are objects for men to exploit, manipulate, and harm. Additionally, men in groups are often more prone to bad behavior—in a group, such as a fraternity, or as part of an athletic team, a man may do things that he might not otherwise do, because he is afraid of the hostility of the other men. The peer pressure is very strong. One of the things we need to do is to teach men how to stand up to other men when they are behaving badly, and to say "don't do that." I myself know of several attempted gang rapes that were stopped, simply because one man was strong enough to say something like "Hey guys, cut it out. Let her alone."

40   Moreover, peer harassment sets the stage for rape. Rape is merely the extreme form of peer harassment. The men who intimidate women are most likely to commit assault on women. Remember earlier I told you that 70–90% of women experience some form of peer harassment. I want to give you the figures for acquaintance rape, when one person forces or intimidates another to have intercourse and where both parties know each other. If you ask the men "Have you ever raped a woman?", most will say "No." But if you ask the question, "Have you ever forced or intimidated a woman to have sexual intercourse with you, between 10–15% will say yes. For women, the figures are more striking. Somewhere between 15 and 25% of undergraduate women have been raped by someone they know. They don't all call it rape, but if you ask them if anyone has ever forced or intimidated them to have sexual intercourse when they did not want to, that is when you get these 15–25% figures. How many is 15–25% of the women on this campus? That is a lot of women. Peer harassment makes it possible.

41   Other factors: Men are generally socialized in our society to be dominant, and that plays a role in peer harassment. Women have been socialized to play a secondary role, so that men are trained to talk, and women are trained to listen. Who has the most power in our society? Who has the most money? The best jobs? Look at our Supreme Court, our Congress, your own institution. Who holds most of the administrative posts? If you do not believe that men have more power, think of the following. You are walking alone on a dark street—it doesn't matter what sex you are. You see six women on the corner. Are you frightened? Same scenario, next night. You are walking alone on a dark street, and you see six men on the corner. Are you frightened? Who has more power in our society—men or women?

42   There are many stereotypes about women being weaker and passive, although these stereotypes interfere with our view of women as equals. We like to think of men and women, at least intellectually, as equals. But in reality, sexual relations—especially those that occur in a context of sexual harassment, sexual teasing and joking to show power, sexual bullying, and sexual assault—these occur within an implicit power relationship where one person, usually the male, has the power to intimidate and cause harm to the other—usually a woman—through physical and social means. Most men are not conscious of their power to intimidate women, although they may use that power often. In contrast women often recognize the power of men. Men and women have very different perceptions of the relationship between the sexes. Just the other day I read a chilling quotation by the author, Margaret Atwood. I found the quotation in some materials put out by a Wisconsin group called Men Stopping Rape. This is the quotation that the men chose to include in their materials. "Why are you afraid of women?" I asked a group of men. "We're afraid they will laugh at us," replied the men. "Why are you afraid of men?" I asked a group of women. "We're afraid they'll kill us," replied the women." End of quote. The quote shows how men and women view each other very differently and that men are not aware of the power that they hold and how they use that power.

43   It makes it difficult for women to say "Stop that, it bothers me." It makes it difficult for women to report harassment and sexual intimidation. Some women are frightened of retaliation. Some may believe that nothing is going to happen, so why bother? Some women begin to believe that this is the way men are, and nothing can change them. Others don't know about or trust their institution's grievance procedure. And sad to say, some women collude in the harassment and intimidation. They have accepted the ideology that any kind of sexual attention is flattery. They may be angry about feminism in part because they have implicitly accepted the myths of men's domination and power—the myths, the beliefs, and the attitudes that support sexual harassment and intimidation that make women believe that they caused the harassment. They may have seen films like "Animal House" and other media which make them believe that this is the way you have a good time. They may not want to antagonize men because they want to be liked and they are fearful of men being angry at them.

44   Peer harassment makes women feel less than equal. They may feel uncomfortable and annoyed. They may feel embarrassed, humiliated or degraded. They may feel disgusted, they may feel helpless, angry, unsure of how to respond. They may feel insulted, and they may be fearful of violence. They may also feel guilty and blame themselves, as if they did something that caused the men to act so badly. The cumulative effect of repeated harassment can be devastating. It reinforces self-doubt, and affects a woman's self-esteem, and even her academic experience. It makes coeducation less equal for women. It makes some women angry at men, and it may make it more difficult for some women to trust men.

45   Peer harassment also affects men. Peer harassment teaches men that relationships based on power are better than those based on intimacy and friendship. It makes it difficult for a man to form a healthy and satisfying relationship with a woman because it is hard to be committed to someone for whom he and others have so little respect. When men view women as objects to be demeaned and scorned, men find it difficult to relate to women as equal human beings—much less as friends or potential romantic partners or as co-workers. Even a man's friendship with other men will be shallow if the way to friendship with his brothers is to ridicule women rather than [build] a friendship based on shared feelings.

46   Let me end with some questions and then we can have some discussion. You are at the beginning of your adulthood. How do you want to relate to members of the other sex while you are in college? How do you want to relate both personally and professionally when you finish college? Do you want to be able to be friends and colleagues? Can you respect someone who is different from you? Can you have a relationship of equality or must it be based on power? Do you want a relationship where sex exists for its own sake and is not for intimacy or caring or sharing? Do we want men to continue to believe that the way to get points with their peers and the way to feel good about themselves and their sexuality is to dominate, to use and exploit women? Do we want men and women to believe that relationships with the other sex that are based on power are better than relationships based on mutual respect and intimacy?

47   The world is changing. The relationships between men and women are changing. Increasingly women are labeling forced sexual activity as rape, and calling peer harassment by name. The days of "boys will be boys" are fast disappearing as young men and young women are learning that the new world is a world in which men and women recognize that whatever their differences, they are equal, and that they must share a world in which they can work together, a world in which men and women are no longer adversarial, a world in which women and men can be friends.

48   Let me close with something that is characteristic of the new mood of women. It is "a newly discovered Biblical revelation," which was discovered in the Middle East by a woman archeologist, of course, assisted by women staff. You'll probably recognize the paraphrase, and it goes like this:

> And they shall beat their pots and pans into printing presses and weave their cloth in protest banners. Nations of women shall lift up their voices with nations of other women, neither shall they suffer discrimination anymore. [By Mary Chagnon]

49   That may sound apocryphal, but I suspect it may yet prove to come from the book of Prophets, for what women are learning is the politics of power and the politics of change, and the campus and the nation, and the world shall never again be the same.

ADDRESS TO THE UNITED NATIONS FOURTH WORLD CONFERENCE ON WOMEN

Hillary Rodham Clinton

Beijing, China, was the site of the United Nations Fourth World Conference on Women, September 4-15, 1995. A parallel meeting approved by the U.N., the Nongovernmental Organizations (NGOs) Forum on Women, was held August 30-September 8 in the town of Huairou about an hour from Beijing. The main issues at the U.N. conference were the stopping of worldwide violence against women, the economic and political empowerment of women, the granting of sexual rights to women, and the funding and implementation of programs to accomplish these goals. Delegates to the conference represented about 185 nations. Among the speakers were Benazir Bhutto, the prime minister of Pakistan, and Winnie Mandela of South Africa.

On September 5, 1995, in a speech interrupted repeatedly by applause, Hillary Rodham Clinton addressed the conference plenary session and attempted to create a common concern for problems facing

---

+The text of this speech was obtained from the office of Hillary Rodham Clinton through its World Wide Web home page.

women worldwide. She stresses commonalties rather than differences (3-6). Throughout the speech, she provides encouragement for necessary efforts by providing examples of the accomplishments of women (13,18-23, 47-49, 53).

Her central assumption is that abuse of women's rights involves abuse of human rights (35-40). Early in the speech she provides a summary forecast of prominent concerns (7) and places them among "the world's most pressing problems" (10). She emphasizes the vast array of "deeply-rooted problems that continue to diminish the potential of half the world's population" (50).

Hillary Rodham Clinton argues a cause-effect connection. Where the situations of women do not flourish the result is that families do not flourish; if women flourish then families flourish 14-15, 52). Using the tests for cause-effect reasoning described earlier in the chapter on Propositions of Fact, evaluate the reasonableness of her argument.

She contends that another problem is that women's work, experience, and problems typically are unnoticed, unheard, and devalued (24, 26). She urges women to give voice to the voiceless and to speak for those not heard; to remain silent is to contribute to the problem (29-32, 41).

In an indirect manner, she criticizes practices in China that harm women and children (42) and denounces Chinese efforts to hinder participation in the NGOs Forum (44-45). Such comments showed courage at a time when U.S.-Chinese diplomatic relations were strained.

Frequently she underscores and illustrates the problems facing women by using brief lists of examples (25, 28, 30, 32, 39, 44, 45, 52). On one occasion she employs a lengthy itemization of problems presented in parallel structure (42). Clearly factual examples are her primary type of evidence. Evaluate her use of examples and specific instances by applying the standard tests for reasonableness: (1) Was a sufficient number of instances presented? (2) Were the instances presented typical/representative ones? (3) Were there any negative of counter-instances that were omitted? But also consider how the use of examples (miniature stories) dramatizes the problems and relates them to the audience's experiences.

Hillary Rodham Clinton effectively employs several language resources to sharpen and strengthen the impact of her arguments. Through alliteration she links together a series of either positive or negative items to make her point more memorable (28, 49, 53). She makes extensive use of parallel phrasing and parallel structure to imbed ideas

> in the audience's memory and to pile example upon example to reinforce significance (8-9, 18–23, 42, 45).

---

1   Mrs. Mongella, distinguished delegates and guests:

2   I would like to thank the Secretary General of the United Nations for inviting me to be part to the United Nations Fourth World Conference on Women. This is truly a celebration — a celebration of the contributions women make in every aspect of life: in the home, on the job, in their communities, as mothers, wives, sisters, daughters, learners, workers, citizens and leaders.

3   It is also a coming together, much the way women come together every day in every country.

4   We come together in fields and in factories. In village markets and supermarkets. In living rooms and board rooms.

5   Whether it is while playing with our children in the park, or washing clothes in a river, or taking a break at the office water cooler, we come together and talk about our aspirations and concerns. And time and again, our talk turns to our children and our families.

6   However different we may be, there is far more that unites us than divides us. We share a common future. And we are here to find common ground so that we may help bring new dignity and respect to women and girls all over the world—and in so doing, bring new strength and stability to families as well.

7   By gathering in Beijing, we are focusing world attention on issues that matter most in the lives of women and their families: access to education, health care, jobs, and credit, the chance to enjoy basic legal and human rights and participate fully in the political life of their countries.

8   There are some who question the reason for this conference. Let them listen to the voices of women in their homes, neighborhoods, and workplaces.

9   There are some who wonder whether the lives of women and girls matter to economic and political progress around the globe . . . Let them look at the women gathered here and at Huairou . . . the homemakers, nurses, teachers, lawyers, policymakers, and women who run their own businesses.

10   It is conferences like this that compel governments and peoples everywhere to listen, look and face the world's most pressing problems.

11   Wasn't it after the women's conference in Nairobi ten years ago that the world focused for the first time on the crisis of domestic violence?

12   Earlier today, I participated in a World Health Organization forum, where government officials, NGOs, and individual citizens are working on ways to address the health problems of women and girls.

13   Tomorrow, I will attend a gathering of the United Nations Development Fund for Women. There, the discussion will focus on local—and highly successful—programs that give hard-working women access to credit so they can improve their own lives and the lives of their families.

14   What we are learning around the world is that, if women are healthy and educated, their families will flourish. If women are free from violence, their families will flourish. If women have a chance to work and earn as full and equal partners in society, their families will flourish.

15   And when families flourish, communities and nations will flourish.

16   That is why every women, every man, every child, every family, and every nation on our planet has a stake in the discussion that takes place here.

17   Over the past 25 years, I have worked persistently on issues relating to women, children and families. Over the past two-and-a-half years, I have had the opportunity to learn more about the challenges facing women in my own country and around the world.

18   I have met new mothers in Jojakarta, Indonesia, who come together regularly in their village to discuss nutrition, family planning, and baby care.

19   I have met working parents in Denmark who talk about the comfort they feel in knowing that their children can be cared for in creative, safe, and nurturing after-school centers.

20   I have met women in south Africa who helped lead the struggle to end apartheid and are now helping build a new democracy.

21   I have met with the leading women of the Western Hemisphere who are working every day to promote literacy and better health care for the children of their countries.

22   I have met women in India and Bangladesh who are taking out small loans to buy milk cows, rickshaws, thread, and other materials to create a livelihood for themselves and their families.

23   I have met doctors and nurses in Belarus and Ukraine who are trying to keep children alive in the aftermath of Chernobyl.

24   The great challenge of this conference is to give voice to women everywhere whose experiences go unnoticed, whose words go unheard.

25   Women comprise more than half the world's population. Women are 70 percent of the world's poor, and two-thirds of those who are not taught to read and write.

26   Women are the primary caretakers for most of the world's children and elderly. Yet much of the work we do is not valued—not by economists, not by historians, not by popular culture, not by government leaders.

27   At this very moment, as we sit here, women around the world are giving birth, raising children, cooking meals, washing clothes, cleaning houses, planting crops, working on assembly lines, running companies, and running countries.

28   Women also are dying from a disease that should have been prevented or treated; they are watching their children succumb to malnutrition caused by poverty and economic deprivation; they are being denied the right to go to school by their own fathers and brothers; they are being forced into prostitution, and they are being barred from the ballot box and the bank lending office.

29   Those of us who have the opportunity to be here have the responsibility to speak for those who could not.

30   As an American, I want to speak up for women in my own country—women who are raising children on the minimum wage, women who can't afford health care or child care, women whose lives are threatened by violence, including violence in their own homes.

31   I want to speak up for mothers who are fighting for good schools, safe neighborhoods, clean air and clean airwaves . . . for older women, some of them widows, who have raised their families and now find that their skills and life experiences are not valued in the workplace . . . for women who are working all night as nurses, hotel clerks, and fast food chefs so that they can be at home during the day with their kids . . . and for women everywhere who simply don't have time to do everything they are called upon to do each day.

32   Speaking to you today, I speak for them, just as each of us speaks for women around the world who are denied the chance to go to school, or see a doctor, or own property, or have a say about the direction of their lives, simply because they are women.

33   The truth is that most women around the world work both inside and outside the home, usually by necessity.

34   We need to understand that there is no formula for how women should lead their lives. That is why we must respect the choices that each woman makes for herself and her family. Every woman deserves the chance to realize her God-given potential.

35   We also must recognize that women will never gain full dignity until their human rights are respected and protected.

36   Our goals for this conference, to strengthen families and societies by empowering women to take greater control over their own destinies, cannot be fully achieved unless all governments—here and around the world—accept their responsibility to protect and promote internationally recognized human rights.

37   The international community has long acknowledged—and recently affirmed at Vienna—that both women and men are entitled to a range of pro-

tections and personal freedoms, from the right of personal security to the right to determine freely the number and spacing of the children they bear.

38 No one should be forced to remain silent for fear of religious or political persecution, arrest, abuse or torture.

39 Tragically, women are most often the ones whose human rights are violated. Even in the late 20th century, the rape of women continues to be used as an instrument of armed conflict. Women and children make up a large majority of the world's refugees. And when women are excluded from the political process, they become even more vulnerable to abuse.

40 I believe that, on the eve of a new millennium, it is time to break our silence. It is time for us to say here in Beijing, and the world to hear, that it is no longer acceptable to discuss women's rights as separate from human rights.

41 These abuses have continued because, for too long, the history of women has been a history of silence. Even today, there are those who are trying to silence our words.

42 The voices of this conference and of the women at Huairou must be heard loud and clear:

- It is a violation of human rights when babies are denied food, or drowned, or suffocated, or their spines broken, simply because they are born girls.
- It is a violation of human rights when women and girls are sold into the slavery of prostitution.
- It is a violation of human rights when women are doused with gasoline, set on fire and burned to death because their marriage dowries are deemed too small.
- It is a violation of human rights when individual women are raped in their own communities and when thousands of women are subjected to rape as a tactic or prize of war.
- It is a violation of human rights when a leading cause of death worldwide among women ages 14 to 44 is the violence they are subjected to in their own homes.
- It is a violation of human rights when young girls are brutalized by the painful and degrading practice of genital mutilation.
- It is a violation of human rights when women are denied the right to plan their own families, and that includes being forced to have abortions or being sterilized against their will.
- If there is one message that echoes forth from this conference, it is that human rights are women's rights . . . And women's rights are human rights.

• Let us not forget that among those rights are the right to speak freely. And the right to be heard.

43   Women must enjoy the right to participate fully in the social and political lives of their countries if we want freedom and democracy to thrive and endure.

44   It is indefensible that many women in non-governmental organizations who wished to participate in this conference have not been able to attend—or have been prohibited from fully taking part.

45   Let me be clear. Freedom means the right of people to assemble, organize, and debate openly. It means respecting the views of those who may disagree with the views of their governments. It means not taking citizens away from their loved ones and jailing them, mistreating them, or denying them their freedom or dignity because of the peaceful expression of their ideas and opinions.

46   In my country, we recently celebrated the 75th anniversary of women's suffrage. It took 150 years after the signing of our Declaration of Independence for women to win the right to vote. It took 72 years of organized struggle on the part of many courageous women and men.

47   It was one of America's most divisive philosophical wars. But it was also a bloodless war. Suffrage was achieved without a shot fired.

48   We have also been reminded, in V-J Day observances last weekend, of the good that comes when men and women join together to combat the forces of tyranny and build a better world.

49   We have seen peace prevail in most places for a half century. We have avoided another world war.

50   But we have not solved other, deeply-rooted problems that continue to diminish the potential of half the world's population.

51   Now it is time to act on behalf of women everywhere.

52   If we take bold steps to better the lives of women, we will be taking bold steps to better the lives of children and families too. Families rely on mothers and wives for emotional support and care; families rely on women for labor in the home; and increasingly, families rely on women for income needed to raise healthy children and care for their relatives.

53   As long as discrimination and inequities remain so commonplace around the world—as long as girls and women are valued less, fed less, fed last, overworked, underpaid, not schooled and subjected to violence in and out of their homes—the potential of the human family to create a peaceful, prosperous world will not be realized.

54   Let this conference be our—and the world's—call to action.

55   And let us heed the call so that we can create a world in which every woman is treated with respect and dignity, every boy and girl is loved and cared for equally, and every family has the hope of a strong and stable future.

56   Thank you very much.

57   God's blessings on you, your work and all who will benefit from it.

CRISIS OF COMMUNITY:
MAKE AMERICA WORK FOR AMERICANS

William K. Raspberry

The Landon Lecture Series at Kansas State University, Manhattan, is one of the most distinguished lecture series in the country. Endowed by the Alf M. Landon Foundation, the university has been able to bring many of America's most distinguished speakers to campus. On April 13, 1995, William Raspberry, columnist for the Washington Post, delivered this lecture on the crisis of community.

Raspberry was born in Okolona, Mississippi, October 12, 1935. He attended Indiana Central College, receiving a B.S. in history in 1958, and an L.H.D. in 1973. He was a reporter for the *Indianapolis Recorder* from 1956-1960. He moved to the *Washington Post* as reporter-editor, and received the designation of urban affairs columnist in 1966, a position he still holds. Raspberry has a special interest in race relations and public education. He taught journalism for two years, 1971-1973, at Howard University, and was a TV commentator on station WTTG in Washington from 1973-1975. He received a Pulitzer Prize for commentary in 1994. His editorial column today appears regularly in many of the nation's most prestigious newspapers.

In this address, he moves directly to the subject he plans to deal with. He distinguishes between "the crisis in the community" and the "crisis of community." His argument will be that we are in danger of national fragmentation rather than focusing on an entity called "American." What does Raspberry say this fragmentation is stemming from?

✝William K. Raspberry, "Crisis of Community: Make America Work for Americans," June 1, 1995, pp. 493-496. Reprinted by permission of *Vital Speeches of the Day* and the authors.

Also, how does he use analogy with the Soviet Union to demonstrate his point? He stresses that we lack honest communication and fail to focus on our problems, but instead look for enemies whom we can blame for our problems. Do you think he develops this idea effectively? Raspberry relies heavily upon the use of example in developing his argument. See for example paragraphs 8, 19, 29 and 46. Discuss how he uses example in these instances.

Relate what Raspberry says about inclusion and cultural isolation with what Molefi Asante is suggesting about education in his address found in this book. Raspberry says that we need national healing rather focusing upon the "politics of difference." We need to focus upon being "Americans". Analyze how he develops this thesis throughout his speech and how his reasoning and use of supporting materials establishes credibility for the idea.

---

1   I've been writing a good deal of late about the violence in our streets, the apathy in our schools, and the hopelessness among our young people—the crisis in our community.

2   America has a crisis of community that is as deep and wide as it is unnoticed. And it threatens to destroy our solidarity as a nation, in much the same fashion as a similar crisis in community has ripped apart the former Soviet Union and what used to be Yugoslavia.

3   I refer, of course, to the gender wars newly resurrected by the latest battles in the Clarence Thomas / Anita Hill holy wars; to the ethnic battles over university; canons and multi-culturalism, to the political warfare that makes party advantage more important than the success of the nation, and to the racial animosities and suspicions fueled by everything from the rantings of Khalid Abdul Muhammed to the O.J. Simpson trial to Charles Murray's pseudo-intellectual call for racial abandonment.

4   But when I express my fear that we are coming unglued, I'm thinking about far more than these things.

5   I'm talking about more even than the normal give and take among the various sectors and ideologies of the society. I am talking about our growing inability to act—even to *think*—in the interest of the nation.

6   It's almost as though there IS no national interest, apart from the aggregate interests of the various components. The whole society seems to be disintegrating into special interests.

7   And not just in politics. College campuses are being ripped apart by the insistence of one group after another on proving their victimization at the

hands of white males, and therefore their right to special exemptions and privileges.

8   One example of what I'm talking about: A few years ago, the Federal Aviation Administration adopted a rule that would bar emergency exit row seating to passengers who are blind, deaf, obese, frail or otherwise likely to inhibit movement during an emergency evacuation. Common sense? Only if you think of the common interests of all the passengers.

9   Surely it is reasonable to have those emergency seats occupied by people who can hear the instructions of the crew, read the directions for operating the emergency doors and assist other passengers in their escape.

10   But some organizations representing the deaf, blind and otherwise disabled reacted to the regulation only as a form of discrimination against their clients who, they insist, have a "right" to the emergency seats.

11   It is true that the majority must never be allowed to run roughshod over the rights of minorities. That is one of the tenets of the American system. But the notion of fairness to particular groups as an element of fairness to the whole has been perverted into a wholesale jockeying for group advantage.

12   Mutual fairness, with regard to both rights and responsibilities, can be the glue that bonds this polyglot society into a nation. Single-minded pursuit of group advantage threatens to rip us apart at the seams. The struggle for group advantage has us so preoccupied with one another's ethnicity that we are losing our ability to deal with each other as fellow humans.

13   What are we to make of this dismaying evidence that the relationships among us are getting worse—even among our college students? I believe two things are happening, and that they reinforce one another. The first is the racism and bigotry that never went away, even though it was relatively quiet for a time.

14   The second is what has been called the politics of difference. There is a pattern I have seen repeated on campuses across America. A black group, perhaps motivated by some combination of discomfort and rejection, goes looking (always successfully) for demonstrable evidence of racism.

15   I used to marvel at this search. Of course there was racism on campus, but what was the point of PROSPECTING for it, as though panning for gold?

16   I mean, where was the assay office to which one took these nuggets of racism and traded them in for something of value?

17   Well, it turns out that there IS such an assay office. It's called the Administration Building. Turn in enough nuggets and you get your reward: a Black Student Union, a special course offering, an African American wing in a preferred dormitory—whatever. All it takes is proof that you are a victim.

18   But despite the reports one hears these days, college students aren't exactly stupid. They are bright enough to see that there are rewards in the politics of difference, in demonstrated victimism. So the victories won by black students become models for similar prizes for gay students or Hispanic students or female students, all of whom gather up their nuggets of victimism and take them to the administration building for redemption.

19   Cornell University, one of the finest institutions in America, has a dormitory called Ujamaa College, a residence for black students; Akwe:kon, a dorm for Native Americans, and also the Latin Living Center.

20   That's the trend when the accent is on difference. And finally, it turns out that everybody gets something out of the politics of difference except white males, who start to feel sorry for themselves.

21   And if they can't find anyone to reward them for their sense of being slighted, they may turn to behavior that was once unthinkable—the "acting out" that manifests itself in incivility, reactionary politics, open bigotry and, on occasion, violence.

22   Every gain by minority groups justifies the sense of victimism on the part of white males, and every repugnant act of white males becomes a new nugget for a minority to take to the assay office.

23   Two things get lost in this sad ritual. The first is that the administration seldom gives up any of its own power: the gains of one group of students are extracted from other groups of students, who then must play up their own disadvantage to wrest some small advantage from another group. The administration's power remains intact.

24   The second overlooked aspect is that the process turns the campus into warring factions—each, no doubt, imagining itself as the moral successor to the heroes of the Civil Rights Movement. There's a difference, though. Dr. King's constantly repeated goal was not special advantage but unity. His dream was not of a time when blacks would finally overcome whites; his dream was that we should overcome, black and white together.

25   His hope was not that we should celebrate our differences but that we should recognize the relative unimportance of these differences. The differences do not *seem* unimportant, of course. Sometimes we seem to notice ONLY our differences.

26   That's why I find it helpful to look at what used to be the Soviet Union and what used to be Yugoslavia. From this distance, it seems clear that the similarities between the Serbs and Croats and other ethnic neighbors in Bosnia-Herzevinia should outweigh their differences.

27　They share the history of a place and indeed many were intermarried. But now that Yugoslavia has broken up, even the marriages have been ripped apart.

28　I find myself wishing these erstwhile Yugoslavs could see for themselves what distance makes clear to us. And I wish we could learn to appreciate how great our similarities and how trivial our differences, and get OUR act together.

29　A "Star Trek" episode of some years ago makes my point. Capt. Kirk and his crew rescue a humanoid who, on his left side, is completely black. His right side, it turns out, is altogether white.

30　They are in the process of trying to learn the origins of this stranger— Lokai, he is called—when they are confronted by a similar humanoid named Bele—this one black on his right side and white on the left. The Enterprise crew, of course, can hardly tell them apart. But the humanoids can see themselves only as complete opposites—which, of course in one sense they are. And not just opposites. Though they are from the same planet, they are also sworn enemies.

31　I won't try to tell you the whole episode, but let me recall this much. Lokai is thought to be a political traitor, and Bele, an official of their home planet's Commission on Political Traitors, has been chasing him throughout the galaxy for a thousand years.

32　Lokai tries to convince the Enterprise crew that Bele and his kind are murderous oppressors. Bele counters that Lokai and his kind are ungrateful savages. The Enterprise crew decides to travel near the strangers' planet.

33　When they come within sensor range they are surprised to learn there is no sapient life there. The cities are intact, vegetation and lower animals abound, but the people are dead. They have annihilated each other. These two have survived only because they happened to be in the business of chasing each other down.

34　And what do they do when they learn what has happened to their planet? They lunge at each other in furious battle. Though the Enterprise crew is appalled, Kirk is unable to convince the two enemies of the futility of their war.

35　"To expect sense from two mentalities of such extreme viewpoints is not logical," says Spock. "They are playing out the drama of which they have become the captives, just as their compatriots did."

36　"But their people are dead," Sulu says slowly. "How can it matter to them now which one is right?"

37　"It does to them," says Spock. "And at the same time, in a sense, it doesn't. A thousand years of hating and running have become all of life."

38   We don't learn from this "Star Trek" episode the nature of the original problem between these warring humanoids, though we can be certain each felt fully justified in continuing the war. They had made a mistake that too many of us make in real life: They had forgotten the difference between problems and enemies.

39   And so have we. Virtually every issue that strikes us as urgent or important is made more intractable by our insistence on seeing it as a matter of us against them.

40   Give us a problem, and we'll find an enemy. Is the U.S. economy in trouble? Make the Japanese the enemy. Are we concerned about the discouraged and dangerous underclass? Blame white racists.

41   Members of my own profession seem unable to tell a story, no matter how significant, unless they can transform it into a case of one person, or one group, against another—unless they can make it a matter of enemies.

42   It is not so much that the enemies we identify are innocent as that identifying and pursuing them takes time and attention away from the search for solutions.

43   It was no trouble at all to come up with evidence that the Japanese were hurting the American economy through predatory pricing, product dumping and nonreciprocity, and certainly all these things merited attention.

44   But the U.S. auto industry improved its position relative to Japan's auto industry not when we all became expert at bashing our Japanese enemy but when Detroit started making better cars.

45   And that's the point. The failure to distinguish between the enemy and the problem has us looking balefully at one another instead of jointly attacking the problem which, in most cases, is as much a problem for us as for those we attack.

46   Take the current fight over affirmative action, for instance. Politicians who lack the imagination to address the *problem* settle for giving us each other to attack. White men—particularly those with a high school education or less—are not imagining things when they feel less secure economically than their fathers were. But they make a mistake when they suppose that their jobs have somehow been handed over to black people in the name of affirmative action. More likely those jobs are in Taiwan or Singapore or have gone up in the smoke of corporate mergers and downsizing. We've got a problem, and we waste our time assaulting enemies.

47   Honest communication about the problem might lead us to look for ways to restore our industrial base, expand our economy, improve the quality of our products and put our people to work. Focusing on enemies produces stirring speeches and little else.

48   You've heard the speeches. You've watched as communities have been ripped apart by those who deliver these speeches. There's how Teresa Heinz, widow of the late Pennsylvania senator, described them in a recent speech:

". . . critical of everything, impossible to please, indifferent to nuance, incapable of compromise. They laud perfection but oddly never see it in anybody but themselves. They are right all the time, eager to say I told you so, and relentlessly unforgiving. They occasionally may mean well, but the effect of even their good intentions is to destroy. They corrode self-confidence and good will; they cultivate guilt; they rule by fear and ridicule.

"They are creatures of opportunity as much as of principles, extremists of the left and the right who feed on our fear and promote it, who dress up their opponents in ugly costumes, who drive a bitter wedge between us and the Other, the one not like us, the one who sees the world just a shade differently. . . . They demonize us by our parts and tear our country to pieces."

49   My own formulation is less eloquent; they focus on enemies rather than on problems. They forget that, at the end of the day, when we've all taken our unfair shots at one another, this simple truth remains: The *problem* is the problem.

50   Our politicians and our factional leaders never miss an opportunity to list the atrocities the *enemy* has committed against us. But nothing changes.

51   Sometimes we're not even sure what we want to change, or what we want the people we call enemies to do. We say we want things to get better, when sometimes I think we only want to score points.

52   We say we want a society in which all of us can live together as brothers and sisters, and the whole time we are saying it we are busy creating another group of barriers to place between us.

53   It's a strange sort of progress we have made since the death of Dr. King. We have "progressed" to the point where we are embarrassed to speak of brotherhood, of black and white together, of our shared status as Americans.

54   That's not an accusation; it's a confession. All of us are capable of getting so caught up in the distance that remains to be run that we forget to give ourselves full credit for the distance we've come.

55   Yet, every now and then, we manage to overcome our embarrassment and see things as from a distance. In that spirit, I'd like to share something I wrote a while back—something I still believe but something I may have trouble saying again.

56   Here it is: The immigration applications, the legal and illegal dodges for getting into this country, the longings you hear in virtually every other part of the world all attest to two astounding facts.

57   The first, widely accepted though not always with good grace, is that "everybody" wants to be an American. The second, of which we take almost no notice, is that virtually anybody can *become* an American.

58   To see just how extraordinary a fact that is, imagine hearing anyone—black, white or Asian—saying he wants to "become Japanese." It sounds like a joke. One can live in Japan (or Ghana or Sweden or Mexico)—can live there permanently, and prosper. But it's essentially impossible to imagine anyone born anywhere else becoming anything else—except American.

59   It's a thought that crosses my mind whenever I hear demands that the government protect the ethnic or language heritage of particular groups: when African Americans demand that the *public* schools adopt an Afrocentric curriculum, for instance, or when immigrants from Latin America are sworn in as American citizens—in Spanish.

60   It crossed my mind again when I came across Jim Sleeper's essay, "In Defense of Civic Culture."

61   I won't try to characterize Sleeper's piece or to summarize its recommendations. [the Washington-based Progressive Foundation] I won't even tell you I agree with everything Sleeper has to say on the subject of race and ethnicity.

62   But he says some things that echo my own feelings, especially when I ponder the extraordinary possibility of becoming American.

63   He acknowledges the obvious: that the America that counted my great-great-grandfather as only three-fifths of a human being has never been free of ethnic and racial bigotry, and that that bigotry has sometimes achieved the status of law, of philosophy—even of religion.

64   But he notes something else: that America is one of the few places on the globe where accusation of such bigotry is a serious indictment. Even when America has been at its ugliest in fact—slavery, the slaughter of Native Americans, the internment of the Japanese and the full range of private and public atrocities, "yet always America held out the promise that, as Ralph Waldo Emerson put it, 'in this asylum of all nations, the energy of . . . all the European tribes [and] of the Africans, and of the Polynesians will construct a new race.'"

65   The civic culture Sleeper writes about includes this notion of Americans as a new and different race, but it also entails what he describes as characteristic American virtues: tolerance, optimism, self-restraint, self-reliance, reason, public-mindedness—virtues that are "taught and caught in the daily life of local institutions and in the examples set by neighbors, co-workers and public leaders."

66   It is, he suggests, the internalizing of these virtues that defines "becoming American."

67   But the transformation works both ways. If people from an awesome range of colors, cultures and ethnicities have become Americans, so has America become what it is (and continues to become) by absorbing and embracing these myriad influences.

68   Some of us are angry, and ought to be, that our academic texts and teachings still disregard or underestimate our part of these influences.

69   Some of us are disappointed that what we bring to the smorgasbord is often undervalued, even brutally rejected.

70   But surely the cure is in working for greater inclusion, not cultural isolation. That's what observers as different as Sleeper, Arthur Schlesinger and John Gardner have been saying. That's what Gary Trudeau was saying in that hilarious (and sobering) series of "Doonesbury" Strips that ended with black students—already having attained their separate courses and dormitories—demanding, at last, separate drinking fountains. Sleeper's insight is that there is nothing "natural" or automatic about those values and attitudes that used to be called "the American way." Educators must teach them, he says, and also "teach that self-esteem is enhanced not simply through pride in one's own cultural origins but, more importantly, by taking pride in one's mastery of civic virtues and graces that all Americans share and admire in building our society."

71   Critics of this view will argue that Sleeper's virtuous and graceful American is a figment, that America is a deeply—perhaps irredeemably—racist society.

72   I prefer to think that Americans are still becoming Americans, just as America is still becoming America.

73   How can we accelerate that becoming? By recognizing its importance, by understanding that hating and running must not become all of life, and by working to grasp the difference between problems and enemies.

74   Confront a difficulty as a problem and you have taken the first steps toward creating the climate for change.

75   Confront it as the work of enemies and you create the necessity for DEFEATING someone, of intimidating someone, of browbeating someone into doing something against his will.

76   Enemies have to be sought out, branded and punished. Which, naturally, gives them one more reason to find an opportunity to strike back at us. And the beat goes on.

77   Problems, on the other hand, admit of cooperative solutions that can help build community.

78   Searching for enemies is most often a pessimist's game, calculated less to resolve difficulties than to establish that the difficulties are someone else's fault. Identifying *problems* is by its very nature optimistic and healing. The whole point of delineating problems is to fashion solutions.

79   Maybe that's what President Clinton had in mind when he called on America to bring back "the old spirit of partnership, of optimism, of renewed dedication to common efforts."

80   "We need," he said, "an array of devoted, visionary, healing leaders throughout this nation, willing to work in their communities to end the long years of denial and neglect and divisiveness and blame, to give the American people their country back."

81   And that is precisely what we need. America has had enough of the politics of difference, the marketing of disadvantage, the search for enemies. It's about time we started to work on what may be the most important problem we face:

82   How to heal our crisis of community and make America work—not for blacks or whites or women or gays; not for ethnics; not for Christians, Moslems or Jews—but for Americans.

ADDRESS ON AIDS TO THE 1992 REPUBLICAN CONVENTION

Mary Fisher

The third night of the 1992 Republican Convention in Houston, Texas, was dubbed "Family Night." On that evening, August 29, the delegates heard speeches from First Lady Barbara Bush, Marilyn Quayle, the vice-president's wife; and the Rev. Pat Robertson. The emotional highlight, however, of the convention speeches delivered in the Astrodome that evening was the short address by Mary Fisher. Fisher, 44 years old, was the daughter of Max Fisher, a wealthy Republican fundraiser and former advisor to President Gerald Ford. One year before her speech, Fisher learned that she had tested positive for the human immunodeficiency virus that causes AIDS.

In her 15-minute speech, broadcast live by the major news networks, Fisher used the rhetorical technique of "enactment" to dramatize the problem of AIDS in America. By presenting herself as an example of

+The text of this speech was obtained from the *Chicago Tribune*, August 23, 1992, section 4, p. 1 & 4.

the point she was trying to prove, Fisher sought a greater national sensitivity to the plight of AIDS victims (1, 2, 5, 15, & 19).

At the beginning of the speech, she used compelling statistics to demonstrate the significance of the growing AIDS epidemic (3&6). Fisher's central thesis was to awaken her immediate convention audience and suggest that the disease was "not a political creature" (4). Since the causes of the AIDS problem are found in ignorance, prejudice and silence (7), she seems to be indirectly attacking the Republican Party's stance on this issue. How well does Fisher establish her case for the true nature of AIDS? Was a national political convention the appropriate forum for this particular message?

Through personal testimony, revealed in balanced antithetical phrasing (12), Fisher issues a national "plea" for greater public awareness of AIDS (12-14). Is Fisher's use of her father's warnings against another Jewish Holocaust an appropriate historical analogy for the current AIDS problem (13)? How can the "shroud of silence" on AIDS (17-18) that she speaks of be finally lifted?

The most compelling part of Fisher's speech came in the closing paragraphs (19-23) designed as a public "letter" to her two young sons, Max and Zachary. Does the emotional power of this conclusion add to or detract from a "reasonable" understanding of the AIDS crisis? How do you finally judge Fisher's role as an enacted "messenger" (20) on this topic?

For a personal account of the events leading up to the composition and delivery of this speech, see Mary Fisher, *My Name is Mary: A Memoir* (New York: Scribner, 1996), pp. 221-244. For a brief analysis of the responses to Fisher's address, see Victoria L. DeFrancisco and Marvin D. Jensen, eds., *Women's Voices in Our Time: Statements by American Leaders* (Prospect Heights, Illinois: Waveland Press, 1994), 267-269.

---

1   Less than three months ago, at platform hearings in Salt Lake City, I asked the Republican Party to lift the shroud of silence which has been draped over the issue of HIV/AIDS. I have come tonight to bring our silence to an end.

2   I bear a message of challenge, not self-congratulation. I want your attention, not your applause. I would never have asked to be HIV-positive. But I believe that in all things there is a purpose, and I stand before you, and before the nation, gladly.

3   The reality of AIDS is brutally clear. Two hundred thousand Americans are dead or dying; a million more are infected. World-wide, 40 million, 60 mil-

lion, or a 100 million infections will be counted in the coming few years. But despite science and research, White House meetings and congressional hearings; despite good intentions and bold initiatives, campaign slogans and hopeful promises, it is, despite it all, the epidemic which is winning tonight.

4   In the context of an election year, I ask you—here, in this great hall, or listening in the quiet of your home—to recognize that the AIDS virus is not a political creature. It does not care whether you are Democrat or Republican. It does not ask whether you are black or white, male or female, gay or straight, young or old.

5   Tonight, I represent an AIDS community whose members have been reluctantly drafted from every segment of American society. Though I am white, and a mother, I am one with a black infant struggling with tubes in a Philadelphia hospital. Though I am female, and contracted this disease in marriage, and enjoy the warm support of my family, I am one with the lonely gay man sheltering a flickering candle from the cold wind of his family's rejection.

6   This is not a distant threat; it is a present danger. The rate of infection is increasing fastest among women and children. Largely unknown a decade ago, AIDS is the third leading killer of young-adult Americans today—but it won't be third for long. Because, unlike other diseases, this one travels.

7   Adolescents don't give each other cancer or heart disease because they are in love. But HIV is different. And we have helped it along—we have killed each other—with our ignorance, our prejudice and our silence. We may take refuge in our stereotypes, but we cannot hide there long. Because HIV asks only one thing of those it attacks: Are you human? And this is the right question: Are you human?

8   Because people with HIV have not entered some alien state of being. They are human. They have not earned cruelty and they do not deserve meanness. They don't benefit from being isolated or treated as outcasts. Each of them is exactly what God made: a person. Not evil, deserving of our judgment; not victims, longing for our pity. People, ready for support and worthy of compassion.

9   My call to you, my party, is to take a public stand no less compassionate than that of the President and Mrs. Bush. They have embraced me and my family in memorable ways. In the place of judgment, they have shown affection. In difficult moments, they have raised our spirits. In the darkest hours, I have seen them reaching not only to me, but also to my parents, armed with that stunning grief and special grace that comes only to parents who have themselves leaned too long over the bedside of a dying child.

10   With the president's leadership, much good has been done: much of the good has gone unheralded, and as the president has insisted, "Much re-

mains to be done." But we do the president's cause no good if we praise the American family but ignore a virus that destroys it.

11 We must be consistent if we are to be believed. We cannot love justice and ignore prejudice, love our children and fear to teach them. Whatever our role, as parent or policymaker, we must act as eloquently as we speak—else we have no integrity.

12 My call to the nation is a plea for awareness. If you believe you are safe, you are in danger. Because I was no hemophiliac, I was not at risk. Because I was not gay, I was not at risk. Because I did not inject drugs, I was not a risk.

13 My father has devoted much of his lifetime guarding against another holocaust. He is part of the generation who heard Pastor Niemoeller come out of the Nazi death camps to say, "They came after the Jews and I was not a Jew, so I did not protest. They came after the trade unionists, and I was not a trade unionist, so I did not protest. They came after the Roman Catholics, and I was not a Roman Catholic, so I did not protest. Then they came after me, and there was no one left to protest."

14 The lesson history teaches is this: If you believe you are safe, you are at risk. If you do not see this killer stalking your children, look again. There is no family or community, no race or religion, no place left in America that is safe. Until we genuinely embrace this message, we are a nation at risk.

15 Tonight, HIV marches resolutely toward AIDS in more than a million American homes, littering its pathway with the bodies of the young. Young men, young women, young parents, young children. One of the families is mine. If it is true that HIV inevitably turns to AIDS, then my children will inevitably turn to orphans.

16 My family has been a rock of support. My 84-year-old father who has pursued the healing of the nations, will not accept the premise that he cannot heal his daughter. My mother refuses to be broken; she still calls at midnight to tell wonderful jokes that make me laugh. Sisters and friends, and my brother, Phillip, whose birthday is today, all have helped carry me over the hardest places. I am blessed, richly and deeply blessed, to have such a family.

17 But not all of you have been so blessed. You are HIV-positive but dare not say it. You have lost loved ones, but you dared not whisper the word AIDS. You weep silently; you grieve alone.

18 I have a message for you: It is not you who should feel shame, it is we. We who tolerate ignorance and practice prejudice, we who have taught you to fear. We must lift our shroud of silence, making it safe for you to reach out for compassion. It is our task to seek safety for our children, not in quiet denial but in effective action.

242 Contemporary American Speeches

19   Some day our children will be grown. My son Max, now 4, will take the measure of his mother; my son Zachary, now 2, will sort through his memories. I may not be here to hear their judgments, but I know already what I hope they are.

20   I want my children to know that their mother was not a victim. She was a messenger. I do not want them to think, as I once did, that courage is the absence of fear; I want them to know that courage is the strength to act wisely when most we are afraid. I want them to have the courage to step forward when called by their nation, or their party, and give leadership—no matter what the personal cost. I ask no more of you than I ask of myself, or of my children.

21   To the millions of you who are grieving, who are frightened, who have suffered the ravages of AIDS firsthand: have courage and you will find support. To the millions who are strong, I issue the plea: Set aside prejudice and politics to make room for compassion and sound policy.

22   To my children, I make this pledge: I will not give in, Zachary, because I draw my courage from you. Your silly giggle gives me hope. Your gentle prayers give me strength. And you, my child, give me reason to say to America, "You are at risk". And I will not rest, Max, until I have done all I can to make your world safe. I will seek a place where intimacy is not the prelude to suffering.

23   I will not hurry to leave you, my children. But when I go, I pray that you will not suffer shame on my account. To all within the sound of my voice, I appeal: Learn with me the lessons of history and of grace, so my children will not be afraid to say the word AIDS when I am gone. Then their children, and yours may not need to whisper it at all. God bless the children, and God bless us all. Good night.

SEX AND VIOLENCE IN
THE ENTERTAINMENT MEDIA

Robert Dole

Concern about casual sex and graphic violence in the entertainment media have been the subject of speeches, off and on, for the past 35 years. Jenkin Lloyd Jones, long-time journalist and editor of the *Tulsa*

+The text of this speech was secured from Robert Dole's Internet presidential campaign World Wide Web site.

Tribune, in the decade of the sixties spoke often about the decay of America's cultural values. Then Vice President Dan Quayle delivered perhaps the most publicized address on the subject, attacking specific television programs such as Murphy Brown. Quayle was subjected to considerable criticism and ridicule.

However, since Quayle's ill-fated address, others have taken up the drum beat. President Clinton expressed his concern about the matter, and Democratic Senators Bill Bradley and Paul Simon spoke out on our nation's crisis of glamorized violence. On May 31, 1995, then the Senate majority leader and leading Republican presidential candidate for the 1996 election, Bob Dole addressed the question in Hollywood's back yard, Los Angeles, California. No longer are such remarks greeted with the same ridicule Dan Quayle received.

Bob Dole was born July 22, 1923, in Russell, Kansas. He attended the University of Kansas from 1941 to 1943, when his studies were interrupted by a stint in the military. He was wounded in the war and lost much of the use of his right hand and arm. He was awarded the Purple Heart and the Bronze Star with two clusters. Leaving the military in 1948, he attended Washburn University in Topeka, graduating with an A.B. in 1950. Two years later he received an LL.B. from Washburn and passed the Kansas bar exam.

Dole's first political office was in the Kansas House of Representatives from 1951–1953. In 1953, he left the legislature and served as county attorney of Russell County until 1961. He was elected and served as representative to the United States' 88th to 90th Congresses. In 1969, he was elected to the United States Senate and rose to the positions of the Senate's Republican leader and, ultimately, the Senate's Majority Leader. In 1976, he was the vice-presidential running mate of President Gerald Ford, but they lost the election to Jimmy Carter. In 1996, Dole became the Republican Party's presidential candidate against the incumbent, Bill Clinton.

In his address on sex and violence in Hollywood, Dole makes a strong appeal to the entertainment industry to put common decency ahead of profit. Dole's introduction identifies the problem he is concerned about and blends criticism with praise of the entertainment industry. What do you see as the essential purpose of Dole's introduction?

Dole clearly states his topic in paragraph 6. He says he has two goals, which he uses as the basic structure of his address. The first goal is to address the effect the media has on the nation's children. Does he support this point to your satisfaction? Do you accept his word for it?

There is strong research evidence on this subject, and you may want to investigate it and report on it for one of your informative speeches.

Dole's second goal is to expose the corporate executives who hide behind "lofty language of free speech." Do you think he is able to generate the guilt he is seeking so as to produce change? He singles out Time Warner (15-16) and addresses them directly. How effective is this approach?

In paragraphs 17-19, Dole is trying to broaden the attack beyond just himself by indicating other responsible people are concerned about the problem. Does he achieve his goal in this respect?

Finally, the speech has interesting stylistic dimensions. Observe the sentence structure in paragraphs 4 and 7.

Do you think that "courage and conscience are alive and well in Hollywood," as Dole desires? Various facets of the subject would be good topics for either informative or persuasive addresses.

---

1   Thank you very much. John, I appreciate that kind introduction. I appreciate all the work that Lod Cook and others have done tonight—Jim Montgomery and many of my friends who are here.

2   I want to talk about a specific matter tonight. I may not win an Oscar, but I'll talk about it anyway. I want to talk to you tonight about the future of America—about issues of moral importance, matters of social consequence.

3   Last month, during my announcement tour, I gave voice to concerns held across this country about what is happening to our popular culture. I made what I thought was an obvious point, a point that worries countless American parents: That one of the greatest threats to American family values is the way our popular culture ridicules them. Our music, movies, television and advertising regularly push the limits of decency, bombarding our children with destructive messages of casual violence and even more casual sex. And I concluded that we must hold Hollywood and the entire entertainment industry accountable for putting profit ahead of common decency.

4   So here I am in California—the home of the entertainment industry and to many of the people who shape our popular culture. And I'm asking for their help. I believe our country is crying out for leaders who will call us as a people to our better nature, not to profit from our weaknesses; who will bring back our confidence in the good, not play on our fears of life's dark corners. This is true for those of us who seek public office. And it is true for those who are blessed with the talent to lead America's vaunted entertainment industry.

5   Actors and producers, writers and directors, people of talent around the world dream of coming to Hollywood. Because if you are the best, this is where you are. Americans were pioneers in film, and dominate world-wide competition today. The American entertainment industry is at the cutting edge of creative excellence, but also too often the leading edge of a culture becoming dangerously coarse.

6   I have two goals tonight. One is to make crystal clear to you the effect this industry has on America's children, in the hope that it will rise to their defense. And the other is to speak more broadly to America about the corporate executives who hide behind the lofty language of free speech in order to profit from the debasing of America.

7   There is often heard in Hollywood a kind of "aw shucks" response to attempts to link societal effects with causes in the culture. It's the "we just make movies people want" response. I'll take that up in a minute. But when they go to work tomorrow, when they sift through competing proposals for their time and money, when they consider how badly they need the next job, I want the leaders of the entertainment industry to think about the influence they have on America's children.

8   Let there be no mistake: televisions and movie screens, boomboxes and headsets are windows on the world for our children. If you are too old, or too sophisticated, or too close to the problem, just ask a parent. What to some is art, to our children is a nightly news report on the world outside their limited experience. What to some is make believe, to them is the "real skinny" on the adult world they are so eager to experience. Kids know firsthand what they see in their families, their schools, their immediate communities. But our popular culture shapes their view of the "real world." Our children believe those paintings in celluloid are reflections of reality. But I don't recognize America in much of what I see.

9   My voice and the rising voices of millions of other Americans who share this view represent more than the codgy old attempt of one generation to steal the fun of another. A line has been crossed—not just of taste, but of human dignity and decency. It is crossed every time sexual violence is given a catchy tune. When teen suicide is set to an appealing beat. When Hollywood's dream factories turn out nightmares of depravity.

10   You know what I mean. I mean "Natural Born Killers." "True Romance." Films that revel in mindless violence and loveless sex. I'm talking about groups like Cannibal Corpse, Geto Boys and 2 Live Crew. About a culture business that makes money from "music" extolling the pleasures of raping, torturing and mutilating women; from "songs" about killing policeman and rejecting law. The mainstreaming of deviancy must come to an end, but it will only stop when the leaders of the entertainment industry recognize and shoulder their responsibility.

11   But let me be very clear: I am not saying that our growing social problems are entirely Hollywood's fault. They are not. People are responsible for their actions. Movies and music do not make children into murderers. But a numbing exposure to graphic violence and immorality does steal away innocence, smothering our instinct for outrage. And I think we have reached the point where our popular culture threatens to undermine our character as a nation.

12   Which brings me to my second point tonight. Our freedom is precious. I have risked my life to defend it, and would do so again. We must always be proud that in America we have the Freedom to speak without Big Brother's permission. Our freedom to reap the reward of our capitalist system has raised the standard of living around the world. The profit motive is the engine of that system, and is honorable. But those who cultivate moral confusion for profit should understand this: we will name their names and shame them as they deserve to be shamed.

13   We will contest them for the heart and soul of every child, in every neighborhood. For we who are outraged also have the freedom to speak. If we refuse to condemn evil, it is not tolerance but surrender. And we will never surrender.

14   Let me be specific. One of the companies on the leading edge of coarseness and violence is Time Warner. It is a symbol of how much we have lost. In the 1930s its corporate predecessor, Warner Brothers, made a series of movies, including "G-Men," for the purpose of restoring "dignity and public confidence in the police." It made movies to help the war effort in the early 1940s. Its company slogan, put on a billboard across from the studio, was "Combining Good Citizenship with Good Picture Making."

15   Today Time Warner owns a company called Interscope Records which columnist John Leo called the "cultural equivalent of owning half the world's mustard gas factories." Ice-T of "Cop Killer" fame is one of Time Warner's "stars." I cannot bring myself to repeat the lyrics of some of the "music" Time Warner promotes. But our children do. There is a difference between the description of evil through art, and the marketing of evil through commerce. I would like to ask the executives of Time Warner a question: Is this what you intended to accomplish with your careers? Must you debase our nation and threaten our children for the sake of corporate profits?

16   And please don't answer that you are simply responding to the market. Because that is not true. In the movie business, as Michael Medved points out, the most profitable films are the ones most friendly to the family. Last year, the top five grossing films were the blockbusters "The Lion King," "Forrest

Gump," "True Lies," "The Santa Clause" and "The Flintstones." To put it in perspective, it has been reported that "The Lion King" made six times as much money as "Natural Born Killers."

17   The corporate executives who dismiss my criticism should not misunderstand. Mine is not the objection of some tiny group of zealots or an ideological fringe. From inner city mothers to suburban mothers to families in rural America—parents are afraid, and growing angry. There once was a time when parents felt the community of adults was on their side. Now they feel surrounded by forces assaulting their children and their code of values.

18   This is not a partisan matter. I am a conservative Republican, but I am joined in this fight by moderates, independents and liberal Democrats. Senator Bill Bradley has spoken eloquently on this subject, as has senator Paul Simon, who talks of our nation's "crisis of glamorized violence." And leaders of the entertainment industry are beginning to speak up, as well.

19   Mark Canton, the president of Universal Pictures, said, "Any smart business person can see what we must do—make more 'PG'-rated films." He said, "Together . . . we can make the needed changes. If we don't, this decade will be noted in the history books as the embarrassing legacy of what began as a great art form. We will be labeled, 'the decline of an empire.'"

20   Change is possible—in Hollywood, and across the entertainment industry. There are few national priorities more urgent. I know that good and caring people work in this industry. If they are deaf to the concerns I have raised tonight, it must be because they do not fully understand what is at stake. But we must make them understand. We must make it clear that tolerance does not mean neutrality between love and cruelty, between peace and violence, between right and wrong. Ours is not a crusade for censorship, it is a call for good citizenship.

21   When I announced I was running for President, I said that my mission is to rein in our government, to reconnect the powerful with the values which have made America strong and to reassert America's place as a great nation in the world. Tonight I am speaking beyond this room to some of the most powerful arbiters of our values. Tonight my challenge to the entertainment industry is to accept a calling above and beyond the bottom line—to fulfill a duty to the society which provides its profits. Help our nation maintain the innocence of its children. Prove to us that courage and conscience are alive and well in Hollywood.

22   Thank you for listening to me tonight. I am grateful for the support you have shown by being here, and feel a great sense of hope and confidence that together we will succeed—not only in this Presidential race, but in our larger mission to reaffirm the goodness and greatness of the United States of America.

23   Thank you very much.

Chapter Seven

Speeches That Affirm Propositions of Policy

. . . I have suspected for some time that the key division of this society, given the awesome rate of change and what it has done to tradition and values, is not a classic ideological or economic split, but how people react to change. Whether they welcome it, merely accept it, or, as in many cases, feel deeply threatened by it.

David Halberstam

The Nature and Importance of Speeches That Affirm Propositions of Policy

Whenever people have been free to choose their personal or collective destinies, speakers have arisen to advocate courses of action. When a President of the United States stands before a television camera to encourage popular approval of a Supreme Court ruling, he or she is proposing a course of action. When a legislator stands at the rostrum of a state senate to recommend adoption of a new taxation program, he or she is advocating a policy. When a social reformer urges the abolition of capital punishment, a union official the rejection of a contract, a theologian an end to doctrinal conflict, or politicians a vote in their behalf, they all are engaged in the affirmation of policies.

Listeners and speakers would benefit from holding a *process view*, rather than a static view, of life. Such a view assumes that change, process, and coping with change are normal rather than exceptional phenomena. There is no "status quo," no static existing state of affairs, to defend. Present policies and programs always evolve, modify, and change to some degree. The choice is not between change and nonchange. The choices center on how to manage the speed, degree, and direction of inevitable change. Solutions and policies never are entirely permanent. No sooner has a program been instituted than the conditions which necessitated it have altered somewhat and new conditions have arisen, thus at least partly rendering the program obsolete.

Although a society's problems have been clearly illuminated, that society will not grow and prosper unless effective courses of action are advocated and undertaken. Some critics of contemporary American society argue that advocates today too seldom conceive and present effective policies. The blunt evaluation in 1951 by William G. Carleton, a professor of political science, still seems remarkably applicable to much public discourse today:

> American speeches . . . for the most part have ceased seriously to examine fundamental policy, to discuss first principles, to isolate and analyze all the possibilities and alternative courses with respect to a given policy. . . . The result is that speeches today are rarely intellectually comprehensive or cogently analytical.

One reason for this shortcoming is the complexity of propositions of policy. The call to take action or change policy is made up of a number of intermediate claims involving all of the intellectual and rhetorical operations identified in the preceding chapters. For example, a speaker who is trying to demonstrate that "It is necessary for the federal government to subsidize the higher education of superior students" might first affirm the proposition of fact that "Many qualified high school graduates are unable to attend college for financial reasons," the proposition of value that "The development of the nation's intellectual resources is socially desirable," and the problem-centered claim that "The loss of intellectual resources constitutes a signifi-cant contemporary social and economic problem."

Speakers try to win acceptance of facts and values and create concern for prob-lems on the basis that they are *true, good,* or *significant.* Speakers advocate policies in belief that they are *necessary* and/or *desirable.* You might note that in the phrasing of propositions of policy, the term *should* (meaning it is necessary or desirable that) ap-pears with great frequency.

Although many persuaders urge *adoption* of a new policy or course of action, in *Perspectives on Persuasion,* Wallace Fotheringham suggests other important categories of action that speakers may seek. In addition to adoption, speakers may defend *con-tinuance* of an existing policy, urge *discontinuance* of an existing policy, or seek *deter-rence* by arguing against adoption of a proposed policy. Sometimes speakers urge re-tention of the basic principles or structure of an existing policy along with *revision* of means and mechanisms of implementing that policy.

All of the following assertions may be classified as propositions of policy:

Proposition A: *The negative income tax should be adopted.*

Proposition B: *The United States should continue its support of the United Nations.*

Proposition C: *The use of marijuana should be decriminalized.*

Proposition D: *Federal regulation of the print mass media should not be adopted.*

If speakers have been intellectually shallow in affirming propositions of policy, at least a portion of the blame must rest with the audiences who place too few demands on the speakers' rhetorical behaviors.

Criteria for Evaluating Speeches That Affirm Propositions of Policy

Although propositions of policy may call for continuance, discontinuance, de-terrence, and revision in addition to adoption, the criteria that follow are written for the speech seeking adoption. The criteria can be made applicable to the other kinds of propositions of policy through modest rephrasing.

1. **Has the speaker demonstrated or is it readily apparent that a need exists for a fundamental change in policy?**

Because programs for action are responses to problems, the critic first should consider whether a legitimate problem exists. Among the subquestions the evalua-tor will wish to consider are the following:

- Are there circumstances that may legitimately be viewed as a problem?
- Is the present policy to blame for such problems?

- Is the problem sufficiently severe to require a change in policy, or may it be met through repairs, adjustments, or improvements in the present program?

In establishing a need for a fundamental change in policy, the speaker may affirm a series of propositions related to facts, values, and problems, each of which may be tested by the listener against criteria developed in earlier chapters.

2.   Has the speaker provided a sufficient view of the nature of the new policy or program?

If a speech affirming a proposition of policy is to have maximum impact, the audience must know exactly what is to be done and how to do it. A sound, well-rounded policy usually encompasses not only the basic principles to guide the course of action but also the specific steps, procedures, or machinery for implementing that policy.

When the speaker describes the nature of a policy, he or she seeks increased understanding and should be assessed by the same criteria outlined in Chapter 3: Has the speaker made the policy meaningful to the audience? Has the speaker explained the policy in a sufficiently interesting way? Has the speaker shown the audience that the information is important?

3.   Has the speaker demonstrated that the new policy will remedy the problem?

If the speaker is to be successful, the audience must believe that the policy will solve the problem and that it realistically can be put into operation. Among the questions that the listener should raise are the following:

- Can the policy be put into effect?
- Is the policy enforceable once it has been instituted?
- Will the policy alleviate the specific problem or problems described by the speaker (by removing the basic causes, or by speedily treating symptoms of a problem the causes of which are unknown)?

In response to such questions, a speaker will affirm one or more propositions of fact by advancing varied arguments. Speakers may argue that the proposed course of action has worked effectively elsewhere in similar situations; that analogous policies have succeeded in remedying similar problems; that experts attest to its ability to solve the problem. The best expert testimony is that which supports the specific program advocated, not just the general principle of the policy. Through word pictures and descriptions the audience should be made to vividly visualize the desirable consequences that will follow if the solution is adopted, and the undesirable consequences that will occur if it is not adopted.

4. Has the speaker demonstrated that the new policy is advantageous?

In addition to showing that the policy will alleviate the problem, the speaker should demonstrate that the policy will produce significant additional benefits and should indicate clearly how the advantages will outweigh any possible disadvantages. A speaker who advocates federal economic aid for public education could show that this policy would not only ease the immediate shortages of facilities and equipment but also would have the additional benefit of helping to equalize educational opportunity throughout the nation. The speaker might stress that the possible remote defect of federal interference in local educational matters is far outweighed by definite immediate advantages and benefits. To demonstrate such benefits, the speaker should employ appropriate examples, statistics, analogies, and expert testimony.

Because people characteristically resist new courses of action in favor of traditional policies, the speaker often will find it wise to recognize in advance and deprecate relevant major policies and arguments that run counter to the proposed policy. Beyond providing adequate reasons for adopting the proposed policy, the speaker frequently must refute alternative programs and opposing arguments. An advocate might directly refute opposing arguments with evidence and reasoning; or show that the arguments, while true in general, really are irrelevant to the specific proposal at hand; or show that the arguments have only minimal validity and are outweighed by other considerations.

People also judge the advantageousness of policies on the basis of personal values and goals. An audience of business people may judge a program partly by the effect it will have on corporate profits. An audience of clergy may judge a policy by its consistency with spiritual values. An audience of minority group members may judge a proposal by the contribution it will make to equality of opportunity. An audience of laborers may judge a program by its effect on their wages. No matter who composes the audience, the speaker advancing propositions of policy must recognize that the values, wants, and goals of listeners influence their evaluation of courses of action. An advantageous policy not only removes the causes of a problem but also harmonizes with such values as efficiency, speed, economy, fairness, humaneness, and legality.

In evaluating speeches affirming propositions of policy, the listener could ask such questions as these:

- Does the policy have significant additional benefits?
- Do the advantages of the policy outweigh its disadvantages?
- Does the policy have greater comparative advantages than other relevant policies?
- Can the policy be experimented with on a limited basis before full-scale adoption is undertaken?

- Is the policy consistent with relevant personal and societal values?

In responding to these questions, the capable speaker will affirm a cluster of evaluative and factual propositions. Such propositions may, in turn, be evaluated in terms of the criteria proposed in earlier chapters.

Although the advocate may sometimes find it wise to fulfill each of the four major criteria in detail, at other times he or she may deem it unnecessary to meet all of them. Speakers may neglect to elaborate on the need or problem because they know the audience already shares their concern for it. A detailed statement of policy may be avoided because the speaker believes it sufficient to show that a general course of action is in some ways superior to one currently pursued. A persuader may avoid mentioning the negative effects of a proposal because its defects are not major. An arguer may pose a theoretical ideal and demonstrate the superiority of the proposal in light of that ideal. Concerning the appropriateness and ethicality of such choices of emphasis as just described, a critical listener may reach judgments differing from the speaker's. But whatever the constraints imposed by audience, setting, and subject, the speaker affirming a proposition of policy must demonstrate to the audience that the proposed course of action is necessary, desirable, and beneficial.

Conclusion

In a free society people often assemble to consider courses of future action. In evaluating such speeches, the listener/critic may raise numerous questions that cluster around the following four criteria. *Has the speaker demonstrated, or is it readily apparent, that a need exists for a fundamental change in policy? Has the speaker provided a sufficient view of the nature of the new policy or program? Has the speaker demonstrated that the new policy will remedy the problem? Has the speaker demonstrated that the new policy is advantageous?*

For Further Reading

Carleton, William G. "Effective Speech in a Democracy." *Vital Speeches of the Day,* June 15, 1951, pp. 540–44.

Gronbeck, Bruce E., et al. *Principles and Types of Speech Communication.* 11th ed. Scott, Foresman, 1990. Chapter 9 explains the nature and uses of the "motivated sequence" structure (attention, need, satisfaction, visualization, action) that is especially useful in speeches advocating policies.

Fotheringham, Wallace C. *Perspectives on Persuasion.* Allyn and Bacon, 1966. Chapters 3 and 11 examine the major goals of persuasive discourse and some undesirable action responses by audiences.

Jensen, J. Vernon. *Argumentation: Reasoning in Communication.* Van Nostrand, 1981. Chapter 5 explains potential lines of argument basic to presenting solutions, policies, and programs.

Leys, Wayne A. R. *Ethics for Policy Decisions.* Prentice-Hall, 1952. Chapters 1, 12, and 22. Pages 189–92 list the critical questions relevant to policy decisions developed in 10 major systems of ethics.

Newman, Robert P., and Newman, Dale. *Evidence.* Houghton Mifflin, 1969. Chapters 1–3 present guidelines for analyzing propositions of policy.

Walter, Otis M., and Scott, Robert L. *Thinking and Speaking.* 5th ed. Macmillan, 1984. Chapter 8 presents suggestions for persuading about solutions to problems.

Walter, Otis M., *Speaking Intelligently.* Macmillan, 1976. Chapters 1 and 5 and pp. 222–24. The author stresses the necessity of high-quality problem-solving for societal survival and growth and suggests strategies for persuading about solutions and policies.

Warnick, Barbara, and Inch, Edward S. *Critical Thinking and Communication: The Use of Reason in Argument.* 2nd ed. Macmillan, 1994. Chapter 10 discusses advocating and opposing policy propositions.

MULTICULTURALISM IN THE PUBLIC SCHOOLS

Diane Ravitch

At a meeting of the New Jersey School Boards Association on November 2, 1990, Diane Ravitch spoke on multiculturalism as an issue and policy for the public schools. She was then an adjunct professor of history and education in the Teachers College of Columbia University in New York City. Diane Ravitch is author of several books, including *The Troubled Crusade: American Education, 1945–1980,* and the California State Board of Education called upon her to structure the state's K-12 history curriculum. Although a Democrat, Ravitch served in the Bush Administration as an Assistant Secretary in the U.S. Department of Education.

What persuasive function might be served by her introductory massing of examples of contemporary European racial, ethnic, and religious conflict and her reassurance that, unlike some European nations,

---

+The text of this speech was provided by Diane Ravitch.

America will not disintegrate (1–4)? Ravitch advocates the general policy of multiculturalism for public school curricula and she specifically advocates adoption of a "pluralist" program to implement that concept (5, 12). She spends little time proving that a need for multiculturalism exists—that there has been a problem requiring a solution (6–11). She seems to assume that her audience of school board members from throughout New Jersey already acknowledge such a need and that they recognize precedents already in place for such a general policy.

Ravitch's major argumentative strategy is to contrast the defining elements of a pluralist and an ethnocentric program of multiculturalism—the former desirable and the latter dangerous (13–15, 26–27)—and also to present the advantages of pluralism and the disadvantages of ethnocentrism (16–22). How clearly and reasonably does she explain and justify the basic components of the pluralist policy? What types of evidence does she use and how soundly does she use them? What values are embodied in pluralism and violated by an ethnocentric approach? Antithesis is a major language resource used to contrast the desirable and undesirable features of the two policies (17–19, 27). How effectively and fairly do you believe that she uses this resource?

At one point Ravitch mentions a "common American culture" embodied in "music, food, clothing, sports, holidays, and customs" that reflects multicultural influences (14). How clearly and adequately is the nature of this common culture demonstrated here and elsewhere in the speech? At another point she poses an either-or-choice with only one of the choices pictured as desirable (22). Must we be forced to choose as she describes? Cannot schools foster *both* pride in heritage *and* knowledge, creativity, and cooperation? Consider her massive accumulation of historical examples of hatred and violence stemming from extreme ethnocentrism (23–25). Does pride in and knowledge about ethnic heritage necessarily result in such barbarism?

Almost in passing, Diane Ravitch mentions Afrocentrism as a type of ethnocentrism and makes an analogy between Afrocentrism and earlier "whites-only" curricula (16). Does she develop this analogy fully and clearly enough to be reasonable? For example, what are the "flaws" and "wild inaccuracies"? Are they simply to be inferred from the following paragraphs? You will want to compare Ravitch's speech with the following speech by Molefi Asante on Afrocentrism. Is Afrocentrism ethnocentric in the major negative ways that Ravitch contends? For a much more complete and detailed defense of the pluralist approach and a more specific attack on the Afrocentric approach, see Diane Ravitch,

"Multiculturalism: E Pluribus Plures," *The American Scholar,* 59 (Summer 1990): 337–354.

1   I recently returned from Eastern Europe, where nationalism and ethnicity are on the rise, in ominous ways. Czechoslovakia may split into two nations, the Czechs and the Slovaks. Armenians and Azerbaijanis are killing each other. The Romanians are unresolved about how to deal with their Hungarian minority; the Hungarians are unresolved about how to deal with their Romanian minority. Yugoslavia may disintegrate if Serbs, Croats, Albanians, Slovenians, Slavonians, and Montenegrens find it impossible to get along together.

2   And of course religious tension is also on the rise. The Poles are reintroducing religious education in their public schools. And ugly manifestations of anti-Semitism are again in the air. Throughout Eastern Europe there is the occasional and amazing phenomenon of anti-Semitism without Jews.

3   Here in the United States, we too are preoccupied with tensions about race, ethnicity, and language. This is inevitable, because we are a multiracial, multiethnic society, and we have people in America who speak the languages of every other nation in the world.

4   And, unlike Yugoslavia, Czechoslovakia, and the Soviet Union, we are not going to disintegrate. First, because we have no territorial basis to our racial-ethnic differences; and second, because racial and ethnic and linguistic issues have been part and parcel of American history from our earliest days.

5   The issue that today confronts the schools is multiculturalism. It is the buzzword of the 1990s. What is it? Why has it become a major controversy? How should the schools respond? Why do some people find it threatening? How can it become a positive force in our schools and society?

6   Due to demographic changes and new immigration of the past generation, there is today widespread cultural diversity in our schools and in our society. Children in American classrooms represent all of the world's races, religions, and ethnic groups.

7   Our greatest concern as educators must be to educate all of these children so that they can enjoy productive lives as Americans citizens. All of our children must be equipped for the demands of the 21st century. In the past few years, demands have been made to change the curriculum to reflect the changing realities of American society.

8   These are not new issues in American education. Twenty years ago, black educators complained about the lily-white textbooks used in the schools. Their complaints were well-founded. The literature textbooks never included a black poet or writer. The history textbooks included slavery as a cause of the

Civil War, but otherwise neglected the lives and experiences of black Americans and ignored the grim realities of racial segregation and discrimination.

9   A generation ago, the city of Detroit inaugurated the first multi-ethnic teaching materials, and other big-city districts began to demand changes in the textbooks. In higher education, scholars advanced the frontiers of knowledge, recovering the long-neglected history of blacks, women, Indians, and immigrants. The work of black leaders like W. E. B. Du Bois, Frederick Douglass, Harriet Tubman, James Weldon Johnson, and Ida B. Wells began to receive new attention. Based on years of solid research, the textbooks in our schools began to reflect a far more interesting America.

10   As a result, the textbooks in our schools today are dramatically different from the textbooks that I read as a child. The most widely used history textbook, Todd and Curti's *Triumph of the American Nation*, presents a picture of a pluralistic America, a nation that is multiracial and multiethnic, a nation built by men and women and people of all different origins.

11   And this approach has become commonplace among today's textbooks. Today our textbooks routinely illustrate children and adults of all races engaged in a variety of occupations, and routinely pay attention to the achievements of people from different backgrounds. Children's reading books include the writings of a wide variety of people, of diverse origins.

12   Given the rapid changes of the past generation, why is multiculturalism a controversial issue today? The controversy arises because the word multiculturalism means different things to different people, and it is being used to describe very different educational approaches. The two basic approaches are either pluralist or ethnocentric. One has the potential to strengthen public education, the other has the potential to harm it.

13   The pluralist approach recognizes that one of the purposes of public education is to create a democratic community and to expand children's knowledge beyond their own home and neighborhood to a larger world. In doing so, education must prepare children to live in a world of competing ideas and values, to be able to live and work with people from different backgrounds, and to learn to examine their own beliefs.

14   The pluralist approach to American culture recognizes that we have a common American culture that was shaped by the contributions of all of many different groups—by American Indians, by Africans, by immigrants from all over the world, and by their descendants. Consider American music, food, clothing, sports, holidays, and customs—all of them demonstrate the commingling of diverse cultures in one nation. We are many peoples, but we are one nation. Paradoxically, we have a common culture that is multicultural. It was shaped by all of us, and we reshape it in every generation.

15   The ethnocentric approach to American culture insists that there is no common culture, and that each of us must trace our origins to the land of our ancestors and identify only with people who have the same skin color or ethnicity. Each of us, by this definition, is defined by who our grandparents were. We must look only to people of the same group for inspiration, for it is they—and they alone—who can offer us role models of achievement. By this approach, I cannot be inspired by Harriet Tubman's bravery or by Zora Neale Hurston's moving prose or by Octavio Paz's eloquence because I am not from their racial/ethnic group. And black children, in turn, cannot be moved by the words of Abraham Lincoln or Elizabeth Cady Stanton or Robert Kennedy because they are of a different race. Ethnocentrism insists that each of us is defined by our race or ethnicity.

16   Some of our schools today have adopted the ethnocentric approach. Sometimes it is called Afrocentrism, and it is modeled on the whites-only curriculum that prevailed in American schools until a generation ago. It contains the same flaws and is equally subject to wild inaccuracies and pervasive bias.

17   What I would suggest to you is that these two approaches—pluralism and ethnocentrism—cannot both be multicultural, because they are completely opposite in purpose. One teaches children that they are part of a multiracial, multiethnic world, the other immerses them in a prideful version of their own race or ethnicity.

18   Pluralism teaches us that we are all part of the great American mosaic and provides us with the glue of civic knowledge that holds the mosaic together. Ethnocentrism teaches children to regard with respect only those of their own particular group.

19   Pluralism teaches that despite our surface differences, we are all human. Ethnocentrism teaches that our differences define us.

20   There is a significant difference in the methods by which these two very different approaches are taught. In the pluralist classroom, the teacher should stress critical thinking. Students should learn about every subject with a critical eye. They should be taught to ask questions, to wonder "How do we know what we know?" "What is the evidence for what we believe?" This is the very opposite of indoctrination. By this approach, it is possible to study the history of religion in a public school classroom, because the object is to learn about it, not to become a member of the faith.

21   By contrast, in the ethnocentric classroom, students are taught to believe in certain truths about their race or ethnic group. They are expected to believe what the teacher and the textbook believes, not to raise doubts or look for alternative explanations. The teacher offers up a pantheon of heroes and stories about the struggles of the faithful, and students are not supposed to disagree.

The message of the ethnocentric classroom is, believe what you are told; do not question or doubt. In the same sense, the ethnocentric classroom resembles a sectarian approach to teaching.

22   Based on method alone, public education must reject ethnocentrism. The public schools do not exist to indoctrinate students into the faith of their ancestors or to instill ethnocentric pride—not for whites, or blacks, or Hispanics, or Asians, or American Indians. The public schools must prepare the younger generation to live in the world of the 21st century, a world of global interdependence, a world of differences—where what will count is what we know, what we can do, and our ability to think creatively and work with others.

23   The history curriculum should not become a tool to build self-esteem or ethnic pride. It is a subject in which to learn about our society and the world, and sometimes the truth can be unpleasant. All of the peoples in the world have been guilty of terrible misdeeds: the Aztecs and Mayans practiced human slavery and human sacrifice; Germans and other Europeans committed genocide against millions of Jews and other Europeans during the Second World War; in Soviet Russia, millions of landowners and political dissidents were killed by their own government; the regime of Idi Amin slaughtered hundreds of thousands of Ugandans; in Nigeria, a million or more Biafrans were murdered by other Africans; in Cambodia, the Pol Pot regime killed more than a million of their fellow Cambodians; the Turks slaughtered hundreds of thousands of Armenians at the time of the First World War; the Chinese Communists murdered millions of Chinese during the 1950s and 1960s; the Iraqis killed thousands of Iraqi Kurds with poison gas in 1982; the Burmese military gunned down thousands of students in 1988.

24   The record of death and genocide and slavery and human suffering is truly universal. The more we learn about history, the more humble we should all become. Human beings, it seems, have always found plenty of reasons to hate and kill other human beings. Differences in the way we look, the way we dress, the god we worship, the language we speak—almost anything has provided grounds for hatred. And if you pick up the daily paper and read the news, you will see that the beat goes on, all over the world—in India, Pakistan, Armenia, Romania, Liberia, Ireland, Burma, China, South Africa, and Lebanon.

25   Given the dismal record of humankind, particularly during the 20th century, it would seem that we as educators should do whatever we can to discourage ethnocentrism and to promote a sense of respect for our common humanity. Ethnocentrism does not belong in public education. It undermines the very purpose of public education, which is to create a community to which we all belong.

26   How can you tell whether a curriculum is pluralist or ethnocentric? It requires thought—it requires intelligence. How can you tell the difference between objective reporting and propaganda? You have to think about it. How can you tell the difference between science and creation science? You have to think about it.

27   Here are some parameters: The pluralist curriculum stresses learning about a subject, while the ethnocentric curriculum indoctrinates students into the tribe or the ways of the elders. The pluralist curriculum promotes mutual respect among people from culturally different backgrounds, while the ethnocentric curriculum promotes feelings of anger, vengeance, bitterness, and hatred. The pluralist curriculum promotes a sense of mutuality and interdependence, while the ethnocentric curriculum promotes racial and ethnic separatism. The pluralist curriculum promotes the building of a community that crosses ethnic/racial/religious lines, while the ethnocentric curriculum builds separate communities based on race or ethnicity or religion.

28   My parents were immigrants, yet I feel that I too inherited Thomas Jefferson's claim that "All men are created equal." I am a woman, yet I feel that I too share Abraham Lincoln's call to rededicate ourselves to the proposition "that government of the people, by the people, for the people, shall not perish from the earth." I am white, yet I celebrate Martin Luther King Jr. as a role model of brevity, profundity, and eloquence.

29   We were not born knowing how to hate those who are different. As the song in *South Pacific* says, you have to be taught to hate, "you have to be carefully taught." It should be our goal as educators to teach respect and mutuality.

30   Culture is not skin color. Culture is history, tradition, and experience. Just as we need to know those experiences that make us different, we need to know the ideas and experiences that hold us together in community. We are all of us—black and white, Hispanic and Asian, American Indian and recent immigrant—in a common project. Education is the means that we have chosen to make it work. It is the spirit of interdependence, the spirit of mutuality, the spirit of respect for our many heritages, and the spirit of common purpose that we must build and cultivate in our schools.

IMPERATIVES OF AN AFROCENTRIC CURRICULUM

Molefi Kete Asante

"When a lot of people, especially white people, hear the word 'Afrocentricity,' they feel threatened, nervous, or both. They shouldn't." This is the reassuring view developed at length in a guest editorial in the *Washington Post National Weekly Edition* (November 26–December 2, 1990, p. 28) by Franklyn G. Jenifer, president of the historically black Howard University in Washington, D.C. In contrast, David Nicholson argues in a commentary essay on multicultural curricula in the *Washington Post National Weekly Edition* (October 8–14, 1990, pp. 23–24): "The question, though, is not whether the curriculum needs to be changed, but whose vision will prevail—that of the nationalists and the zealots, or that of more reasonable people who still believe in a common American culture and shared national values."

When Molefi Kete Asante addressed over two thousand listeners at the Detroit Public Schools Annual Teachers Conference in Cobo Hall in Detroit on February 4, 1991, clearly he was at the center of a national controversy. Asante is chair of the Department of African American Studies at Temple University in Philadelphia, has been a Fulbright professor at the Zimbabwe Institute of Mass Communications, and is chief consultant for the Baltimore public school system's Afrocentric Curriculum Project.

Asante intertwines his presentation of the problem and the proposed solution. The problem—the need to change from a Eurocentric to a truly multicultural curriculum—is described and explained at length (7, 9, 12, 16–17). Asante heightens concern for the problem through examples (10–11) and through an analogy that encourages whites to perceive the issue from an African American viewpoint (4–5). In analyzing this analogy, you are encouraged to apply the relevant standards for soundness of literal analogy discussed in the theory section of Chapter 4 on propositions of fact.

Asante advocates adoption of a multicultural public school curriculum based on the model of an Afrocentric curriculum. In describing

---

+The text of this speech was provided by Molefi Kete Asante.

the basic assumptions and components of the program, how clear are some of the key concepts (8, 19, 21). For example, what does he mean by hegemony (3), or by the subject-object distinction (6)? As another method of defending the components of an Afrocentric curriculum, Asante refutes criticisms by his opponents (4, 12, 18, 22–24). What arguments and evidence does he use in refutation and how reasonably does he use them? Again, consider the clarity of his key concepts. How well would his audience probably understand his criticism of the pluralist-particularist distinction (19)?

Although in this speech Asante does not mention Diane Ravitch by name, in other speeches he does so in refuting his opponents. On some occasions, Ravitch has distinguished her pluralist multicultural program from what she terms Asante's particularist multiculturalism. Without naming them in this speech, Asante characterizes the criticisms by his opponents as hysterical, strident, screaming, and mis-readings (perhaps intentional). Consider in what ways, if any, Ravitch's arguments in the previous speech warrant such labels. Note that like Ravitch, Asante, too, depicts for his audience a stark either-or choice. Here it is between "true multiculturalism" based on the Afrocentric model and "maintenance of the white hegemony" through Ravitch's "pluralist" approach (20). To what degree would you accept this either-or choice as reasonable? Why?

Does an Afrocentric approach to multiculturalism as proposed by Asante seem dangerously ethnocentric in the ways contended by Ravitch in the previous speech? What concrete evidence from Asante's speech would you cite to support your judgment? For example, what is Asante's view on pride and self-esteem, on devaluation of European-heritage contributions to culture, and on a pluralism of respect for all different cultures?

In response to Ravitch's initial article in *The American Scholar,* 59 (Summer 1990), Asante and Ravitch engage in a very heated and more detailed exchange in the same journal (Vol. 60, Spring 1991, pp. 267–276). You are urged to read this exchange with their speeches. Advocates of policies to solve societal problems often argue their cases through varied channels as part of a continuous persuasive campaign: speeches; articles in scholarly journals or popular magazines; books; television talk-show or news program interviews; guest editorials or letters to the editor in newspapers.

1   Since the publication of my first book on centering the educational experience in the child's reality, *Afrocentricity* in 1980 and subsequent works such as *The Afrocentric Idea* (1987) and more recently *Kemet, Afrocentricity, and Knowledge* (1990), there has been quite a lot of controversy about its relationship to the revitalization of curricula at every level of American education. Quite frankly, some of the more hysterical and strident voices against Afrocentricity seem to confirm what Alexander Thomas and Samuel Sillen wrote in their wonderful book, *Racism and Psychiatry,* about the interrelatedness of the idea of African American inferiority and African American pathology in the mainstream thinking.

2   The imperatives of an Afrocentric curriculum are found in three important propositions about education:

1.   **Education is fundamentally a social phenomenon.**

2.   **Schools prepare children for society.**

3.   **Societies develop schools suitable to the societies.**

3   I have argued for an Afrocentric curriculum as a way to systematically augment the teaching of African American children and as a method of centering children in their own historical experiences. Since the primary mode of instruction and the basic design of curriculum are Eurocentric, we have never been in danger of losing the centeredness of white children. An Afrocentric curriculum has to be developed before a general multicultural curriculum can be implemented. If there is no organic presentation of scope and sequence information about the African American, then there can be no multicultural project because most Americans, including African Americans, are woefully ignorant of the African American experience. Educated in the same system of white hegemony as other students, the African American comes out of the experience of school knowing next to nothing about Africa or African Americans. White students, without the benefit of cultural hearsay, know even less.

4   Opposition to the idea of teaching children from the standpoint of their centeredness rather than marginality has reached screaming levels. Those who oppose a centric education for African American children seem to say that content does not matter, yet the same opponents would find it unthinkable to teach white children a curriculum that is not centered in their experiences. For the most part, what we have right this moment in American education is a self-esteem curriculum for white children. It would be interesting to test the theory that self-esteem does not matter in the curriculum by simply eliminating the

Eurocentric basis of the present curriculum and replacing it with, say, an Asio-centric one. Would some white children master such a curriculum? Of course they would. But a larger number would simply find the information, accurate as it might be, about the Vedic Period, varuna, Mokska, Bodhisattva, and the Ulama, a rather dislocating experience for them.

5   Accustomed as they would be to their parents stories about King Henry VIII, Shakespeare, Goethe, Joan of Arc, and Homer, white children in an Asio-centric classroom would find it extremely troubling. Can one expect any less of children of African descent who are fed only Eurocentric information?

6   Across this dynamic nation there is a renewed sense of the possible in education. The reason for the excitement lies in a very simple proposition about education: children will learn with a greater sense of integrity if they view themselves as subjects rather than as objects. When a teacher places a child in the context of the information being taught the child gains a greater sense of self and more enthusiasm for learning. There are enough studies, including those of Dr. Faheem Ashanti of the North Carolina Central University, to demonstrate the value of this proposition.

7   Stated particularly, African American or Latino children should be taught in such a way that they are not alienated from the material they are supposed to be learning. Children of European ancestry do not have to be reinforced in this way because the manner of teaching and the curriculum itself perpetuate a Eurocentric hegemony in education. Furthermore, this view is promoted as a universal truth.

8   Education should reinforce students in their history and heritage as a matter of choice. This does not mean that students should only be taught information that is comfortable and accessible but rather that the teacher should be sensitive to the historical perspectives of the students in the classroom. Any good communicator seeks to know his or her audience.

9   When teachers teach information centered only on the European experience they do not have to make a case about the teaching of European dominance and supremacy; the structure of the curriculum is itself the message of Eurocentric hegemony. What we teach is normally considered what is important and since most schools teach Europe instead of Africa or Asia, students assume that Europe is not only significant but that it is more significant than it ought to be in a multicultural society.

10   When one teaches about Marco Polo, or William of Normandy, or Goethe, or Joan of Arc, one is essentially engaging in the process of transmitting information about a cultural heritage and legacy. The names of the Africans, Ibn Battuta, or King Sundiata of Mali, or Ahmed Baba, or Yenenga, are never spoken in high school classes, and under the current curricular structure, if they

were heard, would lack credibility even though they are by world standards certainly the equal of the Europeans I have mentioned in contrast.

11   The African American child whose parents speak of Sojourner Truth or James Weldon Johnson will most likely never hear those names spoken in any respectable way in a classroom from kindergarten to 12th grade. Instead of being reinforced in cultural heritage, African American children are being placed in crisis. Those who remain in school often have to put up with the total disregard of their own history and heritage. This is not so for white children and should not be so for any children.

12   Our society is multicultural and multi-ethnic and the idea of teaching as if the African American has no historical legacy or to force the discussion of our history to the Enslavement is to teach incorrectly and inadequately. More than this, it reinforces the false notion of white superiority and the equally false notion of black inferiority. We cannot afford to continue to promote the idea that African Americans who demand that an Afrocentric curriculum be infused into the general curriculum are asking amiss. It is the path of folly not just for African Americans but for all of the children of this society who are depending upon us to transmit to them the proper tools for living in this global village.

13   Another point should be made about this project. It is a project about accuracy and fullness in education. The aim of Afrocentric education is not merely to raise self-esteem of African American children. Indeed we have found that few African American children have problems with self-esteem; the real problem is with self-confidence. One can have a good feeling about one's personal attributes but feel a deep lack of confidence brought on by a lack of knowledge. Thus, while self-esteem may be a by-product of the central objective of the Afrocentric method, which is to provide a wholistic, accurate interpretation of the world, self-confidence will certainly be improved by this method.

14   Such an approach will have an impact on white students as well as African American, Latino, and Asian students. For some students it will be the first time that they will have heard the ancient Egyptians discussed as Africans or discovered that Africans played a significant role in the Revolutionary War. It is a fact that we African Americans were here before the United States government and many of our families have lived on this land longer than the families of many presidents of this country.

15   Of course, none of these ideas will have a full impact on education until there are big changes in schools of education throughout the nation. I am not aware of any school of education that has grappled with this problem in any serious manner. In some of the training institutions for teachers it is still possible for a teacher who will eventually teach in an urban setting to complete a degree without ever having taken a course in African American studies! This is truly unbelievable, but it is at the heart of the matter. Certainly the Afrocentric idea ought to be among the perspectives taught in institutions of teacher training.

16 A few months ago I asked fifty principals to identify the names of five African ethnic groups from West Africa. I explained to them that there were no African Americans three hundred and seventy two years ago. Africans who were brought to America against their wills came from particular ethnic groups often with long and important histories. Who are the African Americans you see in your schools? What are some of the names of the groups that combined in the Americas to produce the present African American population?

17 Sadly, almost no one knew the name of an African ethnic group that had become a contributor to the African American gene pool. Names like Yoruba, Hausa, Fulani, Ibo, Baule, Congo, Angola, Serere, Wolof, Mandinka did bring something to mind for a few of the principals when I began to mention them. These are the names of the people, who along with Native Americans and some Europeans, contributed to the present day gene pool of African Americans.

18 Afrocentricity is not an ethnocentric view. While Eurocentric views are often promulgated as universal views, e.g., classical music as European concert music or classical dance as European ballet, etc., the Afrocentric view seeks no valorization of African-centeredness above any other perspective on reality. It is human centered in the sense that no one should be divested of his or her heritage or background. Normally, the only people asked to do so are those who do not hold physical or psychological power. Ethnocentric views valorize themselves and degrade others. Afrocentricity promotes pluralism without hierarchy.

19 To say that we are a multicultural and multi-ethnic society must not mean that we promote a view of these cultures only through the eyes of whites. A true multiculturalism presupposes that we know something about the cultures. Few of those who have spoken or written about multiculturalism seem to understand that the road to a true multiculturalism leads by the way of Afrocentricity. The development of a systematic, organic, wholistic portrayal of the African culture as opposed to a detached, episodic, personality-based version is necessary for a real multicultural project.

20 The idea of a pluralist multiculturalism and a particularist multiculturalism is a non-starter. This first idea is a redundancy and the second is an oxymoron. You either believe in a true multiculturalism or you believe in the maintenance of the white hegemony in education. As a nation we must choose between these positions, there is no other choice.

21 I have made my choice for multiculturalism which means that I need to know all I can about the cultures of the nation. Does it mean that we will now have to know more about Native Americans, Latinos, Asians? Yes, it does and we will be a better nation because of it. Does it mean that the enforcement of a white hegemony on information and process in education is over? Probably not. However, we will never be able to exercise the full potential of this nation until we realize the incredible beauty and value of the collective cultures of America.

22   Finally, Afrocentricity does not negate all Eurocentric views. It should, however, modify those views that are pejorative and stereotypical. By pointing to other perspectives including Native American, Asian, and Latino as well, Afrocentricity suggests a new compact among American peoples. Of course, this means that the Eurocentric idea will not control the structure of knowledge but become, as it should have been all along, one perspective besides many.

23   This should be welcomed in a society such as ours where we will have in fifty years a largely non-European population needing to be educated but needing to be turned on to education by having the same advantage European Americans have had all along, education which centers them in the experience being taught. No one has suggested that this cease being the case with European Americans. However, we have said that where the Eurocentric perspective has turned racist, ethnocentric, or sexist, it should eliminate those attitudes. Pejoratives and racist language should be removed and the curriculum infused with an Afrocentric curriculum. This step is absolutely necessary, otherwise there are those who say that they want multiculturalism without knowing anything about the African American culture. They say they favor multiculturalism and still want to retain the negative expressions about Native Americans or Latinos. The path to multiculturalism goes by the way of cultural respect. This is as true in the United States as it should be in Israel and South Africa, and any other nation where human beings of different heritages live together.

24   It is certainly a misreading, perhaps even a deliberate misreading, of the concept of Afrocentricity to say that it means a blacks-only curriculum. No one that I know has proposed we replace Shakespeare with Ahmed Baba or James Baldwin. We say let us share in the great diversity of everyone. Why not teach Maimonides alongside Frederick Douglass and Wendell Phillips? Why not discuss the contributions of Yenenga, or Yaa Asantewaa, or Nzingha, alongside those of Joan of Arc? If we learn about Marco Polo, what is wrong with learning about the African, Ibn Battuta who travelled farther than Marco Polo and was considered the greatest traveller of the medieval period? Why not alert students to the story of Abubakari II who is reported to have travelled to Mexico from his empire in West Africa in 1312? We must recognize that this nation is an incomplete project whose present is not its past and whose future will not be what we know now. Let us prepare all of our children for the multicultural future that is surely around the turn of the century.

SACRED RIGHTS:
PRESERVING REPRODUCTIVE FREEDOM

Faye Wattleton

Legalized abortion—whether to allow it and, if so, under what restrictions, if any—continues to be a major political and moral issue at the national, state, and local levels. In this continuing debate, advocates of differing positions and policies struggle over fundamental distinctions and concepts: the competing values of life and of freedom of choice; the tension between legal rights and moral responsibilities; the definition of when "life" begins; the constitutional separation of church and state—of religious doctrine and public policy.

In 1973 in *Roe v. Wade,* the U.S. Supreme Court in a 7–2 decision held that a fetus is not a person in a legal sense of the term and that laws restricting women's access to legal abortion violate her constitutional right to privacy. The Court held that a woman had the right to terminate her pregnancy until the final three months of the pregnancy. In July 1989, in *Webster v. Reproductive Health Services,* a 5–4 decision by the U.S. Supreme Court agreed that Missouri had the right to prohibit use of public facilities and personnel to aid abortions that are not necessary to save the mother's life. Without overturning *Roe v. Wade,* the Court opened the option for states to consider more restrictive laws on abortion.

On June 25, 1990, Faye Wattleton accepted the "Ministry to Women Award" of the Unitarian Universalist Women's Federation at their meeting in Milwaukee, Wisconsin. Wattleton holds both Bachelor of Science and Master of Science degrees in nursing and since 1978 she has been President of the Planned Parenthood Federation of America. Planned Parenthood advocates contraception, abortion, sterilization, and infertility services as means of voluntary fertility regulation. In an analysis of Faye Wattleton as "Ms. Family Planning," Paula Span (*Washington Post National Weekly Edition,* November 2, 1987, pp. 8–9) observes: "Both supporters and foes go on at length about her articulateness, her presence, and her forcefulness." Indeed Faye Wattleton may be one of the most prominent and influential black women in America.

+The text of this speech was provided by the national office of the Planned Parenthood Federation of America. After 14 years as President of Planned Parenthood, Faye Wattleton resigned on January 8, 1992.

The Unitarian Universalist Women's Federation supports human rights for all, especially rights of women. The Federation supports the *Roe v. Wade* decision, quality in child care centers, concern for the family, and work for and with the aging. In accepting her award from this favorably disposed audience, Wattleton identifies points of commonality between herself, Planned Parenthood, and the Federation (1–4, 29, 33–34).

The policy that Faye Wattleton advocates and defends is legal protection for reproductive choice and for women's right to privacy (5). She advocates continuation of the *Roe* decision, constitutional protection of fundamental freedoms, and privacy from governmental intrusion (14, 28). She also advocates continued separation of church and state (9–10) and believes that morality should not be legislated (25). The *Webster* decision and the orientation of the current Supreme Court are problems that threaten the *Roe* constitutionally protected policy (6, 8). Through antithetical phrasing, she alludes to other policies advocated by Planned Parenthood: sex education in public schools; adequate adoption and child care; improved birth control methods (27).

Wattleton argues against opposing positions by reducing them to absurdities—by extending them to their logical but ridiculous extremes (11–12)—and by exposing contradictions (18). Evaluate how fairly and reasonably she develops these arguments. What persuasive function might be served by her references to positive political changes in Eastern Europe (15, 23)? She employs statistics to argue that the shepherd has inappropriately strayed from the flock (32). Within a religious context, what objections might there be to the logic of this argument?

Finally, consider some of the distinctive language resources that Wattleton employs. Frequently she uses alliteration to associate a series of positive items (4, 5, 31). Parallel structure is utilized effectively to reinforce a point through a series of examples (13, 14, 21, 25). Note the vivid negative images that Wattleton creates to characterize some of her opponents: under siege (5); zealots (6, 22); fanatics (21); obscene (25); oppressive tyrant, vicious and violent (30). How reasonable and appropriate are these labels for the people she describes? What is your evidence to support your judgment?

---

1   As some of you know, I am a minister's daughter, so addressing a religious gathering always feels like coming home. I'm *especially* comfortable in a Unitarian setting: I've had the honor of speaking from the pulpit of All Souls Church in New York; I've joined Forrest Church in his "All Souls World of Ideas"

discussion programs; and last fall I took part in a sunrise Unitarian service in Kennebunk, Maine.

2   I can honestly say that some of my *best friends* are Unitarian Universalists!—including Planned Parenthood's executive vice president David Andrews. David and I were chatting recently with one of our affiliate presidents, whose husband is the Episcopal bishop of New Mexico. She was telling David that she feels very warmly toward Unitarians. When she and her husband first moved to Albuquerque, their new Episcopal church wasn't ready for use. Since Unitarians don't have summer services, the Unitarian church facility was made available to them. At that point I asked David, "Why don't Unitarians go to church in the summer?" David said, "I don't know, I guess it's just too hot." To which the bishop's wife replied, "Not as hot as it's *gonna* be!"

3   Planned Parenthood's founder Margaret Sanger was herself a Unitarian. In fact, the Brooklyn Unitarian Church gave her both spiritual and financial support back in 1916, when she opened the nation's first birth control clinic—the tiny storefront that grew to become the nation's foremost public health movement.

4   Since that first auspicious alliance, Planned Parenthood has enjoyed a warm partnership with generations of Unitarians the world over. As individuals and as a church, you've shown your commitment to tolerance and compassion—to civil rights and civil liberties—to the free exercise of any religion or *no* religion. Your faith has been a *clarion call to conscience* for women and men in all walks of life.

5   And your uplifted voices have never mattered more than *now*. For one of our most precious, most personal freedoms is imperilled as never before. Reproductive choice—the right that makes all our *other* rights possible—is under siege. Last July—16 years after *Roe v. Wade* recognized women's constitutional right to abortion—the Supreme Court retreated from that historic ruling. In *Webster v. Reproductive Health Services*, the Court severely curbed women's access to abortion—and invited an all-out attack on our cherished right to *privacy*.

6   Plainly put, *Webster* allows state governments to put *fetuses* first. And zealots in *every state* are trying to do just that. More than 450 anti-choice bills have been introduced in the past year in 44 state legislatures. Re-energized pro-choice forces have defeated most such efforts. But in Pennsylvania, Guam, and now Louisiana, legislatures have advanced bills that would virtually eliminate legal abortion.

7   When *Roe v. Wade* was decided in 1973, who could have *imagined* that Americans would be fighting this battle in *1990*? As Yogi Berra said, "It's like *deja vu* all over again!"

8   Historically, we have counted on the courts to *expand* rights that were not explicit in the Constitution—rights for women, minorities, children, the

disabled. But *today's* Court interprets the Constitution the way fundamentalists interpret the Bible—with a stubborn literalism. If a right wasn't *spelled out* by that first quill pen, it doesn't exist! In other words, "If you don't see it on the shelf, we don't carry it—and we won't order it!"

9   One of the *most* troubling aspects of the *Webster* decision is the least-discussed. It concerns the preamble to the Missouri Constitution, which defines *human life* as *beginning at conception.* The Supreme Court refused to rule on this matter—and thus allowed Missouri to make a narrow, *religious* belief *the law of the land!*

10   Preferential treatment for *one* religion over *others* is blatantly unconstitutional. It's like that old bumper sticker from the '60s—"*Your karma* ran over *my dog*ma!" Since when is Roman Catholicism our national faith? The view of the Catholic Church—or any other denomination, for that matter—is valid for those who adhere to it. But Americans must *never* be *governed* by it—or by *any religious doctrine!*

11   We've already seen some *bizarre* legal outcomes of this religious definition of human life. Lawsuits have cropped up claiming fetuses as dependents for tax purposes—or charging "illegal imprisonment" of the fetuses of pregnant inmates—or seeking to reclassify juvenile offenders as adults by tacking an extra nine months onto their age!

12   What's *bizarre* today may turn *grim* by tomorrow. Compulsory pregnancy, forced Caesareans, surveillance and detention of pregnant women—these are the chilling, *logical* outcomes of laws that reduce women to *instruments of the state.*

13   We are *not* instruments of the state! We are *persons,* with human needs and human rights. It is nothing less than *evil* to deny our reproductive autonomy. Without it, our other rights are meaningless. Without it, our dignity is destroyed. And the first victims will be those among us who are already most vulnerable—those whose rights are *already* precarious—those whose access to health care is *already* limited—the young, the poor, and usually that means minorities.

14   But reproductive freedom is an issue that goes *beyond* the disadvantaged, *beyond* state boundaries, *far beyond* abortion itself. It goes to the heart of what this country stands for—to the principles embodied in our *Bill of Rights.* Our Constitution established powers of government and majority rule—and the purpose of the Bill of Rights was to set clear *limits* on those powers. The authors of that great document knew that certain fundamental freedoms must be *guaranteed—insulated* from public debate, *immune* to partisan politics.

15   For over 200 years, America has been "a light unto the nations." How disgraceful, that in *1989,* the year the Berlin Wall came down and the Iron Cur-

tain parted, the only barricade that started to crumble in *this* country was the precious wall protecting our private freedoms!

16   The crack in that wall may soon go even further—this time disenfranchising *teenagers*. Supreme Court rulings are pending in two cases involving mandatory parental notification for minors' abortions.

17   Most of us think parents *should* be involved in such a serious decision. And most pregnant teens *do* tell their parents. But laws that *force a family chat* can be *deadly*—not only for teens in unstable or violent homes—but also for teens with *loving* families. In Indiana, where parental notice is required, one teenager risked an illegal abortion rather than disappoint her parents—and it killed her.

18   It's true that parental involvement laws provide something called a judicial bypass. Minors who feel they *can't* confide in their parents may appear before a judge instead. But the judge is in a hopeless bind: by ruling that a minor is *too immature* to choose an abortion, the judge rules by implication that she is somehow *mature enough to become a mother!* Such a paradox would try the *wisdom of Solomon!*

19   The fact is, judges simply have *no business* making this decision for teens *or* adult women. Any female capable of *becoming* pregnant must have the ability to *prevent* or *end* a pregnancy. That right must never depend on age, race, state residence, wealth—*or* the vagaries of partisan politics. That right is as basic and as precious as our right to assemble here today.

20   Such fundamental freedoms are the proudest heritage of our nation. But our heritage of *Puritanism* also remains deeply rooted. My favorite description of the Puritans is this one, by a 19th century humorist: "The Puritans nobly fled from a land of despotism to a land of freedom—where they could not only enjoy their *own* religion, but where they could prevent everybody *else* from enjoying *theirs!*"

21   The flames of intolerance still burn brightly in this nation. And, like all religious fanatics, *today*'s Puritans subscribe to their own moral code—a code that embraces far more *brutality* than *morality*. To "save lives," they burn clinics. To "defend womanhood," they taunt and threaten pregnant women. To "strengthen the family," they invade our privacy. Blinded by their disregard for the *neediest* of women, they insist that making abortion *harder to get* will make it *go away.*

22   Haven't these zealots learned *anything* from history? Throughout time, women with unwanted pregnancies have *always ended them*, regardless of the law, regardless of the risk to our lives! Throughout the world, women and men equate *freedom* and *democracy* with the right to make private reproductive decisions, *free from government intrusion!*

23   The recent history of Romania is a perfect example. When Ceaucescu was overthrown, two of the *first acts* of the *new* government were to decriminalize abortion—and to deregulate the private ownership of *typewriters*. The new regime clearly recognized that *reproductive choice* is as *fundamental* as *freedom of speech!*

24   If only *our own* government were so wise. On the contrary, our president has taken a *jackhammer* to the bedrock of our basic rights. He has repeatedly asked the Supreme Court to overturn *Roe v. Wade*. He has attacked the federal family planning program, which helps *prevent* half a million abortions each year. And in a recent Supreme Court brief, his administration attacked not only the right to *abortion*, but the very *concept of privacy* that underlies our right to *contraception!*

25   It's nothing short of *obscene* that women are forced to *expose ourselves* to politicians—to submit our *private* matters, our *private* decisions, and our *private* parts to *public* debate! Morality should be taught in the home—it should be preached from the pulpit—it should be practiced in our individual lives—but it must *never* be legislated by lawmakers.

26   *Surely*, America's politicians have more *important* things to do. Like house the homeless, feed the hungry, and educate the ignorant. Like tackle the *root cause* of the abortion issue: *unintended pregnancy.*

27   Instead of compulsory ignorance, we need comprehensive sexuality education—in every home and in every school, from grades K–12. Instead of laws that punish pregnant women, we need our government's commitment to develop better birth control. Instead of pontifications about the *unborn*, we need proper care for the children *already* born.

28   Finally, instead of sermons on the stump, we need to be *left alone by the government*. We need to remove the abortion debate *forever* from the legislative arena. We need a universal recognition that our civil liberties are *off limits to partisan politics!* They are *fundamental* rights! *Indivisible* rights! *Non-negotiable* rights!

29   *Your* advocacy is essential to making these goals a reality. I learned a lot about organized religion from my minister mother. So I know that congregational life can have a profoundly positive impact—not only on our daily lives as individuals—but on the formation of our values and principles as a nation. The best possible wielding of that impact is exemplified by all of you today. You are ever aware that *your* right to freely practice your faith is only as secure as *other* people's right to believe differently. You are eternally *intolerant of intolerance.*

30   When the mechanism of religion goes awry, it is an *oppressive tyrant*. Some fanatics are merely self-righteous. Others are vicious and violent. For *all* those who seek to browbeat the rest of us, I have *these* words, by the folklorist Zora Neale Hurston: "I'll bet you, when you get down on them rusty knees and

get to worrying God, He goes in His privy-house and slams the door. *That's* what He thinks about *you* and *your* prayers!"

31   Those of us who lead spiritual lives have a special responsibility to combat fanaticism. We must remind Americans that *true* morality lies in the freedom to *make* choices—not in *prohibiting* them. We must lift up our voices for liberty—among our families and friends, our colleagues and communities, our pundits and politicians. We must preach from our pulpits that we hold our privacy *sacred!*

32   Happily, the "gospel" *we* are spreading *already* has millions of adherents. The Roman Catholic Church, however, is less fortunate. As I'm sure you've heard, the Church has launched a *$5 million* P.R. campaign to promote its anti-choice message. Questionable priorities aside, this is clearly an act of *desperation.* Has the Church examined its membership lately? Lay Catholics are overwhelmingly *pro-choice!* Three out of four use contraception—77% favor legal abortion in some or all situations—and 85% say a woman can have an abortion and still be a "good Catholic." Clearly, the *shepherd* has strayed from the *flock!*

33   In *this* flock, though, I sense great unity and strength. Maybe that's because you can support reproductive rights and still be a *good Unitarian!* In fact, from what I understand, to be a good Unitarian *by definition* is to support liberty, justice, equality, and a plurality of opinions—and *that's* what *pro-choice really means.*

34   Margaret Sanger, the good Unitarian, once said: "I have always known that it is not enough just to know one great truth. Truth must be *lived*—not merely passively accepted." I know all of you share that courage and that commitment. I am proud to count you among my friends. Thank you for your prestigious award—but much more, for your partnership in our shared faith.

ADDRESS ON ABORTION

Jerry Falwell

As a television evangelist, Jerry Falwell's "Old Time Gospel Hour" reached over 500,000 homes during the mid-1980s. His Moral Majority conservative political organization claimed four million members.

✝The text of this speech was provided by Rev. Falwell's office at Liberty University.

Falwell is founder and pastor of the Thomas Road Baptist Church in Lynchburg, Virginia, with over 20,000 members. Also he is founder and chancellor of Liberty University in Lynchburg. In late 1987 Falwell stepped down as head of the Moral Majority to devote more time to his ministry. In the summer of 1989, Falwell announced that the Moral Majority was being dissolved although the key policies that it had advocated would continue on the public agenda for national debate.

At the Unity '90 Conference in Chicago on June 28, 1990, Falwell addressed a wide range of groups and individuals associated to one degree or another with the pro-life or anti-abortion movement. At such a conference, one natural goal of the speech was to promote social cohesion (8–10). He warns that conflict and bickering among pro-life groups only weakens the effort to reverse *Roe* and to make abortion illegal (4–7). Also he urges cooperation and compromise among the diverse groups in the service of the larger goal (52–54). And of the four "challenges" he describes facing them, the first two stress the social cohesion theme (10–11). Falwell's early massive accumulation of diverse statistics vividly reminds his listeners of the difficulties they still face (3).

But the bulk of Falwell's speech advocates instrumental courses of action that should be adopted to promote significantly the achievement of the ultimate policy—reversal of *Roe* and making abortion illegal. One major action urged by Falwell is opposition to development and distribution of RU 486, the so-called abortion pill (14–15).

Clearly, however, Falwell's primary focus is advocacy of reframing the public debate on the abortion issue and overcoming confusing and misapplied labels (12–13). He offers an extensive plan of argumentation to retake the initiative through refuting ten "myths and misconceptions" that have been "perpetuated for so long by our opponents and the media" (17–50).

Consider, now, the array of rhetorical choices that characterize his speech. Bear in mind that the unspoken definitional assumption that "life" (humanness) begins at conception undergirds his statistics on the "killing" of "innocent and defenseless children" (1, 3). For some of the statistics he uses, he specifies their sources (36, 39–41) while for other statistics he does not specify sources (3, 43). Why should he or should he not have supplied more information on the sources and methods from which the statistics stem? Note also the specifics on several research studies are lacking (18, 19).

You are urged to apply the relevant standard tests for soundness of use of testimony (discussed in Chapter 4 on propositions of fact) to his extensive reliance on various kinds of testimony. Falwell quotes respected religious figures (9, 14, 37, 55), medical experts (35), opponents to use their own words to convict them (15), and journalistic sources that combine judgments with examples (11, 30, 33, 45–46, 49). Especially evaluate the reasonableness of his pervasive use of "reluctant" testimony from persons normally identified with the opposition and normally not expected to say anything favorable to the pro-life cause (20–22, 29, 31–32, 46).

For example, no source is provided for the quotation from Tietze and Henshaw so that a listener might check its accuracy and context (20). The quotation from Dr. Hern's medical textbook (21) should be understood in the context of the chapter in which it appears, where he laments the inadequate training in safe abortion procedures of many surgeons, not that abortion procedures in themselves are unsafe. The quotation by Dr. Calderone (22) represents her personal position and understanding of psychiatric evidence as of 1959, is not an official position of the Planned Parenthood Federation, is part of a speech on the dangers of *illegal* abortion, and is in a context where Calderone advocates reduced need for abortion through increased sex education and contraception availability. (See Calderone, "Illegal Abortion as a Public Health Problem," *American Journal of Public Health,* July 1960, pp. 948–954; Paul K. B. Dagg, "The Psychological Sequelae of Therapeutic Abortion—Denied and Completed," *American Journal of Psychiatry,* May 1991, pp. 578–585.)

Assess, also, the responsibilities of Falwell's interpretation of public opinion poll evidence (24–28) and the soundness of his use of examples (6–7, 37, 42, 44, 48). He argues that morality and religion take precedence over law and human opinion (23, 28). To what extent should this be the case for public policy as well as for private morality? Falwell sometimes uses comparison, analogy, and simile to undercut an opposing argument (15, 21, 50). How fair, accurate, and well-founded are these comparisons?

Among the many books on the abortion controversy, one with special relevance for the rhetorical critic is Celeste Condit, *Decoding Abortion Rhetoric: Communicating Social Change* (University of Illinois Press, 1990).

---

1 January 22, 1973 stands out in my mind as if it were yesterday. I was just 39 years old on the day the United States Supreme Court, by a vote of 7 to 2, struck down state bans on abortion. What has happened "legally" in this

country in the 17 years since that infamous decision is almost incomprehensible. The lives of nearly 25 million innocent and defenseless children have been needlessly and selfishly snuffed out.

2   During these 17 years, the debate on abortion has been raging. Dozens, perhaps hundreds of groups and organizations have been formed to fight this issue from both sides. Countless pieces of legislation have been drafted. Some have been passed, some have been defeated, and virtually all have been challenged. Hundreds of thousands of people have marched and picketed both in opposition to and support of abortion. Thousands have even spent time in jail in defense of their position on this volatile issue.

3   With the exception of preaching the Gospel of Jesus Christ, no single issue has captivated my attention for so long a period of time as has the issue of abortion. This is a good time to stop and take a careful look at this issue and to ask ourselves, "Are we winning or losing the abortion struggle?" Well, let us consider some statistics.

1. **Since 1973, nearly 25 million unborn children have been killed in America by legalized abortion—that is 1.5 million annually and 4,100 daily.**

2. **There were 1,160,389 American casualties from the Revolutionary War, Civil War, World War I, World War II, Korean War and Vietnam War combined. We will kill that many unborn children legally in the next 283 days.**

3. **Nearly 30 percent of all pregnancies end in induced abortion. 81 percent of abortion patients are unmarried. 43 percent of women having abortions have already had one or more abortions.**

4. **Our national bird enjoys better protection than does an unborn child. To damage an eagle's nest or shoot a bird is a crime that carries a maximum penalty of one year in prison and a $250,000 fine.**

5. **13,000 dolphins died in 1989 at the hands of tuna fisherman, prompting a successful consumer boycott of the three major tuna canners. While this issue received tremendous national media coverage, we will kill nearly that many unborn children in this country by the time we wake up on Monday morning.**

6. **While 1.5 million babies are aborted in this country every year, *50 million* are aborted worldwide every year.**

7. **According to the Allan Guttmacher Institute, *46 percent* of American women over the age of 45 have had an abortion.**

4   While I believe we are making progress on many fronts, I must admit that it is difficult to claim that we are "winning" in the "fight for life." That is

why I am excited about UNITY '90. I am proud to join with like-minded people from across the country for this unified strategy session.

5   Unfortunately, it was the call to unity that this conference sent forth which brought to mind the lack of unity within the pro-life ranks which so often besets us. I am ashamed to say that our opponents are publicly far more unified than we are.

6   For example, during debate in the Idaho legislature earlier this year on a bill that would have restricted abortions in that state, a nationally known pro-life organization actually sent a representative to the legislature to testify *against* that bill. That same group later claimed partial credit when Gov. Cecil Andrus vetoed the bill that the legislature had passed. That kind of self-defeating behavior can only drag us down. Whether or not you think that particular bill was the best possible legislation, the fact is that it would have saved lives.

7   Let me give another example. Recently the National Conference of Catholic Bishops announced a $5 million nationwide anti-abortion campaign. NEWSWEEK magazine, April 23, 1990 reported the following about this news, "But surprising criticism came from the non-Catholic anti-abortion activist groups the Bishops hoped to reach." One of our nationally recognized pro-life brothers was quoted as saying, "Christ was in the trenches. The Bishops are not committed to fighting abortion in the most effective way, which is confrontation." That kind of public bickering is at best, counter-productive. There is no room or time for that kind of in-fighting. Unfortunately, our opponents are wise enough to speak with one voice.

8   Let me pause for a few moments to thank many people and organizations who are working faithfully to make a difference in the fight for human life. These people could comprise a Human Life Hall of Fame.

[Editor's Note: At this point Falwell at length praises numerous anti-abortion organizations, their leaders, and other individuals. American Life Lobby; Americans United for Life; Focus on the Family; National Conference of Catholic Bishops; Annual March for Life; Operation Rescue; and Bethany Christian Services. Dr. Bernard Nathanson, producer of the films "Silent Scream" and "Eclipse of Reason." U.S. Senators Jesse Helms, Orin Hatch, Bill Armstrong, and Gordon Humphrey. U.S. Representatives Henry Hyde, Christ Smith, and Bob Doran. Vice-President Dan Quayle and President George Bush.]

9   As far as I am concerned, this is what UNITY '90 is all about—bringing together different people with different strategies for *one* purpose—bringing an end to this holocaust which we call abortion. We may not agree with every person here on every aspect of the abortion debate but we can and *must* agree *on one* thing—that we must use our collective energies and resources to discontinue this national sin. We should also pledge never to publicly disagree with

each other. Dr. Bob Jones, Sr., now in heaven, used to say, "I'd cheer for a hound dog if he came through Greenville barking for Jesus." I feel that way about the abortion issue. I applaud *anyone* who is doing *something* to chip away at this abomination. I appreciate what **Cardinal O'Connor** of New York said last year in an open letter.

> I continue to respect and admire every individual who participates in the Pro-Life Movement in any way—through quiet prayer, through discouraging others through quiet personal persuasion from having abortions, through joining the March for Life in Washington, or in whatever way seems best suited to their own conscience, way of life, or other responsibilities. There is room for all in the Pro-Life Movement. No one need follow the way of others nor should any of us criticize the way of others. United we stand; divided, babies die.

10   Well, what are the challenges that lie before us today? *First* of all, we must develop a unified strategy on every front of the abortion issue. Hopefully, we will begin to put aside our differences and work together with one heart, one mind, and one voice.

11   *Secondly,* we must realize that the Webster decision handed down by the Supreme Court last July and the Minnesota and Ohio decisions handed down Monday did not create an atmosphere in which we could relax but, rather, one in which we must work harder than ever. U.S. NEWS & WORLD REPORT in its April 2, 1990 edition analyzed abortion in this country since the Webster ruling. They reported that "at the time the Court announced its decision in Webster, both pro-life and pro-choice advocates predicted the ruling would mark the denouement of abortion." They went on to quote several prominent leaders on both sides of the issue before drawing this conclusion: "Notwithstanding the hyperbole, the fact is that the right to abortion is just as unencumbered today as it was before the Webster ruling." I say this, not to discourage you, but to challenge all of us to more fervent and diligent work in the months ahead.

12   *Thirdly,* we must re-frame public debate on this issue. We have allowed the debate on abortion to be sidetracked and hijacked from the real issues. Admittedly, we have been virtually helpless on much of this because we do not control the media, but we can do better. For example, we have watched the most basic terminology change before our very eyes. While we were once called "pro-life," we are now routinely referred to as "*anti*-abortion." Likewise, our opponents, rather than being called "pro-abortion," are conveniently referred to as "pro-*choice*." Now, rather than being in *favor* of life, we are "*opposed* to a woman's right to choose." And our opponents, rather than being in favor of abortion are merely in favor of "a woman's right to choose." Let's re-focus the debate—let's debate what abortion *is*, rather than who is for it and who is not.

Let's focus on the number of lives that have been lost rather than the number of people who march at our respective rallies.

13   Two months ago, I was proud to be an observer at the "Rally for Life" in Washington, DC. For over three hours one speaker after another delivered an important message on this issue. Yet throughout the day and in the days that followed, the overriding news story was the running debate over the number of people in attendance. As important as it is to have a strong and public show of support for our cause, it is not nearly as important as spreading the message that abortion is wrong and we have a "better way."

14   *Fourth,* and perhaps our greatest challenge ever, is the development of RU 486—the abortion pill, and its inevitable distribution in this country. As Chuck Colson recently wrote,

> What RU 486 will eventually mean, I fear, is a dramatic shift in the rules of the abortion battle. It will mean that our fight against abortion will no longer focus on the clinic, the dumpster, the Supreme Court steps. It will be relational and educational: Christians persuasively pressing the point among their peers that a life conceived is precious to God and must not be poisoned by a pill. The struggle will no longer be focused on legislatures and suction machines, but on people and the individual values they hold, the values that create their choices. What it means is changing the hearts and minds of a self-centered, callous generation.

15   I recently read, in PEOPLE magazine, an interview with the French medical researcher, Dr. Baulieu who has developed this abortion pill. He talks about abortion as if he were talking about a cure for the common cold, saying, "There is no reason to make a moral debate out of it. If something works, there's no reason to stop it." He goes on to say "there is no reason to be against us. We didn't invent abortion." That is about as logical as a politician supporting the legislation of cocaine and marijuana because he didn't invent the drugs. Some say that Dr. Baulieu may eventually win the Nobel Prize. God help us. If the Nobel Prize is awarded to this Doctor, they might as well award one posthumously to Adolph Hitler.

16   I think you will agree that the task that lies before us is a difficult one. Let's put our heads and hearts together and be heard with one loud voice.

17   How then, can we capture and reframe public debate on the abortion issue? There are many myths and misconceptions about abortion that must be dispelled or corrected. Many of these myths have been perpetrated for so long by our opponents and the media that many people automatically assume them to be accurate. Let me briefly discuss ten of these myths and how we can respond to them.

18   **Myth 1: Making abortion illegal will mean a return to "back alley" abortions.** The fact is that legalized abortion has merely brought "back alley"

abortionists to Main Street. In-depth study shows that maternal deaths resulting from legal abortions are replacing those due to illegal abortions almost one-for-one.

19   Another study comparing the year after Medicaid funding was cut off to the year before showed that the number of abortions decreased dramatically and the number of child births decreased slightly. Instead of abortion, many were exercising greater responsibility in avoiding pregnancy.

20   Abortions may have been safer *prior* to *Roe* than they are now. According to Tietze and Henshaw of the Guttmacher Institute, "it is entirely possible that the death-to-case ratio following illegal abortion in the United States is *higher,* not lower, than it was 15 to 20 years ago."

21   Myth 2: If abortion is legal, it is safe and uncomplicated. Dr. Warren M. Hern, an abortionist and author of a leading text on abortion procedures, has stated that "in medical practice there are few surgical procedures given so little attention and so underrated in its potential hazards as abortion." Abortions can be performed virtually any place someone chooses to perform the procedure. Over three-fourths of abortions are performed in non-hospital facilities.

22   In 1959, Dr. Mary Calderone, Medical Director of Planned Parenthood, made a speech before the American Public Health Association in which she said:

> I ask you not to assume that I am indiscriminately for abortion. Believe me, I am not, for, aside from the fact that abortion is the taking of life, I am mindful of what was brought out by our psychiatrists, that in almost every case, abortion, whether legal or illegal, is a traumatic experience that may have severe kickbacks later on.

23   Also, don't forget that just because something is legal does not mean it is a desirable thing to do. A woman has the legal right to smoke and drink heavily during pregnancy, but no one, including the doctors who perform abortions would recommend such irresponsibility.

24   Myth 3: Americans favor abortion on demand. The most important thing to consider when looking at public opinion polls is the wording of the questions. Simply changing two or three words can dramatically change the results. When worded in a fair and objective way, polls, in fact, reveal that an overwhelming majority of the American people oppose abortion in at least 95% of the cases in which abortion is obtained today. All the controversy we hear about maternal health, rape, and incest amount for less than 5% of the 1.5 million abortions performed annually in this country.

25   A January 1990 Wirthlin Survey asked under which circumstances abortion should be legal. *Only 11%* of Americans said abortion should be legal **"always"**, which is the current solution under Roe. A June 1989 CBS poll asked the question, "What if your state could pass a law that would only permit abortions in the cases of rape, incest, and to save the life of the mother. Would you favor or oppose that law?" 66% said they would favor such a law while only 29% would oppose that law.

26 In March, 1989, a BOSTON GLOBE/WBZ survey on abortion was released. Due to fairly worded questions, this poll showed that abortion for the reasons given by most women seeking abortions is opposed by an overwhelming majority of Americans. This poll listed common reasons for abortion with the percentage of people who opposed abortion in these cases.

Wrong time in life to have a child	82%
Fetus not desired sex	93%
Woman cannot afford a child	75%
As a means of birth control	89%
Pregnancy would cause too much emotional strain	64%
Father unwilling to help raise child	83%
Father absent	81%
Mother wants abortion father wants baby	72%
Father wants abortion mother wants baby	75%

27 It is also interesting to note how few people even know under what conditions abortion is legal today. Most people are surprised to learn that in all 50 states abortion is legal for *any* reason at *any* time including the ninth month of pregnancy.

28 I would be remiss if I did not go a step further and say that even if a majority of Americans favored or supported abortion for any reason, that would not make it right. Let us not lose sight of the fact that regardless of how abortion is considered in the hearts and minds of men, it is murder in the heart of God.

29 Myth 4: Abortion is a feminist issue—a question of women's rights. Modern day feminists either do not realize or simply ignore the fact that abortion is contrary to the original goals of the feminist movement. Early feminists such as Sarah F. Norton, Mattie Brinkerhoff, Susan B. Anthony, Mother Jones, Emma Goldman and Victoria Woodhull all denounced abortion as oppressive to women.

30 Syndicated columnist Steven Chapman said in a April, 1989 column,

Most pro-choice people are libertarian only when it's personally convenient. Women's groups, while adamantly in favor of barring the Government from any role in abortions decisions, are equally insistent that the Government take a *bigger* role in just about everything else. One demonstrator [in a pro-choice march] carried a sign saying, 'My Body, My Baby, My Business.' That's the pro-choice view of abortion. But when a woman chooses to *have* a baby, the cherub suddenly becomes society's concern.

Women's groups endlessly lobby to force taxpayers and employers to bear part of the cost of parenthood. Government subsidies for child care, laws requiring businesses to grant time off to new parents, programs to improve health and welfare of mothers and babies—you name it, they're for it.

31   Juli Loesch, the anti-nuclear activist at Three Mile Island, and now a member of "Feminists for Life," commented in the April, 1989 edition of the WASHINGTON MONTHLY, on her reconsideration of protests against the Vietnam War. She said she found herself being "inconsistent to the point of incoherence. We are saying that killing was not an acceptable solution to conflict situations, yet when we had our own conflict situation, we were willing to go straight to killing as a technical fix."

32   I think we let men off the hook too easily on the abortion issue. Abortion provides a climate that encourages men to abdicate their responsibility to their born, as well as pre-born children. Juli Loesch suggests that the acceptance of abortion actually encourages exploitation of women by men. She says "The idea is that a man can use a woman, vacuum her out, and she is ready to be used again." Men can help make the pro-choice position a responsible one by contributing to a process where the choice is made prior to conception.

33   Jo McGowan is a writer living in India where nearly all abortion cases involve a female fetus. McGowan discusses this in a 1989 NEWSWEEK column where she says:

> Feminists are speaking out of both sides of their mouths. When the issue is sex determination and the 'selective' abortion of girls, they call it female feticide. But when the issue is reproductive freedom and the abortion of male and female fetuses, they call it a 'woman's right to choose.' It won't work. They can't have it both ways. Either they accept abortion or they don't.
>
> She concludes by saying: Perhaps from the undeniable truth that it is wrong to kill a baby simply because she is a girl will emerge the larger truth that it is wrong to kill a baby at all.

34   **Myth 5: Forcing women to carry pregnancies to term will only result in unwanted, abused children.** Legalized abortion has not reduced child abuse problems in this country—in fact, such cases have skyrocketed. According to the U.S. Bureau of the Census, in its 1988 *Statistical Abstract of the United States*, between 1978 and 1985, reported cases of child abuse and neglect rose from 607,000 to 1.3 million annually.

35   There is a lack of statistical research to prove any correlation between child abuse and unwanted pregnancies. Several years ago, Dr. Vincent Fontana, a professor of Clinical Pediatrics and a chairman of the Mayor's task force on Child Abuse and Neglect of the city of New York, stated that:

> Abortion is a 'sweeping and simplistic' solution that fails because the assumption that every battered child is an unwanted child, or that most or even a large proportion of abused children are unwanted children is totally false.

36   **Myth 6: Pro-lifers care only about the baby and aren't extending any help to the pregnant women.** The fact is, there are more crisis pregnancy centers than there are abortion clinics in the United States. The February, 1990 *National Catholic Register* estimates there are over 3,400 pro-life centers in this country, and that 400 new centers are being established each year.

37   I believe that the church of Christ has a better way. I remember 30 years ago, Bishop Fulton Sheen said that the church has no right to preach against abortion unless it is willing to say to that pregnant girl, we have a better way. It was that philosophy that led us through the Thomas Road Baptist Church to start the Liberty Godparent Home in Lynchburg, Virginia eight years ago. This ministry provides housing, medical care counselling, a licensed adoption agency, and an opportunity to continue education, all free of charge to unwed mothers. Through the residence program and the toll-free counselling service, over 3,000 abortions have been prevented since this ministry began in 1982.

38   While much is happening nationwide, much remains to be done. We must establish enough crisis pregnancy homes, adoption agencies, and counselling centers to accommodate the 1.5 million girls and women who, each year, face a traumatic dilemma.

39   **Myth 7: If all the women who are currently seeking abortions were forced to carry their pregnancies to term, there would not be enough adoptive parents to care for these children.** According to the National Committee for Adoption, there have been approximately 50,000 adoptions per year since 1974. However, there are also 2 million childless couples on agency waiting lists or at fertility clinics who would like to adopt. That means 40 couples are waiting to adopt every available baby. Most people wishing to adopt wait anywhere from three to seven years before a baby is available.

40   We need to begin to promote adoption as a viable alternative to abortion. An editorial in *The Wall Street Journal* last year referred to a study conducted by the U.S. Department of Health and Human Services which indicated that 40% of the time, pregnancy counsellors did not even *mention* adoption as an option during discussions with pregnant women.

41   The National Committee for Adoption cites the "legalization of abortion" as a factor that reduces the potential number of adopted children. For example, in 1972, the year before *Roe* v. *Wade*, there were 403,000 out-of-wedlock births and 65,000 unrelated adoptions; but, in 1982 there were 715,000 out-of-wedlock births and only *50,000* unrelated adoptions.

42   I believe there is enough love and care in this country to provide a good home for every baby brought into this world. Even the Spina-Bifida Association of America and the National Down's Syndrome Adoption Exchange report waiting lists for babies they are able to place for adoption.

43   **Myth 8: What we really need is better education about birth control and safe sex.** Rather than teaching young people how to have safe sex, we ought to teach them how to **save** sex for marriage. 81% of all abortion patients are unmarried. This is not how God intended for us to live.

44   There has been much debate in recent years about placing sex clinics in our public schools to make condoms and birth control pills readily available. As far as I am concerned, passing out birth control pills in a public school is like distributing cook books at a fat farm.

45   The April 30 issue of *Insight* magazine recounted an assignment that a *Washington Post* reporter named Leon Dash was given in 1984 to write about teenage pregnancy. He assumed that ignorance about reproduction was the main cause of teenage pregnancy and spent a year living in a neighborhood that had one of the highest numbers of teenage parents. During that year he interviewed his subjects more than 30 hours apiece and reported the following:

> They were all very well-versed in sex education, and those who didn't want children, didn't have them. These girls became mothers to be affirmed as women.
>   Sixteen-year-old Tauscha Vaughn said 'Mr. Dash, will you please stop asking me about birth control? Girls out here know all about birth control. There's too many birth control pills out here. All of them know about it. Even when they're 12, they know what it is.'

46   The magazine went on to say that even the Guttmacher Institute, a leading proponent of education and contraception has been rethinking this issue. Jeannie Rosoff, the institute's president, says "Most of the programs we have had have been preaching sex education. We now know that increasing knowledge does *not* necessarily affect behavior." Finally, this article discussed morality.

> Young people are supposed to find the very idea of morality laughable. But the best indicator these days for not getting pregnant as a teenager is membership in a fundamentalist Protestant church that teaches in no-nonsense fashion that sex outside of marriage is a sin. A study by Sandra Hofferth, an Urban Institute researcher, shows the direct correlation between weekly attendance at religious services and delayed sexual activity.

47   We need *less* sex education and *more* parents, pastors and teachers serving as role models and providing moral education.

48   **Myth 9: You cannot be openly pro-life and win public office in this country.** Contrary to popular opinion, certain pro-life candidates have not lost recent elections because they were pro-life, but rather because they handled the issue poorly. Jim Courter, the GOP gubernatorial candidate in New Jersey last year, did not lose because he was pro-life. He lost because he waffled on his pro-life position and record and eventually abandoned it altogether. Frankly, there really was no pro-life candidate in the New Jersey Governor's race. In the Virginia governor's race, republican Marshall Coleman attempted to hide from the abortion issue by not responding to the media campaign that Wilder and pro-abortion groups launched against him. He too, lost in what turned out to be the narrowest margin in Virginia gubernatorial history.

49   In the January issue of the *American Spectator*, columnist Fred Barnes explains why ducking this issue won't work. He says, "Pro-choice Democrats are unwilling to vote for pro-choice republicans over pro-life democrats. But pro-life Republicans will jump ship in a hurry. Better to stick with the pro-life stand." This is why I have so much respect for men like Ronald Reagan and Jesse Helms. These men and others like them, stand firmly in defense of the unborn without regard for public opinion polls. May God raise up more men and women who are more concerned with the next generation than with the next election.

50   **Myth 10: It's OK to say "I am personally opposed to abortion *but*, I would never force my views on someone else."** That rationale would be like saying in 1860, "I am personally opposed to slavery, but if my neighbor wants to own a few, that's OK." The fact is if abortion is wrong and if abortion is murder, we ought to have the guts to stand up and say so. Imagine the backlash if George Bush one day said during a Press Conference that he was personally opposed to Apartheid but if South Africa wanted to practice it, that was OK. He would be run out of office instantly. Yet, we continue to let politicians off the hook who use this warped logic on the abortion issue. Let's not let them get away with it any longer.

51   Where do we go from here? Perhaps more important than *where* we go is that we go *together*. If anything is obvious from our 17-year struggle, it is that there is no quick or easy solution to this problem.

52   Let's win this fight by changing one heart at a time—saving one baby at a time. Let's agree that preventing *some* abortions is better than preventing none. An "all or nothing" mentality will never succeed in this real world in which we live.

53   I remember appearing on ABC's 20/20 program in 1985 to discuss abortion. On that program I said that I would support *legislation* which would outlaw abortions except in the cases of rape, incest, or when the life of the mother is endangered. Judging from the mail and phone calls we received, you would have thought that I had opened an abortion clinic. I was accused of "selling out" and giving in too easily on this issue. My remarks did not mean that I approve of abortion in some cases and not in others but rather, for the purpose of achieving *some* legislative progress, I would support legislation that would legally prevent over 95% of all abortions. *Any* number of abortions we can prevent legally will be more than we are currently preventing.

54   Let's not argue with each other over anything that would save lives. As each day passes, over 4,000 precious babies are snatched away. Let's covenant together to use every available means—legal, political, and most importantly, spiritual, to reverse this terrible tide.

55   Chuck Colson in a recent column, eloquently articulates the challenge before us. Even if we were to win in the battleground states, that will not be the end of the pro-life struggle. True, we will have brought human law into conformity to God's law—a good end, but not enough. While the law is a moral teacher, law alone cannot change peoples' moral choices. Women will still seek out illegal abortions. So we must work on a more fundamental level than legislation alone, painting a fresh moral vision on our dingy national canvas, a vision of hope and human dignity. We must woo peoples' hearts towards righteousness. But we cannot woo unless we love. It is more than the battle against abortion that suffers when Christians conduct themselves with anger and hate. We wound our witness of the truth and the Gospel and the love of Jesus Christ.

56   In my heart, I question how long God can continue to bless a nation that places as little value on human life as we do in America. It is my prayer that the 1990s will be the decade in which the unborn are emancipated. Let us all pray and work to that end.

Illegal Immigration:
Let's Get on with Solving the Problem

Kathleen Brown

The Town Hall has, for over half a century, been Southern California's leading public issues forum. Because of its reputation for excellence, Town Hall attracts leaders in government, industry, and the arts and sciences from around the world. Town Hall's General Meetings are normally held at luncheon venues attended by leaders from across the professions who value dialogue on contemporary issues.

On September 29, 1993, Kathleen Brown, Treasurer of the State of California, addressed about 500 people at the Town Hall in Los Angeles, California. The *Los Angeles Times,* September 10, 1993, p. A3, reported that this speech, which was interrupted several times by applause, began laying the foundation for a 1994 campaign for Governor against incumbent Pete Wilson. Brown is the daughter of former California governor Edmund G. "Pat" Brown and the sister of former governor Edmund G. "Jerry" Brown, Jr.

As a potential political rival to governor Pete Wilson, Kathleen Brown is arguing an alternative plan on the immigration question. Brown's speech could be evaluated from the "challenger style" of communication proposed by Judith S. Trent and Robert V. Friedenberg in the third edition of their book, *Political Campaign Communication: Principles and Practices* (Westport, Connecticut: 1995), pps. 81–86. According to Trent and Friedenberg, the communication strategies a political challenger can use are the following: 1) Attack the record of opponents, 2) Taking the offensive position on issues, 3) Calling for a change, 4) Emphasizing optimism for the future, 5) Speaking to traditional values rather than calling for value changes, 6) Appearing to represent the philosophical center of the political party, and 7) Delegating personal or harsh attacks to surrogate speakers in an effort to control demagogic rhetoric (p. 81).

Brown begins the speech with optimistic and prideful references to her own immigrant ancestors (7–10). After acknowledging the problem

✝Kathleen Brown, "Illegal Immigration: Let's Get on with Solving the Problem," December 15, 1993, pp. 143–146. Reprinted by permission of *Vital Speeches of the Day* and the author.

of illegal immigration (11–12), she urges a "common sense" approach that hints at her own "centrist" position that specifically avoids "tinkering at the politically charged margins" (18–19). Instead of a radical view, Brown repetitively recommends an approach grounded in the traditional values of common sense, fairness, and responsibility (18, 19, 20, 24–27, 30, 66, 71, 83.)

The cause of the illegal immigration problem is the "prospect of employment" (34–36). Brown's proposed policy takes the offensive on the problem (37–40, 52–56, 58–62, 74–75) and provides reasoned rebuttal arguments (41–48, 63–64). How effectively does Brown argue for her policy?

Finally, Brown specifically attacks Governor Wilson's proposals to deny emergency health services to illegal immigrants (67–70). How well does Brown argue that Wilson's plan does not meet the values she previously stated (69–71)? Are there any hints of demagogic overtones with Brown's rhetorical questions (15, 28) or with the references to Japanese-American internment camps (21)?

---

1 Usually at forums such as these, I dedicate my remarks to the hidden benefits of riding the yield curve, debt ratios and bond ratings.

2 But I want to take this opportunity to begin to address a series of broader policy issues affecting California's future including the economy, education and violence in our communities.

3 Today, I will speak about immigration. First, because it is a major issue in the minds of Californians. Second, because I have been talking about it in bits and pieces over the last several months and it is time to put forth a comprehensive rather than piecemeal statement. And third, because I think it is time to bring the discussion back down to earth.

4 My message is two-fold: first, immigration and immigrants add immeasurable value to California and to our economy and should be celebrated as one of California's greatest assets.

5 Second, illegal immigration is a problem and must be addressed in a responsible and thoughtful manner.

6 Perhaps more than any other force, immigration—legal and illegal—has shaped and will continue to shape California's destiny.

7 Most of us are descendants of immigrants, and one of the reasons I feel strongly about this issue is the pride I feel as a fourth generation Californian.

8 My grandfather's father—Joseph Brown—moved to California from Ireland and became a groundskeeper in Golden Gate Park. My grandmother's

father—August Shuckman—came here from Germany in the 1860s, settled in Colusa County, and ran an inn on the stage coach line. They believed in what California could offer, and ended up giving back far more than was ever given to them.

9   And I also know first-hand about dreams and challenges of newer immigrants—my daughter-in-law is a first generation Filipino-American whose father came to this country to work on the railroads.

10   So I have a personal understanding of the lure of this state—and a determination to build on the dreams of every immigrant.

11   But I also know we can't pretend that illegal immigration isn't a problem. In the past decade, the number of illegal, immigrants in California has doubled, to 2.1 million, equivalent to the population of Arkansas.

12   The increasing numbers of illegal immigrants has, quite properly, raised a growing number of public policy debates touching on issues like jobs, taxes, education, and crime, to name a few.

13   Unfortunately, as the issue of illegal immigration has gained in prominence, it has also gained in virulence. Explosive issues of race, class, employment, and power have all been raised, some with merit, some without, some rationally, and some not.

14   For many years, it was impossible to have a common sense debate about illegal immigration. Anyone who brought it up was immediately branded a racist or kook. Today, it seems we have a different problem: the only way to be heard on this issue is to unveil a new idea that is more punitive than the last one.

15   I gave a great deal of thought to whether another statement at this point in the debate would do more harm than good. Has the dialogue become so overheated that no proposal can receive attention unless it is more extreme than all the previous ones? Have we reached the point where discussion of the illegal immigration issue has become nothing more than an arms race for ambitious politicians?

16   I finally concluded that the most valuable contribution I can make is to try to move the debate from one-upmanship to problem solving. It is no longer acceptable—if it ever was—to throw extreme or impractical proposals on the table just to make those who disagree look soft.

17   What I bring today are not just ideas, but also specific steps to implement them. I have new proposals, but they are grounded in common sense, not news sense.

18   Given the power of immigration to shape the future of this state, it is time to set forward three principles that should guide and ground thoughtful policy: common sense, fairness, and responsibility.

19   Common sense says go to the core of the illegal immigration problem instead of tinkering at the politically charged margins. Common sense says focus on the real reason illegal immigrants come to this country—jobs. And common sense says focus on solutions that have a real chance of being implemented—not unconstitutional approaches that would take years to get resolved.

20   Fairness says that we must go out of our way to prevent an ugly backlash against immigrants that would be both dangerous and shameful.

21   I am mindful that earlier this century, fear of foreigners resulted in thousands of Japanese-Americans being stripped of all their belongings and sent to internment camps. And a year later, that same fear led American servicemen to attack Mexican-Americans in the streets of Los Angeles.

22   That is why I am deeply concerned about the rise in hate crimes committed against foreigners and those perceived to be foreigners, and I want to be unequivocal on this point: immigrants are among California's greatest strengths. Those who commit hate crimes against them should be punished to the full extent of the law.

23   This country was built by immigrants, and there is no difference between a first generation American and fifth generation American.

24   Finally, my third principle: responsibility.

25   *Fiscal* responsibility says that we must avoid solutions with small, short range savings but large, long-term costs.

26   *Corporate* responsibility says businesses must comply with the law, and government must make it painful for those who don't.

27   And perhaps most important, *personal* responsibility says that we must target people who violate the laws, not innocent children who know nothing of borders or documents.

28   Should a small bleeding child be turned away from an emergency room because of who his or her parents are?

29   I believe a fundamental measure of a civilized society is how it treats children and the elderly. Visiting the crimes of an adult upon a child is barbaric, and proposals that do so are based on the coldest and most cynical political calculations.

30   Guided by the principles of common sense, fairness, and responsibility, I see three key elements to an effective plan.

31   First, address the real reason illegal immigrants come here, by cutting off their access to jobs.

32   Second, do a better job of closing off the routes used by illegal immigrants to enter the country.

33   And third, take all rational steps to reduce the economic costs of illegal immigration.

34 I believe the single most important step we can take to reduce illegal immigration is to make it impossible for illegal aliens to get a job in this country. The prospect of employment is what brings people here. The knowledge that employment laws are easy to get around is what brings them here illegally. That's what we've got to stop.

35 I recently read about one undocumented immigrant woman who slipped into California four years ago. She said she had worked for 40 garment sewing shops in Los Angeles.

36 More than three-quarters of the time, employers ignored the law and *never* asked for papers verifying her identity and right to work in the United States. And this is no isolated case: according to I.N.S. officials, about 80 percent of employers in construction and garment manufacturing in Los Angeles and Orange County break immigration regulations.

37 It's painfully clear from what I've just described that it's time we take the following specific steps: First, we must increase penalties for employers who knowingly hire illegal immigrants. Under current federal law, penalties for knowingly hiring undocumented workers are as low as $250. Even a third offense can receive a fine as low as $3,000. These fines must be much higher—$1,000 for the first offense, $5,000 for a second offense, and $10,000 for a third offense.

38 I would prefer that the state of California impose these fines, but federal law prohibits us from doing so. Today I am writing to Attorney General Janet Reno and our congressional delegation to ask for their help in obtaining a waiver from this law.

39 Second, it is unreasonable to impose additional fines on businesses unless we make it possible for them to identify accurately who is legally eligible for work, and who is not.

40 That is why, at a congressional hearing several weeks ago, I proposed the creation of a tamper-proof social security card that every employer must ask of every employee before they are hired. I have tried to tailor my plan so it is easy for small businesses to handle—I want to make it as easy for an employer to check a job applicant's residency status as it is for a grocery clerk to approve a customer's check.

41 A number of concerns have been raised about such a card.

42 First, some say a Social Security card would spur discrimination because only people perceived to be foreigners would be asked to show their cards. I share that concern.

43 So I am proposing the federal law require every employer to ask every employee—both new and existing—for their card. New employees would have to show their cards when they fill out their W-4 form. Existing employees would show their new cards when the Social Security Administration first distributes them.

44   To make the law enforceable without thousands of new inspectors, I would require employers to submit copies of the cards to the IRS along with each employee's W-2 form as proof of compliance. Failure to provide this documentation would be punished by a fine of $1,000 per incident, and the employer's name would be turned over to the I.N.S. for investigation of possible immigration law violations and further penalties.

45   The second concern raised is cost. The Social Security Administration estimates it would cost between $8 and $10 per person to give every eligible citizen a tamper-proof card. California's experience with tamper-proof driver's licenses suggests the costs could even be lower—the DMV estimates that our new licenses, which have a photo and fingerprint cost $7.40 each.

46   I propose that cardholders pay the cost of their own cards. It is a minimal amount, and the benefits of the card to each taxpayer will clearly outweigh this small cost.

47   The third concern is effectiveness. The card is only as reliable as the underlying documents. If the documents used to obtain the card are falsified, then the card itself will have accomplished nothing.

48   But in fact, tamper-proof cards will address the biggest source of the problem: eighty-eight percent of fake cards are completely counterfeit, churned out on unauthorized presses without the knowledge of the Social Security Administration. A tamper-proof card would put an end to that crime.

49   I have one final proposal to address the employment issue. One of the reasons hiring illegal immigrants is attractive to unscrupulous employers is because employers know they can pay below minimum wage, and violate child labor and occupational safely standards without worrying the employees will complain.

50   There are 858,000 employers in California, but do you know how many federal labor inspectors there are?

Sixty two.

There are even fewer full time state field inspectors—seventeen.

51   As a result , there is little chance violators will be caught. And, in the unlikely event they are caught, state fines for violating the minimum wage are as low as $50.

52   So I propose hiring an additional 500 state and federal inspectors for California, to be financed through the enhanced employer fines and a source I will discuss shortly.

53   And, I propose increasing state fines for violations to a minimum of $1,000 per incident. Taking these steps will substantially reduce the economic incentives to hire illegal aliens.

54   Let me now turn to a new point. Along with making it nearly impossible for illegal immigrants to get a job in this country, we must make it nearly impossible for them to cross the border. The only way to do that is with tighter enforcement and increased personnel. This is not complicated; it's simply a matter of finding the resources.

55   I look to two sources.

56   First, I endorse Senator Dianne Feinstein's proposal to charge a $1 toll to all people crossing our borders from Mexico and Canada. This will raise over $400 million a year to fight illegal immigration.

57   I am writing to the Senator today to suggest two additions. First, in order not to overburden people who cross the borders on a daily basis, we should have monthly or annual passes that are available for lower cost. Second, I am asking that a portion of the money raised from the fee be allocated to hire the Department of Labor inspectors I mentioned earlier.

58   The second step we need to take to enforce the borders is to use our military troops for limited backup of the I.N.S. by expanding already-existing cooperative efforts between the Defense Department and the Border Patrol.

59   Let me be clear about this point.

60   I am not proposing militarizing our border, or treating Mexico or Canada, as enemies, or sending armed troops out to arrest illegal aliens. Military troops cannot and would not be used for arrests, or search or seizure.

61   What I am suggesting is treating military troops as an underutilized taxpayer financed resource that can be put to better use.

62   Specifically, we should allow troops to operate in cooperation with the I.N.S., where they can be used for backup purposes including logistical support, communications, transportation, mechanical repairs, and operating equipment.

63   This is not a new role for the military. Under "operation alliance," the military already provides backup assistance to the border patrol and other government agencies involved in drug interdiction. My proposal would expand its role to include illegal immigration.

64   This will free up I.N.S. personnel to tackle enforcement operations. This is just good common sense, and an efficient way to beef up the border patrol with minimal new costs.

65   Along with removing the enticement of jobs, and strengthening our border patrol, there is a third objective we must pursue, and that is to limit the services used—and the costs generated—by illegal immigrants.

66   Once again, I am guided by the principles of common sense, fairness, and responsibility.

67   Those principles, plus simple human decency, are why I oppose Governor Wilson's proposal to deny emergency health services to illegal immigrants. We cannot have people dying on the sidewalk in front of our hospitals. It is shortsighted to allow people with contagious diseases like tuberculosis to spread their illnesses to the rest of the population.

68   And it is both fiscally and morally irresponsible to deny prenatal care to pregnant mothers when the costs of future, preventable ailments will be many times higher.

69   The principles of common sense, fairness, and responsibility are why I also oppose the governor's proposal to deny education to the children of illegal immigrants. In the first place, the Supreme Court has ruled that doing so would be unconstitutional, and changing that will take years, if not longer. Second, schools should devote their scarce resources to education, not to the nearly impossible task of determining the residency status of their students.

70   And most important, it should be obvious that if we deny schooling to children—any children—we contribute to a cycle of illiteracy, hopelessness, drugs, and crime, thereby costing us far more than we will ever save.

71   The principles of common sense, fairness, and responsibility are also why two months ago I wrote to President Clinton suggesting that he initiate a new federal policy that says: every time we negotiate an agreement or treaty with another country, we will add a provision requiring the other country to take back and jail its citizens who have been convicted of crimes in the U.S.

72   Right now, we have 14,000 illegal aliens in California prisons, and another 10,000–15,000 in county jails. It costs the state's taxpayers over $500 million a year to keep them imprisoned, and because the prisons and jails are so overcrowded, we're having to release criminals before they've served their full sentences.

73   We should use the leverage we have during treaty negotiations to force other countries to take back their criminal illegal aliens, with guarantees they will serve the time they're supposed to.

74   I see one other lever that should be used to encourage foreign countries to take back and imprison their nationals who commit crimes here: U.S. foreign aid. Several of the countries that are home to significant numbers of illegal alien convicts are also recipients of U.S. foreign aid.

75   As long as these countries refuse to take back and imprison their nationals, I propose that we deduct the costs of incarceration from their foreign aid allotment, and allocate the money to the states that now bear the costs. For California, that would amount to $47 million a year.

76   There are several other steps that can be taken to reduce the costs of illegal immigrants to California taxpayers. Governor Wilson is now considering two bills that would require people to show proof of legal residency before they can use state job referral agencies and toughen penalties for medical fraud.

77   I urge the governor to sign those bills. Finally, I echo the calls of many other California elected officials in demanding the federal government reimburse California for the full costs of federal immigration policies and policy failures.

78   I've talked a lot about details today; let me conclude by returning to the larger picture.

79   Sometimes in America, important issues can be lost in a sea of rhetoric and conflict. Too many politicians look to divide for political gain; too many reporters look to sensationalize; too many citizens look to blame others for their problems. Illegal immigration need not be one of these issues.

80   We live in times when many of our people are scared. They're scared of losing their health care; they're scared their children can't get a decent education; and they're scared about their personal safety. Illegal immigration is wrongly seen as a cause.

81   When faced with such widespread fears, elected leaders have three choices: we can ignore the problem and hope it goes away, we can exploit those feelings for political gain, or we can try to lead the way to solutions.

82   The first two options cannot work; it's time to try the third. We've had enough meanness and hostility; let's get on with solving the problem.

83   The problems of illegal immigration may strain our patience. But when some exploit that frustration and anger, we must answer with policies drawn from our roots. California's immigrants built—and continue to build—this state with common sense, fairness, and responsibility. Those fundamentals should guide our approach to the challenge of illegal immigration.

84   I thank you very much.

SECURING OUR NATION'S BORDERS: ILLEGAL IMMIGRATION

Pete Wilson

The issue of illegal immigration in the United States has become a major public policy question in the 1990s. While many Americans can trace their ancestral roots to immigrants, the financial drain on some state's resources has become severe. As seen previously in the Kathleen Brown speech, the state of California is now "ground-zero" in the policy debate over how the nation should accommodate illegal immigrants.

Addressing the same Town Hall forum in Los Angeles as did Kathleen Brown, California governor Pete Wilson delivered his view on the illegal immigration question on April 25, 1994. Even though Wilson's speech was delivered one year later than Brown's address, the two speeches should be carefully compared for their opposing viewpoints on the illegal immigration issue.

Born in Lake Forest, Illinois, Pete Wilson grew up in St. Louis, Missouri. After graduating from Yale University and law school at the University of California at Berkeley, Wilson began a career in California politics. Wilson served for twelve years as the mayor of San Diego and one term as United States Senator. While serving in the U.S. Senate, Wilson first entered the national debate on immigration reform. In September 1985, Wilson sponsored a "guest-worker amendment" designed to lessen the harsh migrant-worker restrictions proposed in a landmark immigration reform bill sponsored by Republican senator Alan K. Simpson of Wyoming. (See *Current Biography Yearbook 1991*, New York: H.W. Wilson Company, 1991, p. 619). On February 18, 1989, within weeks after beginning his second term in the Senate, Wilson announced his candidacy for the office of governor. After winning an extremely close race against Dianne Feinstein, former mayor of San Francisco, Pete Wilson was sworn in on January 7, 1991 as the thirty-sixth governor of California. Wilson was re-elected in 1994.

Wilson's presentation on illegal immigration should be analyzed from the stock issues perspective of "need-plan-advantages" frequently

---

+Pete Wilson, "Securing Our Nation's Borders: Illegal Immigration," July 15, 1994, pp. 534–536. Reprinted by permission of *Vital Speeches of the Day* and the author.

applied to policy speeches. The "need" or harmful problem affecting many states, but especially California, is argued early in the speech (9, 11, 12, 13). While Washington's lack of action on the issue is to blame (3) for this problem, Wilson presents his own plan for legal action in well-structured detail (15–18, 28–33). The numerous financial advantages to be accrued from Wilson's plan will ultimately benefit the whole nation, but will especially help the burdened taxpayers of California (48–56).

Aware of potential opposition to his proposals, Wilson's speech clearly anticipates these objections and presents forceful counter-arguments. Wilson denies that the plan is racist (19–21), or is purely partisan (21). He acknowledges that Congress and President Clinton recognize the problem, but their current efforts are inadequate (24–26). In an effort to use Clinton's own words to argue his cause, Wilson contends that even the president admits that California has had to "bear a huge portion of the cost for the failure of federal policy" (35).

Wilson concludes the speech by arguing that his new policy will work and he offers the example of El Paso, Texas as an analogy of a successful blockade (40–41, 43).

Wilson sarcastically observes (44–46), that the people of California can not wait any longer for a "failed policy" in Washington to work. Given the arguments and evidence presented, do you think Wilson's plan will meet its goals (55–56) ? How could Kathleen Brown refute Wilson's position?

---

1   I've come here this afternoon to announce that I will file suit this week against the federal government for its failure to control our nation's borders. It's not a decision I come to lightly. I would rather resolve this crisis in the Congress than in the courts. But the repeated failure of Congress to confront its responsibility to control illegal immigration and to prevent the terrible unfairness to state taxpayers and to needy legal residents—has driven us to seek redress for our injuries in the courts.

2   The federal government's immigration policy is broken and the time to fix it is now.

3   It's hard to blame people who day after day pour across our borders. They're coming to find a better life for themselves and their families. It's easy to sympathize with them and even admire their gumption. It is those in Washington that we should condemn—those who encourage the illegals to break the law by rewarding them for their illegal entry.

4   We are a state and a nation of immigrants, proud of our immigrant traditions. Like many of you, I'm the grandchild of immigrants. My grandmother came to this country in steerage from Ireland at age 16. She came for the same reason any immigrant comes—for a better future than she could hope for in the old country. And America benefited from her and millions like her.

5   But we, as a sovereign nation, have a right and an obligation to determine how and when people come into our country. We are a nation of laws, and people who seek to be a part of this great nation must do so according to the law.

6   The United States already accepts more legal immigrants into our country than the rest of the world combined—1.8 million in 1991 alone.

7   We are a generous people. But there is a limit to what we can absorb and illegal immigration is now taxing us past that limit.

8   Thousands come here illegally every day. In fact, the gaping holes in federal policy have made our borders a sieve. President Clinton has used that very word to describe their porous condition.

9   The results are, in Los Angeles, there's now a community of illegal residents numbering a million people. That's a city the size of San Diego. Alone, it would be the 7th largest city in the nation—half again the population of our nation's capital, Washington, D.C.

10   Two-thirds of all babies born in Los Angeles public hospitals are born to illegal immigrants.

11   As we struggle to keep dangerous criminals off our streets, we find that fourteen percent of California's prison population are illegal immigrants—enough to fill 8 state prisons to design-capacity.

12   And through a recession that has caused the loss of one third the revenues previously received by state government, as we have struggled to maintain per pupil spending and to cover fully enrollment growth with classrooms around the state bursting at the seams, we're forced to spend $1.7 billion each year to educate students who are acknowledged to be in the country illegally.

13   In total, California taxpayers are compelled *by federal law* to spend more than $3 billion to provide services to illegal immigrants—it's approaching 10 percent of our state budget.

14   To ignore this crisis of illegal immigration—as some would have us do—is not irresponsible, but makes a mockery of our laws. It is a slap in the face to the tens of thousands who play by the rules and endure the arduous process of legally immigrating to our country.

15   It's time to restore reason, integrity and fairness to our nation's immigration policy. And we need to do it now. California can't afford to wait.

16   First, the federal government must secure our border. That's the first step in securing our future. They must devote the manpower and the technology necessary to prevent people from crossing the border in the first place.

17   Second, the federal government should turn off the magnetic lure that now rewards people who successfully evade the border patrol and cross the border illegally.

18   And finally, until our representatives in Washington do act, until they secure the border and turn off the magnetic lure, they should pay the full bill for illegal immigration. The states shouldn't be forced to bear the cost for a failed federal policy that gives a free pass to those who breach our borders, then passes the buck to us.

19   Those who oppose reform invariably cry racism. They want to stifle even any discussion of the issue.

20   But this debate isn't about race, it's about responsibility and resources. Washington must accept responsibility for this strictly federal issue, and California must be allowed to devote our limited resources to those people who have come to our country through the legal process.

21   This isn't a partisan issue, or even simply a California issue. Washington's failure to bear responsibility for illegal immigration is forcing states around the nation to bear enormous costs.

22   And we have finally started to see some recognition of the problem in Washington. Working with our Congressional delegation on the Budget Resolution before Congress, we've secured the strongest Congressional statement yet for full reimbursement. It fully acknowledges federal responsibility for criminal aliens who have committed felonies under state law only because they were permitted to enter the country illegally by virtue of federal failure to control the border.

23   In the federal crime bill, the House of Representatives added amendments mandating federal incarceration of criminal aliens or reimbursements to states for the cost of their incarceration—but not until 1998! The official rationale for this four year delay in the arrival of the cavalry is that Congress requires the time to find a way to pay. Meanwhile, the states are to continue patiently laying out what is proportionately a far greater share of our budgets for what is acknowledged to be an exclusively federal duty.

24   On Friday, the Clinton Administration took a positive, but inadequate step towards reimbursing states for the costs of keeping alien felons locked up in state prisons. The $350 million authorized by the White House for all states is little more than half what is required according to the Congressional Budget Office estimate, and in fact is less than they owe California alone.

25   Another amendment to the crime bill authorizes the addition of 6,000 agents to the Border Patrol, but these House authorizations now must pass the Senate to take effect. And even then, they are just *authorizations*, just acknowledgments of the problem. Congress must then take the next step, *appropriation*—which means voting to actually cut a check to pay the costs imposed on the states by federal failure to control the borders and federal mandates to provide services to illegal immigrants.

26   And we've watched, time and time again, as Congress has authorized reimbursement in the spring, but then stripped out or failed to pass an appropriation, and left us holding the bag in the fall.

27   That's why we have launched an unprecedented offensive by a bipartisan coalition of seven states, including the five most populous, to pressure the Administration and Congress to do equity and honor the federal obligation to reimburse us. They should do so in the federal budget and appropriation bills.

28   But, we will not stand by and watch the political process fail once again, when we can wait no longer. So, in addition to pursuing reform in Washington, we are launching a series of lawsuits against the federal government starting this week. Unfortunately, Congress' track record of failure has compelled us to seek a remedy in the courts, even as we continue a bipartisan, multi-state effort to pressure the Administration and Congress to atone for and pay for their sins by corrective action both at the border and in the appropriation process.

29   In court, we'll seek two broad goals. First, that the federal government enforce our nation's immigration laws and secure our nation's border.

30   And second, that the federal government reimburse California fully for costs incurred when it fails to enforce the law.

31   Suing for reimbursement is not only a matter of fairness for state taxpayers, it's a matter of making the political process work for our nation.

32   Immigration and control of our nation's border are, by virtue of the Constitution, a strictly federal responsibility. But today, there is no fiscal accountability for that policy.

33   The Congress is writing blank checks on other people's bank accounts—and one of those accounts belongs to the taxpayers of California.

34   Congress must be forced to bear the fiscal consequences for its immigration policy. If they have to pay the bill for that policy, if they feel the pinch in the federal budget for which they alone are accountable to the voters, then and only then will they have the incentive to fix this policy that simply doesn't work.

35   President Clinton has acknowledged as much himself. Last summer he said,

"One of the reasons the federal government has not been forced to confront this . . . is that the states of California, Texas and Florida have had to bear a huge portion of the costs for the failure of federal policy."

36 It's a fundamental element of democracy—a government must be held accountable for its actions.

37 And if the federal government were held accountable, they would quickly discover that the cost of ignoring the real and explosively growing problem of illegal immigration is far greater than the cost of fixing it.

38 They would see that the federal resources necessary to secure our nation's border are dwarfed by the billions that California and other states spend today in making massive illegal immigration to America a safety-net for the world. What's more, by compelling California to provide this safety-net for illegals, the feds are tearing gaping holes in the safety-net we seek to provide for our own needy legal residents.

39 For next year, the Clinton Administration proposes increasing spending on border enforcement across the country by just $180 million a year. We'll spend nearly 10 times that amount just educating illegal immigrants in California schools.

40 Last week I went to El Paso, where I saw firsthand a program known as Operation Hold the Line that has used a blockade to reduce illegal crossing by 75 percent.

41 I will concede that the same plan that has produced such success for the EL Paso Blockade can't be precisely reproduced everywhere on the border. But the most important lesson to draw from El Paso is that we *can* control our border.

42 Those who say the effort is futile . . . those who say we should simply concede that people who want to cross the border will . . . are wrong.

43 But to secure our border, we first need a plan. Then we must devote the will and resources to carry it out, as they have in El Paso.

44 But the officials responsible in Washington fail to see the urgency of the problem.

45 INS Commissioner Doris Meissner, recently said, and I quote,

"There's nothing wrong in taking a year or two [to enact immigration reform.]"

46 Well, Ms. Meissner, I don't know what border you're looking at, but as the people who bear the cost for your failed policy, we can tell you that two years is too long to wait. Every *day* we wait, the problem grows worse.

47 That's why we're taking our case to court. Since we must, we will force the federal government to bear responsibility for its policies.

48 Our first lawsuit, to be filed this week, will seek reimbursement for the costs California bears for incarcerating alien felons in our state prisons. The price tag this year alone is nearly $400 million, and that doesn't include the costs from previous years, the capital costs for housing these criminals, or the costs to county governments.

49   But our suit will also seek to compel the federal government to do its duty to enforce immigration laws already on the books.

50   Specifically, we'll demand that the federal government be forced to take custody of the thousands of alien felons who have completed their sentences in state prison, but are back on the street, because the INS has failed to deport them. That federal dereliction forces California to supervise parole for 4,400 criminal aliens every day.

51   We'll demand that the federal government begin prosecuting alien felons who return to the U.S., currently a federal offense punishable by up to 15 years in prison, but one routinely ignored by federal officials.

52   And we will demand that federal officials be required to deport alien criminals to the interior of their home country and not continue the absurd practice of simply dumping them at the border, where all too often they simply re-enter the U.S. across the porous border and beat the bus back to L.A.

53   We'll file additional suits in the weeks ahead to address other parts of the federal government's failed policy—a policy that has cost the taxpayers of California more than $10 billion in education, medical and prison costs for illegal immigrants since 1988.

54   And I'm encouraging the cities and counties of California to also file suit to seek reimbursement for the costs owed to them by the federal government.

55   Our goal, though, is larger than simply seeking reimbursement—as important and as urgently needed as it is.

56   Our goal is to force the federal government to accept responsibility for the crisis of illegal immigration. Only when they accept responsibility will Congress finally adopt the reforms necessary to restore integrity and fairness to our immigration laws.

57   Once Congress is forced to confront this problem, I'm sure it will waste no time in doing what's necessary to secure our nation's borders.

58   And securing our nation's borders is the only way we can secure the future we want for California.

59   Thank you very much.

ADDRESS TO THE NATION ON BOSNIA

Bill Clinton

Since the days of Andrew Jackson, an American president has had the symbolic power to "speak" on behalf of the whole nation. In times of domestic or foreign crises, it becomes crucial to evaluate how effectively a president can "rally" the American people to his proposed course of action.

During the twentieth century, scholars in various disciplines have carefully studied the growing rhetorical power of the presidency. Political scientist Jeffrey Tulis argues that "today it is taken for granted that presidents have a *duty* constantly to defend themselves publicly, to promote policy initiatives nationwide, and to inspirit the population." (*The Rhetorical Presidency,* Princeton: Princeton University Press, 1987; p. 4).

President Bill Clinton addressed the nation from the Oval Office on November 27, 1995 to explain the implementation of a new peace agreement in Bosnia that would require the deployment of 20,000 American troops. The 20-minute televised address was widely viewed in the press as one of the most critical of the Clinton presidency as he sought to win bipartisan support for his foreign policy. (See *The New York Times,* November 28, 1995, p.1).

Rhetorical scholar Denise Bostdorff suggests that presidential crisis management can be identified by four rhetorical characteristics: 1) Personification of the competing actors in the conflict; 2) An expressed sense of urgency; 3) Documentation or "proof" of the evil deed about to be done by the "enemy"; and 4) Intervention is described as a dramatization of action to be taken against the enemy. (See Denise M. Bostdorff, "The Presidency and Promoted Crisis: Reagan, Grenada, and Issues Management," *Presidential Studies Quarterly* 21 (Fall 1991), 737–750).

Clinton begins the speech with an announcement of the dramatic actions that have occurred in Bosnia and Dayton, Ohio (1–2). The role of American involvement is hinted at in the introduction (2), but it is precisely defined as not "about fighting a war (3)."

+The text of this speech was obtained from the White House press office through its World Wide Web home page.

While essentially explaining that intervention is justified because "it is the right thing to do," Clinton personifies the American character in value-laden discussions of national ideals (6–8). The true "enemy" of the Bosnian crisis would be "isolationists" urging the withdrawal of American leadership from the world stage (9–13). Clinton does back away from Franklin Roosevelt's metaphor urging that America become the "world's policeman," (14) but the president also invokes World War II-era images to justify involvement in this European situation (17, 29). Europe's future is depicted as being "vital" to American national security (28). Clinton warns that failing to act to secure our interests would have "grave" consequences—such as the collapse of NATO (30–33). How compelling is Clinton's case for American involvement in Bosnia? Has the president clearly defined the nature of the Bosnian crisis?

Clinton argues that American troops are urgently needed (16) to stop the further evils of the "killing fields" and "ethnic cleansing" that previously existed in Bosnia (20–26). Economic sanctions, diplomatic efforts, and even air strikes were not enough to keep "Bosnia's warring ethnic groups" apart (18, 21, 22). America must now honorably respond to the "request" made by the Bosnian people to supply troops to finally "secure its peace" (23–24). What are the implications of Clinton's use of the "Marshall Plan" analogy (29)? Does the president appropriately invoke previous examples of American "partnerships" (33) to support his present policy?

The formal elements of Clinton's policy include precisely defined goals and minimized risks to American troops (34–39). As a result of this plan, Clinton concludes that the people of Bosnia can rebuild their country and their lives (40–41, 43). With the benefits of his plan dramatized, however, Clinton does warn the American people of the potential for casualties (42) and the fact that there is no absolute "guarantee" of peace in the region (43). How do you assess Clinton 's threat that American troops will "fight fire with fire" (42)? Has the president successfully made a case for adoption of his Bosnia policy?

For additional information on the analysis of contemporary presidential crisis rhetoric, see Denise M. Bostdorff, *The Presidency and the Rhetoric of Foreign Crisis* (Columbia: University of South Carolina Press, 1994).

---

1   Good evening. Last week, the warring factions in Bosnia reached a peace agreement as a result of our efforts in Dayton, Ohio.

2 Tonight, I want to speak with you about implementing the Bosnian peace agreement and why our values and interests as Americans require that we do so.

3 Let me say at the outset: America's role will not be about fighting a war.

4 It will be about helping the people of Bosnia to secure their own peace. Our mission will be limited, focused and under the command of an American general. In fulfilling this mission, we will have the chance to help stop the killing of innocent civilians, and especially children, and, at the same time, bring stability to central Europe, a region of the world that is vital to our national interests.

5 And given our responsibility as Americans, it is the right thing to do.

6 From its birth, America has always been more than just a place. America has embodied an idea that has become the ideal for billions of people throughout the world. Our founders said it best: Our ideal is life, liberty and the pursuit of happiness.

7 In this century especially, America has done more than simply stand for these ideals—we have acted on them, and sacrificed for them. Our people fought two world wars so that freedom could triumph over tyranny. After World War I, we pulled back from the world—leaving a vacuum that was filled by the forces of hatred. After World War II, we continued to lead. We made the commitments that kept the peace and secured our interests, that helped spread democracy, that created unparalleled prosperity and that brought victory in the Cold War.

8 Today, because of our dedication, America's ideals—liberty, democracy and peace—are, more and more, the ideals of humanity. It is the power of these ideas, far more than our size, wealth and military might, that makes America a special nation and a uniquely trusted nation.

9 With the Cold War over, some people question the need for our continued, active leadership in the world. They believe that, much like after World War I, America can step back from the responsibilities of leadership. They argue that to be secure, we need only to keep our military strong and our borders safe, and that the time has come to leave for others the hard work of leadership beyond our borders.

10 I strongly disagree.

11 As the Cold War gives way to the global village, American leadership is needed more than ever because problems that start beyond our borders can quickly become problems within them. We are all vulnerable to the organized forces of intolerance and destruction: ethnic, religious and regional rivalries, the spread of weapons of mass destruction, drug trafficking, organized crime and terrorism. Just as surely as fascism and communism, these forces threaten freedom and democracy, peace and prosperity. And they too demand American leadership.

12   As a practical matter, if America does not lead, too often the job will not get done. But if America does lead, we have an unprecedented opportunity to move from war to peace, from oppression to freedom, acting not alone, but with strong partners throughout the world. We see the benefits of our leadership and our partnerships in reducing the threat of dangerous weapons of mass destruction, and in combatting terrorism, organized crime and drug trafficking.

13   But nowhere has the argument for our leadership been more clearly justified than in the struggle to stop or prevent war and ethnic violence, from Iraq to Haiti, from South Africa to Korea, from the Middle East to Northern Ireland. We have stood up for peace and freedom because it is in our interest to do so and because it is the right thing to do .

14   My duty as president is to match the demands for American leadership to our strategic interests and to our ability to make a difference. America cannot and must not be the world's policeman. We cannot stop all war for all time. But we can stop some wars. We cannot save all women and all children. But we can save many. We cannot do everything. But we must do what we can do.

15   There are times and places where our leadership can mean the difference between peace and war, and where we can defend our fundamental values as a people and serve our most basic interests. My fellow Americans, in this new era of peace and hope, there are times when America—and America alone—can and should make a difference.

16   The terrible war in Bosnia is such a case. Nowhere today is the need for American leadership more stark—or more immediate—than in Bosnia.

17   For nearly four years, a terrible war has torn Bosnia apart. This war has wasted thousands of lives and destroyed countless futures. Horrors that we prayed had been banished from Europe forever have been seared into our minds: skeletal prisoners caged behind barbed wire fences, defenseless men and boys shot down into mass graves, evoking vision of World War II concentration camps, endless lines of refugees marching toward a future of despair.

18   When I took office, some were urging immediate intervention in the conflict. I decided that the United States could not force peace on Bosnia's warring ethnic groups—the Serbs, Croats and Muslims—and that American ground troops should not fight a war in Bosnia. Instead, America has worked with our European allies in searching for peace, stopping the war from spreading, and easing the suffering of the Bosnian people.

19   We imposed tough economic sanctions on Serbia. We used our air power to conduct the longest humanitarian air lift in history and to enforce a no-fly zone that took the war out of the skies. We helped to make peace between two of the three warring parties in Bosnia—the Muslims and the Croats.

20   But as months of a terrible conflict turned into years, it became clear that Europe alone could not end the war. This summer, Bosnian Serb shelling once again turned Bosnia's playgrounds and marketplaces into killing fields. The United States led NATO's heavy and continuous air strikes—many of them flown by skilled American pilots.

21   Those air strikes, together with the renewed determination of our European partners and the Bosnian and Croat gains on the battlefield, convinced the Serbs to start thinking about making peace.

22   At the same time, the United States initiated an intensive diplomatic effort that forged a Bosnia-wide cease fire and got the parties to agree to the basic principles of peace. Three dedicated American diplomats—Bob Frasure, Joe Kruzel and Nelson Drew— lost their lives in that effort. We remember their sacrifice and that of their families. And we will never forget their exceptional service to our country.

23   Finally, just three weeks ago, the Muslims, Croats and Serbs came to Dayton, Ohio—in America's heartland—to negotiate a settlement. There, exhausted by war, they made a commitment to peace. They agreed to put down their guns, to preserve Bosnia as a single state, to investigate and prosecute war criminals, to protect the human rights of its citizens, to try to build a peaceful, democratic future. And they asked for America's help as they implement their agreement.

24   America has a responsibility to answer that request—to help turn this moment of hope into an enduring reality. To do that, troops from our country and around the world would go into Bosnia to give them the confidence they need to implement their peace plan. I refused to send American troops to fight a war in Bosnia. But I believe they must help Bosnia secure its peace.

25   I want you to know what is at stake, exactly what our troops will be asked to accomplish, and why we must carry out our responsibility to implement the peace agreement in Bosnia.

26   Implementing the peace in Bosnia can end the terrible suffering of the Bosnian people—the warfare, the mass executions, the ethnic cleansing, the campaigns of rape and terror. Let us never forget: one quarter of a million men, women and children have been shelled, shot and tortured to death. Two million people—half of Bosnia's populations—were forced from their homes and into a miserable life as refugees.

27   These faceless numbers hide millions of personal tragedies. Each of the war's victims was a mother or a daughter, a father or a son, a brother or a sister. Now, American leadership has created the chance to implement the peace agreement—and stop the suffering.

28   Securing peace in Bosnia will also build a free and stable Europe—which has been one of America's most vital interests for nearly a century. Bosnia lies at the very heart of Europe—next door to many of its fragile new democracies and some of America's closest allies. Generations of Americans have understood that Europe's freedom and stability is vital to our own national security.

29   That's why we fought two world wars in Europe. That's why we launched the Marshall Plan to restore Europe. That's why we created NATO and waged the Cold War. That's why we must help the nations of Europe end their worst nightmare since World War II—now.

30   The only force capable of getting the job done is NATO—the powerful military alliance of democracies that has guaranteed our security for half a century. As NATO's leader— and as the primary broker of the peace agreement—the United States must be an essential part of its mission.

31   If we're not there, NATO will not be there. The peace will collapse. The war will reignite. The slaughter of innocents will begin again. A conflict that already has claimed so many victims could spread like poison throughout the region and eat away at Europe's stability, and erode our partnership with our European allies.

32   And America's commitment to leadership will be questioned if we refuse to participate in implementing a peace agreement we brokered in the United States—especially since the presidents of Bosnia, Croatia and Serbia asked us to participate and pledged their best efforts to secure the security of our troops.

33   When America's partnerships are weak and our leadership is in doubt, it undermines our ability to secure our interests and to convince others to work with us to turn back aggressors, to hunt down terrorists and to combat organized crime, drug trafficking and the proliferation of nuclear, chemical and biological weapons. If we maintain our partnership and our leadership, we need not act alone. As we saw in the Gulf War and in Haiti, many other nations who share our goals will share our burdens. But when America does not lead, the consequences can be very grave, not only for others, but eventually for us as well.

34   As I speak to you, NATO is completing its planning for IFOR, an international force for peace in Bosnia of about 60,000 troops. Already, more than 25 nations—including our major NATO allies—have pledged to take part. They will contribute about two-thirds of the implementation force—some 40,000 troops. The United States would contribute the rest—about 20,000 soldiers.

35   Later this week, the final NATO plan will be submitted to me for review and approval. Let me make clear what I expect it to include— and what it must include for me to give final approval to the participation of our armed forces: First, the mission will be precisely defined—with clear, realistic goals that can be achieved in a finite period of time. Our troops will make sure each side withdraws its forces behind the front lines—and keeps them there. They will maintain the cease fire to prevent the war from accidentally starting again. These efforts will help create a secure environment in Bosnia so that its people can return to their homes and begin to rebuild their lives. Our Joint Chiefs of Staff have concluded that this mission should and will take about one year. Second, the risks to our troops will be minimized. American troops will take their orders from the American general who commands NATO. They will be heavily armed and thoroughly trained. By making an overwhelming show of force, they will lessen the need to use force. They will have the authority to respond immediately—and the training and equipment to respond with overwhelming force—to any threat to their safety or violations of the military provisions of the peace agreement.

36   If the NATO plan meets with my approval, I will immediately send it to Congress and request its support. I will also authorize the participation of a small number of American troops in a NATO advance mission that will lay the groundwork for IFOR, starting sometime next week. They will establish headquarters and set up the sophisticated communications systems that must be in place before NATO can send its troops, tanks and trucks into Bosnia.

37   The implementation force itself would begin deploying in Bosnia in the days following the formal signature of the peace agreement in mid-December.

38   The international community will help implement arms control provisions of the agreement so that future hostilities are less likely and armaments limited—while we and others make sure the Bosnian Federation has the means to defend itself once IFOR withdraws. IFOR will not be a part of this effort.

39   Civilian agencies from around the world will begin a separate program of humanitarian relief and reconstruction. The lion's share will be paid for by our European allies and other interested countries. This effort is absolutely essential to making peace endure.

40   It will bring the people of Bosnia the food, shelter, clothing and medicine so many have been denied for so long. It will help them rebuild their roads and schools, their power plants and hospitals, their factories and their shops.

41   It will reunite children with their parents and families with their homes. It will allow the Bosnians freely to choose leaders devoted to reconciliation. It will give all the people of Bosnia a much greater stake in peace than war— so that peace takes on a life and logic of its own.

42   In Bosnia, we can succeed because the mission is clear and limited. Our troops are strong and very well prepared. But no deployment of American troops is risk free and this one may well involve casualties. There may be accidents in the field or incidents with people who have not given up their hatred. I will take every measure possible to minimize risks. But we must be prepared for that possibility. As president, my most difficult duty is to put the men and women who volunteer to serve our nation in harm's way when America's interests and values demand it. I assume full responsibility for any harm that may come to them. But anyone contemplating any action that would endanger our troops should know this: America protects its own. Anyone who takes on our troops will suffer the consequences. We will fight fire with fire—and then some.

43   After so much bloodshed and loss, after so many outrageous acts of inhuman brutality, it will take time— and an extraordinary effort of will—for the people of Bosnia to pull themselves from the past and start building the future. There is no guarantee that Muslims, Serb and Croats will stay together as citizens of a shared state with a common destiny.

44   But thanks to our leadership, and the commitment of our allies, the people of Bosnia have the chance to decide their future peacefully— and in peace. They have a chance to remind the world that, just a few years ago, the mosques, minarets and churches of Sarajevo were a shining symbol of multiethnic tolerance—that Bosnia once found unity in its diversity. We must not turn our backs on Bosnia now. So I ask all Americans—and I ask every member of Congress, Democrats and Republicans alike, to make the choice for peace. In the choice between peace and war, America must choose peace.

45   My fellow Americans, I ask you to think for a moment about the century that is drawing to a close—and the new one that will soon begin.

46   The 20th century has been marked by so much progress, and too much bloodshed. It has been witness to humanity's capacity for the best and its weakness for the worst. Through two world wars and a Cold War, America has stood for freedom and tolerance, and with all those who cherish peace and liberty. We have done so because a world in which nations enjoy peace and people live free will be a much better world for our children to make the most of their God-given potential. And we have done so because it is the right thing to do.

47   Because previous generations of Americans stood up for freedom— and because we continue to do so—the American people are more secure and more prosperous. And more people than ever before live in freedom. More people than ever before are treated with dignity. More people than ever before can hope to build a better life than their parents had—and expect to pass on an even better one to their children.

48   These are the blessings of freedom—and America has always been freedom's greatest champion. If we continue to do everything we can to share these blessings with people around the world—if we continue to be leaders for peace—then the sacrifices that the American people have made this century will be renewed. And the next century can be the greatest our nation has yet known.

49   A few weeks ago, I was privileged to spend time with His Holiness Pope John Paul II when he came to America. At the end of our meeting, the Pope said: "I have lived through most of this century. I remember that it began with a war in Sarajevo. Mr. President, you must not let it end with a war in Sarajevo."

50   In Bosnia, a terrible war has challenged our interests and troubled our souls. Our interests are plain. The cause is right. Our mission will be clear, limited and achievable. The people of Bosnia, our NATO allies and people around the world are looking to America for leadership. Let us lead. That is our responsibility as Americans.

51   Good night. And God bless America.

THE CONTRACT WITH AMERICA

Newt Gingrich

Victory in the 1994 mid-term elections gave the Republican Party control of both houses of Congress and the "heady" feeling of congressional power for the first time in decades. Newt Gingrich observed about his personal meteoric rise to power: "It's amazing. You can go from being a nobody to being one of the leaders of the country" (U.S. News, April 10,1995, p. 26). During the first one hundred days following the Republican ascendancy, Gingrich, as Speaker, pushed through a bold agenda of legislative action in the House of Representatives. As the one hundred day self-imposed deadline neared, he was afforded the opportunity on April 7 to "play president" by delivering a live, prime time televised speech on CNN. Similar in tone to the annual presidential State of

---

✝Newt Gingrich, "The Contract with America: A Report on the New Congress," May 1, 1995, pp. 423–426. Reprinted by permission of *Vital Speeches of the Day* and the author.

the Union address, this state of the new Congress address reviews the achievements of the first hundred days before moving to a discussion of remaining challenges.

The much publicized Contract with America was the product of a working retreat in Maryland involving Gingrich and forty other House Republicans. The contract served as a set of promises around which campaign rhetoric could be organized. Following the Republican victory, it also served as a coherent legislative agenda for both the House and the Senate.

This speech occasion marked a moment of personal triumph for the Speaker. In ninety-three days many of the promises of the "contract" were kept through major legislative victories in the House. This nationally televised address enabled Gingrich to enumerate the legislative successes of the new Congress and to demonstrate that "even in Washington you can do what you say you're going to do." The achievements of the new Congress, briefly reviewed in paragraph 3 of the introduction, were given more detailed consideration in paragraphs 13 through 18. What separates the cursory and the detailed enumerations of "promises kept" is a call for a total remaking of the federal government to render it capable of dealing with such societal problems as teenage pregnancy, gang violence, AIDS, and drugs. All of these problems are viewed under the shadow of an enormous national debt that is being passed to future generations. What function is served by separating the initial statement of promises kept (paragraph 3) from the more detailed treatment (paragraphs 13 through 18)?

Paragraph 19 serves as the major transition between the discussion of previous successes and the discussion of future challenges—"the big battles yet to come." The first challenge, to render government more cost efficient and contemporary, is carried by a single example involving delays in replacing vacuum tubes with microchips. Is this single example adequate support for the argument that obsolescence "pervades most of the federal government"?

The second challenge, to replace the welfare state with opportunity, justifies such an action by suggesting that the welfare system is causally related to such social ills as violence, brutality, child abuse, and drug addiction. To what extent has the speaker demonstrated that the welfare system is the direct cause of such social ills?

The third challenge involves "ending bureaucratic micromanagement in Washington" by returning power to individuals and local and state governments, and by "reducing regulation, taxation, and frivolous lawsuits." Does the speaker sufficiently demonstrate how these changes are to be made?

The fourth through seventh challenges, seen as opportunities, involve the creative use of: information technologies, breakthroughs in molecular medicine, new Medicare options, and systems for creating new jobs, new health programs, and new learning. Again, the second test of a speech that affirms a policy proposition pertains: Has the speaker provided a sufficient view of the nature of the policy?

The speaker saves the biggest challenge for last, that being, getting our nation's finances in order by balancing the budget. How effectively does the speaker demonstrate the need for such a policy? Underlying the need argument is the motivational appeal that "we" are being unfair to our children and grandchildren by piling up trillions in debt that they will eventually have to replay. How effective do you find this appeal to fairness?

The speech ends with a strong concluding appeal filled with idealism, optimism, romanticism, and patriotism. How realistic is this appeal given the severity and complexity of the problems detailed earlier in the speech?

---

1   Good evening. I want to thank you for joining me tonight and for this chance to give you, the American people, a report on the new Congress—what we've been doing, what we hope to do and how we're working to keep faith with what you sent us here to do.

2   But first let me thank the hundreds of thousands of Americans who've written me over the past few months. Your letters are full of good ideas and often moving words of encouragement. This letter, addressed to "Dear Mr. Newt," included a portrait of George Washington. It was sent to me by first grader Steven Franzkowiak from Georgia. And I thank each and every one of you.

3   Last September the House Republicans signed a Contract with America. We signed this contract and made some promises to you and to ourselves. You elected us and for the last 93 days we have been keeping our word. With your help we're bringing about real change. We made Congress subject to the same laws as everyone else, we cut congressional committee staffs and budgets by 30 percent and voted on every item in the Contract. And I can tell you tonight we are going to sell one Congressional building and privatize a Congressional parking lot.

4   While we've done a lot, this contract has never been about curing all the ills of the nation. One hundred days cannot overturn the neglect of decades.

The contract's purpose has been to show that change is possible, that even in Washington you can do what you say you're going to do. In short, we've wanted to prove to you that democracy still has the vitality and the will to do something about the problems facing our nation. And it seems to me, whether you are conservative or liberal, that is a very positive thing.

5   And so I want to talk about the Contract tonight—our successes and our failures, but I also want to talk about something much larger. Because although I've spent the last six months of my life living and breathing and fighting for what's written in this Contract, I know the American people want more than these ten things.

6   So what I want to talk with you about tonight is not just what a new political majority on Capitol Hill has accomplished in 100 days, but how all of us together—Republicans and Democrats alike—must totally remake the federal government—to change the very way it thinks, the way it does business, the way it treats its citizens. After all, the purpose of changing government is to improve the lives of our citizens, strengthen the future of our children, make our neighborhoods safe and build a better country. Government is not the end, it is the means.

7   We Americans wake up every morning, go to work, take our kids to school, fix dinner, do all the things we expect of ourselves and yet something isn't quite right. There is no confidence that government understands the values and realities of our lives. The government is out of touch and out of control. It is in need of deep and deliberate change. Now when that change is accomplished, then perhaps Americans will be able to sleep a little better at night and wake up feeling less anxious about their futures.

8   I represented the people who worked at the Ford plant in Hapeville, Georgia. The Ford Motor Company, like all of the domestic auto industry, faced the need to change in order to keep up with tougher competition. Today, they produce twice as many cars per employee at three times the quality. General Motors and Chrysler are doing the same thing. So are America's small businesses. They're all rethinking the way they operate. Should government be any different? . . . Of course not.

9   We sincerely believe we can reduce spending and at the same time make government better. Virtually every institution in America, except government, has reengineered themselves to become more efficient over the last decade. They cut spending, provided better products, better education and better service for less.

10   But I believe we must remake government for reasons much larger than saving money or improving services. No civilization can survive with 12-year-olds having babies, with 15-year-olds killing each other, with 17-year-olds

dying of AIDS, with 18-year-olds getting diplomas they can't read. Every night on every local news we see human tragedies that have grown out of the current welfare state.

11   And as a father of two daughters, I cannot ignore the terror and worry parents in our inner cities must feel for their children. Within a half mile of this Capitol, drug, violence and despair threaten the lives of our citizens. We cannot ignore our fellow Americans in such desperate straits by thinking that huge amounts of tax dollars release us from our moral responsibility to help these parents and children. There is no reason the federal government must keep an allegiance to failure. With goodwill, with common sense, with the courage to change, we can do better for all Americans.

12   Another fact we cannot turn our head away from is this, no truly moral civilization would burden its children with the economic excesses of the parents and grandparents. This talk of burdening future generations is not just rhetoric; we're talking about hard, economic consequences that will limit our children's and grandchildren's standard of living. Yet that is what we are doing. For the children trapped in poverty, for the children whose futures are trapped by a government debt they're going to have to pay, we have an obligation tonight to talk about the legacy we're leaving our children and grandchildren, an obligation to talk about the deliberate remaking of our government. This change will not be accomplished in the next 100 days, but we must start by recognizing the moral and economic failure of the current methods of government.

13   In these last 100 days, we have begun to change these failed methods. We outlined 10 major proposals in the Contract that would begin to break the logjam of the past; the House passed nine of them.

14   First, we passed the Shays Act which makes the Congress obey all the laws that other Americans have to obey. The house passed it, the Senate passed it and the President signed it. So that's one law signed, sealed and delivered.

15   We passed a balanced budget amendment in the House with bipartisan support; it has been temporarily defeated in the Senate by one vote. Although constitutional amendments are harder to get through Congress because they require two-thirds vote rather than a simple majority, don't be discouraged. Senator Dole has said he will call it up for another vote. The momentum is with us and with your help and your voice I believe it is possible this amendment will pass later this Congress.

16   As promised, we introduced a constitutional amendment on term limits, but we failed even though 85 percent of House Republicans voted for it. Again, that two-thirds vote. There have been 180 bills introduced to limit congressional terms over America's history, but not one of them ever made it to the

House floor . . . until last week. I pledge to you that term limits will be the first vote of the next Congress so keep the pressure on, keep your hopes up.

17   In both the House and the Senate we passed a line item veto, just as you asked. It's remarkable that a Republican House and a Republican Senate are giving such a strong tool to a president of the other party. I believe it shows our good faith and determination to cut spending.

18   Other contract proposals have passed the House and are being worked on in the Senate. We passed regulatory reform, legal reform and welfare reform. We passed a $500 tax credit per child. We passed an increase in the earning limit for senior citizens, so they won't have their social security checks cut if they earn extra money. We passed a capital gains tax cut and indexed these gains to spur the savings and investments that create jobs.

19   Even with all these successes and others, the Contract with America is only a beginning. It is the preliminary skirmish to the big battles yet to come.

20   The big battles will deal with how we remake the Government of the United States. The measure of everything we do will be whether we are creating a better future with more opportunities for our children.

21   New ideas, new ways and old-fashioned common sense can improve government while reducing its costs. Let me give you an example. The United States Government is the largest purchaser of vacuum tubes in the Western world. This is a Federal Aviation Administration vacuum tube. Good solid 1895 technology. This is the updated mid-1950s version. When you fly in America, vacuum tubes in the air traffic control system keep you safe. Our purchasing rules are so complicated and so wasteful that our government has not been able, in seven years, to figure out how to replace vacuum tubes with this. This is a microchip that has the computing power of 3 million vacuum tubes. So today's government operates this way; after we remake it, the government of the future will operate this way.

22   My point is this: this same reliance on the obsolete pervades most of the federal government—not just in regard to computers but in regard to its thinking, its attitudes, its approaches to problems.

23   It's one thing if we're talking about vacuum tubes, but this backward thinking is entirely something else if we're talking about human lives. The purpose of all this change is not simply a better government; it is a better America.

24   A truly compassionate government would replace the welfare state with opportunity. The welfare system's greatest cost is the human cost to the poor. In the name of "compassion" we have funded a system that is cruel and destroys families. Its failure is reflected by the violence, brutality, child abuse and drug addiction in every local TV news broadcast.

25   Poor Americans are trapped in unsafe government housing, saddled with rules that are anti-work, anti-family and anti-property. Let me give you some statistics on this failure. Welfare spending now exceeds $300 billion a year. Yet despite all the trillions that have been spent since 1970, the number of children in poverty has increased 40 percent.

26   On this chart, you'll notice that welfare spending goes up, and so does children born outside marriage. Year by year they track each other. The more tax money we spend on welfare, the more children who are born without benefit of family and without strong bonds of love and nurturing. If money alone were the answer, this would be a paradise.

27   Since money is not the answer, it should be clear we have a moral imperative to remake the welfare system so every American can lead a full life. After all, we believe that all men and women are endowed by our Creator with certain unalienable rights among which are life, liberty and the pursuit of happiness. We are determined to remake this government until every child of every racial background, in every neighborhood in America, knows that he or she has all the opportunities of an American.

28   I believe we have to do a number of things to become an opportunity society. We must restore freedom by ending bureaucratic micromanagement here in Washington. As any good business leader will tell you, decisions should be made as closely as possible to the source of the problem. This country is too big and too diverse for Washington to have the knowledge to make the right decision on local matters; we've got to return power back to you—to your families, your neighborhoods, your local and state governments. We need to promote economic growth by reducing regulation, taxation and frivolous lawsuits. Everywhere I go Americans complain about an overly complicated tax code and an arrogant, unpredictable and unfair Internal Revenue Service. This summer we will begin hearings on bold, decisive reform of the income tax system. We're looking at a simplified flat tax and other ways to bring some sense to the disorder and inequity of our tax system.

29   Another reason for optimism is the tremendous opportunities being created by the information technologies. Tremendous is a big word so let me show you an example. This is a traditional telephone cable. This is a fiber optic cable. You can barely see it. This almost invisible fiber optic cable is equal to 64 of these bulky traditional cables. Now that is a tremendous opportunity. With these breakthroughs the most rural parts of America can be connected electronically to the best learning, the best health care and the best work opportunities in the world. Distance learning can offer new hope to the present inner city neighborhood, the poorest Indian reservation and the smallest rural com-

munity. Distance medicine can bring the best specialists in the world to your health clinic, your hospital.

30   Furthermore, the breakthroughs in molecular medicine may cure Alzheimer's, eliminate many genetic defects and offer new cures for diabetes, cancer and heart disease. These breakthroughs combined with preventive care and medical innovations can create better health for all Americans. And we will pass a reform so that when you change jobs you can't be denied insurance even if you or your family have health problems.

31   We will improve Medicare by offering a series of new Medicare options that will increase senior citizens control over their own health care and guarantee them access to the best and most modern systems of health research and health innovation. My father, my mother, and my mother-in-law all rely on Medicare. I know how crucial the Medicare system is to senior Americans, and we will insure that it continues to provide the care our seniors need with more choices at less cost to the elderly.

32   All around us opportunities for a better life are being developed but our government all too often ignores or even blocks them. We need those breakthroughs which create new jobs, new health, and new learning, to give us the opportunity and growth to deal with our budgetary problems. We must get our national finances in order. The time has come to balance the federal budget and to free our children from the burdens upon their prosperity and their lives.

33   This is a Congressional voting card. This card goes into a box on the House floor and the computer records the members' vote. The Congressional voting card is the most expensive credit card in the world. For two generations it has been used to pile up trillions in debt that our children and grandchildren will eventually have to pay.

34   Now a big debt has a big impact. To make such numbers real, let me give you an example. If you have a child or grandchild born this year, that child is going to pay $187,000 in taxes in their lifetime to pay their share of the interest on the debt. Yes, you heard me right, $187,000 in taxes, in their lifetime—that's over $3,500 in taxes every year of their working lives just to pay interest on the debt we are leaving them. That's before they are taxed to pay for Social Security or Medicare, education or highways or police or the national defense. You know and I know, that's just not fair.

35   It was once an American tradition to pay off the mortgage and leave the children the farm. Now we seem to be selling the farm and leaving our children the mortgage.

36   By 1997, we will pay more for interest on the debt than for the national defense. That's right, more of our tax money will be spent to pay interest on

government bonds than we'll pay for the Army, the Navy, the Air Force, and the Marine Corps, the intelligence agencies and the defense bureaucracy combined.

37 Okay, Social Security. I want to reassure all of you who are on Social Security, or will soon retire, that your Social Security is fine. No one will touch your Social Security, period. But we must make sure that the baby boomers' retirements, which are coming up in the next century, are as secure as their parents'. Because the money the government supposedly has been putting aside from the baby boomers Social Security taxes is not there. The government has been borrowing that money to pay for the budget deficit. The Social Security trust fund is simply I.O.U.s from the U.S. Treasury. So when the baby boomers get set to retire, where's the money to pay them going to come from? Well, can't the government just borrow more money? The honest answer is no. No system, no country is weathly enough to have unlimited borrowing.

38 But the answer is clear. The key to protecting the baby boomers Social Security is to balance the budget. That way by the time the baby boomers retire the government will be financially sound enough to pay them. The problem is not Social Security. After all, Social Security would be fine if the federal government would stop borrowing the money. The government can stop borrowing the money when we balance the budget. It is just that simple.

39 Our goals are simple. We don't want our children to drown in debt. We want baby boomers to be able to retire with the same security as their parents. We want our senior Americans to be able to rely on Medicare without fear.

40 These are the reasons why, as Franklin Delano Roosevelt said, "Our generation has a rendezvous with destiny." This is the year we rendezvous with our destiny to establish a clear plan to balance the budget. It can no longer be put off. That is why I am speaking to you so frankly.

41 Next month we will propose a budget that is balanced over seven years. The budget can be balanced even with the problems of the federal government. It can be balanced without touching a penny of Social Security and without raising taxes. In fact, spending overall can go up every year. We simply must limit annual spending increases to about 3 percent between now and 2002.

42 The key is the willingness to change, to set priorities, to redesign the government, to recognize that this is not the 1960s or '70s but the 1990s and we need a government to match the times. As I've said, Social Security is off the table. But that leaves a lot on the table—corporate welfare, subsidies of every special interest. Defense is on the table. I'm a hawk, but a cheap hawk.

43 As the budget battle rages over the coming months, you will hear screams from the special interest groups. I'm sure you've already heard the dire cries that we were going to take food out of the mouths of schoolchildren. That we were going to feed them ketchup. The fact of the matter is that all we did was vote to increase school lunch money four and a half percent every year for five years and give the money to the states to spend because we thought they would do a better job than the federal government of ensuring that the children's meals were nutritional.

44   We believe that if local parents, local school boards and local state legislators visit their children's local schools, they will know firsthand about their children's lunches. Our critics believe that if the school hires a clerk, who doesn't cook anything, to fill out a report to go back to the state clerk, who doesn't cook anything but fills out a report so that the national clerk in Washington, who doesn't cook anything, can write you a letter about the school they didn't visit in the county they've never been to, to reassure you about the lunch they've never seen. That is the difference in our two approaches.

45   All I ask is that as we work to balance the budget that you verify the facts on both sides. And then you decide which approach is best.

46   Whatever the arguments this remains a country of unparalleled possibilities. I was talking the other day to a fellow who does business in Europe. He said what impresses people overseas is that Americans can change faster than anybody. That's why we're competitive once again in the world. We as a people have the natural ability to respond to change. That is what we do best when the government is not in the way. Our potential is as great and prosperous as it's ever been in our history. From now on all roads lead forward.

47   This job can't be done in Washington. We need your participation in a new dialogue. I hope every high school and college student will spend some class time in April or early May looking at the impact of the deficit on their young lives. We are making this speech and our briefing on the budget available through the Library of Congress at Thomas on the Internet. Both are also available from your congressman or congresswoman's office. We want every American to have the facts and participate in the new dialogue.

48   If I had one message for this country on this day when we celebrate the act of keeping our word, it would be a simple message: Idealism is American. To be romantic is American. It's okay to be a skeptic, but don't be a cynic. It's okay to raise good questions, but don't assume the worst. It's okay to report difficulties, but it's equally good to report victories.

49   Yes, we have problems, and of course it's going to be difficult to enact these things. That's the American way. And of course, we're going to have to work hard, and of course we're going to have to negotiate with the President, and of course the American people are going to have to let their will be known. But why should we be afraid of that? That is freedom.

50   I am here tonight to say that we're going to open a dialogue, because we want to create a new partnership with the American people, a plan to remake the government and balance the budget that is the American peoples' plan—not the House Republican plan, not the Gingrich plan, but the plan of the American people. And it is in the spirit of committing ourselves idealistically, committing ourselves romantically, believing in America, that we celebrate having kept our word. And we promise to begin a new partnership, so that together we and the American people can give our children and our country a new birth of freedom.

51   Thank you, and good night.

VIOLENT CRIME:
MYTHS, FACTS, AND SOLUTIONS

D. Stanley Eitzen

Dr. D. Stanley Eitzen, John H. Stern Distinguished Professor of Sociology, Colorado State University, is one of the most prominent academic public speakers of the time. He regularly takes his academic expertise and his messages about societal problems to the public. In this instance, he spoke at a symposium titled, "The Shadow of Violence: Unconsidered Perspectives," at Hastings College, Hastings, Nebraska, March 15, 1995.

Dr. Eitzen was born in Glendale, California. He received a B.A. degree from Bethel College in Kansas in 1952, an M.S. from Emporia State University in 1952, and a Ph.D. from the University of Kansas in 1966. He was a high school teacher in Kansas from 1958–1965, first at Galva and then at Turner High in Kansas City. When he received his doctorate, he was appointed assistant professor of sociology at the University of Kansas where he taught until 1974, when he moved to Colorado State University, where he has taught ever since.

Much of Dr. Eitzen's study has focused on the sociology of sport and on various social problems, with a special emphasis on crime. He is the author of a number of books, including *Sociology of North Amer-*

✝D. Stanley Eitzen, "Violent Crime: Myths, Facts, and Solutions: The Conservative and Progressive Answers," May 15, 1995, pp. 469–472. Reprinted by permission of *Vital Speeches of the Day* and the author.

ican Sport; Criminology; and *Crime in the Streets* and *Crime in the Suites.*

Propositions of policy draw on all the previous forms of address that we have examined in this book. Policy addresses require accurate information, information that is used to establish a fact or facts, then those facts must be shown to constitute a problem that should concern the audience. Finally, the speaker must present a plausible approach or plan of action that will solve or alleviate the problem. The section of the speech that Dr. Eitzen presents in the form of "myths" (4–12) seeks to demonstrate a proposition of fact. It is here that you will want to raise questions about the speaker's use of supporting information. First of all, what kind of information does he use? Is the information fully relevant to the issue? Is the information sufficient to constitute credibility?

You may note that Dr. Eitzen does not cite sources for the information he uses in exploding the four myths. Can one assume that his research and scholarly credentials provide the necessary credibility. Remember that he has written widely on the topic.

In the solution phase of the speech (13), Dr. Eitzen identifies two kinds of answers to the problem. He then seeks to eliminate the conservative approach by showing that available evidence does not support that position, and argues that conservative measures are fundamentally "after the fact" solutions. He then contends that progressive measures are geared to preventing the fact, and that they come in two types: 1) Measures to protect society immediately, and 2) Long term preventive measures to reduce violent crime. Do you think that he is able to make his measures sufficiently compelling to convince the average listener? If so why? If not, why not?

The final paragraph of the speech seeks to lift the address to a level beyond reason and argument to a more philosophical realm. The speaker states that "Everyone needs a dream" and that "Many young people act in antisocial ways because they have lost their dreams." What is your opinion of this matter? Has the speaker convinced you that the loss of a life's dream is the essence of the problem?

---

1   My remarks are limited to violent street crimes (assault, robbery, rape, and murder). We should not forget that there are other types of violent crimes that are just as violent and actually greater in magnitude than street crimes: corporate, political, organized, and white collar. But that is another subject for another time. Our attention this morning is on violent street crime, which has made our cities unsafe and our citizens extremely fearful. What are the facts about violent crime and violent criminals and what do we, as a society, do about them?

2   I am going to critique the prevailing thought about violent crime and its control because our perceptions about violent crime and much of what our government officials do about it is wrong. My discipline—sociology—knows a lot about crime but what we know does not seem to affect public perceptions and public policies. Not all of the answers, however, are always crystal clear. There are disagreements among reasonable and thoughtful people, coming from different theoretical and ideological perspectives. You may, difficult as it seems to me, actually disagree with my analysis. That's all right. The key is for us to address this serious problem, determine the facts, engage in dialogue, and then work toward logical and just solutions.

3   What do criminologists know about violent crime? Much of what we know is counter intuitive; it flies in the face of the public's understanding. So, let me begin with some demythologizing.

4   *Myth 1: As a Christian nation with high moral principles, we rank relatively low in the amount of violent crime.* Compared with the other industrialized nations of the world, we rank number one in belief in God, "the importance of God in our lives," and church attendance. We also rank first in murder rates, robbery rates, and rape rates. Take homicide, for example: the U.S. rate of 10 per 100,000 is three times that of Finland, five times that of Canada, and nine times greater than found in Norway, the Netherlands, Germany, and Great Britain. In 1992, for example, Chicago, a city about one-fifth the population of the Netherlands had nine times more gun-related deaths than occurred in the Netherlands.

5   *Myth 2: We are in the midst of a crime wave.* When it comes to crime rates we are misled by our politicians, and the media. Government data indicate that between 1960 and 1970 crime rates doubled, then continued to climb through the 1970s. From 1970 to 1990 the rates remained about the same. The problem is with violent crime by youth, which has increased dramatically. Despite the rise in violent crime among youth, however, the *overall* violent crime rate actually has decreased in the 1990s.

6   Our perceptions are affected especially by the media. While crime rates have leveled and slightly declined during the 1990s, the media have given us a different picture. In 1993, for example, the three major networks doubled their crime stories and tripled their coverage of murders. This distortion of reality results, of course, in a general perception that we are in the midst of a crime wave.

7   *Myth 3: Serious violent crime is found throughout the age structure.* Crime is mainly a problem of male youths. Violent criminal behaviors peak at age 17

and by age 24 it is one-half the rate. Young males have always posed a special crime problem. There are some differences now, however. Most significant, young males and the gangs to which they often belong now have much greater firepower. Alienated and angry youth once used clubs, knives, brass knuckles, and fists but now they use Uzis, AK47s, and "streetsweepers." The result is that since 1985, the murder rate for 18–24 year-olds has risen 65 percent while the rate for 14–17 year-olds has increased 165 percent.

8   The frightening demographic fact is that between now and the year 2005, the number of teenagers in the U.S. will grow by 23 percent. During the next ten years, black teenagers will increase by 28 percent and the Hispanic teenage population will grow by about 50 percent. The obvious prediction is that violent crime will increase dramatically over this period.

9   *Myth 4: The most dangerous place in America is in the streets where strangers threaten, hit, stab, or shoot each other.* The streets in our urban places are dangerous, as rival gangs fight, and drive-by shootings occur. But, statistically, the most dangerous place is in your own home, or when you are with a boyfriend or girlfriend, family member, or acquaintance.

10   *Myth 5: Violent criminals are born with certain predispositions toward violence.* Criminals are not born with a criminal gene. If crime were just a function of biology, then we would expect crime rates to be more or less the same for all social categories, times, and places. In fact, violent crime rates vary considerably by social class, race, unemployment, poverty, geographical place, and other social variables. Research on these variables is the special contribution of sociology to the understanding of criminal behavior.

11   Let's elaborate on these social variables because these have so much to do with solutions. Here is what we know about these social variables:

1.   **The more people in poverty, the higher the rate of street crime.**

2.   **The higher the unemployment rate in an area, the higher the crime rate. Sociologist William J. Wilson says that black and white youths at age 11 are equally likely to commit violent crimes but by their late 20's, blacks are four times more likely to be violent offenders. However, when blacks and whites in their late 20s are employed, they differ hardly at all in violent behavior.**

3.   **The greater the racial segregation in an area, the higher the crime rate. Sociologist Doug Massey argues that urban poverty and urban crime are the consequences of extremely high levels of black residential segregation and racial discrimination. Massey says,**

"Take a group of people, segregate them, cut off their capital and guess what? The neighborhoods go downhill. There's no other outcome possible."

As these neighborhoods go downhill and economic opportunities evaporate, crime rates go up.

4. **The greater the family instability, the higher the probability of crimes by juveniles. Research is sketchy, but it appears that the following conditions are related to delinquent behaviors: (a) intense parental conflict; (b) lack of parental supervision; (c) parental neglect and abuse; and (d) failure of parents to discipline their children.**

5. **The greater the inequality in a neighborhood, city, region, or society, the higher the crime rate. In other words, the greater the disparities between rich and poor, the greater the probability of crime. Of all the industrialized nations, the U.S. has the greatest degree of inequality. For example, one percent of Americans own 40 percent of all the wealth. At the other extreme, 14 1/2 percent of all Americans live below the poverty line and 5 percent of all Americans live below *one-half* of the poverty line.**

   12   When these social variables converge, they interact to increase crime rates. Thus, there is a relatively high probability of criminal behavior—violent criminal behavior—among young, black, impoverished males in inner cities where poverty, unemployment, and racial segregation are concentrated. There are about 5 million of these high-risk young men. In addition, we have other problem people. What do we do? How do we create a safer America?

   13   To oversimplify a difficult and contentious debate, there are two answers—the conservative and progressive answers. The conservative answer has been to get tough with criminals. This involves mandatory sentences, longer sentences, putting more people in prison, and greater use of the death penalty. This strategy has accelerated with laws such as "three strikes and you're out (actually in)," and the passage of expensive prison building programs to house the new prisoners.

   14   In my view, this approach is wrong-headed. Of course, some individuals must be put in prison to protect the members of society. Our policies, however, indiscriminately put too many people in prison at too high a cost. Here are some facts about prisons:

1. **Our current incarceration rate is 455 per 100,000 (in 1971 it was 96 per 100,000). The rate in Japan and the Netherlands is one-tenth ours. Currently, there are 1.2 million Americans in prisons and jails (equivalent to the population of Philadelphia).**

2.   The cost is prohibitive, taking huge amounts of money that could be spent on other programs. It costs about $60,000 to build a prison cell and $20,000 to keep a prisoner for a year. Currently the overall cost of prisons and jails (federal, state, and local) is $29 billion annually. The willingness to spend for punishment reduces money that could be spent to alleviate other social problems. For example, eight years ago Texas spent $7 dollars on education for every dollar spent on prisons. Now the ratio is 4 to 1. Meanwhile, Texas ranks 37th among the states in per pupil spending.

3.   As mentioned earlier, violent crimes tend to occur in the teenage years with a rapid drop off afterwards. Often, for example, imprisonment under "3 strikes and you're out" laws gives life imprisonment to many who are in the twilight of their criminal careers. We, and they, would be better off if we found alternatives to prison for them.

4.   Prisons do not rehabilitate. Actually, prisons have the opposite effect. The prison experience tends to increase the likelihood of further criminal behavior. Prisons are overcrowded, mean, gloomy, brutal places that change people, but usually for the worse, not the better. Moreover, prisoners usually believe that their confinement is unjust because of the bias in the criminal justice system toward the poor and racial minorities. Finally, prisoners do not ever pay their debt to society. Rather they are forever stigmatized as "ex-cons" and, therefore, considered unreliable and dangerous by their neighbors, employers, fellow workers, and acquaintances. Also, they are harassed by the police as "likely suspects." The result is that they are often driven into a deviant subculture and eventually caught—about two-thirds are arrested within three years of leaving prison.

    15   Progressives argue that conservative crime control measures are fundamentally flawed because they are "after the fact" solutions. Like a janitor mopping up the floor while the sink continues to overflow; he or she may even redouble the effort with some success but the source of the flooding has not been addressed. If I might mix metaphors here (although keeping with the aquatic theme), the obvious place to begin the attack on crime is *upstream*, before the criminal has been formed and the crimes have been committed.

    16   We must concentrate our efforts on high-risk individuals before they become criminals (in particular, impoverished young inner city males). These prevention proposals take time, are very costly, and out-of-favor politically, but they are the only realistic solutions to reduce violent street crime.

    17   The problem with the conservative "after the fact" crime fighting proposals is that while promoting criminal justice, these programs dismantle social justice. Thus, they enhance a criminogenic climate. During the Reagan years, for example, $51 billion dollars were removed from various poverty programs. Now,

under the "Contract for America" the Republicans in Congress propose to reduce subsidized housing, to eliminate nutrition programs through WIC (Women, Infants, and Children), to let the states take care of subsidized school lunches, and to eliminate welfare for unmarried mothers under 18 who do not live with their parents or a responsible guardian.

18   Progressives argue that we abandon these children at our own peril. The current Republican proposals forsake the 26 percent of American children under six who live in poverty including 54 percent of all African American children and 44 percent of all Latino children under the age of six. Will we be safer as these millions of children in poverty grow to physical maturity?

19   Before I address specific solutions, I want to emphasize that sociologists examine the structural reason for crime. This focus on factors outside the individual does not excuse criminal behavior, it tries to understand how certain structural factors *increase* the proportion of people who choose criminal options.

20   Knowing what we know about crime, the implications for policy are clear. These proposals, as you will note, are easy to suggest but they are very difficult to implement. I will divide my proposals into immediate actions to deal with crime now and long-term preventive measure:

21   *Measures to protect society immediately:*

1. **The first step is to protect society from predatory sociopaths. This does not mean imprisoning more people. We should, rather, only imprison the truly dangerous. The criminal law should be redrawn so that the list of crimes reflects the real dangers that individuals pose to society. Since prison does more harm than good, we should provide reasonable alternatives such as house arrest, half-way houses, boot camps, electronic surveillance, job corps, and drug/alcohol treatment.**

2. **We must reduce the number of handguns and assault weapons by enacting and vigorously enforcing stringent gun controls at the federal level. The United States is an armed camp with 210 million guns in circulation. Jeffrey Reiman has put it this way:**

   "Trying to fight crime while allowing such easy access to guns is like trying to teach a child to walk and tripping him each time he stands up. In its most charitable light, it is hypocrisy. Less charitably, it is complicity in murder."

3. **We must make a special effort to get guns out of the hands of juveniles. Research by James Wright and his colleagues at Tulane University found that juveniles are much more likely to have guns for protection than for status and power. They suggest that we must restore order in the inner cities so that fewer young people do not feel the need to provide their own protection. They argue that a perceived sense of security by youth can be accomplished**

if there is a greater emphasis on community policing, more cooperation between police departments and inner city residents, and greater investment by businesses, banks, and cities in the inner city.

4   We must reinvent the criminal justice system so that it commands the respect of youth and adults. The obvious unfairness by race and social class must be addressed. Some laws are unfair. For example, the federal law requires a five-year, no-parole sentence for possession of five grams of crack cocaine, worth about $400. However, it takes 100 times as much powder cocaine—500 grams, worth $10,000—and a selling conviction to get the same sentence. Is this fair? Of course not. Is it racist? It is racist since crack is primarily used by African Americans while powder cocaine is more likely used by whites. There are also differences by race and social class in arrest patterns, plea bargain arrangements, sentencing, parole, and imposition of the death penalty. These differences provided convincing evidence that the poor and racial minorities are discriminated against in the criminal justice system. As long as the criminal justice system is perceived as unfair by the disadvantaged, that system will not exert any moral authority over them.

5   We must rehabilitate as many criminals as possible. Prisons should be more humane. Prisoners should leave prison with vocational skills useful in the real world. Prisoners should leave prison literate and with a high school degree. And, society should formally adopt the concept of "forgiveness" saying to ex-prisoners, in effect, you have been punished for your crime, we want you to begin a new life with a "clean" record.

6   We must legalize the production and sale of "illicit drugs" and treat addiction as a medical problem rather than a criminal problem. If drugs were legalized or decriminalized, crimes would be reduced in several ways: (a) By eliminating drug use as a criminal problem, we would have 1.12 million *fewer* arrests each year. (b) There would be many *fewer* prisoners (currently about 60 percent of all federal prisoners and 25 percent of all state prisoners are incarcerated for drug offenses). (c) Money now spent on the drug war ($31 billion annually, not counting prison construction) could be spent for other crime control programs such as police patrols, treatment of drug users, and jobs programs. (d) Drugs could be regulated and taxed, generating revenues of about $5 billion a year. (e) It would end the illicit drug trade that provides tremendous profits to organized crime, violent gangs, and other traffickers. (f) It would eliminate considerable corruption of the police and other authorities. (g) There would be many fewer homicides. Somewhere between one-fourth and one-half of the killings in the inner cities are drug-related. (h) The lower cost of purchasing drugs reduces the need to commit crimes to pay for drug habits.

22 *Long-term preventive measures to reduce violent crime:*

1. The link between poverty and street crime is indisputable. In the long run, reducing poverty will be the most effective crime fighting tool. Thus, as a society, we need to intensify our efforts to break the cycle of poverty. This means providing a universal and comprehensive health care system, low-cost housing, job training, and decent compensation for work. There must be pay equity for women. And, there must be an unwavering commitment to eradicate institutional sexism and racism. Among other benefits, such a strategy will strengthen families and give children resources, positive role models, and hope.

2. Families must be strengthened. Single-parent families and the working poor need subsidized child care, flexible work schedules, and leave for maternity and family emergencies at a reasonable proportion of their wages. Adolescent parents need the resources to stay in school. They need job training. We need to increase the commitment to family planning. This means providing contraceptives and birth control counseling to adolescents. This means using federal funds to pay for legal abortions when they are requested by poor women.

3. There must be a societal commitment to full and decent employment. Meaningful work at decent pay integrates individuals into society. It is a source of positive identity. Employed parents are respected by their children. Good paying jobs provide hope for the future. They also are essential to keep families together.

4. There must be a societal commitment to education. This requires two different programs. The first is to help at-risk children, beginning at an early age. As it is now, when poor children start school, they are already behind. As Sylvia Ann Hewlett has said:

"At age five, poor children are often less alert, less curious, and less effective at interacting with their peers than are more privileged youngsters."

This means that they are doomed to be underachievers. To overcome this we need intervention programs that prepare children for school. Research shows that Head Start and other programs can raise IQ scores significantly. There are two problems with Head Start, however. First, the current funding only covers 40 percent of eligible youngsters. And second, the positive effects from Head Start program are sometimes short-lived because the children then attend schools that are poorly staffed, overcrowded, and ill-equipped.

23   This brings us to the second education program to help at-risk children. The government must equalize the resources of school districts, rather than the current situation where the wealth of school districts determines the amount spent per pupil. Actually, equalization is not the answer. I believe that there should be special commitment to invest *extra* resources in at-risk children. If we do, we will have a safer society in the long run.

24   These proposals seem laughable in the current political climate, where politicians——Republicans *and* Democrats—try to outdo each other in their toughness on crime and their disdain for preventive programs. They are wrong, however, and society is going to pay in higher crime rates in the future. I am convinced that the political agenda of the conservatives is absolutely heading us in the wrong direction—toward more violent crime rather than less.

25   The proposals that I have suggested are based on what we sociologists know about crime. They should be taken seriously, but they are not. The proposals are also based on the assumption that if we can give at-risk young people hope, they will become a part of the community rather than alienated from it. My premise is this: Everyone needs a dream. Without a dream, we become apathetic. Without a dream, we become fatalistic. Without a dream, and the hope of attaining it, society becomes our enemy. Many young people act in antisocial ways because they have lost their dream. These troubled and troublesome people are society's creations because we have not given them the opportunity to achieve their dreams—instead society has structured the situation so that they will fail. Until they feel that they have a stake in society, they will fail, and so will we.

SHOULD MEDIA SEX AND VIOLENCE
BE CENSORED OR CENSURED?

Nadine Strossen

Nadine Strossen is a Professor of Law at New York Law School. In 1991 she was the first woman to be elected president of the American Civil Liberties Union, a position she held at the time of the following speech. Also, she has been active in such organizations as National

---

+Reprinted by permission of Nadine Strossen.

Coalition Against Censorship and Feminists for Free Expression. The American Civil Liberties Union (ACLU) is a non-profit, nonpartisan, 250,000 member public interest organization devoted to protecting basic civil liberties of all Americans (freedom of speech, press, religion, and assembly; equal protection of the law; legal due process; and rights to privacy). And the ACLU works to extend these civil liberties to groups that traditionally have been denied them. According to an *ACLU Briefing Paper,* the organization "defends the right of people to express their views, not the views that they express."

On October 18, 1995 Nadine Strossen presented the Tenth Annual Otto Silha Lecture at the Silha Center for the Study of Media Law and Ethics at the University of Minnesota. Founded in 1984, the Silha Center promotes research about the First Amendment, about critical legal studies, and about media ethics.

At the start of her 50-minute lecture, she reassures her audience that her topic of legal and ethical issues of sex and violence in the media clearly relates to the focus of the Center. She uses examples and expert interpretation to illuminate the current widespread political impulse to censor the entertainment media (8-10). Her policy position of opposing censorship and favoring responsible censuring of media is clear. Indeed throughout her speech in various ways she explores the continuing tension in American society between First Amendment rights of freedom of expression and the ethically responsible exercise of those rights. More extensive analysis of this tension as related to campus hate speech, pornography, and obscene rock and rap music lyrics can be found in Richard L. Johannesen, "Diversity, Freedom, and Responsibility in Tension," in Josina M. Makau and Ronald C. Arnett, eds., *Communication Ethics in An Age of Diversity* (University of Illinois Press, forthcoming, Chapter 9).

Strossen employs several organizational techniques to promote clear audience comprehension and logicality of argument structure. She explicitly "forecasts" the number and nature of arguments to come (13, 32). Verbal "signposts" that enumerate her main points within major sections of the speech are found throughout (14, 16, 17, 19, 22, 27, 32, 39, 47, 52, 54). The so-called "this-or-nothing" pattern is used (14-31). In this pattern a speaker examines, each in turn, several potential solutions or courses of action and shows why each is defective, inappropriate, or irrelevant. Then the speaker presents her or his own proposal as the only remaining reasonable one—in effect it is either "this or nothing at all." How adequately does she use this pattern? Are there other alternatives that should be explored? Does she justify as reasonable her alternative as the best one? Concerning the difference between Strossen and Mackinnon the pornography issue, see Strossen's book, *Defending Pornography: Free Speech, Sex, and the Fight for Women's Rights* (1995) and two books by Catherine Mackinnon, *Feminism Unmodified* (1987) and *Only Words* (1993).

An overarching argumentative strategy for Strossen, one so obvious that it demands attention by the rhetorical critic, is the attempt again and again to draw careful distinction between concepts or approaches. She distinguishes between "obscenity" and "intentional incitement to imminent violence" that have no First Amendment protection and other descriptions and depictions of sex and violence that do have such protection (14). She differentiates between processes of censoring and censuring (13, 27). She draws distinctions between supposedly harmful depictions of sex and violence in the *entertainment* media (54-65) and the probably more harmful inaccurate and exaggerated depictions of sex and violence in the *news* media (40-46). You are urged to evaluate her use of statistics and expert testimony in drawing this distinction concerning news media. Strossen also differentiates between responsible (ethical) censure or criticism of the media (34-38, 47-49) and irresponsible (ethically suspect, hypocritical) criticism of the media (54-64).

You may want to do a comparative evaluation of Strossen's speech with Senator Bob Dole's speech on "Sex and Violence in the Entertainment Media" (mentioned by Strossen) printed earlier in this book in Chapter 7 on Speeches that Create Concern for Problems. In Dole's speech what position does he take on government censorship of the entertainment media?

In addition to advocating responsible criticism as a course of action, Strossen concludes by advocating educational programs as one policy for addressing causes of the problem (65-69). Through expert testimony (66, 68, 69), she argues that education is better then censorship "both in principle and in practice." Compare the specificity of her description of the expert testimony here with her vague "experts note" elsewhere (59).

The text of this speech was provided by Nadine Strossen. For this lecture she acknowledges the research assistance of Kurt Stuckel, Ralph S. Toss, and Donna Wasserman. For sake of brevity, the editors of this book have omitted the documentation note numbers and documentation sources appended to the speech.

1   I am delighted to be your Silha Lecturer. Professionally, I am honored to follow my distinguished predecessors in this prestigious lecture series. And personally, I am always happy to be back in Minnesota, where I grew up, and which I still consider my heart's home.

2   Since the Silha Center focuses on media ethics and law, I want to address a very current topic, at the forefront of a nationwide debate, that involves both law and ethics: the controversy of sex and violence in the media. This is a perennial controversy, as old as the communications media themselves. The invention of each new medium has always ignited public anxieties about its more vivid, more readily disseminated descriptions or depictions concerning controversial subjects—and in our society, sex and violence are always at the top of the list, given our simultaneous fascination and aversion.

3   Consistent with our fascination, the earliest and heaviest uses of each new medium are for communications concerning sex and violence. For example, pornographic videos are widely credited with helping to make the VCR a household appliance. And now sexual and violent words and images are burgeoning on the newest communications frontiers, in cyberspace. The human desire for sexually oriented words and images is so consistently strong that some experts see it as a major motivating force behind the development and use of all new communications media, throughout history, beginning with Stone Age sculpture and cave drawings. A recent *New York Times* story made this point about CD-ROM technology. It quoted experts who believe that the lure of virtual porn is spearheading much of the innovation in this field. As the *Times* observed, "Hard core meets hard drive."!

4   But now let's turn to the other side of our society's paradoxical attitudes toward sex and violence, its aversion. Just as each new communications medium is soon used for sexual and violent expression, such use in turn soon leads to calls for censorship. We saw this phenomenon very vividly this summer. Reports about the widespread availability of sexual and violent expression on the Internet spurred Congressional efforts to impose sweeping new cyber-censorship.

5   Americans' paradoxical love-hate attitude toward sexual and violent expression was well-captured by my fellow Minnesotan, Garrison Keillor, when testifying in Congress in defense of the National Endowment for the Arts several years ago. The NEA, of course, has been repeatedly attacked for funding sexually oriented art. Keillor quipped:

> My ancestors were Puritans from England, (who) arrived here in 1648 in the hope of finding greater restrictions than were permissible under English law at the time.

6   Marcia Pally's recent comprehensive analysis of studies about the alleged adverse impact of television violence—which debunks the claim that any such adverse impact has been shown—notes that television violence has been attacked ever since the advent of television itself, even when neither violence nor television were very prevalent in our society. She observes:

> The first Congressional hearings on television violence were held in 1952, when fewer then 25 percent of households had television sets and the violence rates were among the lowest in the century. Among youth, violence rates were on the decline. . . . so eager were the public and its leaders to blame television for something that they attacked it for problems they did not have.

7   So media sex and violence, along with attempted censorship of them, have been with us as long as the media themselves.

8   Lately, though, we have seen a stepped-up wave of censorial measures, coming from virtually every government agency, and supported by many segments of the public, from across the political spectrum. This past summer, we heard highly-publicized, harsh attacks on the media by politicians from Bob Dole to Bill Clinton, who both gave major speeches attacking sex and violence on TV and in films. Last summer we also heard similar critiques by citizens from William Bennett to C. Delores Tucker, who have attacked rap and rock lyrics as misogynistic and violent.

9   ABC commentator Jeff Greenfield aptly explained the broad political support for censoring TV violence, for example, as follows:

> Conservatives are allowed to hate TV violence because it's produced in Hollywood and sold in New York. Now that Moscow isn't an issue, those are the two

> least favorite cities of cultural conservatives. Liberals are allowed to hate it because it's produced and programmed by powerful corporate interests supported by corporate advertisers. . . . In other words, attacking TV violence, as a political matter, is about as risky as attacking illegal aliens who commit environmental crimes.

(Of course, the ACLU would defend *them,* too!)

10   Jeff's point has recently been reconfirmed, since broad bipartisan majorities in Congress have passed several sweeping censorial measures. For example, the Senate voted 84-16 for the "Communications Decency Act,"

Nadine Strossen, Professor of Law at New York Law School.

which would vastly suppress sexually oriented expression in all telecommunications, including in cyberspace. And other provisions of the comprehensive telecommunications bills that the Senate and the House both passed this summer would severely restrict the televising not only of material that is inappropriately "violent," according to some media or government official, but also of material that such officials might deem "indecent" or otherwise "objectionable." Moreover, many state legislatures have passed, or are seriously considering, similar repressive measures.

11 All of these assaults on media sex and violence raise important questions of both law and ethics—or professional responsibility—for lawyers, journalists, politicians, and others. In the remainder of my talk, I will discuss some of these questions.

12 While the legal issues are hotly debated, I actually think they are quite simple. In my view—and that of many, if not most, constitutional scholars—censoring media sex or violence is unconstitutional. I will briefly explain why, and then turn to what I think is the more difficult and subtle aspect of the analysis—the ethical questions.

13 Let me lay out my basic conclusions in a nutshell, and then I will elaborate on each of them. First, media sex or violence is constitutionally protected free speech. But that does not necessarily mean that it is positive or should be insulated from criticism. Second, *criticizing* media sex or violence is also constitutionally protected free speech. But, again, that does not necessarily mean that *it* is positive, or should be insulated from criticism. In other words, let's not *censor anything* in the realm of media sex or violence. But let's *censure everything* in that realm, including *both* some media depictions *and* some criticisms of them.

14 I will now briefly elaborate on my first conclusion: that media sex or violence is constitutionally protected free speech, and that censoring it is therefore unconstitutional. I am excluding from my remarks the relatively narrow categories of sexual and violent speech that the Supreme Court currently holds to have no constitutional protection in any medium, including print: the subset of sexual expression that satisfies the current definition of "obscenity," which requires (among other things) that it lack serious literary, artistic, political or scientific value; and the subset of violent expression that constitutes an intentional incitement to imminent violence.

15 Beyond these specific exceptions, though, sexual and violent media expression is constitutionally protected. The simplest way to summarize the basis for this conclusion is by quoting from a letter that I co-authored and sent to Congress in October, 1995, in opposition to all four currently pending measures to restrict TV violence.

16   Let me briefly outline those measures. The first would establish a federal Television Ratings Commission to create rating guidelines for "violent and objectionable" programming; it would require that such ratings be part of the broadcast signals; and it would mandate that new TV sets contain a chip capable of blocking out the rated programs. (This is the so-called "V-Chip" legislation.) A second bill is essentially identical to the first, except that the ratings guidelines would be issued by the Federal Communications Commission. A third would authorize the FCC to prohibit "violent. . . programming" during hours when children comprise a substantial portion of the viewing audience. Finally, the fourth pending proposal would establish a federally funded "report card" that would identify the most violent programs and their sponsors.

17   We enlisted several dozen distinguished constitutional law professors and other First Amendment experts to sign our letter to Congress opposing all four measures. Here is a portion of our explanation for that opposition:

> These bills suffer from several common constitutional defects. First, they . . . restrict violent expression fully protected by the First Amendment, which . . . may only be restricted when it is both intended and likely to incite imminent violence. No programming on television rises to the level of that exacting standard.

18   As an aside, I should note that some studies are said to show that TV sex and violence does have other, less direct, adverse impacts on viewers. Even those claims are hotly contested by many experts. Indeed, some maintain that that there are even positive social and psychological impacts from exposure to such images. But, for the moment, let's put aside these debatable points. There's no serious debate on the narrower kind of causal relationship that our First Amendment precedents require as a prerequisite for censoring: intentional, direct, and immediate. No credible authority contends that even massive exposure to TV creates this kind of "clear and present danger."

19   Now I'll turn back to the constitutional scholars' letter to Congress:

> Second, the First Amendment does not merely prevent censorship at it is commonly understood, but it also prevents government from creating obstacles, additional financial encumbrances, or discouragements for speech that falls fully within its protection. Finally, the proposals also involve a content and viewpoint bias that cannot be reconciled with the Constitution. . . . Any definition of violence that. . . failed to follow the incitement standard would be fatally overbroad, encompassing expression that would almost universally be seen as socially beneficial.

20   Here in Minnesota, I want to stress that the letter illustrated this last conclusion by citing a recent study involving students at Concordia College in Moorhead. The students were enlisted to demonstrate how the "report card" proposal would work, by rating the most violent programs on TV during a recent time period. They concluded that the ten most violent programs on cable TV during that timeframe included some historical documentaries and the acclaimed biographical movie about Helen Keller, "The Miracle Worker." The letter continues and concludes as follows:

> Even if [these proposals had] no other constitutional [flaws], none would satisfy the requirement that [any such] regulations [must] be the least restrictive means of furthering a compelling state interest. . . . This is particularly true since there are technical means that are not dependent on government intervention and better facilitate parental control of children's viewing . . . blocking devices that . . . allow parents to restrict access to material they select without relying on subjective and ad hoc determinations made through government initiative. . . .
>
> It remains axiomatic that the First Amendment is violated when government seeks to regulate speech because "it is thought unwise, unfair, false or dangerous." Expressly listing "violence on television" among categories of controversial speech that is [nonetheless] constitutionally protected, "however insidious" it might be, the [U. S. Court of Appeals for the] Seventh Circuit eloquently explained, "Any other answer leaves government in control of . . . the institutions of culture, the great censor and director of which thoughts are good for us."

21 In light of the foregoing clear constitutional principles, censorship is not an appropriate response to media sex and violence that we might dislike or even believe to be "fraught with danger" of a more subtle nature than incitement of imminent violence.

22 This leaves us with two options: first, we could change our current legal standards, and lower the First Amendment barrier to censorship. This is exactly the argument made by those feminists who want to censor what they call "pornography"—sexually explicit expression that is "subordinating" or "degrading" to women. They contend that such expression leads to discrimination and violence against women. Significantly, though, they concede that there is not proof that such expression satisfies the "clear and present danger" test, and therefore fall back on the argument that it should be accepted "on faith." For example, in her latest book advocating censorship of pornography, University of Michigan Law Professor Catharine Mackinnon well-captured this fallback position through a defensive double-negative: "There is no evidence that pornography does no harm." In its 1992 decision in *Butler v. The Queen,* accepting the anti-pornography feminist position, the Canadian Supreme Court also accepted this dangerous intuitive approach to limiting sexual expression, stating:

> It might be suggested that proof of actual harm should be required. . . . [I]t is sufficient. . . for Parliament to have a reasonable basis for concluding that harm will result and this requirement does not demand actual proof of harm.

23   Of course, given the impossibility of *disproving* that *any* expression causes any harm, or of showing that there is no "reasonable basis" for this conclusion, we would have no free speech were such a burden of proof actually to be imposed. To appreciate this, just substitute for the word "pornography" in Mackinnon's pronouncement any other type of expression or medium. We would have to acknowledge that "there is no evidence" that media violence does no harm, or that television in general does no harm, or that editorials criticizing government officials do no harm, or that religious sermons do no harm, and so forth. There certainly is no evidence that feminist writing in general, or MacKinnon's in particular, does no harm.

24   To accept the MacKinnon or Canadian Supreme Court formulation would be a reversion to the discredited "bad tendency" test that was to suppress a wide range of controversial expression earlier in our history, before the U.S. Supreme Court supplanted it with the clear and present danger test. Allowing speech to be curtailed on the speculative basis that it might indirectly lead to possible harm would inevitably unravel free speech protection. *All* speech might lead to potential danger at some future point. Justice Oliver Wendell Holmes recognized this fact in an important 1925 opinion. Holmes rejected the argument that pacifist and socialist ideas should be repressed because they might incite young men to resist the draft or to oppose the U.S. system of government—actions and views that many thought might ultimately undermine national interests. As Holmes noted, "Every idea is an incitement."

25   If we banned the expression of all ideas that might lead individuals to actions that might have an adverse impact even on important interests such as national security or public safety, then scarcely any idea would be safe, and surely no idea that challenged the status quo would be. Precisely for this reason, and to avoid reverting to the "bad tendency" test, Seventh Circuit Judge Frank Easterbrook struck down an anti-pornography law that had been drafted by Catharine MacKinnon and passed by the City of Indianapolis. (As many of you know, MacKinnon had originally drafted that law, together with Andrea Dworkin, right here in Minnesota, but it never went into effect here because it was twice vetoed by then-Mayor Don Fraser.)

26   The law suppressed sexually explicit depictions of "subordination." For the sake of argument, Judge Easterbrook accepted the cornerstone assumption underlying the law—namely, that "depictions of subordination tend to perpetuate subordination." Even so, he ruled, the law would still be unconstitutional, because it revived the discredited and dangerous "bad tendency" doctrine:

> If pornography is what pornography does, so is other speech. . . . Efforts to suppress communist speech in the United States were based on the belief that the

public acceptability of such ideas would increase the likelihood of totalitarian government. Religions affect socialization in the most pervasive way. . . . The Alien and Sedition Acts passed during the administration of John Adams rested on a sincerely held belief that disrespect for the government leads to social collapse and revolution—a belief with support in the history of many nations.

Racial bigotry, anti-Semitism, *violence on television*, reporters' biases—these and many more influence the culture and shape our socialization. . . . Yet all is protected as speech, however insidious. Any other answer leaves the government in control of all of the institutions of culture, the great censor and director of which thoughts are good for us.

Sexual responses often are unthinking responses, and the association of sexual arousal with the subordination of women therefore may have a substantial effect. But almost all cultural stimuli provoke unconscious responses. Religious ceremonies condition their participants. Teachers convey messages by selecting what not to cover; the implicit message about what is off limits or unthinkable may be more powerful than the messages for which they present rational argument. . . . If the fact that speech plays a role in a process of conditioning were enough to permit governmental regulation, that would be the end of freedom of speech.

27   For these reasons, we must focus on our second option for responding to media fare we don't like—and that we believe might well have some serious negative impacts, even if they don't rise to the level of a clear and present danger. This is what I call cen*suring*, as opposed to cen*soring*—exercising our own free speech rights rather than terminating someone else's.

28   Media executives and journalists exercise *their* First Amendment rights—and also act in an ethical and responsible fashion—when they voluntarily decide not to publish or air certain material that they think might have adverse consequences.

29   And readers and viewers exercise *their* First Amendment rights when they criticize certain materials and urge the media not to disseminate them. If viewers band together to organize demonstrations and even boycotts against certain media presentations, or their sponsors, those activities are protected by the First Amendment freedoms of speech and association, despite the economic pressure they exert.

30   As the Supreme Court has often said, in a free society, the appropriate response to speech you find offensive or dangerous is not censorship, but counterspeech—more speech, not less. So, the fact that the media have free speech rights certainly doesn't mean that we have to agree with or approve of what they choose to say in exercising those rights. To the contrary, we are free to exercise our own free speech rights to express our disagreement, disapproval, even our discouragement. We may try to persuade the media not to exercise their

rights—or, one could also say, not to wield their *power*—in certain ways. Such private persuasion is as consistent with the First Amendment as government coercion is inconsistent.

31   Strongly as I support counterspeech or censuring, as a *legal* or *constitutional* matter, I also believe it raises some important and difficult *ethical* issues. Lately, these have generated a lot of confusion, so I would like to lay out some observations and guiding principles. Some of these weigh in favor of criticizing the media, but some weigh against it.

32   Let me start with three observations on the positive side. First, criticism of media depictions may well lead to the chilling or even cutting off of the criticized expression. Still, it is not only constitutionally protected, but also, in many instances, ethically justified. I have to stress that this potentially suppressive impact of criticism of media expression is an important concern; in some cases, it should counsel self-restraint and deter us from engaging in censure. I will discuss that further later, when I come to the considerations that weigh against criticizing the media. In the present context, though, I want to stress that criticizing the media is ethically justified precisely *because of* its impact in stifling expression that has adverse impacts.

33   Lately, we have seen some confusion between constitutionally protected censorship and constitutionally prohibited criticism, and I recognize that there might well be some troubling borderline situations. After all, as I have already explained, the First Amendment can be violated through government measures that indirectly suppress speech as well as by heavy-handed, overt censorship. But government officials have free speech rights too. And they are free to use those rights to express their individual opinions about the media—including critical opinions—so long as they don't impose those opinions through government regulations.

34   In one recent situation, too many government officials, journalists, and others falsely accused President Clinton of violating First Amendment rights when he simply criticized certain media expression. But, in so doing, he acted in a manner that was perfectly constitutional—and, in my view, ethical and responsible as well. Five days after the Oklahoma City bombing last April, Clinton gave a speech right here in Minneapolis, in which he strongly criticized hate-mongering over the airwaves, suggesting that it had helped to create an atmosphere conducive to actual violence. Clinton emphasized that he was not advocating any government censorship, but rather only criticism by concerned citizens. Nevertheless, he was immediately accused of endangering freedom of speech. The next day, at Iowa State University, he again explained why his criticism was completely consistent with both free speech and responsibility—in other words, it was justified as a matter of both law and ethics:

Yes, stand up for freedom of speech. Yes, stand up for all of our freedoms, [including] the freedom of assembly [and] the freedom to bear arms. . . . But remember this: with freedom . . . comes responsibility. And that means that even as others discharge their freedom of speech, if we think they are being irresponsible, then we have the duty to stand up and say so to protect our own freedom of speech.

35   No less staunch a free speech advocate than journalist Molly Ivins made the very same point in a column she wrote just a few days after Clinton's Minneapolis and Iowa speeches (April 18, 1995):

The phenomenal torrent of rhetoric unleashed by the Republican right lately on the theme that Government Is the Enemy plays right into the hands of the haters. The more people talk about government as Them, some unreachable, uncontrollable Other, the more extreme the haters get. . . . Does this mean that anyone who criticizes the gummint should now shut up, lest we somehow encourage the scum who are willing to kill children in their blind hatred? Of course not . . . .

Do I think the climate of hate speech, hate radio and hate politics contributed to the torn, tiny bodies in Oklahoma City? I know they did . . . . Hate speech is fertilizer for bombs. So should we limit freedom of speech? Of course not. But with freedom comes responsibility, and people should be held accountable for their words. And the rest of us have a responsibility, too: to use our own freedom to speak out against the haters.

36   I would like to cite another example of speech by an official that simply criticizes other speech and that should be protected despite its potential impact in stifling certain ideas. Indeed, it should be *encouraged precisely because of* that potential impact.

37   The ACLU has been the leading opponent of campus hate speech codes that punish students who make racist and other biased statements. We have won federal court lawsuits against hate speech codes at the nearby Universities of Wisconsin and Michigan, for example. But while we oppose such direct suppression of campus hate speech, we have advocated other measures that may well indirectly lead to its suppression. Among other things, we urge university officials to denounce the ideas conveyed by hate speech. A few years ago, the President of my alma mater, Harvard University, did precisely that in a statement that cogently discussed the pertinent constitutional and ethical considerations. A student club at Harvard had circulated a letter that was viciously demeaning to women. Harvard's then-President, Derek Bok, issued a strong public criticism of the sexist views conveyed in the letter. He also explained why his doing so was completely consistent with the letter writers' freedom of speech, as follows:

The wording of the letter was so extreme and derogatory to women that I wanted to communicate my disapproval publicly, if only to make sure that no one could gain the false impression that the Harvard administration harbored any sympathy or complacency toward the tone and substance of the letter. Such action does not infringe on free speech. Indeed, statements of disagreement are part and parcel of the open debate that freedom of speech is meant to encourage; the right to condemn a point of view is as protected as the right to express it. Of course, I recognize that even verbal disapproval by persons in positions of authority may have inhibiting effects on students. Nevertheless, this possibility is not sufficient to outweigh the need for officials to speak out on matters of significance to the community—provided, of course, that they take no action to penalize the speech of others.

38   In sum, criticisms of media content, including media sex and violence, can well be ethically justified, not just constitutionally permitted.

39   A second positive aspect of such media criticisms is that they may well promote other civil liberties, in addition to free speech. As I have made clear, I completely defend the media's free speech rights to depict violence. But I think there is a specific danger to civil liberties that flows from some such depictions, so I certainly exercise my free speech rights to criticize those. Moreover, if that criticism would lead to fewer violent depictions of the sort that concern me, I believe that would have a net positive impact on civil liberties.

40   The focus of my concern is the exaggerated, distorted depiction of crime in television news coverage. This creates an unwarranted panic and hysteria about crime in general. Moreover, it creates unwarranted fears of and by particular groups of the population in particular. Women are depicted disproportionately as crime victims, and black men as crime perpetrators. Such distorted depictions unduly inhibit people's freedom of movement, heighten racial and gender tensions, and lead to repressive ineffective anti-crime measures.

41   National statistics show that a person's chances of becoming a victim of a violent crime actually have decreased since 1981. Yet, across the country, fear of crime is rising. Sociologists pin the bulk of the blame for the current national obsession with crime on the mass media's increasingly extensive, relentless coverage of it. In short, while we don't have an actual crime wave, we do have a media crime wave.

42   Let me cite just a few statistics to demonstrate this. Since the early 1990s, TV's attention to crime has more than tripled. In 1994, the three major broadcast networks aired more stories on crime than on the economy, health care reform, and the midterm elections *combined*. In 1994, there were nine times as many murder stories as in 1990. But during this same time period, the actual crime rates were decreasing, including for murder and other violent crimes. To distort their crime coverage even more, the national and local news often focus on the most gruesome, atypical crimes committed. A full 30% of the media coverage is aimed at a mere .3% of all the crimes committed.

43   The foregoing numbers are not skewed by the national obsession with the O.J. Simpson case. To be sure, the networks gave as much nightly coverage to the O.J. case as they did to *all* crime news as recently as 1992, when the current media crime wave began. For all its hype, though, the Simpson case accounted for only a fraction of TV's crime news. Even without that case, crime news had doubled between 1992 and 1993, and murder news had trebled.

44   Professor George Gerbner, a pioneering scholar of the effects of exposure to media violence, has noted the potential adverse impact that this kind of exaggerated crime coverage can have specifically on people's civil liberties. In a recent article, George and his coauthors concluded that, by teaching that the world is violent and frightening, TV fuels feelings of anxiety, insecurity, and mistrust. According to these experts, this sense of "danger, vulnerability, and general malaise" in turn invites exploitation and repression. As they explain:

> [Fearful people are] more dependent, more easily manipulated and controlled, more susceptible to deceptively simple, strong, tough measures and hard-line postures—both political and religious. They may accept and even welcome repression if it promises to relieve their insecurities and other anxieties.

45   This certainly sounds like exactly the mindset that has generated public support for so many repressive measures lately, from the draconian "Crime bill" to the so-called "Omnibus Counterterrorism Act," which the ACLU maintains is more accurately named the "Ominous Counter-Constitution Act." Thus, the exaggerated, distorted media coverage of actual violent crime can play a role in undermining our civil liberties.

46   Accordingly, as a civil libertarian, I enthusiastically welcome the voluntary decision that certain media have made to tailor their own crime coverage accordingly. This is a decision that is completely consistent with professional ethics and responsibility, as well as with constitutional rights. According to news reports I've read, some of the media outlets that have made such decisions are right here in the Twin Cities. For example, in January 1994, WCCO-TV announced that it was going to cut back on its violent and graphic crime coverage, thus defying the adage for most local TV news, "If it bleeds, it leads." And KARE-TV unleashed "KARE about Crime," in which each crime story it reports contains a solution-oriented element.

47   This leads to my third point on the positive side of the media criticism ledger. Not only do free speech advocates such as Yours Truly have the same *right* as everyone else does to criticize media depictions that we believe have some negative effect. Beyond that, we also have a special *responsibility* to engage in such criticism. The ACLU always does this when we defend the First Amendment rights of speakers whose views are contrary to civil liberties, for example, the Ku Klux Klan or Nazis. The relevant ACLU policy provides:

> The right of all groups to express their opinions must be defended regardless of the point of view they express . . . .However, when a group espouses positions adversely affecting civil liberties . . . the [ACLU] should vigorously present its position, while defending the group's right to speak. The [ACLU] should also emphasize . . . that the loose accusations of these groups can create an atmosphere of caution in which dissident views will not be expressed.

48   That last point is very important; in this context, as always, the touchstone is responsibility. While some criticisms of expression may be responsible, some may well be irresponsible. And loose, irresponsible accusations against broad groups can suppress legitimate dissent, which would be antithetical to free speech in a democracy. But, to cite a previous example, I don't think that Clinton's criticisms of hatemongering were in that vein. Indeed, far from stifling criticisms of him and of our government, his Minneapolis speech unleashed an outpouring of more such criticisms.

49   And the ACLU's point about the special duty of free speech defenders to raise our own voices against messages we see as dangerous and destructive, was also made by Bill Clinton in his Minneapolis speech after the Oklahoma City bombing:

> If they insist on being irresponsible with our common liberties, then we must be all the more responsible with our liberties. . . . When they say things that are irresponsible, that may have egregious consequences, we must call them on it. The exercise of their freedom of speech makes our silence all the more unforgivable.

50   Now let me turn to the other side of the ledger on censuring or criticizing media sex or violence. I have just explained why media violence and other expression might not be beneficial, and therefore should be critcized, even though it is constitutionally protected. But turnabout is fair play. Criticism of media violence and other expression likewise might not be beneficial, and therefore should itself be criticized, even though it too is constitutionally protected. So, just as media self-restraint might well be the ethical response regarding violent, sexual or other images, likewise, individuals' self-restraint might well be the principled response regarding criticism of violent, sexual, or other images.

51   While media critics certainly have the free speech right to voice their criticisms, that does not mean their criticisms are either correct or constructive. To the contrary, we are all free to express our disagreement, disapproval, and discouragement of what the media critics are saying. We are certainly free to criticize the critics, and in some instances, we also have an ethical responsibility to do so. Just as many critics contend that media images cause certain dangers of which we should be aware, I maintain that criticisms and private protests against media images also cause certain dangers, of which we should also be aware.

52   First, as I have already noted, private pressures may well have the very same end-result as government censorship: namely, banning particular types of expression. Indeed, some forms of private pressure are at least as potent as direct government regulation—for example, consumer or advertiser boycotts.

53   For those who want to preserve the fullest possible diversity of information, ideas, and perspectives, private economic coercion should be no more palatable than governmental coercion. Recall, for example, that the most vicious attacks on free expression during the McCarthy period resulted from private actions, such as blacklisting in the TV and film industries. This point was made by Marjorie Heins, the Director of the ACLU's Arts Censorship Project, a few years ago, when some feminists were boycotting the publisher of *American Psycho* by Bret Easton Ellis, due to its gory descriptions of brutal misogynistic violence. In urging feminists to "think twice about boycotting books," Margie made the following observations:

> [T]he goal of boycotting a bookseller is to suppress, or censor, some literature, because of its offensive content . . . . Although censorship by private individuals or groups doesn't raise the same legal questions as government censorship . . . it does raise some of the same moral and political questions. [In both cases,] censorship has the same dangerous purpose: To shrink the expressive landscape. [T]he boycotters hope, through economic coercion, to . . . impose an ideological litmus test on works that [publishers and booksellers] consider for sale or publication.

54   Criticism of the media entails a second major danger, which is well-illustrated by what is going on throughout our political system right now: the danger of diversion. Protests against expression are always motivated by concern about some serious underlying societal problem, and certainly increasing violence, especially among our youth, is a terrible, tragic problem. As always, politicians are eager to offer a "quick-fix" solution to such pressing problems, and censoring descriptions and depictions is the oldest, cheapest "quick-fix" available. Advocating censorship allows politicians to claim they are "doing something" about the underlying problem, without raising taxes.

55   The problem is that this scapegoating of expression, blaming images and words, is doubly flawed. Not only does it violate our cherished freedom of speech, but it also does not meaningfully address the underlying problems that gave rise to it. Thus, such scapegoating is at best ineffective. At worst, it is counterproductive, since it diverts attention and resources from the actual problems at hand, and constructive means of addressing them, sometimes in blatantly hypocritical ways.

56   For example, politicians of all stripes have been hypocrtically hiding behind a purported concern for children as an alleged justification for censorship. The many pending censorship measures specifically target media and entertainment forms that are particularly appealing to young people, including TV, video games, computer networks, and rap and rock music. In addition to the legislative measures that I previously described, in June, a federal court in Washington, D.C. upheld unprecedented federal restrictions on cable and broadcast TV and radio, ostensibly to protect children from exposure to vaguely defined "indecent" material.

57   However, these measures violate not only the rights of the putatively benefited children, but also the rights of adults, all without doing anything meaningful for children's welfare. Restrictions such as those approved by the D.C. court deprive parents of the right to shape the upbringing of their own children by making their own decisions as to what cable or broadcast material their children will or will not be allowed to see. And they also deprive all adults of the right to decide what they will or won't view or listen to; all of us are relegated to seeing or hearing only the material that the government deems fit for some children.

58   Often politicians and others who say they are seeking to protect children are really aiming to restrict adults' rights, too; that is why I said earlier that they are "hiding behind" their purported concern with children's well-being. For example, this summer's massive attack on "cyberporn" was heralded by lurid images of children being unwittingly bombarded by sexual images on the computer screen. *Time* magazine's July 3, 1995 cover, for instance, featured a horror-stricken, zombie-like child mesmerized by a computer screen. The headline blared: "CYBERPORN: EXCLUSIVE. A new study shows how pervasive and wild it really is. Can we protect our kids—and free speech?"

59   Yet experts note how inaccessible sexual and other controversial material is on computer networks. In contrast with TV images, which flood the screen at the touch of a button, this computerized material may only be obtained by going through such steps as submitting credit card numbers and access codes, all designed to make them available to consenting adults only.

60   Moreover, software companies are developing increasingly sophisticated blocking or filtering devices, to let parents screen out selected sexual and other materials to which they do not want their children to have access.

61   As an aside, this points to another example of how certain media coverage of sex and violence can have an adverse impact on civil liberties, and hence should be criticized. *Time* magazine was roundly—and in my view

rightly—criticized for "Feeding the Internet Porn Panic," to quote a *Harper's* magazine story by that name. It's sensational pictures actually included one of a man copulating with a computer! As one critic quoted in *Harper's* said: "There's just no way that the story as published by *Time* is anything other than a huge gift to those who want to censor the Internet." To his credit, the reporter who wrote the story was receptive to this criticism, and expressly said that he would write it differently if he had it to do all over again. As he said in the *Harper's* piece: "There is nothing I more wish I had than another week to work on that story."

62   In light of the actual facts about the relative inaccessibility of cyber-porn, the alleged desire to shield children from certain material falls flat as a rationale for curbing content in cyberspace; what's really at stake is the desire to deprive adults of access to that material too. When I recently debated Christian Coalition Executive Director Ralph Reed on this issue, he essentially admitted as much, invoking concerns about making cyberspace "family friendly," and thus raising the spectre of imposing "traditional family values" on everyone in the U.S. This point was noted in a recent article in *The American Spectator* as follows:

> Passions [surrounding censorship issues] are rising, and some of them are unhealthy. Ralph Reed grew so testy on "Crossfire" that he accused Nadine Strossen of advocating "bestiality." The ACLU President, of course, had done no such thing, and it may be that Reed was angry because only minutes before he had been made to look foolish and perhaps even sinister. Michael Kinsley had asked him whether he wanted to keep smut away from adults as well as from children. Reed gave an ambiguous answer, and so Kinsley asked him again. In fact, he repeated the question three times, but Reed remained ambiguous.

63   The tendency to use a purported protection of children as a smoke-screen for directly curbing adults' rights is accompanied by blatant hypocrisy as far as children themselves are concerned. While politicians are eager to cite their devotion to children as an excuse for limiting the civil liberties of young and old alike, they are far less eager to adopt constructive measures that will actually advance young people's current well-being or future prospects. Our recent budget-slashing frenzy has been particularly devastating to education; we are channeling more and more of our young people into prisons rather than colleges, and state and local governments are spending more and more of their money on building more and larger jails and prisons, while public schools are crumbling.

64   Some prominent politicians have provided particularly blatant examples of the hypocritical hiding behind an asserted concern with children's well-being to sabotage rights of children and adults, without in fact advancing children's well-being. For example, in June, Senate Majority Leader, and leading Republican Presidential contender, Bob Dole, gave a well-publicized speech assailing violence in the media and its asserted negative impact on our nation's youth. Yet, while Dole is thus leading the charge to remove images of guns from TV screens, he has also led the charge to reinstate real assault weapons on the street!

65   If we are going to constructively respond to the actual causes of actual violence, what should we do? What are the constructive alternatives from which our focus on media violence has been diverting us?

66   Experts who have recently studied causes of violence, and constructive approaches to reducing it, have advocated education and other measures. They haven't focused on TV at all. For example, in 1993, the American Psychological Association issued a study on children and violence. It concluded that the central causes of violence in children are abuse, rejection and neglect by parents, as well as violence between parents. Other factors it cited were: poverty; the belief that educational and job opportunities are closed because of racial or ethnic discrimination; the failure to learn nonaggressive ways to deal with frustration; and poor performance in school. Correspondingly, to reduce violence in children, the APA recommended most highly school programs that teach children such social and emotional skills as managing anger, negotiating, and solving disagreements in ways that do not involve intimidation or violence.

67   So, according to the experts, the most effective measures for reducing violence in children would have absolutely nothing to do with media. Thus, rather than continuing to hold hearing after hearing on TV violence, our government resources would be far better spent on combatting domestic violence and rebuilding our crumbling public education system. As journalist Kurt Anderson warned, it's time to stop shouting "theater" in a crowded fire.

68   Moreover, even if one focused specifically on media-related strategies for reducing violence, these still would not include changing the con*tent* of media depictions. Rather, they would aim at the con*text* in which those depictions are seen—specifically, the attitudes and awareness that the viewer brings to bear upon them. Such educational measures have been recommended by a wide range of experts, including the American Psychological Association, the National Research Council, and the Surgeon General's Workshop that reported to the Meese Pornography Commission about sexually violent media images. All these experts endorsed what have been termed "media literacy programs," which would educate in critical viewing skills.

69   In 1992, three leading experts on the alleged links between exposure to televised violence and actual violence—Professors Daniel Linz, Barbara Wilson, and Ed Donnerstein—studied the comparative effectiveness of three pos-

sible approaches for severing such links: government restrictions on media; voluntary labeling by the entertainment industry; and media education. They unanimously concluded: "The solution we find most promising is educational interventions . . . ." This is social science confirmation of the actual efficacy of the approach favored by free speech theory: more speech. Thus, the more-speech or educational strategy is better both in principle and in practice.

70   I would like to end with a quote that has been attributed to former Supreme Court Justice William O. Douglas, a great free speech champion, which aptly capsulizes the spirit of my remarks: "Freedom of speech is a dangerous thing. But it's the safest thing we've got."

Chapter Eight

Speeches That Intensify Social Cohesion

Social cohesion, any social order, rests on shared values, customs, and traditions which identify us in our roles as members of a society. We are disposed accordingly to empathy, cooperation, lawful behavior, and even altruistic acts. We understand each other, for we "speak the same language," that is, we share the same values, perceptions, identifications, ideals, reactions, and rules of action. A social order is both the effect and the source of shared values and beliefs.

Ernest van de Haag

The Nature and Importance of Speeches That Intensify Social Cohesion

At the heart of any social order is a set of values that constitutes the basis for all social action. In recognition of the importance of values, Chapter 5 discussed the nature of speeches that seek to establish propositions of value. However, once values have been established, the perpetuation of social order demands that these values periodically be reaffirmed and intensified. A rhetorical critic, Ronald F. Reid, reminds us: "Building and maintaining social cohesion is an ever present need; for although individuals within society are obviously not all alike, they must transcend their differences if they are to function as a viable social unit."

There are numerous occasions in our society on which speeches that intensify social cohesion are given; church services, victory celebrations, awards convocations, retirement luncheons, funeral services, nominating conventions, fund-raising rallies, sales promotion meetings, and commencements are such occasions. At moments like these, speakers address audiences about the values that both share as members of a common group. The speeches given in such moments are noncontroversial for a specific audience. They do not urge adoption of new values or rejection of old values. Rather, they seek to reinforce and revitalize existing audience values. Speakers seek unity of spirit or a reenergizing of effort or commitment; they try to inspire, to kindle enthusiasm, or to deepen feelings of awe, respect, and devotion.

Among the types of speeches that intensify social cohesion are the following:

- *Sermons:* A sermon articulates the tenets of a faith. It is designed to inspire stronger commitment to religious beliefs and values.
- *Eulogies:* A eulogy pays tribute to the dead. It identifies, in the life of the departed, qualities which those who remain behind should value and emulate.
- *Dedication Speeches:* A dedication speech marks the completion of a group project. It praises group achievement and stresses the importance of the object being dedicated to future group endeavors.
- *Commemorative Speeches:* A commemorative speech marks the anniversary of an event. It demonstrates the significance of the event in the light of present group values, beliefs, and goals.
- *Commencement Speeches:* A commencement speech signals the completion of a course of study. It praises those being graduated and speaks to the values that should be reflected in their future lives.
- *Keynote Speeches:* A keynote speech serves as a preface to a meeting, conference, or convention. It stresses the social worth and importance of the work to be done by those assembled.
- *Welcoming Speeches:* A speech of welcome extends a greeting to people who are new to a group. It expresses satisfaction with the presence of new mem-

bers or visitors and relates the values of the group to the values of those joining or visiting the group.

- *Farewell Speeches:* A farewell speech is given by a person who is leaving a
  group. The speaker usually reflects on the quality of the experiences that were
  shared with the group and the emotions he or she is experiencing at the moment of departure.
- *Presentation Speeches:* A presentation speech accompanies the presentation of
  an award to a group member. It specifies the qualities the award is meant to
  symbolize and justifies the presentation of the award to the person being
  honored.
- *Nomination Speeches:* A nominating speech places the name of a person before
  a group of voters as a candidate for an elective office. It describes the requirements of the office (abilities, personal qualities, duties, problems to be
  faced), praises the virtues, accomplishments, and experiences of the person
  being nominated, and depicts the success the group will have under the leadership of the nominee if he or she is elected.
- *Acceptance Speeches:* An acceptance speech is given by the recipient of an
  award or honor. In accepting an award, a speaker is expected to express gratitude and to demonstrate the personal qualities the award is intended to
  symbolize.
- *Inaugural Addresses:* An inaugural address is given by a person as he or she
  is about to assume a position of leadership in a group. The speaker normally
  acknowledges the passing of leadership, praises past group performance
  and achievements, and identifies the values and goals of future group
  activities.

Each of these types of speeches serves a different immediate purpose. However,
all share the larger social purpose of intensifying social cohesion by paying tribute
to the values of the group. By nature, the speech that intensifies social cohesion invites members to reaffirm their commitment to the values, customs, and traditions
that are at the heart of group life.

Students often assign less importance to this form than to informative or persuasive communication. Drawing on their past experiences with ceremonial gatherings, they conclude that speeches that intensify social cohesion are often "flowery"
and trite—given more to affected *or* artificial flourishes than to substantive issues.
However, sociologist Robert Bellah warns against taking this speech form lightly. He
observes:

> . . . we know enough about the function of ceremonial and ritual in various soci-
> eties to make us suspicious of dismissing something as unimportant because it is
> "only a ritual." What people say on solemn occasions need not be taken at face

value, but it is often indicative of deep-seated values and commitments that are not made explicit in the course of everyday life. [1]

Careful students will recognize that ceremonial speeches often capture the essence of a social fabric. Such speeches help to illuminate the central values that undergird group traditions, procedures, and goals. In fact, many of the greatest speeches of recorded history have sought to intensify social cohesion.

Criteria for Evaluating Speeches That Intensify Social Cohesion

Although one could devise discrete criteria for the evaluation of each type of speech discussed in the previous section, each type may be meaningfully considered by applying criteria common to them all.

1.   Has the speaker satisfied the ceremonial purpose(s) of the gathering?

Because speeches that intensify social cohesion are usually given at ceremonial gatherings, the first question to be asked is whether the speech has satisfied the ceremonial purpose. For example, when one attends a dedication ceremony, it is expected that the speaker will praise the object being dedicated. When one attends a commencement, it is expected that the graduating seniors will be appropriately honored and advised. A welcoming ceremony calls for a tribute to both the person being welcomed and the institution extending the welcome. A presentation ceremony calls for a speech in praise of the person being awarded a tribute.

Whenever the speaker prepares a speech designed to intensify social cohesion, the audience's expectations at that moment must be considered. The Christian minister who on Easter Sunday ignores the meanings of the resurrection, the commencement speaker who ignores the graduating seniors assembled, and the eulogist who ignores or condemns the life of the departed all err in their omissions by failing to meet the ceremonial demands of the occasion. Whatever their personal reasons for speaking, speakers must conform to the particular expectations of their audiences on specific occasions if their speeches are to succeed.

2.   Has the speaker selected group values worthy of perpetuation?

Although the ceremonial demands of the occasion strongly constrain the speaker's behavior when seeking to intensify social cohesion, the speaker should still be held responsible for the substantive worth of the message. Because speeches

---

[1]Cited in Michael Novak, *Choosing Our King: Powerful Symbols in Presidential Politics* (New York: Macmillan, 1974), p. 142.

that intensify social cohesion attempt to strengthen group values, the speaker should be expected to identify values worthy of esteem and perpetuation by the audience.

In applying this criterion, the enlightened listener or reader will test the values selected by the speaker. Has the eulogist selected the finer values examplified by a person's life? Has the inaugural speaker identified the most significant and worthy values as guides for future group action? Has the commencement speaker identified relevant and meaningful values for his audience of graduates? In evaluating Douglas MacArthur's speech "Farewell to the Cadets," reprinted later in this chapter, the reader should ask, "Are 'duty, honor, country' the finer values to which a soldier should subscribe in a free society?" In evaluating Martin Luther King's speech "I Have a Dream," also reprinted later, the reader should question whether the values of creative suffering and nonviolent resistance were those most relevant and wise for the black minority in a "white" America in 1963.

3.   Has the speaker given impelling expression to the values selected?

Many critics have condemned speeches of this type because they tend to reexpress the commonplace values of our social order. For example, many critics have condemned the commencement speech as a genre. Such speeches, they claim, are seldom more than dull rearticulations of established truths. Born of truisms, these speeches are infrequently more than trite reexpressions of the public mind. Although such charges are too often justified, they are not inherent indictments of the speech form. Rather, they are criticisms made valid by speakers who are incapable of giving impelling expression and redefinition to the values that bind our society together.

Because speeches that intensify social cohesion must by definition treat shared values, speakers must exercise special skill in giving new meaning and purpose to old values. Speakers have succeeded in accomplishing this difficult task. Through incisive analysis and amplification and through vivid and compelling language, gifted speakers succeed in gaining renewed audience commitment to old values without seeming trite.

Through the process of analysis, speakers must determine the particular relevance of cherished values to contemporary events and problems. Through the process of amplification, speakers must select those anecdotes, comparisons, contrasts, descriptions, examples, restatements, and definitions that make their contemporary analyses come alive. In the process, they must also demonstrate that their analyses are appropriate to the emotions that the nature of the occasion naturally evokes— whether elation, hope, gratitude, affection, pride, sympathy, anger, hate, shame, remorse, or grief. Speakers must also select vivid and compelling language to clothe their ideas. Through such stylistic devices as metaphor, vivid imagery, alliteration, parallelism, antithesis, hyperbole, and personification, gifted speakers can find ways for language to give new excitement and meaning to old values.

Conclusion

Many situations call for speeches that urge audience recommitment to social values. Among the common types of speeches that intensify social cohesion are sermons, eulogies, dedication speeches, commemorative speeches, commencement speeches, keynote speeches, welcoming speeches, farewell speeches, presentation speeches, acceptance speeches, and inaugural speeches.

In evaluating speeches of this form, the critic must consider *whether the speaker has met the ceremonial purpose of the gathering, whether the speaker has selected group values worthy of perpetuation, and whether the speaker has given impelling expression to the values selected.*

For Further Reading

Allen, R. R., and McKerrow, Ray E. *The Pragmatics of Public Communication.* 3rd ed. Kendall/Hunt Publishing Company, 1985. Chapter 9 examines ceremonial speaking and offers guidelines for building social cohesion.

Carlile, Clark S. and Daniel, Arlie V. *A Project Text for Public Speaking.* 6th ed. Harper/Collins, 1991. Some projects involve speeches that aim primarily at social cohesion, including farewell, eulogy, dedication, anniversary, and nomination acceptance.

Condit, Celeste. "The Function of Epideictic: The Boston Massacre Orations as Exemplar." *Communication Quarterly,* 33 (Fall 1985): 284–298. Describes the functions of epideictic/ceremonial discourse as definition/understanding, shaping/sharing community, and display/entertainment. Suggests "communal definition" as the aim of a "complete" epideictic speech.

Gronbeck, Bruce, et al. *Principles and Types of Speech Communication.* 11th ed. Scott, Foresman, 1990. Ch. 18 discusses varied types of speeches for ceremonial purposes, many of which seek social cohesion.

Gronbeck, Bruce E. *The Articulate Person.* 2nd ed. Scott, Foresman, 1983. Chapter 7 discusses speeches that reinforce existing audience values and beliefs. Pages 248–257 describe the cultural functions of speeches at public ceremonies. Chapter 12 examines speeches for various special occasions.

Hart, Roderick P. "The Functions of Human Communication in the Maintenance of Public Values." In Carroll Arnold and John Bowers, eds. *Handbook of Rhetorical and Communication Theory,* Allyn and Bacon, 1984, Chapter 12.

Osborn, Michael, and Osborn, Suzanne. *Public Speaking.* 2nd ed. Houghton Mifflin, 1991. Chapter 15 examines various types of ceremonial speaking and their functions in reinforcing existing values and promoting group and cultural cohesion. Pages 256–259 illustrate language techniques that create cohesion.

Perelman, Chaim, and Olbrechts-Tyteca, L. *The New Rhetoric.* Trans. John Wilkinson and Purcell Weaver. University of Notre Dame Press, 1969. Pages 47–54 discuss types of discourse that "establish a sense of communion centered around particular values recognized by the audience."

Reid, Ronald F. *The American Revolution and the Rhetoric of History.* Speech Communication Association, 1978. Ch. 3 analyzes ways in which present societal values are reinforced through appeals to noble Revolutionary forebearers and to noble Revolutionary principles.

Rosenfield, Lawrence W. "The Practical Celebration of Epideictic." In Eugene White, ed. *Rhetoric in Transition.* Pennsylvania State University Press, 1980, pp. 131–155. A scholarly reinterpretation of the nature and function of speeches in honor of excellence, speeches that acknowledge goodness, grace, and intrinsic excellence rather than merely praise achievements and accomplishments.

Walter, Otis M. *Speaking Intelligently.* Macmillan, 1976. Pages 185–92 examine the nature of discourse which seeks to intensify social cohesion and offer specific strategies for increasing group pride and identity.

INAUGURAL ADDRESS

John F. Kennedy

On January 20, 1961, the late John Fitzgerald Kennedy delivered his Presidential inaugural address to a large outdoor audience before the nation's Capitol on a cold, clear day. In contrast to his rapid-fire delivery during the campaign, Kennedy spoke slowly, giving careful emphasis to special phrases and the cadence of his prose.

An inaugural address by an American President typically reflects some now-traditional expectations and characteristics. Multiple audiences are addressed directly or indirectly: the inaugural crowd, Americans everywhere, world heads-of-state, and the people of the world. One major function is to set the general tone of the new administration. On social, economic, and military matters domestically and internationally, the President usually outlines in broad strokes some intended stances. But advocacy of specific, detailed policies and programs is not expected and abstract language may be more acceptable here than in

---

✝The text of this speech was taken from a recording of the address.

other kinds of political discourse. A second major function is to promote social cohesion. The President seeks to heal the wounds and antagonisms of the recent political campaign, to urge reenergized commitment to central societal values and goals, and to promote a feeling of national unity. In an inaugural address, the President frequently will cite or adapt the words and wisdom of revered past Presidents and leaders. And such a speech may praise noble elements of America's heritage and applaud America's destiny. Both the introductions and conclusions of inaugural addresses typically call upon the blessings of God.

Kennedy's address demonstrates that effective style is not bombast or artificial ornament. Perhaps the most important stylistic quality of his speech is his sentence construction. Observe that his sentence length varies widely and that he employs many abstract and few concrete words. Is abstractness perhaps a natural quality of an inaugural address? What role do antithesis, parallelism, rhythm, and energy and movement play in this speech? Kennedy utilizes numerous metaphors, some rather hackneyed, but some fresh and subtle. Can you identify metaphors of each type?

The passage most frequently quoted from this speech is "Ask not what your country can do for you—ask what you can do for your country." Examine the context in which this sentence is used. Does it appear to be a natural outgrowth from the flow of ideas in the speech? Notice also phrases that echo passages in speeches by Abraham Lincoln (paragraphs 6 and 22) and by Franklin D. Roosevelt (10 and 25). Kennedy uses Biblical allusions (19 and 23) and images reflecting his Navy days in the South Pacific (20).

For a detailed analysis of the functions and techniques of American Presidential inaugural addresses, see Karyln Kohrs Campbell and Kathleen Hall Jamieson, *Deeds Done In Words: Presidential Rhetoric and the Genres of Governance* (University of Chicago Press, 1990), Ch. 2.

---

1   *Vice President Johnson, Mr. Speaker, Mr. Chief Justice, President Eisenhower, Vice President Nixon, President Truman, Reverend Clergy, Fellow Citizens:* We observe today not a victory of party but a celebration of freedom—symbolizing an end as well as a beginning—signifying renewal as well as change. For I have sworn before you and Almighty God the same solemn oath our forebears prescribed nearly a century and three quarters ago.

2   The world is very different now. For man holds in his mortal hands the power to abolish all forms of human poverty and all forms of human life. And

yet the same revolutionary beliefs for which our forebears fought are still at issue around the globe—the belief that the rights of man come not from the generosity of the state but from the hand of God.

3 We dare not forget today that we are the heirs of that first revolution. Let the word go forth from this time and place, to friend and foe alike, that the torch has been passed to a new generation of Americans—born in this century, tempered by war, disciplined by a hard and bitter peace, proud of our ancient heritage—and unwilling to witness or permit the slow undoing of those human rights to which this nation has always been committed, and to which we are committed today, at home and around the world.

Photo. No. KNC-20213, John F. Kennedy Library

4 Let every nation know, whether it wishes us well or ill, that we shall pay any price, bear any burden, meet any hardship, support any friend, or oppose any foe to assure the survival and the success of liberty.

5 This much we pledge—and more.

6 To those old allies whose cultural and spiritual origins we share, we pledge the loyalty of faithful friends. United, there is little we cannot do in a host of cooperative ventures. Divided, there is little we can do—for we dare not meet a powerful challenge at odds and split asunder.

7 To those new states whom we welcome to the ranks of the free, we pledge our word

President John F. Kennedy speaking on the White House lawn.

that one form of colonial control shall not have passed away merely to be replaced by a far more iron tyranny. We shall not always expect to find them supporting our view.

8 But we shall always hope to find them strongly supporting their own freedom—and to remember that, in the past, those who foolishly sought power by riding the back of the tiger ended up inside.

9 To those people in the huts and villages of half the globe struggling to break the bonds of mass misery, we pledge our best efforts to help them help themselves, for whatever period is required—not because the Communists may be doing it, not because we seek their votes, but because it is right. If a free society cannot help the many who are poor, it cannot save the few who are rich.

10 To our sister republics south of our border, we offer a special pledge—to convert our good words into good deeds—in a new alliance for progress—to assist free men and free governments in casting off the chains of poverty. But this peaceful revolution of hope cannot become the prey of hostile powers. Let all our neighbors know that we shall join with them to oppose aggression or subversion anywhere in the Americas. And let every other power know that this hemisphere intends to remain the master of its own house.

11 To that world assembly of sovereign states, the United Nations, our last best hope in an age where the instruments of war have far outpaced the instruments of peace, we renew our pledge of support—to prevent it from becoming merely a forum for invective—to strengthen its shield of the new and the weak—and to enlarge the area in which its writ may run.

12 Finally, to those nations who would make themselves our adversary, we offer not a pledge but a request: That both sides begin anew the quest for peace, before the dark powers of destruction unleashed by science engulf all humanity in planned or accidental self-destruction.

13 We dare not tempt them with weakness. For only when our arms are sufficient beyond doubt can we be certain beyond doubt that they will never be employed.

14 But neither can two great and powerful groups of nations take comfort from our present course—both sides overburdened by the cost of modern weapons, both rightly alarmed by the steady spread of the deadly atom, yet both racing to alter that uncertain balance of terror that stays the hand of mankind's final war.

15 So let us begin anew—remembering on both sides that civility is not a sign of weakness, and sincerity is always subject to proof. Let us never negotiate out of fear. But let us never fear to negotiate.

16 Let both sides explore what problems unite us instead of belaboring those problems which divide us.

17   Let both sides, for the first time, formulate serious and precise proposals for the inspection and control of arms—and bring the absolute power to destroy other nations under the absolute control of all nations.

18   Let both sides seek to invoke the wonders of science instead of its terrors. Together let us explore the stars, conquer the deserts, eradicate disease, tap the ocean depths, and encourage the arts and commerce.

19   Let both sides unite to heed in all corners of the earth the command of Isaiah—to "undo the heavy burdens . . . [and] let the oppressed go free."

20   And if a beachhead of cooperation may push back the jungle of suspicion, let both sides join in creating a new endeavor: not a new balance of power, but a new world of law, where the strong are just and the weak secure and the peace preserved.

21   All this will not be finished in the first one hundred days. Nor will it be finished in the first one thousand days, not in the life of this administration, nor even perhaps in our lifetime on this planet. But let us begin.

22   In your hands, my fellow citizens, more than mine, will rest the final success or failure of our course. Since this country was founded, each generation of Americans has been summoned to give testimony to its national loyalty. The graves of young Americans who answered the call to service surround the globe.

23   Now the trumpet summons us again—not as a call to bear arms, though arms we need—not as a call to battle, though embattled we are—but a call to bear the burden of a long twilight struggle, year in and year out, "rejoicing in hope, patient in tribulation"—a struggle against the common enemies of man: Tyranny, poverty, disease and war itself.

24   Can we forge against these enemies a grand and global alliance, North and South, East and West, that can assure a more fruitful life for all mankind? Will you join in that historic effort?

25   In the long history of the world, only a few generations have been granted the role of defending freedom in its hour of maximum danger.

26   I do not shrink from this responsibility—I welcome it. I do not believe that any of us would exchange places with any other people or any other generation. The energy, the faith, the devotion which we bring to this endeavor will light our country and all who serve it—and the glow from that fire can truly light the world.

27   And so, my fellow Americans: Ask not what your country can do for you—ask what you can do for your country.

28   My fellow citizens of the world: Ask not what America will do for you, but what together we can do for the freedom of man.

29   Finally, whether you are citizens of America or citizens of the world, ask of us here the same high standards of strength and sacrifice which we ask of you. With a good conscience our only sure reward, with history the final judge of our deeds, let us go forth to lead the land we love, asking His blessing and His help, but knowing that here on earth God's work must truly be our own.

I Have a Dream

Martin Luther King, Jr.

Late in August 1963, more than 200,000 people held a peaceful demonstration in the nation's capital to focus attention on Negro demands for equality in jobs and civil rights. The marchers assembled at the Washington Monument on the morning of the 28th and filed in two columns down to the Lincoln Memorial. A little later, 10 civil-rights leaders met with President Kennedy at the White House and subsequently returned to the Lincoln memorial, where each of them addressed the assembled throng. As measured by crowd reaction, this speech by Martin Luther King was the high point of the day. In the months prior to his assassination in April, 1968, King broadened his advocacy to include the rights of poor people of all races and ethnic groups and to condemn continued American involvement in the Vietnam War.

One way to assess this speech would be to apply the criteria suggested at the start of this chapter for evaluating speeches that intensify social cohesion. Has the speech satisfied the cermonial purpose(s) of the gathering? Has the speaker selected group values worthy of perpetuation? Has the speaker given impelling expression to the values selected? Or this speech might be examined as a particular type of social cohesion speech, namely a *rally speech* that arouses enthusiasm for tasks ahead through uplifting sagging spirits and through deepening of commitments. Rally speeches occur on various occasions, such as keynote addresses at political and professional conventions, sales promotion speeches at meetings of company sales personnel, and speeches to civic

---

action groups. Speakers at rallies typically utilize some combination of the following approaches: (1) Stress the importance, the value, of the work the group has been doing. (2) Promote group self-confidence by praising their past success, dedication, and sacrifice and by praising their basic values, principles, and goals. (3) Outline the tasks, opportunities, and challenges ahead. (4) Use vivid imagery and emotionally stimulating language to paint word pictures of the better future achievable through united, sustained group effort.

In this speech, King urges rededication to the black non-violent civil rights movement and reinforces values central to this view of that movement: courage, faith, hope, freedom, justice, equality, non-violence, sacrifice, dignity, and discipline. He sees these values as rooted in the traditional American Dream. Early in the speech, King balances pleas for non-violence and for cooperation between blacks and whites with a strong sense of urgency to achieve results. Perhaps to blunt the charges of gradualism and overmoderation made by some black leaders such as Malcolm X, King stresses the "fierce urgency of now."

King's audience on this occasion would have attributed to him a very high level of ethos, a very positive degree of speaker credibility. His followers saw him as an expert, trustworthy, dynamic leader of their movement. In the speech and setting themselves, echos of Abraham Lincoln further reinforce his high ethos with this particular audience. As the Lincoln Memorial provides the physical setting, echos of the Gettysburg Address come through the structure of the speech (past, present, future) and in paragraphs two and five.

King utilizes varied language resources to lend power, motivation, and inspiration to his message. Consider where, for what possible functions, and how effectively he uses such stylistic devices as repetition, parallelism, and refrain. Consider especially the "I have a dream" and "Let freedom ring" passages. In the same manner, examine his use of antithetical phrasing, including "meeting physical force with soul force," "heat of oppression. . . oasis of freedom and justice," and "jangling discords . . . beautiful symphony." How appropriate to the occasion and to King as a Southern Baptist minister was his frequent use of imagery, paraphrases, and direct quotations from the Bible? Finally, assess his heavy use of metaphors throughout the speech. Would the audience probably experience them as natural to the topic, as artificial, as fresh and stimulating, as trite and dull, or as familiar and reassuring? What functions might have been served by particular metaphors? Note especially the early extended metaphor (figurative analogy) of cashing a check.

Rhetorical scholar Keith D. Miller has explored the ways in which King in his speeches, as one thoroughly exposed to the heritage of black folk preaching, reflected the tradition of "voice merging." In voice merging, black ministers created their own identities "not through original language but through identifying themselves with a hallowed tradition"—often by "borrowing homiletic material from many sources, including the sermons of their predecessors and peers."

In his speeches King typically both explicitly capitalized on revered biblical and national traditions with which his audiences agreed and "borrowed without acknowledgement from the sermons of both black and white Protestant ministers." In this way much of King's rhetoric had "been tested—often repeatedly tested—with both listeners and readers before King employed it." After extensive analysis, Miller argues that rhetorical critics should reconsider their "unqualified remonstrations against plagiarism and the use of cliches." See Keith D. Miller, "Voice Merging and Self-Making: The Epistemology of 'I Have A Dream'," *Rhetoric Society Quarterly,* 19(Winter 1989): 23–32; Miller, "Martin Luther King Borrows a Revolution: Argument, Audience, and Implications of a Second Hand Universe," *College English, 48(March 1986):* 249–265. Also see Richard L. Johannesen, "The Ethics of Plagiarism Reconsidered: The Oratory of Martin Luther King, Jr.," *Southern Communication Journal,* 60 (Spring 1995): 185–194.

---

1   I am happy to join with you today in what will go down in history as the greatest demonstration for freedom in this history of our nation.

2   Five score years ago, a great American, in whose symbolic shadow we stand today, signed the Emancipation Proclamation. This momentous decree came as a great beacon light of hope to millions of Negro slaves, who had been seared in the flames of withering injustice. It came as a joyous daybreak to end the long night of their captivity.

3   But one hundred years later, the Negro is still not free. One hundred years later, the life of the Negro is still sadly crippled by the manacles of segregation and the chains of discrimination. One hundred years later, the Negro lives on a lonely island of poverty in the midst of a vast ocean of material prosperity. One hundred years later, the Negro is still languished in the corners of American society and finds himself an exile in his own land. So we have come here today to dramatize a shameful condition.

4   In a sense, we've come to our nation's Capitol to cash a check. When the architects of our republic wrote the magnificent words of the Constitution

and the Declaration of Independence, they were signing a promissory note to which every American was to fall heir. This note was a promise that all men—yes, black men and well as white men—would be guaranteed the unalienable rights of life, liberty, and the pursuit of happiness.

5   It is obvious today that America has defaulted on this promissory note insofar as her citizens of color are concerned. Instead of honoring this sacred obligation, America has given the Negro people a bad check; a check which has come back marked "insufficient funds." But we refuse to believe that the bank of justice is bankrupt. We refuse to believe that there are insufficient funds in the great vaults of opportunity of this nation. So we've come to cash this check—a check that will give us upon demand the riches of freedom and the security of justice. We have also come to this hallowed spot to remind America of the fierce urgency of *now*. This is no time to engage in the luxury of cooling off to take the tranquilizing drug of gradualism. *Now is the time* to make real the promises of Democracy. *Now is the time* to rise from the dark and desolate valley of segregation to the sunlight of racial justice. *Now is the time* to lift our nation from the quicksands of racial injustice to the solid rock of brotherhood. *Now is the time* to make justice a reality for all of God's children.

6   It would be fatal for the nation to overlook the urgency of the moment. This sweltering summer of the Negro's legitimate discontent will not pass until there is an invigorating autumn of freedom and equality. Nineteen sixty-three is not an end, but a beginning. Those who hope that the Negro needed to blow off steam and will now be content will have a rude awakening if the nation returns to business as usual. There will be neither rest nor tranquility in America until the Negro is granted his citizenship rights. The whirlwinds of revolt will continue to shake the foundations of our nation until the bright day of justice emerges.

7   But there is something that I must say to my people who stand on the warm threshold which leads into the palace of justice. In the process of gaining our rightful place we must not be guilty of wrongful deeds. Let us not seek to satisfy our thirst for freedom by drinking from the cup of bitterness and hatred.

8   We must forever conduct our struggle on the high plane of dignity and discipline. We must not allow our creative protest to degenerate into physical violence. Again and again we must rise to the majestic heights of meeting physical force with soul force. The marvelous new militancy which has engulfed the Negro community must not lead us to a distrust of all white people, for many of our white brothers, as evidenced by their presence here today, have come to realize that their destiny is tied up with our destiny. And they have come to realize that their freedom is inextricably bound to our freedom. We cannot walk alone.

9   And as we walk we must make the pledge that we shall always march ahead. We cannot turn back. There are those who ask the devotees of civil rights, "When will you be satisfied?" We can never be satisfied as long as the Negro is the victim of the unspeakable horrors of police brutality. We can never be satisfied as long as our bodies, heavy with the fatigue of travel, cannot gain lodging in the motels of the highways and the hotels of the cities. We cannot be satisfied as long as the Negro's basic mobility is from a smaller ghetto to a larger one. We can never be satisfied as long as our children are stripped of their selfhood and robbed of their dignity by signs stating "For Whites Only." We cannot be satisfied as long as a Negro in Mississippi cannot vote and a Negro in New York believes he has nothing for which to vote. No, no, we are not satisfied, and we will not be satisfied until justice rolls down like waters and righteousness like a mighty stream.

10   I am not unmindful that some of you have come here out of great trials and tribulations. Some of you have come fresh from narrow jail cells. Some of you have come from areas where your quest for freedom left you battered by the storms of persecution and staggered by the winds of police brutality. You have been the veterans of creative suffering. Continue to work with the faith that unearned suffering is redemptive.

11   Go back to Mississippi, go back to Alabama, go back to South Carolina, go back to Georgia, go back to Louisiana, go back to the slums and ghettos of our Northern cities knowing that somehow this situation can and will be changed. Let us not wallow in the valley of despair.

12   I say to you today, my friends, so even though we face the difficulties of today and tomorrow, I still have a dream. It is a dream deeply rooted in the American dream.

13   I have a dream that one day this nation will rise up and live out the true meaning of its creed: "We hold these truths to be self-evident; that all men are created equal."

14   I have a dream that one day on the red hills of Georgia the sons of former slaves and the sons of former slaveowners will be able to sit down together at the table of brotherhood; I have a dream—

15   That one day even the state of Mississippi, a state sweltering with the heat of injustice, sweltering with the heat of oppression, will be transformed into an oasis of freedom and justice; I have a dream—

16   That my four little children will one day live in a nation where they will not be judged by the color of their skin but by the content of their character; I have a dream today.

17   I have a dream that one day down in Alabama with its vicious racists, with its governor having his lips dripping with the words of interposition and nullification, one day right there in Alabama little black boys and black girls will be able to join hands with little white boys and white girls as sisters and brother; I have a dream today.

18 I have a dream that one day every valley shall be exalted, every hill and mountain shall be made low, and rough places will be made plane and crooked places will be made straight, and the glory of the Lord shall be revealed, and all flesh shall see it together.

19 This is our hope. This is the faith that I go back to the South with. With this faith we will be able to hew out of the mountain of despair a stone of hope. With this faith we will be able to transform the jangling discords of our nation into a beautiful symphony of brotherhood. With this faith we will be able to work together, to pray together, to struggle together, to go to jail together, to stand up for freedom together, knowing that we will be free one day.

20 This will be the day. . . . This will be the day when all of God's children will be able to sing with new meaning. "My country 'tis of thee, sweet land of liberty, of thee I sing. Land where my fathers died, land of the pilgrim's pride, from every mountainside, let freedom ring," and if America is to be a great nation—this must become true.

21 So let freedom ring—from the prodigious hilltops of New Hampshire, let freedom ring; from the mighty mountains of New York, let freedom ring—from the heightening Alleghenies of Pennsylvania!

22 Let freedom ring from the snowcapped Rockies of Colorado!

23 Let freedom ring from the curvaceous slopes of California!

24 But not only that; let freedom ring from Stone Mountain of Georgia!

25 Let freedom ring from Lookout Mountain of Tennessee!

26 Let freedom ring from every hill and molehill of Mississippi. From every mountainside, let freedom ring, and when this happens. . . .

27 When we allow freedom ring, when we let it ring from every village and every hamlet, from every state and every city, we will be able to speed up that day when all of God's children, black men and white men, Jews and Gentiles, protestants and Catholics, will be able to join hands and sing in the words of the old Negro spiritual, "Free at last! free at last! thank God almighty, we are free at last!"

Democratic Convention Keynote Address

Barbara Jordan

On July 12, 1976, Barbara Jordan, U.S. Congresswoman from Texas, delivered this nationally televised keynote address to the Democratic National Convention in New York City. A lawyer, Jordan was the first black woman elected to the Texas state senate. She came to national public prominence on July 25, 1974, with her eloquent and impassioned defense of the Constitution as a committee speaker during the televised hearings of the U.S. House of Representatives committee on President Nixon's impeachment. Her 21 minute speech at the 1976 Democratic convention followed a comparatively lackluster keynote speech by Sen. John Glenn, the astronaut hero. She was introduced via a film biography of her life and career and was greeted by the convention audience with a three minute standing ovation. In keeping with her reputation as an excellent public speaker, Jordan delivered the speech in a clear, forceful, and dramatic manner. A *New York Times* reporter (July 13, 1976, p. 24) describes the audience reaction: "Time and again, they interrupted her keynote speech with applause. And, after it was all over . . . she was brought back for a final curtain call and for the loudest ovation of all."

Clearly a political convention keynote address seeks to mold social cohesion. Typically the keynote speaker stresses the importance of the convention and the deliberations of the delegates, castigates the opposing party, praises the heritage, values, and policies of their own party, and exhorts the convention delegates and all party members to unite in a vigorous, successful campaign. A keynote speaker attempts to inspire and reenergize members by setting a theme, a tone, a *key note,* for the convention.

Jordan left the Congress in 1978 to become a professor at the University of Texas. After enduring a progressively worsening case of multiple sclerosis, Barbara Jordan died, at age 59, on January 17, 1996.

Throughout the speech Jordan develops the central theme of a people in search of a national community, in search of the common good.

+Reprinted by permission from *Vital Speeches of the Day,* August 15, 1976, pp. 645–46.

This note of cohesiveness is reflected in her choice of phrases: one nation; common spirit; common endeavor; common ties; each person do his or her part. Frequently she justifies a position or judgment as harmonious with the will or interests of "the people." She attributes to "the people" such values as common sense and generosity. (For an analysis of the socially cohesive function served by appeals to "the people" in political discourse, see Michael C. McGee, "In Search of 'The People'," *Quarterly Journal of Speech,* October 1975.)

In a major section of the speech, Jordan utilizes parallel phrasing (we believe, we are, we have) to outline the Democratic Party's concept of governing—its basic beliefs that reflect its view of human nature. She metaphorically ("bedrock") stresses the fundamental nature of these beliefs and claims that they are not negotiable. The beliefs have explicit or implicit values imbedded in them: equality (note the double antithetical phrasing of the first belief); opportunity; government of, by, and for the people; activity; innovativeness; adaptability; sacrifice for a good cause; optimism.

Note that Jordan frequently repeats words, rephrases ideas, and in vocal delivery overenunciates the pronunciation of words (gov-er-ning; hyp-o-crit-i-cal). She may have intentionally used such techniques of redundancy and emphasis to overcome the physical noise and listener inattention typical of political conventions. Some in the audience, most likely the television audience, may have felt that her attitude toward them was one of superiority, as if they were simpleminded folk who needed everything spelled out and overemphasized for comprehension.

In at least two ways, Jordan's address differs slightly from the expectations or traditions associated with political convention keynote speeches. First, she makes virtually no direct attacks on the Republicans. Her apparent attacks are implied. By metaphorically characterizing past Democratic mistakes as those "of the heart," she may be indirectly asserting calculating, devious mistakes by the Nixon Administration. By arguing that no President can veto the decision of the American people to forge a national community, she indirectly may be attacking President Ford's heavy use of the veto to block Congressional legislation.

In a second departure from tradition, she does criticize her own party, but in such a moderate way as to freshen the speech without weakening her praise of party principles or generating negative audience reaction. She admits the Democratic Party has made past mistakes, but they were in behalf of the common good and the Party was willing later to confess them. Metaphorically she underscores the point by saying that Party "deafness" to the will of the people was only temporary. Her warning that the Democratic Party at times has attempted to be "all things to all people" may be indirect criticism of Jimmy Carter who was faulted during the primaries for making that kind of appeal. As a final analytic consideration here, assess whether this warning against being "all things to all people" is to some degree inconsistent with her point earlier in the speech that the Democratic Party is an inclusive party ("Let everybody come").

Two prominent rhetorical critics have said of Jordan's speech: "Many critics who watched and heard her speak will have recognized a recurrent rhetorical form, a reflexive form, a form called 'enactment' in which the speaker incarnates the argument, *is* the proof of the truth of what is said." (Karlyn Kohrs Campbell and Kathleen Hall Jamieson, *Form and Genre, Shaping Rhetorical Action* (Falls Church, VA: The Speech Communication Association, n.d., p. 9.) Discuss the speech from this perspective of rhetorical enactment by the speaker. Does it help you to understand the power of Jordan's words?

---

1   One hundred and forty-four years ago, members of the Democratic Party first met in convention to select a Presidential candidate. Since that time, Democrats have continued to convene once every four years and draft a party platform and nominate a Presidential candidate. And our meeting this week is a continuation of that tradition.

2   But there is something different about tonight. There is something special about tonight. What is different? What is special? I, Barbara Jordan, am a keynote speaker.

3   A lot of years passed since 1832, and during that time it would have been most unusual for any national political party to ask that a Barbara Jordan deliver a keynote address . . . but tonight here I am. And I feel that notwithstanding the past that my presence here is one additional bit of evidence that the American Dream need not forever be deferred.

4   Now that I have this grand distinction what in the world am I supposed to say?

5   I could easily spend this time praising the accomplishments of this party and attacking the Republicans, but I don't choose to do that.

6   I could list the many problems which Americans have. I could list the problems which cause people to feel cynical, angry, frustrated: problems which include lack of integrity in government; the feeling that the individual no longer counts; the reality of material and spiritual poverty; the feeling that the grand

American experiment is failing or has failed. I could recite these problems and then I could sit down and offer no solutions. But I don't choose to do that either.

7   The citizens of America expect more. They deserve and they want more than a recital of problems.

8   We are a people in a quandary about the present. We are a people in search of our future. We are a people in search of a national community.

9   We are a people trying not to solve the problems of the present—unemployment, inflation—but we are attempting on a larger scale to fulfill the promise of America. We are attempting to fulfill our national purpose: to create and sustain a society in which all of us are equal.

10   Throughout our history, when people have looked for new ways to solve their problems, and to uphold the principles of this nation, many times they have turned to political parties. They have often turned to the Democratic Party.

11   What is it, what is it about the Democratice Party that makes it the instrument that people use when they search for ways to shape their future? Well I believe the answer to that question lies in our concept of governing. Our concept of governing is derived from our view of people. It is a concept deeply rooted in a set of beliefs firmly etched in the national conscience of all of us.

12   Now what are these beliefs?

13   First, we believe in equality for all and privileges for none. This is a belief that each American regardless of background has equal standing in the public forum, all of us. Because we believe this idea so firmly, we are an inclusive rather than an exclusive party. Let everybody come.

14   I think it no accident that most of those emigrating to America in the 19th century identified with the Democratic Party. We are a heterogenous party made up of Americans of diverse backgrounds.

15   We believe that the people are the source of all governmental power; that the authority of the people is to be extended, not restricted. This can be accomplished only by providing each citizen with every opportunity to participate in the management of the government. They must have that.

16   We believe that the government which represents the authority of all the people, not just one interest group, but all the people, has an obligation to actively, underscore actively, seek to remove those obstacles which would block individual achievement . . . obstacles emanating from race, sex, economic condition. The government must seek to remove them.

17   We are a party of innovation. We do not reject our traditions, but we are willing to adapt to changing circumstances, when change we must. We are willing to suffer the discomfort of change in order to achieve a better future.

18   We have a positive vision of the future founded on the belief that the gap between the promise and reality of America can one day be finally closed. We believe that.

19   This my friends, is the bedrock of our concept of governing. This is a part of the reason why Americans have turned to the Democratic Party. These are the foundations upon which a national community can be built.

20   Let's all understand that these guiding principles cannot be discarded for short-term political gains. They represent what this country is all about. They are indigenous to the American idea. And these are principles which are not negotiable.

21   In other times, I could stand here and give this kind of exposition on the beliefs of the Democratic Party and that would be enough. But today that is not enough. People want more. That is not sufficient reason for the majority of the people of this country to vote Democratic. We have made mistakes. In our haste to do all things for all people, we did not foresee the full consequences of our actions. And when the people raised their voices, we didn't hear. But our deafness was only a temporary condition, and not an irreversible condition.

22   Even as I stand here and admit that we have made mistakes I still believe that as the people of America sit in judgment on each party, they will recognize that our mistakes were mistakes of the heart. They'll recognize that.

23   And now we must look to the future. Let us heed the voice of the people and recognize their common sense. If we do not, we not only blaspheme our political heritage, we ignore the common ties that bind all Americans.

24   Many fear the future. Many are distrustful of their leaders, and believe that their voices are never heard. Many seek only to satisfy their private work wants. To satisfy private interests.

25   But this is the great danger America faces. That we will cease to be one nation and become instead a collection of interest groups: city against suburb, region against region, individual against individual. Each seeking to satisfy private wants.

26   If that happens, who then will speak for America?

27   Who then will speak for the common good?

28   This is the question which must be answered in 1976.

29   Are we to be one people bound together by common spirit sharing in a common endeavor or will we become a divided nation?

30   For all of its uncertainty, we cannot flee the future. We must not become the new puritans and reject our society. We must address and master the future together. It can be done if we restore the belief that we share a sense of national community, that we share a common national endeavor. It can be done.

31 There is no executive order: there is no law that can require the American people to form a national community. This we must do as individuals and if we do it as individuals, there is no President of the United States who can veto that decision.

32 As a first step, we must restore our belief in ourselves. We are a generous people so why can't we be generous with each other? We need to take to heart the words spoken by Thomas Jefferson:

33 "Let us restore to social intercourse that harmony and that affection without which liberty and even life are but dreary things."

34 A nation is formed by the willingness of each of us to share in the responsibility for upholding the common good.

35 A government is invigorated when each of us is willing to participate in shaping the future of this nation.

36 In this election year we must define the common good and begin again to shape a common future. Let each person do his or her part. If one citizen is unwilling to participate, all of us are going to suffer. For the American idea, though it is shared by all of us, is realized in each one of us.

37 And now, what are those of us who are elected public officials supposed to do? We call ourselves public servants but I'll tell you this: we as public servants must set an example for the rest of the nation. It is hypocritical for the public official to admonish and exhort the people to uphold the common good if we are derelict in upholding the common good. More is required of public officials than slogans and handshakes and press releases. More is required. We must hold ourselves strictly accountable. We must provide the people with a vision of the future.

38 If we promise as public officials, we must deliver. If we as public officials propose, we must produce. If we say to the American people it is time for you to be sacrificial; sacrifice. If the public official says that, we (public officials) must be the first to give. We must be. And again, if we make mistakes, we must be willing to admit them. We have to do that. What we have to do is strike a balance between the idea that government should do everything and the idea, the belief, that government ought to do nothing. Strike a balance.

39 Let there be no illusions about the difficulty of forming this kind of a national community. It's tough, difficult, not easy. But a spirit of harmony will survive in America only if each of us remembers that we share a common destiny. If each of us remembers, when self-interest and bitterness seem to prevail, that we share a common destiny.

40 I have confidence that we can form this kind of national community.

41 I have confidence that the Democratic Party can lead the way. I have that confidence. We cannot improve on the system of government handed down to us by the founders of the Republic, there is no way to improve upon that. But what we can do is to find new ways to implement that system and realize our destiny.

42   Now, I began this speech by commenting to you on the uniqueness of a Barbara Jordan making the keynote address. Well I am going to close my speech by quoting a Republican President and I ask you that as you listen to these words of Abraham Lincoln, relate them to the concept of a national community in which every last one of us participates: "As I would not be slave, so I would not be master. This expresses my idea of Democracy. Whatever differs from this, to the extent of the difference is no Democracy."

OPPORTUNITIES FOR HISPANIC WOMEN:
IT'S UP TO US

Janice Payan

A keynote speech serves as a motivational preface to a meeting, conference, or convention. Typically it stresses the social importance of the work to be done by those assembled. A keynote speaker attempts to inspire and re-energize the audience by setting a theme, a tone, a *key note,* for the meeting. Janice Payan, a Vice President of U.S. West Communications, presented this keynote address on May 19, 1990 at the Adelante Mujer (Onward Women) Conference in Denver, Colorado. U.S. West Communications specializes in telecommunications products and services, including cellular telephones.

One of the most noteworthy features of this speech is Payan's pervasive use of personal narrative—the telling of personal stories (19–20, 22–24, 26–36). What are some of the persuasive functions that these stories seem to aim at accomplishing? How well do they accomplish those functions? In what ways do they reflect the values she stresses in the speech? Payan frequently relates personal stories that serve the special function of enhancing identification between her audience and herself; these stories emphasize experiences that she and the audience

---

+The text of this speech is reprinted with permission from *Vital Speeches of the Day,* September 1, 1990, pp. 697–700.

have in common (1, 10–13, 15, 17, 21). How well do you think they accomplish this purpose of identification?

The key values that Payan attempts to reinforce and re-energize in her audience are hard work/perseverance (4, 21, 32); self-confidence (6, 28, 30, 32); united effort (20, 31, 34, 36); cooperation (33); pride in heritage (20); fulfilling ones potential (10, 16, 26, 38); and taking action (6). To further underscore hard work and perseverance as values, she tells stories of three Hispanic women as examples or role models of success due to determination (7–9). She reassures her listeners that these examples are representative ones (10): "Virtually every Hispanic woman in America started with a similar slate." To emphasize taking action as a value, Payan uses a refrain to motivate action (29, 32, 33, 36): "What are you going to do about it?"

Two additional aspects of Payan's speech invite comment. First, consider her use of humor—both obvious and subtle (3–4, 16, 22, 24, 31). For any particular instance, to what extent does the humor seem a natural part of the point she is making and seem to flow naturally from the subject matter? Does any of the humor seem artificial, irrelevant, or "tacked-on"? How much does the humor add to or detract from her point? Are there other places where humor is used that we have overlooked? Second, of the "five things I wish I had known," Payan clearly enumerates the first four. What, specifically, is the fifth one? Should she have enumerated it for clarity and completeness? Why or why not?

---

1   Thank you. I felt as if you were introducing someone else because my mind was racing back 10 years, when I was sitting out there in the audience at the Adelante Mujer conference. Anonymous. *Comfortable.* Trying hard to relate to our "successful" speaker, but mostly feeling like Janice Payan, working mother, *glad for a chance to sit down.*

2   I'll let you in on a little secret. I *still am* Janice Payan, working mother. The only difference is that I have a longer job title, and that I've made a few discoveries these past 10 years that I'm eager to share with you.

3   The first is that keynote speakers at conferences like this are *not* some sort of alien creatures. Nor were they born under a lucky star. They are ordinary *Hispanic Women* who have stumbled onto an extraordinary discovery.

4   And that is: *Society lied to us.* We *do* have something up here! We *can* have not only a happy family but also a fulfilling career. We *can* succeed in *school* and *work* and *community life,* because the key is not supernatural powers, it is *perseverance.* Also known as *hard work! And God knows Hispanic women can do*

hard work!!! We've been working hard for centuries, from sun-up 'til daughter-down!

5   One of the biggest secrets around is that successful Anglos were not born under lucky stars, either. The chairman of my company, Jack MacAllister, grew up in a small town in eastern Iowa. His dad was a teacher; his mom was a mom. Jack worked, after school, sorting potatoes in the basement of a grocery store. Of course I realize, *he could have been hoeing them,* like our migrant workers. Nevertheless, Jack came from humble beginnings. And so did virtually every other corporate officer I work with. The major advantage they had was living in a culture that allowed them to *believe* they would get ahead. So more of them did.

6   It's time for *Hispanic women* to believe we can get ahead, *because we can.* And because *we must.* Our families and work-places and communities and nation need us to reach our full potential. There are jobs to be done, children to be raised, opportunities to be seized. We must look at those opportunities, choose the ones we will respond to, and *do something about them.* We must do so, for others. And we must do so, for ourselves. *Yes,* there are barriers. You're up against racism, sexism, and too much month at the end of the money. *But so was any role model you choose.*

7   Look at Patricia Diaz-Denis. Patricia was one of nine or ten children in a Mexican-American family that had low means, but high hopes. Her parents said Patricia should go to college. But they had no money. So, little by little, Patricia scraped up the money to send herself. Her boyfriend was going to be a lawyer. And he told Patricia, "You should be a lawyer, too, because *nobody can argue like you do!*" Well, Patricia didn't even know what a lawyer was, but she became one—so successful that she eventually was appointed to the Federal Communications Commission in Washington D.C.

8   Or look at Toni Pantcha, a Puerto Rican who grew up in a shack with dirt floors, no father, and often no food. But through looking and listening, she realized the power of *community*—the fact that people with very little, when working together, can create much. Dr. Pantcha has created several successful institutions in Puerto Rico, and to me, *she* is an institution. I can see the wisdom in her eyes, hear it in her voice, wisdom far beyond herself, like Mother Teresa.

9   Or look at Ada Kirby, a Cuban girl whose parents put her on a boat for Miami. Mom and Dad were to follow on the next boat, but they never arrived. So Ada grew up in an orphanage in Pueblo, and set some goals, and today is an executive director at U.S. WEST's research laboratories.

10   Each of these women was Hispanic, physically deprived, but *mentally awakened to the possibilities of building a better world,* both for others and for themselves. Virtually every Hispanic woman in America started with a similar slate. In fact, let's do a quick survey. If you were born into a home whose economic

status was something *less than rich* . . . please raise your hand. It's a good thing I didn't ask the *rich* to raise their hands. I wouldn't have known if anyone was listening. All right. So you were not born rich. As Patricia, Toni, and Ada have shown us, it doesn't matter. It's the choices we make from there on, that make the difference.

11   If you're thinking, "that's easy for *you* to say, Payan," then I'm thinking: "little do you know. . . ." If you think I got where I am because I'm smarter than you, or have more energy than you, you're wrong. If I'm so smart, why can't I parallel park? If I'm so energetic, why do I still need eight hours of sleep a night? And I mean *need*. If I hadn't had my eight hours last night, you wouldn't even want to *hear* what I'd be saying this morning!

12   I am more like you and you are more like me than you would guess. I'm a third-generation Mexican-American . . . born into a lower middle-class family right here in Denver. My parents married young; she was pregnant. My father worked only about half the time during my growing-up years. He was short on education, skills, and confidence. There were drug and alcohol problems in the family. My parents finally sent my older brother to a Catholic high school, in hopes that would help him. They sent me to the same school, to *watch* him. That was okay.

13   In public school I never could choose between the "Greasers" and the "Soshes." I wanted desperately to feel that I "belonged." *But did not like feeling that I had to deny my past to have a future.* Anybody here ever feel that way?

14   Anyway, the more troubles my brother had, the more I vowed to avoid them. So, in a way, he was my inspiration. As Victor Frankl says, there is meaning in every life. By the way, that brother later died after returning from Vietnam.

15   I was raised with typical Hispanic female expectations. In other words: If you want to *do* well in life, you'd better . . . can anybody finish that sentence? Right! *Marry well.* I liked the idea of loving and marrying someone, but I felt like he should be more than a "meal ticket." And I felt like *I* should be more than a leech. I didn't want to feel so dependent. So I set my goals on having a marriage, a family, *and* a career. I didn't talk too much about those goals, so nobody told me they bordered on *insanity* for a Hispanic woman in the 1960s.

16   At one point, I even planned to become a doctor. But Mom and Dad said "wait a minute. That takes something like 12 years of college." I had no idea how I was going to pay for *four* years of college, let alone 12. But what scared me more than the cost was the *time:* In 12 years I'd be an *old woman.* Time certainly changes your perspective on that. My advice to you is, if you want to be a doctor, go for it! It doesn't take 12 years, anyway. If your dreams include a career that requires college . . . go for it! You may be several years older when you finish, but by that time you'd be several years older if you *don't* finish college, too.

17   For all my suffering in high school, I finished near the top of my graduating class. I dreamed of attending the University of Colorado at Boulder. You want to know what my counselor said? You already know. That I should go to a business college for secretaries, at most. But I went to the University of Colorado, anyway. I arranged my own financial aid: a small grant, a low paying job, and a *big* loan. I just thank God that this was the era when jeans and sweatshirts were getting popular. That was all I had!

18   I'm going to spare you any description of my class work, except to say that it was difficult—and worth every painful minute. What I want to share with you is three of my strongest memories—and strongest learning experiences—which have nothing to do with books.

19   One concerns a philosophy professor who, I was sure, was a genius. What I liked best about this man was not the answers he had—but the questions. He asked questions about the Bible, about classic literature, about our place in the universe. He would even jot questions in the margins of our papers. And I give him a lot of credit for helping me examine my own life. I'm telling you about him because I think each of us encounter people who make us think—sometimes painfully. And I feel, very strongly, that we should listen to their questions and suffer through that thinking. We may decide everything in our lives is just like we want it. But we may also decide to change something.

20   My second big "non-book" experience was in UMAS—the United Mexican American Students. Lost in what seemed like a rich Anglo campus, UMAS was an island of familarity: people who looked like me, talked like me, and *felt* like me. We shared our fears and hopes and hurts—and did something about them. We worked hard to deal with racism on campus, persuading the university to offer Chicano studies classes. But the more racism we experienced, the angrier we became. Some members made bombs. Two of those members died. And I remember asking myself: "Am I willing to go up in smoke over my anger? Or is there another way to make a difference?" We talked a lot about this, and concluded that two wrongs don't make a right. Most of us agreed that working *within* the system was the thing to do. We also agreed not to deny our Hispanic heritage: not to become "coconuts"—brown on the outside and white on the inside—but to look for every opportunity to bring *our* culture to a table of many cultures. That outlook has helped me a great deal as a manager, because it opened me to listening to all points of view. And when a group is open to all points of view, it usually chooses the right course.

21   The third experience I wanted to share from my college days was the time they came nearest to ending prematurely. During my freshman year, I re-

ceived a call that my mother had been seriously injured in a traffic accident. Both of her legs were broken. So was her pelvis. My younger brother and sister were still at home. My father was unemployed at the time, and I was off at college. So who do you think was elected to take on the housework? Raise your hand if you think it was my father. No??? Does anybody think it was *me*? I am truly amazed at your guessing ability. Or is there something in our Hispanic culture that says the women do the housework? Of course there is. So I drove home from Boulder every weekend; shopped, cleaned, cooked, froze meals for the next week, did the laundry, you know the list. And the truth is, it did not occur to me until some time later that my father could have done some of that. I had a problem, but I was part of the problem. I *did* resist when my parents suggested I should quit school. It seemed better to try doing everything, than to give up my dream. And it was the better choice. But it was also very difficult.

22   Which reminds me of another experience. Would it be too much like a soap opera if I told you about a personal crisis? Anybody want to hear a story about myself that I've never before told in public? While still in college, I married my high school sweetheart. We were both completing our college degrees. My husband's family could not figure out why I was pursuing college instead of kids, but I was. However, it seemed like my schoolwork always came last.

23   One Saturday night I had come home from helping my Mom, dragged into our tiny married-student apartment, cooked a big dinner for my husband, and as I stood there washing the dishes, I felt a teardrop trickle down my face. Followed by a flood. Followed by sobbing. *Heaving.* If you ranked crying on a scale of 1 to 10, this was an 11. My husband came rushing in with that . . . you know . . . that "puzzled-husband" look. He asked what was wrong. Well, it took me awhile to figure it out, to be able to put it into words. When I did, they were 12 words: "I just realized I'll be doing dishes the rest of my life."

24   Now, if I thought you'd believe me, I'd tell you *my husband finished the dishes.* He did not. But we both did some thinking and talking about roles and expectations, and, over the years, have learned to share the domestic responsibilities. We realized that we were both carrying a lot of old, cultural "baggage" through life. *And so are you.*

25   I'm not going to tell you what to do about it. But I am going to urge you to realize it, think about it, and even to cry over the dishes, if you need to. You may be glad you did. As for me, *What have I learned from all this?* I've learned, as I suggested earlier, that Hispanic women have bought into a lot of myths, through the years. Or at least *I* did. And I want to tell you now, especially you younger women, the "five things I wish I had known" when I was 20, 25, even 30. In fact, some of these things I'm *still* learning—at 37. Now for that list of "five things I wish I had known."

26   First: I wish I had known that I—like most Hispanic women—was underestimating my capabilities. When I first went to work for Mountain Bell, which has since become U.S. WEST Communications—I thought the "ultimate" job I could aspire to, would be district manager. So I signed up for the courses I knew would help me achieve and handle that kind of responsibility. I watched various district managers, forming my own ideas of who was most effective—and why. I accepted whatever responsibilities and opportunities were thrown my way, generally preparing myself to be district manager.

27   My dream came true. But then it almost became a nightmare. After only 18 months on the job, the president of the company called me and asked me to go interview with *his* boss—the president of our parent company. And the next thing I knew, I had been promoted to a job *above* that of district manager. Suddenly, I was stranded in unfamiliar territory. They gave me a big office at U.S. WEST headquarters down in Englewood, where I pulled all the furniture into one corner. In fact, I sort of made a little "fort." From this direction, I could hide behind the computer. From that direction, the plants. From over here, the file cabinet. Safe at last. *Until*, a friend from downtown came to visit me. She walked in, looked around, and demanded to know: *"What is going on here?* Why was your door closed? Why are you all scrunched up in the corner?" I had all kinds of excuses. But she said: "You know what I think? I think you're afraid you don't deserve this office!"

28   As she spoke, she started dragging the plants away from my desk. For a moment, I was angry. Then afraid. Then we started laughing, and I helped her stretch my furnishings—and my confidence. And it occurred to me that had I pictured, from the beginning, that I could become an executive director, I would have been better prepared. I would have pictured myself in that big office. I would have spent more time learning executive public speaking. I would have done a lot of things. And I began to do them with my new, expanded vision of becoming an officer—which subsequently happened.

29   I just wish that I had known, in those early years, how I was underestimating my capabilities. I suspect that *you are, too.* And I wonder: *What are you going to do about it?*

30   Second: I wish I had known that power is not something others give you. It is something that comes from *within yourself . . .* and which you can then share with others.

31   In 1984, a group of minority women at U.S. WEST got together and did some arithmetic to confirm what we already knew. Minority women were woefully underrepresented in the ranks of middle and upper management. We had a better chance of winning the lottery! So we gathered our courage and took our case to the top. Fortunately, we found a sympathetic ear. The top man told us to take our case to *all* the officers. We did. But we were scared. And it

showed. We sort of "begged" for time on their calendars. We apologized for in-
terrupting their work. Asked for a little more recognition of our plight. And the
first few interviews went terribly. Then we realized: we deserve to be on their
calendars as much as anyone else does. We realized that under-utilizing a group
of employees is not an interruption of the officers' work—it *is* the officers'
work. We realized that we should not be asking for help—we should be *telling*
how *we could help*. So we did.

32   And it worked. The company implemented a special program to help
minority women achieve their full potential. Since then, several of us have moved
into middle and upper management, and more are on the way. I just wish we
had realized, in the beginning, where power really comes from. It comes from
within yourself . . . and which you can then share with others. I suspect *you* need
to be reminded of that, too. And I wonder: *What are you going to do about it?*

33   Third: I wish I had known that when I feel envious of others, I'm really just showing my lack of confidence in myself. A few years ago, I worked
closely with one of my co-workers in an employee organization. She is Hispanic. Confident. Outgoing. In fact, she's so likeable I could hardly stand her!
But as we worked together, I finally realized: She has those attributes; I have
others. And I had to ask myself: do I want to spend the time it would take to develop her attributes, or enjoy what we can accomplish by teaming-up our different skills? I realized that is the better way. I suspect that you may encounter
envy from time to time. And I wonder: *What are you going to do about it?*

34   Fourth: I wish I had realized that true success is never something you
earn single-handedly. We hear people talk about "networking" and "community" and "team-building." What they mean is an extension of my previous
idea: We can be a lot more effective working in a group than working alone.

35   This was brought home to me when I was president of our Hispanic
employees' organization at U.S. WEST Communications. I wanted my administration to be the best. So I tried to do everything myself, to be sure it was done
right. I wrote the newsletter, planned the fund-raiser, scheduled the meetings,
booked the speakers, everything. For our big annual meeting, I got the chairman of the company to speak. By then, the other officers of the group were feeling left out. Come to think of it, they *were* left out. Anyway, we were haggling
over who got to introduce our big speaker. I was determined it should be me,
since I so "obviously" had done all the work.

36   As it turned out, I missed the big meeting altogether. My older brother
died. And I did a lot of painful thinking. For one thing: I was glad my team was
there to keep things going while I dealt with my family crisis. But more important: I thought about life and death and what people would be saying if *I* had
died. Would I prefer they remember that "good ol' Janice sure did a terrific job
of arranging every last detail of the meeting?" Or that "we really enjoyed work-

ing with her?" "Together, we did a lot." All of us need to ask ourselves that question from time to time. And I wonder: *What are you going to do about it?*

37   Hispanic women in America have been victims of racism, sexism, and poverty for a long, long time. I know, because I was one of them. I also know that when you stop being a victim is largely up to you. I don't mean you should run out of here, quit your job, divorce your husband, farm out your kids, or run for President of the United States.

38   But I *do* mean that "whatever" you can dream, you can become. A couple of years ago, I came across a poem by an Augsburg College student, Devoney K. Looser, which I want to share with you now.

"I wish someone had taught me long ago
"How to touch mountains
"Instead of watching them from breathtakingly safe distances.
"I wish someone had told me sooner
"That cliffs were neither so sharp nor so distant nor so solid as they seemed.
"I wish someone had told me years ago
"That only through touching mountains can we reach peaks called beginnings, endings or exhilarating points of no return.
"I wish I had learned earlier that ten fingers and the world shout more brightly from the tops of mountains
"While life below only sighs with echoing cries.
"I wish I had realized before today
"That I can touch mountains
"But now that I know, my fingers will never cease the climb."
Please, my sisters, never, ever, cease the climb.

39   Adelante Mujer!

THE RAINBOW COALITION

Jesse Jackson

On July 17, 1984, the evening following Mario Cuomo's eloquent keynote speech, candidate Jesse Jackson addressed the Democratic National Convention. Although now it was clear that Walter Mondale would receive the nomination for president, the convention audience was very

+With some corrections added based on a recording of the speech, the text is reprinted with permission from *Vital Speeches of the Day*, November 15, 1984, pp. 77–81.

uncertain what the tone and substance of Rev. Jackson's message might be. His campaign rhetoric often was characterized by the press as confrontative and divisive. During the campaign Jackson won seven presidential primaries, brought some prisoners home after visiting Fidel Castro in Cuba, and secured freedom for an American naval pilot shot down over Syria. Delegates and viewers on national television would recall his early ethnic slur against Jews ("Hymies") and his refusal for much of the campaign to reject the support and views of Louis Farrakhan, the Black Muslim leader.

But Jackson's speech in San Francisco was one of conciliation rather than division. *Newsweek* (July 30, 1984, p. 23) observed that "without departing from the dictates of his conscience, he said nearly all the things party leaders had hoped for." *Newsweek* also contended that his speech "brought a new music to the mainstream of American oratory, stirring the spirit and wrenching the emotions in a way more reminiscent of the revival tent than the convention hall." Florida's Governor Bob Graham, according to *Newsweek,* declared: "If you are a human being and weren't affected by what you just heard, you may be beyond redemption."

Clearly Jackson's general purpose was social cohesion. He sought to re-energize the commitment of his followers in the Rainbow Coalition, to heal divisive wounds that he and others had inflicted during the campaign, and to unite all Democrats around shared values and against a common enemy, Reaganism. Justifiably his address also could be analyzed as an unofficial keynote speech (see introduction to speech by Barbara Jordan in this chapter) or as a rally speech (see introduction to Martin Luther King, Jr. speech in this chapter).

Throughout the speech he stresses the need for unity (6, 12, 14–16, 25–26, 31–33, 39, 76, 84), even to the extent of setting a personal example through apology (20–21). Fundamental values shared by Democrats are emphasized: justice, fairness, humaneness, sharing, conscience, and inclusiveness. Jackson depicts the role of diversity and competition as healthy (12, 25) and describes the inclusiveness of the Rainbow Coalition and of the Democratice Party (27–28, 34–38, 71, 86).

To demonstrate that he has a firm command of political and economic realities, both domestic and foreign, Jackson relies heavily on two forms of support for his contentions. He employs statistics to quantify the seriousness of problems (42, 44–51, 61–67). Often he supports a judgment or defines a concept by itemization of examples or qualities (2, 6, 9, 18, 22, 56, 63, 76). To what extent are his uses of statistics and examples appropriate and reasonable?

In a very real sense, Jackson's speech can be characterized as a political sermon. Much more so than is typical of American political discourse, Jackson overtly preaches. He frequently describes God's nature and role. Allusions are made to the Bible (10, 12, 34, 76, 81) and religious concepts are employed (6, 24, 79, 85), including being called to redemption and to a mission. Search Jackson's address for additional illustrations of these, or other, sermonic features. For purposes of clarity and emphasis, Jackson often structures a series of ideas in parallel sequence (33, 34–38, 44–50, 77). Indeed parallelism in the form of repetition (54, 71, 73) and refrain provide stress on some central themes, such as the need to "dream" and his view that "our time has come" (78–79, 80–84).

Metaphorical imagery is a stylistic tactic important to the power of Jackson's message. The cumulative metaphorical image, developed in different ways at various points, is of movement upward and into the light (10, 22, 32, 71, 76–77). This movement takes the form of a journey (10, 69), a rising boat (10, 42–43), and progress to higher ground (32–33, 84). In paragraph 26 Jackson vividly captures his theme of unity-in-diversity through the metaphors of the rainbow and the quilt. Alliteration is used to associate in a memorable way clusters of things or ideas, either all positive or all negative (4, 5, 20, 37, 62–63, 72). Antithesis is the phrasing of two opposing or competing items into sharp, terse contrast with one item of the pair given clear preference over the other. Jackson frequently employs antithesis to crystalize value judgements (2, 8, 18, 20–21, 37–38, 52, 54, 69, 73, 77, 79, 84–85). Pervasive antithesis is such a marked feature of the speech that the rhetorical critic cannot ignore assessing the appropriateness, clarity, and persuasive functions of specific usages.

Parts of this analysis of Jackson's speech are indebted to two insightful essays: Martha Cooper and John Makay, "Political Rhetoric and the Gospel According to Jesse Jackson," in Charles W. Kneupper, ed., *Visions of Rhetoric* (Rhetoric Society of America, 1987), pp. 208–218; Leslie A. DiMare, "Functionalizing Conflict: Jesse Jackson's Rhetorical Strategy at the 1984 Democratic National Convention," *Western Journal of Speech Communication,* 51 (Spring 1987): 218–226.

1   Tonight we come together bound by our faith in a mighty God, with genuine respect for our country, and inheriting the legacy of a great party—a Democratic Party—which is the best hope for redirecting our nation on a more humane, just, and peaceful course.

2   This is not a perfect party. We are not a perfect people. Yet, we are called to a perfect mission: our mission, to feed the hungry, to clothe the naked, to house the homeless, to teach the illiterate, to provide jobs for the jobless, and to choose the human race over the nuclear race.

3   We are gathered here this week to nominate a candidate and write a platform which will expand, unify, direct, and inspire our party and the nation to fulfill this mission.

4   My constituency is the damned, disinherited, disrespected, and the despised.

5   They are restless and seek relief. They've voted in record numbers. They have invested the faith, hope, and trust that they have in us. The Democratic Party must send them a signal that we care. I pledge my best not to let them down.

6   There is the call of conscience: redemption, expansion, healing, and unity. Leadership must heed the call of conscience, redemption, expansion, healing, and unity, for they are the key to achieving our mission.

7   Time is neutral and does not change things.

8   With courage and initiative leaders change things. No generation can choose the age or circumstances in which it is born, but through leadership it can

African-American civil rights leader Jesse Jackson speaking at a news conference.

Photo courtesy of Bettman Archive

choose to make the age in which it is born an age of enlightenment—an age of jobs, and peace, and justice.

9   Only leadership—that intangible combination of gifts, discipline, information, circumstance, courage, timing, will, and divine inspiration—can lead us out of the crisis in which we find ourselves.

10   Leadership can mitigate the misery of our nation. Leadership can part the waters and lead our nation in the direction of the Promised Land. Leadership can lift the boats stuck at the bottom.

11   I have had the rare opportunity to watch seven men, and then two, pour out their souls, offer their service, and heed the call of duty to direct the course of our nation.

12   There is a proper season for everything. There is a time to sow and a time to reap. There is a time to compete, and a time to cooperate.

13   I ask for your vote on the ballot as a vote for a new direction for this party and this nation: a vote for conviction, a vote for conscience.

14   But I will be proud to support the nominee of this convention for the president of the United States of America.

15   I have watched the leadership of our party develop and grow. My respect for both Mr. Mondale and Mr. Hart is great.

16   I have watched them struggle with the cross-winds and cross-fires of being public servants, and I believe that they will both continue to try to serve us faithfully. I am elated by the knowledge that for the first time in our history a woman, Geraldine Ferraro, will be recommended to share our ticket.

17   Throughout this campaign, I have tried to offer leadership to the Democratic Party and the nation.

18   If in my high moments, I have done some good, offered some service, shed some light, healed some wounds, rekindled some hope, or stirred someone from apathy and indifference, or in any way along the way helped somebody, then this campaign has not been in vain.

19   For friends who loved and cared for me, and for a God who spared me, and for a family who understood, I am eternally grateful.

20   If in my low moments, in word, deed, or attitude, through some error of temper, taste, or tone, I have caused anyone discomfort, created pain, or revived someone's fears, that was not my truest self.

21   If there were occasions when my grape turned into a raisin and my joy bell lost its resonance, please forgive me. Charge it to my head and not to my heart. My head is so limited in its finitude; my heart is boundless in its love for the human family. I am not a perfect servant. I am a public servant. I'm doing my best against the odds. As I develop and serve, be patient. God is not finished with me yet.

22 This campaign has taught me much: that leaders must be tough enough to fight, tender enough to cry, human enough to make mistakes, humble enough to admit them, strong enough to absorb the pain, and resilient enough to bounce back and keep on moving. For leaders, the pain is often intense. But you must smile through your tears and keep moving with the faith that there is a brighter side somewhere.

23 I went to see Hubert Humphrey three days before he died. He had just called Richard Nixon from his dying bed, and many people wondered why. And, I asked him.

24 He said, "Jesse, from this vantage point, with the sun setting in my life, all of the speeches, the political conventions, the crowds, and the great fights are behind me now. At a time like this you are forced to deal with your irreducible essence, forced to grapple with that which is really important to you. And what I have concluded about life," Hubert Humphrey said, "when all is said and done, we must forgive each other, and redeem each other, and move on."

25 Our party is emerging from one of its most hard-fought battles for the Democratic Party's presidential nomination in our history. But our healthy competition should make us better, not bitter. We must use the insight, wisdom, and experience of the late Hubert Humphrey as a balm for the wounds in our party, this nation, and the world. We must forgive each other, redeem each other, regroup, and move on.

26 Our flag is red, white, and blue, but our nation is rainbow—red, yellow, brown, black, and white—we're all precious in God's sight. America is not like a blanket—one piece of unbroken cloth, the same color, the same texture, the same size. America is more like a quilt—many patches, many pieces, many colors, many sizes, all woven and held together by a common thread.

27 The white, the Hispanic, the black, the Arab, the Jew, the woman, the Native American, the small farmer, the businessperson, the environmentalist, the peace activist, the young, the old, the lesbian, the gay, and the disabled make up the American quilt.

28 Even in our fractured state, all of us count and fit somewhere. We have proven that we can survive without each other. But we have not proven that we can win or make progress without each other. We must come together.

29 From Fannie Lee Hamer in Atlantic City in 1964 to the Rainbow Coalition in San Francisco today; from the Atlantic to the Pacific, we have experienced pain but progress as we ended American apartheid laws; we got public accommodations; we secured voting rights; we obtained open housing; as young people got the right to vote; we lost Malcolm, Martin, Medgar, Bobby and John and Viola.

30   The team that got us here must be expanded, not abandoned. Twenty years ago, tears welled up in our eyes as the bodies of Schwerner, Goodman, and Chaney were dredged from the depths of a river in Mississippi. Twenty years later, our communities, black and Jewish, are in anguish, anger, and pain.

31   Feelings have been hurt on both sides. There is a crisis in communication. Confusion is in the air. We cannot afford to lose our way. We may agree to agree, or agree to disagree on issues; we must bring back civility to these tensions.

32   We are co-partners in a long and rich religious history—the Judeo-Christian traditions. Many blacks and Jews have a shared passion for social justice at home and peace abroad. We must seek a revival of the spirit, inspired by a new vision and new possibilities. We must return to higher ground. We are bound by Moses and Jesus, but also connected to Islam and Mohammed.

33   These three great religions—Judaism, Christianity, and Islam—were all born in the revered and holy city of Jerusalem. We are bound by Dr. Martin Luther King, Jr. and Rabbi Abraham Heschel, crying out from their graves for us to reach common ground. We are bound by shared blood and shared sacrifices. We are much too intelligent; much too bound by our Judeo-Christian heritage; much too victimized by racism, sexism, militarism, and anti-Semitism; much too threatened as historical scapegoats to go on divided one from another. We must turn from finger-pointing to clasped hands. We must share our burdens and our joys with each other once again. We must turn to each other and not on each other and choose higher ground.

34   Twenty years later, we cannot be satisfied by just restoring the old coalition. Old wine skins must make room for new wine. We must heal and expand. The Rainbow Coalition is making room for Arab-Americans. They too know the pain and hurt of racial and religious rejection. They must not continue to be made pariahs. The Rainbow Coalition is making room for Hispanic-Americans who this very night are living under the threat of the Simpson-Mazzoli bill, and farm workers from Ohio who are fighting the Campbell Soup Company with a boycott to achieve legitimate workers rights.

35   The Rainbow is making room for the Native Americans, the most exploited people of all, a people with the greatest moral claim amongst us. We support them as they seek the restoration of their ancient land and claim amongst us. We support them as they seek the restoration of land and water rights, as they seek to preserve their ancestral homelands and the beauty of a land that was once all theirs. They can never receive a fair share for all that they have given us, but they must finally have a fair chance to develop their great resources and to preserve their people and their culture.

36   The Rainbow Coalition includes Asian-Americans, now being killed in our streets—scapegoats for the failures of corporate, industrial, and economic policies. The Rainbow is making room for the young Americans. Twenty years ago, our young people were dying in a war for which they could not even vote. But 20 years later, Young America has the power to stop a war in Central America and the responsibility to vote in great numbers. Young America must be politically active in 1984. The choice is war or peace. We must make room for Young America.

37   The Rainbow includes disabled veterans. The color scheme fits in the Rainbow. The disabled have their handicap revealed and their genius concealed; while the able-bodied have their genius revealed and their disability concealed. But ultimately we must judge people by their values and their contribution. Don't leave anybody out. I would rather have Roosevelt in a wheelchair than Reagan on a horse.

38   The Rainbow is making room for small farmers. They have suffered tremendously under the Reagan regime. They will either receive 90 percent parity or 100 percent charity. We must address their concerns and make room for them. The Rainbow includes lesbians and gays. No American citizen ought be denied equal protection under the law.

39   We must be unusually committed and caring as we expand our family to include new members. All of us must be tolerant and understanding as the fears and anxieties of the rejected and of the party leadership express themselves in many different ways. Too often what we call hate—as if it were deeply rooted in some philosophy or strategy—is simply ignorance, anxiety, paranoia, fear, and insecurity. To be strong leaders, we must be long-suffering as we seek to right the wrongs of our party and our nation. We must expand our party, heal our party, and unify our party. That is our mission in 1984.

40   We are often reminded that we live in a great nation—and we do. But it can be greater still. The Rainbow is mandating a new definition of greatness. We must not measure greatness from the mansion down, but the manger up.

41   Jesus said that we should not be judged by the bark we wear but by the fruit that we bear. Jesus said that we must measure greatness by how we treat the least of these.

42   President Reagan says the nation is in recovery. Those 90,000 corporations that made a profit last year but paid no federal taxes are recovering. The 37,000 military contractors who have benefited from Reagan's more than doubling the military budget in peacetime, surely they are recovering. The big corporations and rich individuals who received the bulk of the three-year, multibillion tax cut from Mr. Reagan are recovering. But no such recovery is under way for the least of these. Rising tides don't lift all boats, particularly those stuck on the bottom.

43   For the boats stuck at the bottom there is a misery index. This administration has made life more miserable for the poor. Its attitude has been contemptuous. Its policies and programs have been cruel and unfair to working people. They must be held accountable in November for increasing infant mortality among the poor. In Detroit, one of the great cities of the Western world, babies are dying at the same rate as Honduras, the most underdeveloped nation in our hemisphere.

44   This administration must be held accountable for policies that contribute to the growing poverty in America. Under President Reagan, there are now 34 million people in poverty, 15 percent of our nation. Twenty-three million are white, 11 million black, Hispanic, Asian, and others. Mostly women and children. By the end of this year, there will be 41 million people in poverty. We cannot stand idly by. We must fight for change, now.

45   Under this regime we look at Social Security. The 1981 budget cuts included nine permanent Social Security benefit cuts totaling $20 billion over five years.

46   Small businesses have suffered under Reagan tax cuts. Only 18 percent of total business tax cuts went to them—82 percent to big business.

47   Health care under Mr. Reagan has been sharply cut.

48   Education under Mr. Reagan has been cut 25 percent.

49   Under Mr. Reagan there are now 9.7 million female-head families. They represent 16 percent of all families, half of all of them are poor. Seventy percent of all poor children live in a house headed by a woman, where there is no man.

50   Under Mr. Reagan, the administration has cleaned up only 6 of 546 priority toxic waste dumps.

51   Farmers' real net income was only about half its level in 1979.

52   Many say that the race in November will be decided in the South. President Reagan is depending on the conservative South to return him to office. But the South, I tell you, is unnaturally conservative. The South is the poorest region in our nation and, therefore, has the least to conserve. In his appeal to the South, Mr. Reagan is trying to substitute flags and prayer cloths for food, and clothing, and education, health care, and housing. But President Reagan who asks us to pray, and I believe in prayer—I've come this way by the power of prayer. But, we must watch false prophecy.

53   He cuts energy assistance to the poor, cuts breakfast programs from children, cuts lunch programs from children, cuts job training from children and then says, to an empty table, "let us pray." Apparently he is not familiar with the structure of a prayer. You thank the Lord for the food that you are about to receive, not the food that just left.

54   I think that we should pray. But don't pray for the food that left, pray for the man that took the food to leave. We need a change. We need a change in November.

55   Under President Reagan, the misery index has risen for the poor, but the danger index has risen for everybody.

56   Under this administration we've lost the lives of our boys in Central America, in Honduras, in Granada, in Lebanon.

57   A nuclear standoff in Europe. Under this administration, one-third of our children believe they will die in a nuclear war. The danger index is increasing in this world.

58   With all the talk about defense against Russia, the Russian submarines are closer and their missiles are more accurate. We live in a world tonight more miserable and a world more dangerous.

59   While Reagonomics and Reaganism is talked about often, so often we miss the real meaning. Reaganism is a spirit. Reaganomics represents the real economic facts of life.

60   In 1980, Mr. George Bush, a man with reasonable access to Mr. Reagan, did an analysis of Mr. Reagan's economic plan. Mr. Bush concluded Reagan's plan was "voodoo economics." He was right. Third-party candidate John Anderson said that the combination of military spending, tax cuts, and a balanced budget by '84 could be accomplished with blue smoke and mirrors. They were both right.

61   Mr. Reagan talks about a dynamic recovery. There is some measure of recovery, three and a half years later. Unemployment has inched just below where it was when he took office in 1981. But there are still 8.1 million people officially unemployed, 11 million working only parttime jobs. Inflation has come down, but let's analyze for a moment who has paid the price for this superficial economic recovery.

62   Mr. Reagan curbed inflation by cutting consumer demand. He cut consumer demand with conscious and callous fiscal and monetary policy. He used the federal budget to deliberately induce unemployment and curb social spending. He then waged and supported tight monetary policies of the Federal Reserve Board to deliberately drive up interest rates—again to curb consumer demand created through borrowing.

63   Unemployment reached 10.7 percent; we experienced skyrocketing interest rates; our dollar inflated abroad; there were record bank failures; record farm foreclosures; record business bankruptcies; record budget deficits; record trade deficits. Mr. Reagan brought inflation down by destablizing our economy and distrupting family life.

64   He promised in 1980 a balanced budget, but instead we now have a record $200 billion budget deficit. Under President Reagan, the cumulative budget deficit for his four years is more than the sum total of deficits from George Washington to Jimmy Carter combined. I tell you, we need a change.

65   How is he paying for these short-term jobs? Reagan's economic recovery is being financed by deficit spending—$200 billion a year. Military spending, a major cause of this deficit, is projected over the next five years to be nearly $2 trillion, and will cost about $40,000 for every taxpaying family.

66   When the government borrows $200 billion annually to finance the deficit, this encourages the private sector to make its money off of interest rates as opposed to development and economic growth. Even money abroad—we don't have enough money domestically to finance the debt, so we are now borrowing money abroad, from foreign banks, government, and financial institutions—$40 billion in 1983; $70 to $80 billion in 1984 (40 percent of our total); over $100 billion (50 percent of our total) in 1985.

67   By 1989, it is projected that 50 percent of all individual income taxes will be going to pay just for the interest on that debt. The U.S. used to be the largest exporter of capital, but under Mr. Reagan we will quite likely become the largest debtor nation. About two weeks ago, on July 4, we celebrated our Declaration of Independence. Yet every day, supply-side economics is making our nation more economically dependent and less economically free. Five to six percent of our gross national product is now being eaten up with President Reagan's budget deficit.

68   To depend on foreign military powers to protect our national security would be foolish, making us dependent and less secure. Yet Reaganomics has us increasingly dependent on foreign economic sources. This consumer-led but deficit-financed recovery is unbalanced and artificial.

69   We have a challenge as Democrats: to point a way out. Democracy guarantees opportunity, not success. Democracy guarantees the right to participate, not a license for either the majority or a minority to dominate. The victory for the Rainbow Coalition in the platform debates today was not whether we won or lost; but that we raised the right issues. We can afford to lose the vote; issues are non-negotiable. We cannot afford to avoid raising the right questions. Our self respect and our moral integrity were at stake. Our heads are perhaps bloodied but now bowed. Our backs are straight. We can go home and face our people. Our vision is clear. When we think, on this journey from slaveship to championship, we've gone from the planks of the boardwalk in Atlantic City in 1964 to fighting to have the right planks in the platform in San Francisco in '84. There is a deep and abiding sense of joy in our soul, despite the tears in our eyes. For while there are missing planks, there is a solid foundation upon which to build. Our party can win. But we must provide hope that will inspire people to struggle and achieve; provide a plan to show the way out of our dilemma, and then lead the way.

70   In 1984, my heart is made to feel glad because I know there is a way out. Justice. The requirement for rebuilding America is justice. The linchpin of progressive politics in our nation will not come from the North; they in fact will come from the South. That is why I argue over and over again—from Lynchburg, Va., down to Texas, there is only one black congressperson out of 115. Nineteen years later, we're locked out of the Congress, the Senate, and the governor's mansion. What does this large black vote mean? Why do I fight to end second primaries and fight gerrymandering and annexation and at large. Why do we fight over that? Because I tell you, you cannot hold someone in the ditch unless you linger there with them. If we want a change in this nation, reinforce that Voting Rights Act—we'll get 12 to 20 black, Hispanic, female, and progressive congresspersons from the South. We can save the cotton, but we've got to fight the boll weevil—we've got to make a judgment.

71   It's not enough to hope ERA will pass; how can we pass ERA? If blacks vote in great numbers, progressive whites win. It's the only way progressive whites win. If blacks vote in great numbers, Hispanics win. If blacks, Hispanics, and progressive whites vote, women win. When women win, children win. When women and children win, workers win. We must all come up together. We must come up together.

72   I tell you, with all of our joy and excitement, we must not save the world and lose our souls; we should never short-circuit enforcement of the Voting Rights Act at every level. If one of us rises, all of us must rise. Justice is the way out. Peace is a way out. We should not act as if nuclear weaponry is negotiable and debatable. In this world in which we live, we dropped the bomb on Japan and felt guilty. But in 1984, other folks also got bombs. This time, if we drop the bomb, six minutes later, we, too, will be destroyed. It's not about dropping the bomb on somebody; it's about dropping the bomb on everybody. We must choose developed minds over guided missiles, and think it out and not fight it out. It's time for a change.

73   Our foreign policy must be characterized by mutual respect, not by gunboat diplomacy, big stick diplomacy, and threats. Our nation at its best feeds the hungry. Our nation at its worst will mine the harbors of Nicaragua; at its worst, will try to overthrow that government; at its worst, will cut aid to American education and increase aid to El Salvador; at its worst our nation will have partnership with South Africa. That's a moral disgrace. It's a moral disgrace. It's a moral disgrace.

74   When we look at Africa, we cannot just focus on apartheid in southern Africa. We must fight for trade with Africa, and not just aid to Africa. We cannot stand idly by and say we will not relate to Nicaragua unless they have elections there and then embrace military regimes in Africa, overthrowing Democratic governments in Nigeria and Liberia and Ghana. We must fight for democracy all around the world, and play the game by one set of rules.

75   Peace in this world. Our present formula for peace in the Middle East is inadequate; it will not work. There are 22 nations in the Middle East. Our nation must be able to talk and act and influence all of them. We must build upon Camp David and measure human rights by one yardstick. In that region we have too many interests and too few friends.

76   There is a way out. Jobs. Put Americans back to work. When I was a child growing up in Greenville, S.C. the Rev. Sample who used to preach every so often a sermon linked to Jesus. He said, if I be lifted up, I'll draw all men unto me. I didn't quite understand what he meant as a child growing up. But I understand a little better now. If you raise up truth, it's magnetic. It has a way of drawing people. With all this confusion in this convention—the bright lights and parties and big fun—we must raise up the simple proposition: if we lift up a program to feed the hungry, they'll come running. If we lift up a program to study war no more, our youth will come running. If we lift up a program to put America back to work, an alternative to welfare and despair, they will come working. If we cut that military budget without cutting our defense, and use that money to rebuild bridges and put steelworkers back to work, and use that money, and provide jobs for our cities, and use that money to build schools and train teachers and educate our children, and build hospitals and train doctors and train nurses, the whole nation will come running to us.

77   As I leave you now, and we vote in this convention and get ready to go back across this nation in a couple of days, in this campaign, I'll try to be faithful to my promise. I'll live in the old barrios, and ghettos and reservations, and housing projects. I have a message for our youth. I challenge them to put hope in their brains, and not dope in their veins. I told them like Jesus, I, too, was born in a slum, but just because you're born in a slum, does not mean the slum is born in you, and you can rise above it if your mind is made up. I told them in every slum, there are two sides. When I see a broken window, that's the slummy side. Train that youth to be a glazier, that's the sunny side. When I see a missing brick, that's the slummy side. Let that child in the union, and become a brickmason, and build, that's the sunny side. When I see a missing door, that's the slummy side. Train some youth to become a carpenter, that's the sunny side. When I see the vulgar words and hieroglyphics of destitution on the walls, that's the slummy side. Train some youth to be a painter, an artist—that's the sunny

side. We need this place looking for the sunny side because there's a brighter side somewhere. I am more convinced than ever that we can win. We'll vault up the rough side of the mountain; we can win. I just want young America to do me one favor. Just one favor.

78   Exercise the right to dream. You must face reality—that which is. But then dream of the reality that ought to be, that must be. Live beyond the pain of reality with the dream of a bright tomorrow. Use hope and imagination as weapons of survival and progress. Use love to motivate you and obligate you to serve the human family.

79   Young America, dream! Choose the human race over the nuclear race. Bury the weapons and don't burn the people. Dream of a new value system. Teachers, who teach for life, and not just for a living, teach because they can't help it. Dream of lawyers more concerned about justice than a judgeship. Dream of doctors more concerned about public health than personal wealth. Dream of preachers and priests who will prophesy and not just profiteer. Preach and dream. Our time has come.

80   Our time has come. Suffering breeds character. Character breeds faith. And in the end, faith will not disappoint.

81   Our time has come. Our faith, hope, and dreams will prevail. Our time has come. Weeping has endured for the night. And, now joy cometh in the morning.

82   Our time has come. No graves can hold our body down.

83   Our time has come. No lie can live forever.

84   Our time has come. We must leave racial battleground and come to economic common ground and moral higher ground. America, our time has come.

85   We've come from disgrace to Amazing Grace, our time has come.

86   Give me your tired, give me your poor, your huddled masses who yearn to breathe free, and come November, there will be a change because our time has come.

87   Thank you and God bless you.

FAREWELL TO THE CADETS

Douglas MacArthur

General Douglas MacArthur became a national hero during World War II as the Supreme Allied Commander in the Pacific. Perhaps his greatest moment was when he successfully returned to Manila after the Japanese early in the war had driven American forces from the Phillippines. Upon leaving Manila, MacArthur had vowed, "I shall return." At the close of the war, he commanded the Allied occupational forces in Japan, and his skillful supervision of the restoration of the Japanese nation was widely acclaimed, even by the Japanese. When President Truman ordered American forces into Korea in 1950 to stop the invasion of the South by the North, General MacArthur was again placed in command of the expedition. However, he became an outspoken critic of the administration's Korean policy, and, as a consequence, President Truman relieved General MacArthur of his command in 1951. MacArthur returned to America to a hero's welcome. He accepted an invitation to address a joint session of Congress, and his concluding remarks on the ballad of the "Old Soldier" captured the imagination of the American people. He died on April 5, 1964.

In leaving formal, active association with a group or position, persons sometimes deliver farewell speeches; at times the farewell is combined with an acceptance of an award from the group for outstanding service. In such a situation a critic could assess the ways in which the speaker satisfies various expectations probably held by audiences on such occasions: (1) Expression of gratitude for the award presented and/or for the cooperation and opportunities provided by the group. (2) Expression of sadness and other emotions on leaving the group or position. (3) Recollection of praiseworthy accomplishments or memorable events shared with the group. (4) Praise for the group's values, principles, and goals, along with urging rededication to their continuation. (5) Discussion of the speaker's reasons for leaving: sometimes this even may mean discussion of disagreements or conflicts with superiors or

---

+This speech was taken from a recording of the address and is printed by permission of the MacArthur Memorial Foundation.

others that led to the departure. (6) Description of the future in broad, sometimes vivid, terms if the group's values and efforts are perpetuated.

On May 12, 1962, General MacArthur, an honor graduate of the United States Military Academy at West Point, went there to receive the Sylvanus Thayer award for service to his nation. The Old Soldier, then 82, accepted the award and, despite failing health, made a moving and inspirational farewell speech to the cadets of the academy, an institution he had served earlier as superintendent. He sought to reinforce and defend the cadets' commitment to the values of "duty, honor, country," the motto inscribed on the academy coat of arms. Although MacArthur originally was gifted with an exceptionally rich and resonant voice, it was now hoarse and often faint. He spoke slowly and deliberately, gaining intensity with phrases such as "faint bugles blowing reveille" and "the strange, mournful mutter of the battlefield."

MacArthur had employed many of the key ideas and vivid phrases in this speech repeatedly in varied contexts in earlier speeches throughout his career. And parts of two paragraphs (9, 25) were derived, without acknowledging the sources, from the previously published words of other people.[1] Although his powers of rhetorical invention might be criticized as being limited, an ability to combine rhetorical elements for moving impact nevertheless is reflected in this address.

As you analyze this speech, you should focus upon several important rhetorical factors. The first is credibility of source. MacArthur, a legendary war hero, doubtlessly enjoyed high ethos with the cadets. Moreover, the text of the speech reveals that MacArthur was fully aware of ethos factors. Second, MacArthur was a conscious speech stylist, a fact readily apparent in this address; imagery, metaphor, antithesis, parallelism, and elegance of language are pronounced. Do any of his images seem strained, or are any of his metaphors mixed? Third, note his strategy of linking "duty, honor, country" with desirable consequences (paragraphs 7–10) and with valiant men (11–18). And in paragraph 6 he promotes these values by asserting that blameworthy men consistently downgrade them. Finally, to what higher values does MacArthur relate "duty, honor, country" in order to defend the worth of the cadets' motto?

---

[1]Stephen Robb, "Pre-Inventional Criticism: The Speaking of Douglas MacArthur," in G. P. Mohrmann et al., eds., *Explorations in Rhetorical Criticism* (University Park: Pennsylvania State University Press, 1973), pp. 178–90.

1   As I was leaving the hotel this morning, a doorman asked me, "Where are you bound for, General?" And when I replied, "West Point," he remarked, "Beautiful place. Have you ever been there before?"

2   No human being could fail to be deeply moved by such a tribute as this, coming from a profession I have served so long and a people I have loved so well.

3   It fills me with an emotion I cannot express. But this award is not intended primarily to honor a personality, but to symbolize a great moral code— the code of conduct and chivalry of those who guard this beloved land of culture and ancient descent. That is the animation of this medallion. For all eyes and for all time it is an expression of the ethics of the American soldier. That I should be integrated in this way with so noble an ideal arouses a sense of pride and yet of humility, which will be with me always.

4   Duty, honor, country: those three hallowed words reverently dictate what you want to be, what you can be, what you will be. They are your rallying points to build courage when courage seems to fail, to regain faith when there seems to be little cause for faith, to create hope when hope becomes forlorn.

5   Unhappily, I possess neither that eloquence of diction, that poetry of imagination, nor that brilliance of metaphor to tell you all that they mean.

6   The unbelievers will say they are but words, but a slogan, but a flamboyant phrase. Every pedant, every demogogue, every cynic, every hypocrite, every troublemaker, and, I am sorry to say, some others of an entirely different character, will try to downgrade them even to the extent of mockery and ridicule.

7   But these are some of the things they do. They build your basic character. They mold you for your future roles as the custodians of the nation's defense. They make you strong enough to know when you are weak and brave enough to face yourself when you are afraid.

8   They teach you to be proud and unbending in honest failure, but humble and gentle in success; not to substitute words for action; not to seek the path of comfort, but to face the stress and spur of difficulty and challenge; to learn to stand up in the storm, but to have compassion on those who fall; to master yourself before you seek to master others; to have a heart that is clean, a goal that is high; to learn to laugh, yet never forget how to weep; to reach into the future, yet never neglect the past; to be serious, yet never take yourself too seriously; to be modest so that you will remember the simplicity of true greatness, the open mind of true wisdom, the meekness of true strength.

9   They give you a temper of the will, a quality of the imagination, a vigor of the emotions, a freshness of the deep springs of life, a temperamental predominance of courage over timidity, of an appetite for adventure over love of ease.

10   They create in your heart the sense of wonder, the unfailing hope of what next, and the joy and inspiration of life. They teach you this way to be an officer and a gentleman.

11   And what sort of soldiers are those you are to lead? Are they reliable? Are they brave? Are they capable of victory? Their story is known to all of you. It is the story of the American man-at-arms. My estimate of him was formed on the battlefields many, many years ago, and has never changed. I regarded him then, as I regard him now, as one of the world's noblest figures—not only as one of the finest military characters but also as one of the most stainless.

12   His name and fame are the birthright of every American citizen. In his youth and strength, his love and loyalty, he gave all that mortality can give. He needs no eulogy from me or from any other man. He has written his own history and written it in red on his enemy's breast.

13   But when I think of his patience under adversity, of his courage under fire, and his modesty in victory, I am filled with an emotion of admiration I cannot put into words. He belongs to history as furnishing one of the greatest examples of successful patriotism. He belongs to posterity as the instructor of future generations in the principles of liberty and freedom. He belongs to the present—to us—by his virtues and by his achievements.

14   In twenty campaigns, on a hundred battlefields, around a thousand campfires, I have witnessed that enduring fortitude, that patriotic self-abnegation, and that invincible determination which have carved his statue in the hearts of his people.

15   From one end of the world to the other, he has drained deep the chalice of courage. As I listened to those songs, in memory's eye I could see those staggering columns of the First World War, bending under soggy packs on many a weary march, from dripping dusk to drizzling dawn, slogging ankle-deep through the mire of shell-shocked roads; to form grimly for the attack, blue-lipped, covered with sludge and mud, chilled by the wind and rain, driving home to their objective, and, for many, to the judgment seat of God.

16   I do not know the dignity of their birth, but I do know the glory of their death. They died unquestioning, uncomplaining, with faith in their hearts, and on their lips the hope that we would go on to victory.

17   Always for them: duty, honor, country. Always their blood, and sweat, and tears, as we sought the way and the light and the truth. And 20 years after, on the other side of the globe, again the filth of murky foxholes, the stench of ghostly trenches, the slime of dripping dugouts, those boiling suns of relentless heat, those torrential rains of devastating storms, the loneliness and utter desolation of jungle trails, the bitterness of long separation from those they loved

and cherished, the deadly pestilence of tropical disease, the horror of stricken areas of war.

18   Their resolute and determined defense, their swift and sure attack, their indomitable purpose, their complete and decisive victory—always victory, always through the bloody haze of their last reverberating shot, the vision of gaunt, ghastly men, reverently following your password of duty, honor, country.

19   The code which those words perpetuate embraces the highest moral law and will stand the test of any ethics or philosophies ever promulgated for the uplift of mankind. Its requirements are for the things that are right and its restraints are from the things that are wrong. The soldier, above all other men, is required to practice the greatest act of religious training—sacrifice. In battle and in the face of danger and death he discloses those divine attributes which his Maker gave when he created man in his own image. No physical courage and no brute instinct can take the place of the divine help, which alone can sustain him. However horrible the incidents of war may be, the soldier who is called upon to offer and to give his life for his country is the noblest development of mankind.

20   You now face a new world, a world of change. The thrust into outer space of the satellite spheres and missiles marks a beginning of another epoch in the long story of mankind. In the five-or-more billions of years the scientists tell us it has taken to form the earth, in the three-or-more billion years of development of the human race, there has never been a more abrupt or staggering evolution.

21   We deal now, not with things of this world alone, but with the illimitable distances and as yet unfathomed distances of the universe. We are reaching out for a new and boundless frontier. We speak in strange terms of harnessing the cosmic energy; of making winds and tides work for us; of creating synthetic materials to supplement or even replace our old standard basics; to purify sea water for our drink; of mining ocean floors for new fields of wealth and food; of disease preventatives to expand life into the hundreds of years; of controlling the weather for a more equitable distribution of heat and cold, of rain and shine; of space ships to the moon; of the primary target in war no longer limited to the armed forces of an enemy, but instead to include his civil populations; of ultimate conflict between a united human race and the sinister forces of some other planetary galaxy; of such dreams and fantasies as to make life the most exciting of all times.

22   And though all this welter of change and development your mission remains fixed, determined, inviolable. It is to win our wars. Everything else in your professional career is but corollary to this vital dedication. All other public purposes, all other public projects, all other public needs, great or small, will

find others for their accomplishments; but you are the ones who are trained to fight.

23   Yours is the profession of arms, the will to win, the sure knowledge that in war there is no substitute for victory, that if you lose the nation will be destroyed, that the very obsession of your public service must be duty, honor, country.

24   Others will debate the controversial issues, national and international, which divide men's minds. But serene, calm, aloof, you stand as the nation's war guardians, as its lifeguard from the raging tides of international conflict, as its gladiator in the arena of battle. For a century-and-a-half you have defended, guarded, and protected its hallowed traditions of liberty and freedom, of right and justice.

25   Let civilian voices argue the merits or demerits of our processes of government: whether our strength is being sapped by deficit financing indulged in too long; by federal paternalism grown too mighty; by power groups grown too arrogant; by politics grown too corrupt; by crime grown too rampant; by morals grown too low; by taxes grown too high; by extremists grown too violent; whether our personal liberties are as firm and complete as they should be.

26   These great national problems are not for your professional participation or military solution. Your guidepost stands out like a tenfold beacon in the night: duty, honor, country.

27   You are the leaven which binds together the entire fabric of our national system of defense. From your ranks come the great captains who hold the nation's destiny in their hands the moment the war tocsin sounds.

28   The long, gray line has never failed us. Were you to do so, a million ghosts in olive drab, in brown khaki, in blue and gray, would rise from their white crosses, thundering those magic words: duty, honor, country.

29   This does not mean that you are warmongers. On the contrary, the soldier above all other people prays for peace, for he must suffer and bear the deepest wounds and scars of war. But always in our ears ring the ominous words of Plato, that wisest of all philosophers: "Only the dead have seen the end of war."

30   The shadows are lengthening for me. The twilight is here. My days of old have vanished—tone and tints. They have gone glimmering through the dreams of things that were. Their memory is one of wondrous beauty watered by tears and coaxed and caressed by the smiles of yesterday. I listen vainly, but with thirsty ear, for the witching melody of faint bugles blowing reveille, of far drums beating the long roll.

31   In my dreams I hear again the crash of guns, the rattle of musketry, the strange, mournful mutter of the battlefield. But in the evening of my memory

always I come back to West Point. Always there echoes and reechoes: duty, honor, country.

32 Today marks my final roll call with you. But I want you to know that when I cross the river, my last conscious thoughts will be of the Corps, and the Corps, and the Corps.

33 I bid you farewell.

Eulogies for the *Challenger* Astronauts

Ronald Reagan

On January 28, 1986, at 11:39 A.M. EST, only 70 seconds after lift-off from Cape Canaveral, Florida, flying at almost 2000 miles per hour, the space shuttle, *Challenger,* exploded and all seven crew members were killed. The flight was being shown live on national television and the tragedy stunned the nation. President Ronald Reagan delivered two eulogies in response to the disaster.

Speeches of tribute, such as testimonials for living persons and eulogies for the dead, typically reflect rather traditional rhetorical resources to praise accomplishments and acknowledge virtues. The speaker may remind us that the person being paid tribute possesses various qualities of character, such as courage, justice, wisdom, temperance, concern for others, faith, charity, generosity, courtesy, dedication, honesty, industriousness, or humility. The speaker could describe qualities of the person's accomplishments: bravery: extreme difficulty; acknowledgement of excellence by others; personal harm incurred; a "first"; the "best"; the unexpected; the "only"; frequency of achievement; a "last" time ever. Immediate and longterm influences could be stressed, perhaps by describing the "debts" that society owes the person and how we can continue to "repay" that indebtedness through our attitudes and actions, how we can carry on the person's values and commitments. Speakers frequently emphasize the praiseworthy values, ideals, motives, and life goals held by the person. Among the kinds of rhetorical supporting ma-

---

✝These eulogies are reprinted from *Weekly Compilation of Presidential Documents*, 22 (February 3, 1986), pp. 104–105, 117–119.

terials typically used in speeches of tribute are factual examples, testimony from notables, experts, or literary sources, narration of incidents, comparison to other persons, Biblical quotations or allusions, and quotations or paraphrases of the person's own words.

By summarizing and slightly modifying the extensive research of Kathleen Jamieson, we can describe four characteristic functions of eulogies in European-American cultures.[1] First, by publicly confirming the person's death, the eulogy helps us overcome our temporary denial of the reality of the death; we overcome our initial reaction of "I just don't believe it." Second, the uneasy realization of our own eventual death is lessened by descriptions of ways in which the deceased "lives on" in history, in heaven, through good works, through followers, or through the person's family. Third, a recounting of the life and virtues of the person *in the past tense* allows us to reorient our own relationship with the deceased from present to past and from physical encounter to memory. Finally, by expressing community solidarity and social cohesion, the eulogy reassures us that our community or group will survive the death. To promote such social cohesion, audiences expect that the eulogist will not "speak ill of the dead," although some eulogists may mentioned modest "faults" in order to "humanize" the person. Sometimes the eulogist provides a rationale for the death so that we do not feel the death was in vain or due to pure chance. Such reasons might include God's will, fulfillment of destiny, evil conditions in society, or even a conspiratorial plot. Another study of eulogies describes three major purposes of the eulogistic form: (1) to express appropriate personal and audience grief; (2) to deepen appreciaton and respect for the deceased; and (3) to give the audience strength for the present and inspiration for the future.[2]

At 5:00 P.M. on the same day of the *Challenger* tragedy, the day on which he was scheduled to present his annual State of the Union address, President Ronald Reagan offered a brief eulogy nationally televised from the oval Office at the White House. At the outset he expresses appropriate personal grief (1–2) and grief on behalf of the audience (3–4). He deepens respect and appreciation for the dead by praising their courage (3–4) and by depicting them as pioneers (5) and explorers (6). He promotes solidarity in the "community" of space program employees by expressing faith and respect for the program (7) and

[1]Kathleen M. Jamieson, *Critical Anthology of Public Speech* (Chicago: Science Research Associates, 1978), pp. 40–41.

[2]Paul C. Brownlow and Beth Davis, "'A Certainty of Honor': The Eulogies of Adlai Stevenson," *Central States Speech Journal*, 25 (Fall 1974), 217–24.

by praising their dedication and professionalism (9). Reagan reassures American citizens that in a sense the astronauts' example and efforts will "live on" through the continuation of a vigorous manned space program; they will not have died in vain (8).

Reagan mentions two coincidences, one directly (10) and one indirectly (3). They place the tragedy in a larger historical context of exploration. They may even imply that fate or destiny was at work. The conclusion (11) is a moving and poetic confirmation of the astronauts' death. The quotation is paraphrased from "High Flight," a sonnet by John Gillespie Magee, Jr., a World War II American airman who died in the service of the Royal Canadian Air Force.

Peggy Noonan, a member of Reagan's speechwriting staff, wrote most of the January 28 eulogy. For her account, see Peggy Noonan, *What I Saw at the Revolution* (Random House, 1990), pp. 252–259. For an extensive analysis of the January 28 eulogy, see Steven M. Minter, "Reagan's Challenger Tribute: Combing Generic Constraints and Situational Demands," *Central States Speech Journal,* 37 (Fall 1986): 158–165.

Shortly before noon on January 31, 1986, President Reagan delivered a second and longer eulogy (10 minutes) at the formal memorial service for the *Challenger* astronauts. The scene was the mall in front of the Avionics Building at the Johnson Space Center in Houston, Texas, and the audience was estimated at 10,000, including 2000 space program employees, 90 members of the House and Senate, and 200 relatives of the astronauts. The memorial service was nationally televised.

Reagan's introductory sentence succinctly reflects two purposes of any eulogy: to express personal and collective grief and to give the audience strength for the present and hope for the future. Use of the parallel structure, "we remember" (6–12), forcefully confirms the reality of their deaths, a reality made more emotionally moving through the personal details provided about each of their lives. The President praises values and virtues exemplified in the way "they led . . . and lost their lives" (3), especially perseverance (10, 12) and heroism (7–8, 13, 15). As in the first eulogy, he honors the astronauts' achievement by comparison to the explorations of American pioneers (16). Again Reagan reassures Americans that the astronauts will continue to live in several ways: in heaven (21); through our following their example of courage and character (17); and through continuation of the space shuttle program (10, 18–20).

Address to the Nation. January 28, 1986

1   Ladies and gentlemen, I'd planned to speak to you tonight to report on the state of the Union, but the events of earlier today have led me to change those plans. Today is a day for mourning and remembering.

2   Nancy and I are pained to the core by the tragedy of the shuttle *Challenger*. We know we share this pain with all of the people of our country. This is truly a national loss.

3   Nineteen years ago, almost to the day, we lost three astronauts in a terrible accident on the ground. But we've never lost an astronaut in flight; we've never had a tragedy like this. And perhaps we've forgotten the courage it took for the crew of the shuttle; but they, the *Challenger* Seven, were aware of the dangers, but overcame them and did their jobs brilliantly. We mourn seven heroes: Michael Smith, Dick Scobee, Judith Resnik, Ronald McNair, Ellison Onizuka, Gregory Jarvis, and Christa McAuliffe. We mourn their loss as a nation together.

4   For the family of the seven, we cannot bear, as you do, the full impact of this tragedy. But we feel the loss, and we're thinking about you so very much. Your loved ones were daring and brave, and they had that special grace, that special spirit that says, "Give me a challenge and I'll meet it with joy." They had a hunger to explore the universe and discover its truths. They wished to serve, and they did. They served all of us.

5   We've grown used to wonders in this century. It's hard to dazzle us. But for 25 years the United States space program has been doing just that. We've grown used to the idea of space, and perhaps we forget that we've only just begun. We're still pioneers. They, the members of the *Challenger* crew, were pioneers.

6   And I want to say something to the school children of America who were watching the live coverage of the shuttle's takeoff. I know it is hard to understand, but sometimes painful things like this happen. It's all part of the process of exploration and discovery. It's all part of taking a chance and expanding man's horizons. The future doesn't belong to the fainthearted; it belongs to the brave. The *Challenger* crew was pulling us into the future, and we'll continue to follow them.

7   I've always had great faith in and respect for our space program, and what happened today does nothing to diminish it. We don't hide our space program. We don't keep secrets and cover things up. We do it all up front and in public. That's the way freedom is, and we wouldn't change it for a minute.

8   We'll continue our quest in space. There will be more shuttle flights and more shuttle crews, and yes, more volunteers, more civilians, more teachers in space. Nothing ends here; our hopes and our journeys continue.

9   I want to add that I wish I could talk to every man and woman who works for NASA or who worked on this mission and tell them: "Your dedication and professionalism have moved and impressed us for decades. And we know of your anguish. We share it."

10   There's a coincidence today. On this day 390 years ago, the great explorer Sir Francis Drake died aboard ship off the coast of Panama. In his lifetime the great frontiers were the oceans, and an historian later said, "He lived by the sea, died on it, and was buried in it." Well, today we can say of the *Challenger* crew: Their dedication was, like Drake's, complete.

11   The crew of the space shuttle *Challenger* honored us by the manner in which they lived their lives. We will never forget them, nor the last time we saw them, this morning, as they prepared for their journey and waved goodbye and "slipped the surly bonds of earth" to "touch the face of God."

Rich Scobee and Kathie Krause, children of astronaut Francis Scobee; June Scobee, the astronaut's widow; Nancy Reagan; President Ronald Reagan; Jane Smith, widow of astronaut Michael Smith; and two of Smiths' children, Scott and Alison, listen to a memorial service for the seven dead astronauts killed in the 1/28/86 shuttle explosion.

Remarks at the Johnson Space Center in Houston, TX. January 31, 1986

1   We come together today to mourn the loss of seven brave Americans, to share the grief that we all feel, and perhaps in that sharing, to find the strength to bear our sorrow and the courage to look for the seeds of hope.

2   Our nation's loss is first a profound personal loss to the family and the friends and the loved ones of our shuttle astronauts. To those they left behind— the mothers, the fathers, the husbands and wives, brothers and sisters, yes, and especially the children—all of America stands beside you in your time of sorrow.

3   What we say today is only an inadequate expression of what we carry in our hearts. Words pale in the shadow of grief; they seem insufficient even to measure the brave sacrifice of those you loved and we so admired. Their truest testimony will not be in the words we speak, but in the way they led their lives and in the way they lost their lives—with dedication, honor, and an unquenchable desire to explore this mysterious and beautiful universe.

4   The best we can do is remember our seven astronauts, our *Challenger* Seven, remember them as they lived, bringing life and love and joy to those who knew them and pride to a nation.

5   They came from all parts of this great country—from South Carolina to Washington State; Ohio to Mohawk, New York; Hawaii to North Carolina to Concord, New Hampshire. They were so different; yet in their mission, their quest, they held so much in common.

6   We remember Dick Scobee, the commander who spoke the last words we heard from the space shuttle *Challenger*. He served as a fighter pilot in Vietnam earning many medals for bravery and later as a test pilot of advanced aircraft before joining the space program. Danger was a familiar companion to Commander Scobee.

7   We remember Michael Smith, who earned enough medals as a combat pilot to cover his chest, including the Navy Distinguished Flying Cross, three Air Medals, and the Vietnamese Cross of Gallantry with Silver Star in gratitude from a nation he fought to keep free.

8   We remember Judith Resnik, known as J.R. to her friends, always smiling, always eager to make a contribution, finding beauty in the music she played on her piano in her off-hours.

9   We remember Ellison Onizuka, who as a child running barefoot through the coffee fields and macadamia groves of Hawaii dreamed of someday traveling to the Moon. Being an Eagle Scout, he said, had helped him soar to the impressive achievements of his career.

10   We remember Ronald McNair, who said that he learned perseverance in the cottonfields of South Carolina. His dream was to live aboard the space station, performing experiments and playing his saxophone in the weightless-

ness of space. Well, Ron, we will miss your saxophone, and we *will* build your space station.

11   We remember Gregory Jarvis. On that ill-fated flight he was carrying with him a flag of his university in Buffalo, New York—a small token, he said, to the people who unlocked his future.

12   We remember Christa McAuliffe, who captured the imagination of the entire nation; inspiring us with her pluck, her restless spirit of discovery; a teacher, not just to her students, but to an entire people, instilling us all with the excitement of this journey we ride into the future.

13   We will always remember them, these skilled professionals, scientists, and adventurers, these artists and teachers and family men and women; and we will cherish each of their stories, stories of triumph and bravery, stories of true American heroes.

14   On the day of the disaster, our nation held a vigil by our televison sets. In one cruel moment our exhilaration turned to horror; we waited and watched and tried to make sense of what we had seen. That night I listened to a call-in program on the radio; people of every age spoke of their sadness and the pride they felt in our astronauts. Across America we are reaching out, holding hands, and finding comfort in one another.

15   The sacrifice of your loved ones has stirred the soul of our nation and through the pain our hearts have been opened to a profound truth. The future is not free; the story of all human progress is one of a struggle against all odds. We learned again that this America, which Abraham Lincoln called the last, best hope of man on Earth, was built on heroism and noble sacrifice. It was built by men and women like our seven star voyagers, who answered a call beyond duty, who gave more than was expected or required, and who gave it little thought of worldly reward.

16   We think back to the pioneers of an earlier century, the sturdy souls who took their families and their belongings and set out into the frontier of the American West. Often they met with terrible hardship. Along the Oregon Trail, you could still see the gravemarkers of those who fell on the way. But grief only steeled them to the journey ahead.

17   Today the frontier is space and the boundaries of human knowledge. Sometimes when we reach for the stars, we fall short. But we must pick ourselves up again and press on despite the pain. Our nation is indeed fortunate that we can still draw on immense reservoirs of courage, character, and fortitude—that we're still blessed with heroes like those in the space shuttle *Challenger.*

18   Dick Scobee knew that every launching of a space shuttle is a techno-logical miracle. And he said, "If something ever does go wrong, I hope that

doesn't mean the end to the space shuttle program." Every family member I talked to asked specifically that we continue the program, that that is what their departed loved one would want above all else. We will not disappoint them.

19   Today we promise Dick Scobee and his crew that their dream lives on, that the future they worked so hard to build will become reality. The dedicated men and women of NASA have lost seven members of their family. Still, they, too, must forge ahead with a space program that is effective, safe, and efficient, but bold and committed.

20   Man will continue his conquest of space. To reach out for new goals and ever greater achievements—that is the way we shall commemorate our seven *Challenger* heroes.

21   Dick, Mike, Judy, El, Ron, Greg, and Christa—your families and your country mourn your passing. We bid you goodbye; we will never forget you. For those who knew you well and loved you, the pain will be deep and enduring. A nation, too, will long feel the loss of her seven sons and daughters, her seven good friends. We can find consolation only in faith, for we know in our hearts that you who flew so high and so proud now make your home beyond the stars, safe in God's promise of eternal life.

22   May God bless you all and give you comfort in this difficult time.

FEAR AND TERROR

F. Forrester Church IV

Four days after the April 19, 1995 bombing of the Federal Building in Oklahoma City, Frank Forrester Church IV, minister of the Unitarian Church of All Souls in New York City, sought to find meaning in "this terrible tragedy" for himself and for his congregation. Having experienced the bombing of the World Trade Center in New York City two years earlier, Reverend Church and his parishoners had cause to feel special empathy for the victims of the Oklahoma blast—empathy communicated to members of the First Unitarian Church of Oklahoma City by way of a letter Dr. Church chose to share in the introduction to his sermon.

✝This speech is printed by permission of Forrester Church IV.

Coming as it did just three days after the celebration of Easter, this calamity was viewed as turning Easter "on its head, the holy calendar reversed, resurrection first and then, three days later, the crucifixion." This juxtaposition of the week preceding and the holy calendar emphasizes the inhumanity of the act being deplored—an act that demanded consideration above the themes normally addressed on the Sunday following Easter. How does the introduction emphasize the significance of the event and justify the diversion from traditional sermon themes at Eastertide?

The most unusual feature of this sermon is its candor. Dr. Church expresses his personal feelings and reactions to the bombing, almost to the point of revealing shortcomings in his character. What effect are such personal revelations likely to have on an audience? Do they help his parishoners sort through the "rubble and carnage" of their own feelings? Is this speech likely to increase or decrease the ethos assigned to the speaker by his immediate audience, liberals, conservatives, Muslims, or you?

---

1   How very long ago Easter seems. Only a week ago we gathered in this peaceful sanctuary to trumpet the victory of love over death. One week later we are left to sort through the rubble and carnage that litter the once quiet streets of Oklahoma City, our hearts possessed with grief, anger, and fear. It's as if Easter this year has been turned on its head, the holy calendar reversed, resurrection first and then, three days later, the crucifixion.

2   Obviously, whatever I had planned to speak about this morning is of no consequence in light of the week's events. In a single blast, the world we live in is unalterably changed.

3   There is little we can do about this. In fact, apart from the perilous, if completely understandable, urge for retribution, our grief, anger, and fear are accompanied by a hollow sense of powerlessness. I did send, on your behalf, the following overnight letter to our fellow Unitarian Universalists at the First Unitarian Church in Oklahoma City. It's only a gesture, but at times like this, watching at a distance, we are sometimes forced to rely on mere gestures. At least they connect us to those whose pain is more immediate than our own.

Dear Unitarian Universalist Friends in Oklahoma City:

Please know how deeply we feel for you and your neighbors in the wake of the terrible tragedy that has befallen you, and indeed, our entire country. Having struggled with our own fears following the World Trade Center bombing two years ago, we in New York have at least a sense of the bewilderment you must surely be experiencing. Our prayers this Sunday are with you and the loved ones of those members of your congregation whose lives have been affected or swept away by this senseless, evil act. If we can be of any assistance whatsoever, please do not hesitate to call.

In faith and with profound sorrow,

Forrest Church (on behalf of the congregation of All Souls in New York City)

4   First Unitarian Church is near the Federal Building in Oklahoma City. The impact of the bomb caused some structural damage. Two members of the church are among the missing, and therefore are presumed dead. Carolyn and I will send a check directly to the church for their relief fund. I invite you to join us. Give it or send it to me and I'll pass it along. This too is a small thing, a gesture, but it connects us with our religious family. It permits us to do something, however small, at a time when so little we can say or do seems to matter all that much.

5   The question remains, how do we sort through the rubble and carnage? How can we extricate some meaning or guidance from this terrible tragedy? I am as off balance as you are. Having been transfixed by the television reports, I now want to run from them, from the images of horror, from the tears and the anger. I am looking for a good movie, even a bad movie, anything to take me away. And I will find one. I found one yesterday. I will find one today. But I also know that I must look deeper and further, both into myself and into the life we share as citizens of this country, even of the world.

6   I must look deeper into myself, in part because my initial response to the Oklahoma City bombing was to fix my attention and fear on a composite, stereotypical image of a Muslim terrorist: bearded, wiry, dark-eyed, alien, inscrutable, fanatical, terrifying. Even after I saw the composite drawings of the two suspects, I thought to myself, "Well, the one could be Arab. Perhaps the other is a bad rendering. After all, they caught that man on his way from Oklahoma City to Jordan, his bags filled with bomb-making material and photographs of American military sites."

7   His name was Amad Abrahim. They held him for sixteen hours. He was very cooperative. His bags were not filled with bomb-making material and photographs of American military sites. Nor did the other suspects I read about, Asad and Anis Siddiqy, have anything to do with the bombing. They were Queens taxi drivers working on an immigration problem. They lived with Mohammed Chaff. He too was grilled for fifteen hours. I understand that. All leads had to be scrupulously followed. But I also know that if I were given a multiple choice terrorist quiz two days ago, and asked to guess between Asad Siddiqy, Mohammed Chaff, Amad Abrahim, Timothy McVeigh, and Terry Nichols, I would have failed the test.

8   The threat of internationally sponsored murder and mayhem by such groups as the Hamas and Hesbollah is very real. An old friend of mine, Steve Emerson, author of the now-famous documentary "Jihad in America" presents the evidence in convincing detail. But I also know, or should know, that no people, no faith, have anything like a corner on hatred. Take the woman who said of our Muslim neighbors on a talk show this week, "No wonder this happened. These countries, their culture, have no respect for human life." Or the caller who threatened to blow up a discount variety store on Fifth Avenue owned by a Syrian-born Albert Cabal. "We're going to get you and we're going to get your family." "This is not a question of anybody's origin," President Clinton reminds us. "This was murder, this was evil, this was wrong. Human beings everywhere, all over the world, will condemn this out of their own religious convictions."

9   So I am troubled, deeply troubled by my knee-jerk reaction. All of us are prejudiced. But when thoughtful people do not work hard to temper their prejudices, bigots—those who celebrate prejudice—will only be vested with more power. Bigots like Timothy McVeigh and Terry Nichols.

10   I've noticed that a favorite question posed by reporters to people on the street is some variation of, "Does it bother you that Americans are responsible for this?" "It devastates me," one woman replied. "I just can't believe that an American, that a human being, could do this." There are millions of Arab Americans, millions of Muslim Americans—Muslim American human beings. They are only as likely to buy the hatred spewed by the Hamas or Hesbollah as are white-bread Mid-Western Christian Americans likely to feed on the equally bigoted and dangerous paranoia fostered by groups like the Michigan Militia, led by Norman Olson, self-styled "pistol-packin' preacher," and gun store owner. Or the Arizona patriots, whose members believe that the United States is being run by the protocol of Zion or about to be conquered by the United Nations.

11   Friday's *New York Post* [April 23, 1995] ran a cartoon of three Muslims laughing and burning an American flag at the base of the Statue of Liberty, which read "Give us your tired, your poor, your huddled masses, your terrorists, your murderers, your slime, your evil cowards, your religious fanatics, your welfare cheats." I can think of at least two flag-waving Christians wedded to their own perverse reading of the Bill of Rights, who would have laughed knowingly at that cartoon. Believing that our government has fallen prey to foreigners, welfare cheats, and slime, among whom they numbered Blacks and Jews, and obsessed with their guns, these two unimaginably sick Americans are responsible for the death of some two hundred innocent people, victims of the same kind of hate that such a cartoon unwittingly fosters.

12   Timothy McVeigh, a "quiet, shy church-going youth from upstate New York, who liked computers, basketball, and cars." Terry Nichols, a "good neigh-

bor," with a bumper-sticker on his car that boasted the words, "American and Proud." The former, arrested carrying a licensed Glock semi-automatic pistol, loaded with hollow point bullets, known as cop-killers, slept with his guns. The latter was known to have experimented with fertilizer bombs in his barn.

13   Tom Metzger, head of something call the White Aryan Resistance, said yesterday: " I have told people for years, at least since 1984, when The Order declared war on the central government of the United States that the government of this country—what we call the criminals—had better start listening to the dispossessed white people, the dispossessed majority. There was a hot war in the 1980s, and since then there's been a cold war, and now things are heating up again."

14   We don't need to look outside our borders or to another faith to discover our common enemy. He also lurks within, inspired not by the Koran but by the book of Revelation, his hatred of the government fed by the incendiary, divisive anti-government rhetoric empoloyed so successfully by certain of our political leaders, his fears fomented into paranoia and then violence by the American gun lobby.

15   We don't have to look any further than The Turner Diaries, a hateful, frightening book deemed the Bible of the survivalist movement. Positing the secret take-over of the government by Jews seeking to strip good Americans of their guns in an attempt to establish a new world order, the book begins with these words: "Today it finally began. After all those years of talking—and nothing but talking—we have finally taken our first action. We are at war with the system, and it is no longer a war of words." Extremists blow up a federal office building at 9:15 this morning. "Our worries about the relatively small size of the bomb were unfounded; the damage is immense. The scene in the courtyard was one of utter devastation. Overturned trucks and automobiles, smashed office furniture and building rubble were strewn wildly about—and so were the shockingly large number of victims. They have clearly made the decision to portray the bombing of the FBI building as the atrocity of the century. All the bombings, arsons and assassinations carried out by the Left in this country have been rather small time in comparison."

16   And so we come to April 19th. The day that American patriots defended Lexington and Concord against the Redcoats in 1775. The day that survivalist Randy Weaver, holed up in Ruby Ridge, Idaho, was informed by compatriots of a government plot against him in 1992. The day that the Branch Davidians immolated themselves in 1993. And the day that white-supremacist, Richard Snell, who murdered a black police officer and a Jewish business man was to be executed in Arkansas in 1995. That was last Wednesday. With this date as a mantra, one right-wing newsletter, *The Montana Militia,* warned that

Snell would die, "unless we act now!!!" Snell, a murderer, did die. So did 200 innocents. Two centuries after the first minutemen bravely fought at the Lexington bridge, two centuries after our founders, mindful of events leading up to the shot heard round the world, passed the second amendment to our nation's constitution establishing our right to a citizen's militia, a far deadlier blast in Oklahoma City has been heard round the world, and history itself, our own nation's history, lies twisted in the wreckage.

17   There will be great pressure in the days ahead to enact an Omnibus Counter-terrorism Act to protect us from Muslim fanatics. I wish only that certain of the most vociferous proponents of this legislation would examine their own consciences to ponder how their support for lifting a ban on semi-automatic weapons actually enhances the opportunity for terrorism to occur in this country. I hope they will hear their own words about protecting our sacred right to buy and keep arms echo back from the writings and voices of the hate mongers actually responsible for the tragedy in Oklahoma City. I hope they will think, at least a little, about how the seeds of division grow, how rhetoric that plays on our fears of one another, on our differences, the rhetoric that scapegoats, that pits neighbor against neighbor, can so easily blossom into full-blown bigotry, and with such devastating consequences.

18   One final thought. When we try to fight hatred with hate and fire with fire, we do not lessen but only compound the object of our enmity. We do not destroy the Randy Weavers of this world by sending federal agents to storm their Idaho shack, killing his wife and child in the crossfire. We do not extirpate the power expressed in David Koresh's paranoia and fascination with violence by killing four of his followers and then embargoing his compound until he and his sect immolate themselves. We do nothing to diminish the white-supremicism and anti-Semitism spewed by Richard Snell when we execute him for his heinous crimes. As the tragedy in Oklahoma City reminds us, violence only begets more violence. Even the most just violence, whether institutional or accidental, only contributes to the climate of fear and hatred which spawns yet more violence in an endless spiral.

19   If we have learned anything, we should have learned this from the endless succession of terrorist activity in the Middle East. Now we can study it on our own soil. If I were asked yesterday whether the perpetrators of this unimaginably evil act should receive the death penalty, I would have said yes. Today, I say no. I couldn't bear for them to become martyrs for the next wave of Timothy McVeighs and Terry Nichols. Let the blood be on their hands, not ours.

20   I expect that we will execute them. When we do, even as I have wrestled this week with my own prejudice against Arab Americans, I will again, I am sure, wrestle against, and perhaps unsuccessfully, my own primitive,

human desire for vengeance. Not my finest part, but part of me will cheer when there brutal men die. I am ashamed of that, but it is so.

21   What I will be far more ashamed of is this. I will be far more ashamed if I do not dedicate a greater part of my energy to combating—and that is not too strong a word—the climate of violence that is poisoning this country. Begin with guns. Ban more. Restrict others. Enforce and enhance licensing procedures. Make them difficult to buy. Enact severe penalties for illegal sale or possession. And drive every lackey of the American gun lobby from office, however high-minded and perversely patriotic his or her rhetoric.

22   I will also be ashamed if I do not do everything in my small power to reclaim the history and symbols of this great nation from the anti-American, anti-Christian white supremacist and survivalist zealots who have turned the courageous minutemen of Concord and the American Bill of Rights into fertilizer for their bombs. So far as it is in our power, and while admitting some necessary abridgment forced by prudence, we must not permit ourselves to be held hostage by our fears, driven to compromise precious American rights far more essential to the survival of this republic than the right to bear arms. The only way to do this is to answer fear, the fear these zealots and their unwitting political champions foment so successfully, with greater faith, the faith of our founders, a faith in one nation, indivisible, with liberty and justice for all. We must answer in the spirit of the people of Oklahoma City, whose courage, bravery, self-sacrifice, and neighborly love remind us once again of what it really means to be a true American. We must answer according to the best that is within the human heart, not imitate the worst.

23   Perhaps the best way to counter fear with faith is to begin with our own prejudices. These we can do something about, something more than a gesture. Tomorrow I shall call a Muslim cleric, Shaykh Abd'Allah Ali, Leader of the Admiral Family Circle, and invite him to preach at All Souls as soon as possible. This afternoon, at the Adult Education Committee meeting, I will urge that we devote a month next fall to the study of Islam. Most of us are profoundly ignorant about the teachings of Islam, an ignorance that feeds our prejudice.

24   In the meantime, mindful of life's fragility, let us remember how fortunate we are. Please, treat one another with kindness. Be thankful for the days we are given. There is time for us, there is still time, time to love and also time to learn.

Index of Rhetorical Principles ■